Gridiron Gypsies

Carlisle, Pennsylvania

Copyright 2022, 2023, 2025 © Tom Benjey

Published by Tuxedo Press
Carlisle, PA 17015
TuxedoPress.com

Fourth printing, 2025

All rights reserved. No part of this publication may be reproduced, stored in a retrieval system, or transmitted, in any form or by any means, electronic, mechanical, photocopying, recording, or otherwise, without the prior permission of Tuxedo Press.

ISBN 978-1-936161-06-5
Library of Congress Control Number 2022940665

Gridiron Gypsies
How The Carlisle Indians Shaped Modern Football

Tom Benjey

Carlisle, Pennsylvania

Contents

	Acknowledgements	vii
	Introduction	1
1	Football Begins at Carlisle	
	1893	7
	1894	13
	1895	18
2	Playing the Best	
	1896	27
	1897	35
	1898	44
3	A Coach of Their Own – 1899	51
4	Athletic Director, Too – 1900	63
5	A Search for Talent – 1901	71
6	The Walking Wounded – 1902	83
7	Coast to Coast – 1903	94
8	Captain Leadership	107
9	Major Changes – 1904	115
10	Hoo-ah! – 1905	125
11	Football Goes Airborne – 1906	139
12	Warner Returns to His Favorite Players – 1907	153
13	Go West Young Men – 1908	171

14	Thorpe Bolts – 1909	187
15	Major Rule Change – 1910	199
16	Carlisle's Best – 1911	211
17	An Olympic Year – 1912	225
18	Three in a Row – 1913	241
19	A Cure for All Diseases – 1914	255
20	The Decline – 1915	271
21	The Season That Almost Wasn't – 1916	283
22	The Last Dance – 1917	291
23	The End of It All – 1918	301
	Epilog	311
A	Origin of the School	316
B	Players with Years Played	324
	Notes	337
	Illustrations	362
	Index	366

Acknowledgements

Putting together such a book as this requires input from numerous expert sources. Jeffrey J. Miller, author of *Pop Warner: A Life on the Gridiron*, identified the source of the score for the 1908 game with Haskell Institute, a discussion of why Pop left Carlisle in 1904, and much, much more. Ken Frew, Archivist for Historical Society of Dauphin County, clarified the names used to reference Harrisburg High School in the 1890s. Ken Ackerman, who has written about such figures as Boss Tweed, Leon Trotsky, and J. Edgar Hoover, gave me considerable help in writing a synopsis for my book proposal.

Kent Stephens, historian for the College Football Hall of Fame, took considerable time out of his packed schedule to summarize the material regarding Carlisle in *Spalding's Football Guides* for the years 1893 through 1898 and to photocopy article discussing rules changes occurring during that time period. James G. Sweeney, Army's most loyal fan and author of articles for the College Football Historical Society, for reviewing the drafts of the introduction and preface, pointing out how some of it would bore the reader. He also read the 1915 chapter for flow.

Jeff Mann, collector of all things Spalding, for weighing his Spalding J ball to help in determining the difference in weights in it and the Victor ball used in the 1899 Cal game. James Campbell, author of several books on pro football, for assistance in figuring out the weight of an inflated football, serving as an early reader, and pointed out an error.

Kristin Rodgers, Collections Curator at Ohio State University's Health Sciences Library Medical Heritage Center, provided the proper names of a team and of the field on which Carlisle played in 1897. Scout Noffke, Reference & Administrative Specialist with Rauner Special Collections Library at Dartmouth College, for researching a possible 1898 game with Carlisle. Robert A. Dunkleberger, Bloomsburg University Archivist, provided the name of the field and some history regarding the Carlisle-Bloomsburg Normal games. Catherine Perry, Digital Projects and Collections Manager at Gettysburg College, provided names, including students' slang names, and history of Gettysburg College's athletic fields.

Jerry Price, Senior Communications Advisor/Historian at Princeton University, provided historic field names. Jim Gerencser, Dickinson College Archivist, provided the name or lack thereof for the athletic field used before Biddle Field and pointed me to the place where I could find the cost of tuition at Dickinson Law School. He also oversaw the scanning of the National Archives files for Carlisle Indian School. Louise LoBello, Research and Collections Management Specialist at Franklin & Marshall College, provided the names for the football fields at the times Carlisle played F&M. Laurie Lounsberry Meehan, University Archivist & Librarian, Alfred University, for researching the name of the University's football field. Patricia Higo, Archives and Special Collections Librarian, University of Detroit Mercy, for researching the name of the University of Detroit's football field in 1918. Charles Bare, Director of Athletic Media Relations at The College of the Holy Cross for providing the name of the College's football field in 1915.

Ives Goddard, Smithsonian Institution Linguist Emeritus, for explaining how Bemus Pierce (Seneca) and Wallace Denny (Oneida) could have set up code words to sneak plays to players on the field. Jessica Boyer, Director of the Library, Mount Saint Mary's College, provided information on the 1911 game with Mt. St. Mary's College.

Timothy Brown, author of *How Football Became Football: 150 Years of the Game's Evolution*, for continued assistance in understanding early football rules and their impact on how players played the game. He also reviewed the manuscript for errors and set me straight where I misunderstood things. Jim Thorpe expert Robert W. Wheeler saved me from embarrassment by finding numerous typographical errors and giving me encouragement to continue. Beside editing my manuscript, Susan Mary Malone provided invaluable advice suggesting I include more about the players, the addition of which made my book more interesting reading. Anne R. Keene, author of *The Cloudbuster Nine: The Untold Story of Ted Williams and the Baseball Team That Helped Win World War II*, put me in touch with a traditional publisher.

Cathy Jimerson and Dennis Parrish provided invaluable advice concerning the actual names of several Carlisle players. Dennis Parrish provides helpful information on Grandchildren and great grandchildren of Carlisle players have shared stories and photographs. They include Diane Garrard (William and George Gardner), Geoffrey Johnston (Louis Island), Liane Johnson and Stan Juneau (Sampson Bird), James Brown (James Phillips), Jay Garvie (James Garvie), Cecilia Balenti-Moddelmog (Mike Balenti), and all the others whose emails were lost in a system crash. Special thanks to Freddie Wardecker for making his photograph and document collection available to me to illustrate my books.

Jeff Wood, proprietor of Whistlestop Bookshop in Carlisle, provided publishing advice and news. If it wasn't for Raymond Schmidt, editor for the

College Football Historical Society, this book wouldn't have been written. He cajoled me into writing it. So, if you don't like it, blame Ray. Last but far from least, my wife Ann read and reread, pointing out the boring parts and finding my cut-and-paste errors. Without her patient and loyal support, this book would never have been finished.

Introduction

"The only good Indian is a dead Indian" was the prevailing view in 1879, just three years after what the popular media called "Custer's Last Stand" and a decade before Wounded Knee.

Civil War hero and veteran of the Indian wars cavalry officer Richard Henry Pratt thought differently: Indians were educable. He was ridiculed when he started Carlisle Indian School with the express purpose of educating Indians in order for them to enjoy the full fruits of citizenship. His position was as unpopular then as is voicing controversial opinions in this current time of heightened sensitivities. Critics dubbed this heretic "an honest lunatic" for espousing the belief that Indians could do anything whites could do, given proper training and opportunity. He based his philosophy on what he had observed firsthand, watching how his Black troops, called Buffalo Soldiers by the Indians, and his Indian scouts performed militarily. He saw no reason they couldn't also function well in the white man's society. Endlessly promoting the school, he gave speeches around the country, wrote articles for major newspapers and magazines, and lobbied government officials.

The Carlisle Indian School newspaper echoed his position and provided examples of students' and former students' excellence. In great demand, the school's popular band marched in several inaugural parades and played at world fairs and other major events to show the general populace what Indians could do if given the chances whites had. So, even though he abhorred the violence in the game, it was totally in character for him to demand that, if Carlisle boys were to play football, they must soon play and beat the best college elevens.

Some others cited reasons why they thought Indian athletes should outperform their white counterparts. R. Meade Bache, a longtime scientist with the U. S. Coast and Geodetic Survey, wrote articles about the physical force imparted by boxers' muscles and got them published in scientific journals. His 1895 paper on reaction times by race attracted the attention of University of Pennsylvania Professor of Psychology Lightner Witmer, who applied an electrical shock to the wrists of a dozen young men of three races and timed how soon they responded using a telegrapher's key. In Witmer's experiment, whites had the slowest reaction times and Indians the quickest. Blacks' times were in between. Bache explained away the Indians' faster reaction times than Blacks as the result of the Blacks having had intermarried more with whites than had Indians.

The Philadelphia Inquirer reporter covering Penn's football game with Carlisle that fall shifted the differences from genetics to culture: "[The Indians] saw more quickly, heard and responded to all sensations more quickly. Mr. Bache's theory is that the higher the civilization the greater the loss in quickness of automatic movements." After the game, long-time Penn football Coach George Woodruff reportedly said "[H]e would rather train the Indian boys than his own team and that they composed the ideal team for which he has been long looking would seem to sustain the purely scientific experiments." It seems logical that young men who have spent their lives living in nature and observing animals while hunting would develop quicker reflexes than those who lived in towns and cities.

Later, Pop Warner made observations of his own players. He noticed both physical and cultural differences. He claimed that Indians' lower legs dropped straight down from the knee where whites' lower legs curved slightly outward. Carlisle publicist Hugh R. Miller maintained that most Indians' feet were flat, parallel to each other, and pointed straight ahead where whites' pointed outward. (The author, a subject group of one white person, noticed the reasons he was a poor kicker. His lower legs curve slightly and that his toes point outward.) Warner thought straight lower legs gave Indian kickers an advantage. And Indians could get kicks off slightly quicker because their feet were already pointed straight ahead where white kickers had to turn their foot to put it in the proper position.[1] To the author's knowledge, this claim hasn't been researched. His experience coaching Indian players led Warner to observe how they learned:

> While at Carlisle, I had developed a theory that the Indians boys had been trained by their forefathers to be keen observers. Often when the Indian boys were exposed to a new sport or game, they would usually refuse to participate. Instead they would stand and watch the older, more experienced Indian boys, who were participating in the new sport or game, demonstrate how it was to be played.
>
> Then after having studied the play or actions of the elders, they would attempt to mimic those same actions, or motions, and would usually be almost as accomplished as those who they had just observed.

---

[1] A tracker in an old Hollywood western opined that a white man had joined a group he was trailing because his toes pointed outward where the others pointed straight ahead. Warner's belief may not have been as uncommon as it seemed.

Gridiron Gypsies was written because no existing book covered the complete Carlisle football story. It includes games not in the previous attempt and corrects scores and locations that were reported incorrectly. Information not easily found seventy years ago was located using technology not available to the earlier writer. The title is a shortened form of the nickname given to the team by sportswriters who observed Carlisle's coast-to-coast travel to play the best teams on their home turf: "Gypsies of the Gridiron."

Carlisle Indian School, created and operated by cavalry officer Richard Henry Pratt and located on the Army's second-oldest post, was a construct of the Federal Government. Dependent on government funding, it was an endangered species on the edge of extinction its entire existence. As early as 1898, success on the football field aided its survival against political opposition. This was not the last time football came to the school's assistance.

During his twenty-five-year tenure as superintendent, the school and everything it did reflected Pratt's views and opinions. Following superintendents were either cavalry officers or government employees, and the football team, although "owned" by the athletic association, was not exempt from government influence and policies, which changed over time.

This book is also about the players themselves, the most colorful to ever don football togs, and not just because several were inducted into the Hall of Fame. Their lives and personalities were much more interesting than the scions of the wealthy they played against.

Pratt's history leading up to forming Carlisle Indian School is essential to understanding why the school was founded and what it attempted to accomplish. This and why he was reluctant to allow a football team to compete with other schools is included as Appendix A. Chapter 1 tells the story of how the football program started in 1893 and began competing in earnest in 1894. The early years are covered two per chapter. Beginning with 1897, Carlisle's first winning season, a chapter is devoted to each year. Coverage for each season begins with a list of important rule changes that went into effect that year. (Rule changes came fast and furious in those days.) Team photos are available for most years. A summary of the games played that season follows the narrative. Each chapter ends with postseason evaluations, such as All-America honors where appropriate. Things happening after the season's end that impact the upcoming season are generally, but not always, considered part of the next year.

Individual and action photos as well as period cartoons help illustrate the text. Identifying players on photos was a challenge for a number of reasons, with the absence of many student records the largest. Mischievous players sometimes gave photographers and reporters made-up names like Yahoo and Waukesha. Nicknames were sometimes used, confusing matters worse because one person's nickname might be another's actual name. Barrel was one such example. When two or more with the same last name were on the team, initials often weren't included in newspaper articles if only one of them got into the game. Using the positions played wasn't infallible because they were so versatile.

Newspaper accounts of a game often varied significantly, including the scores. Misspelled names were the norm, nicknames weren't unusual, and first names were usually missing. The most troublesome of the errors was when different players were credited for having made a certain play or score. In the 1911 Johns Hopkins game, for example, *The Baltimore Sun* listed the following as having scored touchdowns: Thorpe, Powell, Williams, Vedernack, and Broker. The *Pittsburgh Daily Post* credited the touchdowns to: Thorpe, Powell, Williams, Vedernack, and Bergie. In this case as in many, I chose a local paper's coverage because its reporters would have been more familiar with the players than out-of-town scribes. Since no Carlisle or Harrisburg paper gave this game much ink, I relied on the *Baltimore Sun*'s coverage of the action because it went into greater detail.

Something the modern reader might find confusing is the lengths of halves. In the early years, although the rules specified the length of halves, coaches often negotiated how many minutes each one was to be. One half being longer than the other wasn't uncommon. Games that had gotten out of hand or if the visiting team had to catch a train, were abbreviated before time had expired. Cartoons and articles cut from period newspapers are sprinkled across the chapters. Modern readers might find many of them to be racist. Not including them would paper over important history.

The school's demise and end of the football team are covered in the last chapter. The epilogue covers attempts to reopen the school after WWI.

In recent years, Carlisle and other off-reservation government Indian boarding schools have been strongly criticized for several things and Indian graves at boarding schools are being moved to reservations. The implication in the popular press is that these schools were unhealthy places. This book only looks at Carlisle and no study of health conditions there as compared to the reservations has been made. What is known is that the world was an unhealthy place and reservations were particularly unhealthy. The average life span for all Americans wasn't much more than half of what it is in the early twenty-first century and for Indians it was less than that.

Trachoma, a disease of the eye that left untreated could cause blindness, was rampant on the reservations and many Carlisle students were afflicted with it. Superintendent Pratt arranged for noted eye specialists in Philadelphia and New York City to treat afflicted students for a minimal fee. This quality of care would not have been available to most Americans at that time and definitely not on reservations.

Carlisle has been criticized for forcing students to speak English but Pratt didn't have to force them. Early on, he convinced chiefs to send their children to his school so they could learn English and no longer be cheated when signing treaties. With boys and girls from over seventy tribes on campus and no two from the same tribe allowed to room together, they had to learn English if they wanted to communicate with each other.

Pratt believed that complete immersion was the best way to assimilate the Indians and instituted outing periods, during which students lived and worked with families in eastern Pennsylvania and New Jersey and earned some money while there. Carlisle students weren't forced to go on outings. In fact, they were required to apply and qualify for them if they wanted to go. Not all were accepted and appropriate host families couldn't be found for some. Students out on outings during the school year attended public schools with the children of the host families.

At the end of the enrollment period, usually three or five years, students were free to leave or reenroll. They weren't forced to assimilate into the majority culture but many chose to do that.

Student outcomes ranged widely. In general, those who flourished at Carlisle had good outcomes afterward. Those who "went back to the blanket" didn't usually do as well due to the lack of resources and opportunities on the reservations. Students who did well academically and learned their trades had good chances for productive lives as did musicians and football players. Carlisle's players were generally good students and were active in the debating societies and other extra-curricular activities. Football players became celebrities because their names were printed in newspapers from coast to coast. Integrating into the majority society was easier for them than others because of this. Many of them didn't return to the reservation. A few even married white women. Some of their grandchildren didn't even know their grandfathers had played football at Carlisle.

Looking back in later years after winning national championships and the Rose Bowl while leading other teams, Warner fondly remembered the Indians:

> Great teams, those Carlisle elevens that I coached, and what was even finer, sportsmen all. There wasn't an Indian of the lot who didn't love to win and hate to lose, but to a man they were modest in victory and resolute in defeat. They never gloated, they never whined, and no matter how bitter the contest, they played cheerfully, squarely and cleanly.

Superintendent Pratt with young student.

1
Football Begins at Carlisle

Rules in 1893:

Touchdown:	4 points
Kick after touchdown:	2 points
Field goal:	5 points
Safety:	2 points
Distance for first down:	5 yards
Attempts to make first down:	3 downs

Kickoffs: Team giving up field goal or touchdown kicks off to other team
Game length: 2 halves of forty-five minutes each
Field: 110 yards long by 160 feet wide with goal posts 18 ½ feet apart centered on the goal lines and crossbars 10 feet above the ground.
The Intercollegiate Football Association (IFA) adopted a standard that limited sports to undergraduates. Some schools refused to comply.
Notes.
Balls fumbled out of bounds are live. Players from both teams would hurdle or run over benches, water jugs, people who happened to be between them and the ball, tracks surrounding the field, and anything else that impeded their ability to corral the loose spheroid. This rule did not change **until 1926.**

One fall afternoon in 1893, Richard Henry Pratt, superintendent of Carlisle Indian School, worked at his desk in the headquarters building on Carlisle Barracks, the army's second-oldest installation behind West Point. Established in 1787 by British Col. John Stanwix and nestled in picturesque Cumberland Valley, Carlisle Barracks served as a supply post during the French and Indian War. Prior to the Civil War, it housed a cavalry school. The headquarters building, like almost everything on the base, was relatively new, built after 1863. The only pre-Civil War structure remaining was the limestone powder magazine built by Hessian soldiers taken prisoner by Washington at Trenton. Everything else was burned in July 1863 by J. E. B. Stuart's Confederate troops while the Battle of Gettysburg raged in the next county south.

A knock on the door interrupted this Civil War hero and leader of Buffalo Soldiers. Dressed in his blue cavalry officer's uniform, although working at detached assignments since 1878, Richard Henry Pratt, the epitome of *loco parentis,* considered the students, who ranged in age from four to twenty-four, as his children and believed it was his responsibility to look after them. He often referred to himself as their "school father." Capt. Pratt even gave the brides away in his full dress uniform when they married. Wanting to give students educational experiences similar to what whites got, a range of clubs and activities such as the YMCA and debating societies were organized. He succeeded in getting a Quaker lady to donate the money to start a school band. Pratt allowed the boys to form intramural football teams representing the various shops, clubs, and even the band. He could control what happened on campus but not elsewhere. In 1890, Stacy Matlock's leg was badly broken in a sandlot game with the Dickinson College team. Helping the school physician set the compound fracture revulsed Pratt so terribly he banned off-campus football.

The superintendent told the unseen visitor to enter and his door opened, revealing forty of the school's finest athletes dressed in their best military uniforms with something on their minds. At over six feet tall and with a face that reflected his near-death experience with smallpox as a child, Capt. Pratt presented a commanding appearance. In spite of this, students felt comfortable approaching him with their problems and requests. He invited the boys into his office where they stood around his desk, their black eyes intensely focused on him. The school's champion orator, possibly Benjamin Caswell, stepped forward and presented himself as a descendent of Chief Logan.

He began, "I appeal to any white man to say that ever he entered Logan's cabin hungry and he gave him no meat, came cold and naked and he clothed him not." The boy then presented the case for playing football against other schools eloquently.

Pratt recalled: "...[T]he genius of his argument almost compelled me to relax the judicial mien and release any pent-up laughter. When he had finished, I waited a little and then said: 'Boys, I begin to realize that I must surrender and give you the opportunities you so earnestly desire. I will let you take up outside football again, under two conditions.'

"'First, that you will never, under any circumstances, slug. That you will play fair straight through. And if the other fellows slug you will in no case return it. Can't you see that if you slug, people who are looking on will say, 'There, that's the Indian of it. Just see them. They are savages and you can't get it out of them.' Our white fellows may do a lot of slugging and it causes little or no remark, but you have to make a record for your race. If the other fellows slug and you do not return it, very soon you will be the most famous football team in the country. If you can set an example of that kind for the white race, you will do a work in the highest interests of your people.'"

The boys responded in unison, "All right, Captain. We agree to that."

"My other condition is this. That, in the course of two, three, or four years, you will develop your strength and ability to such a degree that you will whip the biggest football team in the country. Well, what do you say to that?"

The boys stood silent before their spokesman said, "Well, Captain, we will try."

Pratt responded, "I don't want you to promise to try. I want you to say that you will do it. The man who only thinks of trying to do a thing admits to himself that he may fail, while the sure winner is the man who will not admit to failure. You must get your determination up to that point."

Looking serious, they thought for a while before answering, "Yes sir, we will agree to that."

Pleased, Pratt said, "Very well, now I know that you cannot win unless you have as good or better instruction than your opponents, and I will write to Walter Camp, the great football authority, and ask him to name me the best coach in the United States and, if possible to get him, he will be your instructor."

Ecstatic, the boys left.

Pratt followed through and wrote Camp. "The father of American football" responded promptly with the name Glenn Scobey "Pop" Warner, who was then engaged as the head coach of his alma mater, Cornell. The ingenious Warner sounded like the right man but he wasn't available. So, Pratt delegated the job to his second-in-command, Disciplinarian William G. Thompson. He had no known experience coaching football; he was an administrator and taught business courses. But it was much too late in the season for anything resembling a full schedule. So, Thompson hurriedly arranged three games, two of which were with area high school teams.

With only 250 to 300 boys of age to play on the school's football team, Carlisle was at a disadvantage to the colleges and universities the Indians would be playing. Those schools generally had largely male student bodies numbering in the thousands and footballers who had played on their high school or prep school teams. Many of the Carlislian eleven hadn't even seen a football before coming to the Indian School.

One advantage Carlisle had before 1914 was, because many of its players were older than white children when they began their education, they were older and more physically and emotionally mature than their opponents. Another reason for Carlisle having older players was that it wasn't unusual for its students to re-enroll for an additional period to continue their education.

Although Carlisle was a vocational school in which students spent half the day in academic classes, the other half learning a trade, some graduated from high school and a few graduated from college. Dickinson School of Law was where most Carlisle players who earned degrees got theirs. They chose the Law School because they could start earning money immediately after graduating. A couple went to dental school later.

Over half of Carlisle's players had lost at least one parent and several had lost both. The Indian School gave them places to live and, in some cases, opportunities to earn money to pay tuition at an off-campus institution. To some extent, Carlisle served as an orphanage because the reservations had limited finances and little to support orphaned children.

Team captains in those days were much more important than today, where the title is mostly ceremonial. In the early years of American football, the captain was responsible for running the team during games. Coaching from the sidelines and sending in plays was barred. Players were supposed to be smart enough to call their own plays.

Cheating on this rule was common as players, coaches, and water boys concocted ways of communicating from the sidelines to the players on the field. Carlisle was no different from the colleges in this regard.

The players elected a member as their leader and followed his directions. The captain could play any position as leadership qualities were the most important factor. Benjamin Caswell, class of '92, then attending the Dickinson College prep school, was selected as Carlisle's first captain, probably because of having experience playing college football on the Dickinson team the year before.

Football was a violent games in those days. Players were frequently maimed and some died each year. Opposing teams lined-up against each other literally toe-to-toe, waiting for the ball to be snapped. Mass plays, in which punching, kicking, and biting were largely hidden from officials, dominated the game. Brutal wedge plays, in which players would lock arms or hang onto each other to produce an impregnable wall in front of the ballcarrier, had been introduced the year before, and experts expected them to be used more widely this year. Had Pratt known that, he might have made a different decision. Regardless, Carlisle was soon using the V, as some reporters called it, in their offense.

On Saturday, November 11, 1893, the Carlisle Indians took the field as an official NCAA (retroactively) team when they faced off against Harrisburg High School. *The Philadelphia Inquirer* listed the game as a scoreless tie between Carlisle Training School and Harrisburg High. *The Harrisburg Patriot* gave the Indians the win at 10-0, listing the Harrisburg players' names but not Carlisle's.

Two days later, the Indians played Dickinson College on its own field. The college's newspaper, *The Dickinsonian,* reported, "Quite a large crowd passed through the gates for the main purpose of seeing the Indians play football [sic], and all went away with the knowledge that Indians can play this exceedingly popular game as well as base-ball [sic]." Fumbles were the Indians' downfall but they fought to the end of the forty-minute skirmish. Benjamin Caswell had to leave the game due to a serious leg injury. "The Indians played a plucky, obstinate game from start to finish." The college boys beat their neighbors but considered this to be a practice game and didn't compile detailed statistics.

The Dickinsonian gave the score as 16-0, but the text of the article suggested that the published result omitted a touchdown the Indians scored: "The Indian perseverance and determination then showed itself. They bucked our centre [sic] until they carried the ball over the line but failed to kick goal."[2]

---

[2] At that time, extra points after touchdowns required a player from the team scoring the touchdown to punt the ball from the spot behind the goal line where

Making a touchdown was worth four points, six if the kick after was successful. *The Patriot* reported the score as 16-4, as the game coverage supported.

On Thanksgiving Day, November 30, Carlisle played another Indian school, Educational Home (later Lincoln Institute) of Philadelphia, on the Dickinson College field. (The future Red Devils were away at Harrisburg's Island Park playing Bucknell that day.) Carlisle easily shut out the visiting Indians, scoring six touchdowns and kicking five field goals for a total of thirty-four points in the forty-five-minute first half. They pushed across two more touchdowns and made both kicks after touchdown in the twenty-minute second half for a total of seven out of eight attempts for the game. These scores totaled forty-six points for Carlisle, instead of the fifty *The Sentinel* headline blared. Perhaps they made another touchdown or two safeties the reporter missed. The fifty probably came from the scoreboard, so we'll use that until more information is uncovered.

Caswell, Jonas Metoxen, Bemus Pierce, and Laban Locojim starred for Carlisle. Fairbanks and Peake did well for Philadelphia, but Carlisle's line was too heavy for them.

Position	Player
Right End	Laban Locojim (Apache)
Right Tackle	Joseph Irwin (Gros Ventre)
Right Guard	Bemus Pierce (Seneca)
Center	Benjamin Doxtator (Oneida)
Left Guard	Martin Wheelock (Oneida)
Left Tackle	Charles Buck (Piegan)
Left End	Anthony Austin (Piegan)
Quarterback	Harvey Warner (Omaha)
Right Halfback	Benjamin Caswell (Chippewa)
Left Halfback	Frank Cayou (Omaha)
Fullback	Jonas Metoxen (Oneida)

A number of young men wanting to see the game without paying the fifteen-cent ticket price tried to scale the fence surrounding the Dickinson College athletic field. One who succeeded was captured by an Indian guard and ordered to get out. The man refused and started a fight that drew in several others. When policemen stopped the melee, a crowd outside hurled

---

the ball was touched down to a teammate a prescribed distance away. The person receiving the punt would call a fair catch. A dropkick or placekick would be attempted from that spot.

stones onto the field. Officer Jackson approached the fence to get the people to stop. Instead, someone threw a large stone that hit him between the eyes. The unfortunate policeman was knocked unconscious. The attending physician feared that Jackson's skull was fractured. Luckily, it wasn't. After that, Pratt attended as many games as practical to prevent future problems.

Intercollegiate football at Carlisle was born, although Carlisle Indian Industrial School was never a college, but the vast majority of the opponents they would soon be scheduling most certainly were.

1893 Summary

Date	Opponent	Location	Indians	Opp.
Nov. 11	Harrisburg High School	Athletic Field, Carlisle Barracks, PA	10	0
Nov. 13	Dickinson College	Dickinson College Athletic Field, Carlisle, PA	4	16
Nov. 30	Educational Home	Dickinson College Athletic Field, Carlisle, PA	50	0

Won 2; Lost 1; Tied 0

Carlisle's First Full Season

Rule Changes for 1894:

The flying wedge was allowed, as were plays in which three players could be in motion as a mass when the ball was snapped. Considerable brutality resulted. Referee and umpire were to use whistles to stop play. Halves shortened to 35 minutes.

In the fall of 1894, Luck was a lady in the form of Nancy Luckenbaugh, a teacher at the Indian School. The football team had no coach but she had a friend in Harrisburg by the name of Vance McCormick. The 1892 Walter Camp First Team All-America halfback and captain of the national championship Yale team had graduated in 1893 to return home to assist his wealthy father manage the family's businesses. Miss Luckenbaugh invited him to give the Carlisle team a look. He liked what he saw well enough to agree to coach them for free—but with what time he had available. Carlisle Indian School had its first football coach.

Vance offset his lack of experience at coaching somewhat with his enthusiasm. He impressed Superintendent Pratt by how he threw himself into teaching the boys the rudiments of the game. When they didn't grasp how to capture a loose football, McCormick demonstrated how to do it properly by diving onto the muddy ground with no regard for what it would do to his clothing. Capturing a loose football properly was an important skill because the football was hard to keep under control. The ball they played with was much larger and shaped more like a watermelon than a modern-day football. Fumbles were so common that books teaching football skills included sections on falling on errant spheroids.

Fumbles hurt teams so badly that coaches warned players of the hazards of dropping the ball. John Heisman, Georgia Tech coach, reputedly held up a football at the beginning of the season's practices and said, "Gentlemen, it is better to have died as a small boy than to fumble this football." Still, fumbles persisted and plagued most teams.

1894 Carlisle Indians

The players made good advantage of the half-dozen times Vance was able to come to campus. Most of the responsibility for running the team fell on Benjamin Caswell, who had been elected to serve as captain again. The Indians' 1894 season, their first real one, started with a high school team, the last they would schedule. Although *The Sentinel* announced a game with "a Harrisburg team" to be played on September 29, the Indians didn't take the field until October 6. The lighter Harrisburg boys were no match for them and never threatened their goal line. Caswell and Jonas Metoxen scored touchdowns in the first half but Bemus Pierce's kicks after failed. Metoxen snared a fumble and raced fifty yards for a touchdown in the second half. Pierce made the kick. *The Philadelphia Inquirer* opined, "The Indian pupils at the Carlisle School by defeating at football the team of the Harrisburg High School show that they can absorb civilization as well as anybody."

Cross-town rival Dickinson College kicked off a string of college opponents. Anthony Austin, David McFarland, Metoxen, and Caswell stood out in the 12-12 tie played out over two twenty-minute halves. Things got tougher after that when they faced Lehigh University. Even though the Brown and White's performance "was not up to the standard" and the "Indians play[ed] a snappy game," Carlisle lost 22-12 in "the most exciting game played at Bethlehem this season." The Indians' teamwork was good, with Caswell and Metoxen standing out and Pierce making both goals after touchdown. Their weakest point was the inability to tackle a runner low.

The next game required the Indians to leave Pennsylvania for the first time. Soon, out-of-state games would become routine. After touring the Naval Academy, by the time the game started they seemed dazed. The shock of quickly giving up a touchdown jolted them awake. Carlisle moved the ball but failed to put it across the goal line. Navy's second score came after the Indians thought the play had been whistled dead, but it was allowed. Both kicks after touchdowns failed. The Indians were shut out for the first time 8-0.

The next day, *The Harrisburg Patriot* reported that the Indians would play Yale in mid-November. The evening after that, the entire Carlisle team attended a lecture given by Minnesota's head coach, Thomas Cochran, about Yale's way of training players. The Minnesota football program was so strapped for cash at the time that Cochran toured the country raising money for it through speaking fees. The audience applauded portraits of Frank Butterworth, William Orville "Wild Bill" Hickok III, and Vance McCormick, all of whom starred for Yale after attending nearby Harrisburg Academy.

Three days after the Navy game, the Indians traveled to Lancaster, Pennsylvania to play Franklin and Marshall College. They played a strong first half, scoring three touchdowns, but the college boys rallied in the second thirty-minute half to win the exciting and hotly contested game 28-18. Harman (2), Long, Baker, and Stroup made touchdowns for the home team. Caswell (2) and Metoxen made them for Carlisle. Cremer kicked five conversions, Metoxen three.

The following Saturday found Carlisle playing at Bucknell. Their coach, Bill Young, reportedly said, "They are the cleverest tacklers he ever saw. They do not know the meaning of the word fear and when running with the ball will never cry down until all hope for squirming or twisting a foot or two further is gone." In spite of this, Bucknell won 10-0 in "...the hardest fought game ever played in Lewisburg." The Orange and Blue's superior teamwork overcame Carlisle's weight and tackling advantages. *The Lewisburg Journal* observed, "[T]he Indians showed better civilization than many of the white clubs that have contended on the same field. There was no howling and hooting by them and no disposition to break the limbs or necks of their competitors; but they played well and fairly, and commanded the respect of all who witnessed the game."

With the games against college teams under their belts, the Indians turned to athletic clubs for opponents. First up was the Pittsburgh A. C. *The Pittsburg Press* gave this game the first play-by-play coverage given to any Carlisle Indians game. Early on, the paper said, it "...was one of the best ever seen in Pittsburg [sic]. The Indians can play football. There is no doubt in the world about that, and they put up as clean and gentlemanly an article in that line as any Pittsburg ever witnessed....The play was hard and fast from start to finish and was marked by clever team and individual work on both sides. The tackling of the Indians was a particularly brilliant feature. They never think of letting a man get past them, yet they seem to have a knack of downing him without hurting him."

The first half, in which P.A.C. scored its first touchdown, was almost entirely played in Carlisle's half of the field. Ten minutes into the game, Pittsburgh's McNeil ran it in from ten yards out for the game's first score. Reed's kick after touchdown failed. P.A.C. led 4-0. Later in the half, a short, high Carlisle punt gave the home team the ball again. McNeil went around left end for ten yards, then for fifteen more. Brown ran around the other end for ten more. Steen gained twenty yards, putting the ball at Carlisle's fifteen-yard line. Mallett bulled over for the touchdown, and Reed again missed the kick. P.A.C. 8-Carlisle 0.

The second half was a defensive struggle with no scoring and players on both teams leaving the game because of injuries. Caswell was replaced by Presley Houk, and P.A.C. substituted Paisley for Steen. The game ended with the ball on Carlisle's fifty-yard line. Since the length of the halves wasn't given, one assumes they were according to regulations. After the game, Anthony

Austin was elected captain to replace Benjamin Caswell, whose ankle was injured too badly for him to continue playing the rest of the season.

Carlisle's next game was against Columbia Athletic Club in the nation's capital on the field used by the Washington National League baseball team. Among the unusually large crowd sitting in the bleachers were several chiefs then in Washington to negotiate treaties. The *Washington Times* reported, "The spectators were rewarded by a snappy, well-played contest, in which the aborginies [sic] fought with bull-like determination, but had to yield by a score of 18 to 0, principally because of lack of competent interference and tackling on their part." Metoxen's rushes were Carlisle's strong point. McFarland, American Horse, and several others were injured, weakening the team, allowing Columbia to score with relative ease in the second half. Carlisle lost 15-0.

The Indians' next, and last, game that year almost did not happen. Rev. Dr. H. E. Niles demanded that York Y.M.C.A. cancel its Thanksgiving Day game and rallied other ministers to support him. The association board did as he wished and issued a statement to that effect on November 9th. The players howled at this decision, and the York City team offered to play Carlisle in place of the Y.M.C. A. The next day, several ministers pushed back against Niles' claims, leaving only Rev. Bell, Dr. Freas, and Dr. Lilly supporting him. Ministers supporting the ban received some pushback from their congregants. "A lady of the congregation whom he tried to convince that Thanksgiving foot ball [sic] was wrong refused to be convinced, on the ground that if it was not sinful for the minister's son to go hunting on that day, neither was football deserving of his denunciation."

Opposition against holding the game evaporated and 2,500 people came out to watch York Y.M.C.A. play the Carlisle Indian School. At the end of two twenty-five-minute halves, the score was knotted at 6-6. Each team had scored a touchdown and made the kick after. This tie brought Carlisle's first full season of football to a close without the Yale game materializing—at least for that year.

After the end of the school year, Benjamin Caswell left Carlisle and Conway Hall to serve as an assistant instructor of carpentry at Fort Belknap Boarding School near Harlem, Montana to start his career in the Indian Bureau. Caswell's talent was lost to the team but the Indian School was hardly bereft of fine athletes. Bemus Pierce (Seneca, New York) was elected captain for the first time.

1894 Season Summary

Date	Opponent	Location	Indians	Opp.
Oct. 6	Harrisburg High School	6th Street Grounds, Harrisburg, PA	14	0*
Oct. 13	Dickinson College	Dickinson College Athletic Field, Carlisle, PA	12	12
Oct. 20	Lehigh University	Athletic Grounds, Bethlehem, PA	12	22
Oct. 31	Naval Academy	Worden Field, USNA, Annapolis, MD	0	8
Nov. 3	Franklin & Marshall College	New Athletic Field, Lancaster, PA	18	28
Nov. 10	Bucknell University	Athletic Field, Lewisburg, PA	0	10
Nov. 17	Pittsburgh Athletic Club	East Liberty Park, Pittsburgh, PA	0	8
Nov. 24	Columbia Athletic Club	Boundary Field, Washington, DC	0	15†
Nov. 29	York Y.M.C.A.	Y.M.C.A. Grounds, York, PA	6	6

Won 1; Lost 6; Tied 2

*Some reports identify the opponent as Harrisburg High School, others as Central High School because the school was referred to as Central (colloquially) by many at that time.

† *The Washington Times* had the score as 15-0, but *The Philadelphia Times'* brief piece had 18-0. Sportswriters placed the game site as National Park or Baseball Park, but the official name was Boundary Field.

Tackling Colleges

Rules Changes for 1895:

The Intercollegiate Rules Committee became dysfunctional, leaving a void. Two sets of college representatives stepped in to fill the vacuum: Princeton and Yale abolished mass momentum plays by limiting the number of men in motion when the ball is snapped to one. Cornell, Harvard, and Penn placed no restrictions on these dangerous plays. Teams could choose to play their games according to either set of rules or the previous year's version.

The September 20 edition of *The Indian Helper* announced that eight games had been arranged for the 1895 season, and with the return of the farm boys, football practice had begun in earnest. Carlisle students often returned after the start of football practice because they were away during the summers, either vacationing at their homes or working at farms and businesses in eastern Pennsylvania or New Jersey under Carlisle's outing program. An integral part of Pratt's educational program, outings gave students the opportunity to earn money while being immersed in the majority culture. It also celebrated Walter Camp's inclusion of the team's 1894 record in the *1895 Spalding's Football Guide*. Carlisle was recognized as a legitimate power, even before having won a single important game, as acknowledgement of the potential for greatness experts had observed. *Spalding's Guides*, produced at the beginning of each season, now included the team's schedule for the upcoming season, results for the previous season, and a team photo with the names of the players noted.

Vance McCormick returned as a part-time coach, with much of the responsibility for running the team again falling on the captain. After the previous season's end, players elected Bemus Pierce as captain. With only six returning starters and few experienced substitutes to tackle much tougher opponents, Captain Pierce faced a huge task.

On October 3, Carlisle accepted York Y.M.C.A.'s invitation to again play on Thanksgiving Day. Unclear was whether they were just acknowledging the last game on the schedule or was York Y.M.C.A. actually replacing another team in a game previously arranged. Since Dickinson College did not field a team that year, it might have been to replace an anticipated game with them.

The Indians opened the season against a college team this year, Pennsylvania College (later Gettysburg College), quickly making booking high school opponents a thing of the past. "The Swamp," as Gettysburg students called their field due to its propensity to flood, was so beastly hot they shortened the halves to twenty minutes. The outmatched home team seldom made a first down and had some of its kicks blocked. The Indians played well together. Their interference around the ends was fine, they bucked the line and tackled well but fumbled too often. Players attributed these miscues to the new game ball being slick as opposed to the well-used practice balls they were accustomed to handling. Bemus Pierce scored a touchdown in each half but only one of the kicks after was successful. Carlisle 10–Pennsylvania College 0.

Next up on this home-game-less season was Duquesne Country and Athletic Club, a team that featured former college players. *The Pittsburg Press* writer observed considerable improvement since the Indians last played in the Iron City: "Their business-like methods and utter disregard for bumps and knocks received while the teams were in action won for them the admiration of the spectators who saw the game at close range....It seemed next to impossible to stop them, especially when they tried the revolving wedge, which they did several times."

After a fumble exchange on the initial possessions, the Indians marched steadily down the field, with McFarland ultimately pushed over the goal line for a touchdown. Bemus Pierce kicked the goal after touchdown for a 6–0

Carlisle lead. After receiving the kickoff, Captain Pierce directed his men to play fast. The Indians steamed down the field, seldom being held for no gain, until the Duquesne line stiffened at its own twenty-five-yard line. The half ended with the ball on the fifteen.

Duquesne moved the ball better in the second half, particularly with end runs. After recovering an Indian fumble on their own eighteen-yard line, Van Cleve followed his interference and dashed around his right end for a touchdown. Young's kick after failed. Carlisle 6-Duquesne 4. In a later possession, McFarland set up a Metoxen touchdown with a ten-yard run around his right end. Pierce's kick failed. Carlisle 10-Duquesne 4. Later, McFarland scored another touchdown and Pierce kicked the goal after. Carlisle 16-Duquesne 4. Duquesne threatened to score once more but were repulsed at Carlisle's seven.

After the game was over and Carlisle had left for home, Duquesne C. & A. C. member Charles M. Payne sent David McFarland a cartoon he had drawn with the inscription: "From one of the many friends you boys have made here by your gentlemanly playing." Perhaps he was inspired by a filler piece in *The Pittsburg Press*: "Those were not good Indians that tackled the

"REVENGE!"

Duquesnes yesterday. They were avenging the occurrences of a century or so just around the same diggings." His was the earliest known cartoon of the team.

Four days after the Duquesne game, the Indians invaded the City of Brotherly Love. An advertisement for the game made clear that mass momentum plays would be the order of the day. Penn was famous for its guards-back mass formation. The Indians found little love on the University of Pennsylvania's brand-new Franklin Field.

However, *The Philadelphia Inquirer* had some kind words for their efforts:

> The game yesterday was by long odds the hardest Pennsylvania has had this season. The Indians showed up surprisingly strong in defensive play, and with good coaching they would defeat Lehigh, Lafayette or any team outside of the larger colleges. Vance McCormick, the old Yale quarterback [sic], was at Carlisle one day this fall, and that was the only time on which the Indians have received any instructions in the strategic points of play. They played the game in a style peculiar to themselves, relying mainly on their strength and grit to carry them through.

After Quaker Scalps.

Carlisle came close to scoring in the first half but failed to be the first to score on the Quakers that year. The first half ended with the score 12-0, Penn having scored two touchdowns.

The Quakers' rapid onslaught in the second half overwhelmed the Indians. The first touchdown of the half was scored after only thirty seconds of play and the rout was on. The eventual national champions won 36-0 in the closest game they had played up to this point in the season.

After the game, *The Inquirer* ran the first known newspaper cartoons of the Indian squad. *The Carlisle Sentinel* opined, "The Indian football team gets high marks for its work in Philadelphia yesterday. They may yet carry off all honors in that direction. If they do, they can, perhaps, the sooner convince the general public of their great advance in civilization."

Penn's future hall-of-fame Coach George Woodruff remarked that he would rather train the Indian boys than his own athletes because they composed the ideal team for which he had been looking for a long time. They would also seem to sustain the purely scientific experiments of R. Meade Bache, the Penn researcher who had observed quicker reaction times from Indians than for whites. The Indian saw more quickly, heard and responded to all sensations faster.

An outcome of the game was that perennial power Yale agreed to face Carlisle on November 6, an open date for both teams. But before meeting the Eli, the Midshipmen of Annapolis awaited. *The Indian Helper* considered the game a disappointment as the previous year's game had been close. The Carlisle boys had an off day, allowing Navy to roll up thirty-four unanswered points. *The Baltimore Sun observed,* "A noticeable feature was the cleanness of the Indians' game, slugging and fouling seem to be civilized arts which they have not yet learned." The game was halted ten minutes into the second half when the Indians were about to score, the reason given was that it was to keep them from missing the train back to Carlisle.

On the Warpath.

The Yale game, although another shutout loss at 18–0, was more encouraging. The Indians moved the ball to Yale's ten-yard line twice but didn't score. Frank Cayou's forty-five-yard run around end was the highlight of the game. Metoxen's bucking and Pierce's line play were good. Yale was held scoreless until the second half. Jakey Jamison was injured and Bemus Pierce was ejected after "...[He] and Bass of Yale got into a little scrap...," weakening the team. Overall, the team played well and gave Yale a tussle. Yale's hometown paper wrote, "The Indians have had very few hours of coaching, though this was by McCormick, and they made a very creditable showing. They are intelligent, agreeable men, and made a favorable impression." *The New York Herald* wrote, "The Indian backs were superior to Yale's, and the well-drilled teamwork was a revelation to the 2,000 spectators, who expected to see nothing but war-dance playing and to hear war-cry signaling."

Bucknell, another team the Indians had held to a low score in 1894, was their next opponent. Laid up in the hospital, Metoxen's absence weakened the Indians' backfield. Bucknell's Coach Young introduced a new interference scheme that stymied the Indians' defense and implemented a scheme of his own design they couldn't penetrate. Bucknell scored three touchdowns in the thirty-minute first half. All three kicks after were successful. Bucknell 18-Carlisle 0. In the thirty-five-minute second half, Carlisle didn't let Bucknell cross its goal line and scored its touchdown near the end of the period using a variation of the old crisscross play. Final score: Bucknell 18–Carlisle 4.

Next up for the Indians was the previously undefeated York Y.M.C.A. team they had played the previous Thanksgiving. This year's meeting was moved up from its originally scheduled date, perhaps to avoid the controversy of the year before. Metoxen was still out but the team was otherwise intact. *The York Daily* described Carlisle's peculiar approach to play calling: "It is a notable fact that the Indians have no code or signals. Their style of play

The Modern Hiawatha.

is peculiar. Every member knows exactly what he must do as soon as the centre stoops to snap the ball back. There is no word passed nor sign given, or if there are, they have been kept so concealed that nobody has heard or seen either." It is unlikely they had ESP, so signals of some sort had to be used.

Hand signals or words from a language unknown to the white men would be likely guesses. Smithsonian Linguist Emeritus Ives Goddard conjectured that, because Carlisle's players couldn't understand each other's native languages, specific words were assigned to plays, much like what was done later by Navajo Code Talkers in WWII.

An enthusiastic crowd braved the cold but was soon disappointed as the game quickly became a rout as the Indians made touchdown after touchdown in rapid succession. Results varied by newspaper report. *The Philadelphia Times* had this scoring: Seneca, Bemus Pierce, Jamison, and Seneca. Goals after were kicked by Hawley and Bemus Pierce, putting Carlisle ahead 24-0 at halftime. The onslaught continued in the second half with Cayou, Seneca, and Seneca scoring again, with the kicks after touchdown by Bemus Pierce. *The Sentinel* credited the scoring as follows: "Touchdowns—Cayou 1; Seneca 1; Hudson 1; B. Pierce 3; H. Pierce 1. Goals kicked, H. Pierce 7." One would expect the Carlisle newspaper to be more familiar with the players than either York or Philadelphia. York Y.M.C.A. got no closer to the Indians' goal than the fifteen-yard line. Carlisle won 42-0.

The Indians closed their season on Thanksgiving Day in their first appearance in the nation's largest city. The Manhattan Y.M.C.A., augmented with Crescent Athletic Club players, provided the opposition. New Yorkers expected to see bare-chested braves in warpaint and feathers. Instead, they saw athletes outfitted the same as white players. Cayou capped Carlisle's impressive opening drive with a two-yard dash into the end zone. Bemus Pierce made the kick after touchdown. Carlisle 6-Y.M.C.A. 0. The Indians' second drive was made with "...a dash and skill that temporarily dazed their opponents." Then Cayou was pushed over for the score. Carlisle 12-Y.M.C.A. 0. "At times the back work of the visitors was remarkable, and they showed a skill in the perfection of their mass plays little short of perfection." Later, the Manhattanites recovered a Carlisle fumble on the Indians' forty-yard line. They then battered the left side of Carlisle's line until Manhattan's Vermilyea scored. The kick after was unsuccessful. Carlisle 12-Y.M.C.A. 4. The second half was a field-position game with frequent punts, but Seneca was able to score another touchdown. Carlisle 16-Y.M.C.A. 4. The *New York Tribune* observed, "There were no serious accidents, and the game was unusually free from slugging."

On Friday, the Indians toured the *New York Tribune*, the Brooklyn Bridge, and a large city fire house before departing for home. The Indian

School band and several hundred students met their train. *The Indian Helper* reported,

> Our stay-at-homes were so elated at the New York victory on Thanksgiving Day on Friday evening when the team arrived, half the school turned out with the band and the four-horse herdic without horses. They met the victors at the train in town, piled them into the herdic and literally dragged them out to the school, while the band played them in, in grand style. Their yell—"Hello! Hellee! Who are we? Hello! Hellee! Who are we? Hello! Hellee! Who are we? IN-DIANS, C-A-R-L-I-S-L-E!" was repeated time and time again with a vim that must have been heard for miles around.

The players were becoming known nationally, as well as on campus, due to coverage of their games being circulated in newspapers across the country.

Carlisle ended their second season with a .500 record, including losses to two of the Big Four: Penn and Yale. The Indians were on the way to fulfilling the first part of Pratt's admonition. They had started playing the best teams in the country. Beating them would have to come later.

1895 Season Summary

Date	Opponent	Location	Indians	Opp.
Oct. 5	Pennsylvania College	Prep Field, Gettysburg, PA	10	0
Oct. 12	Duquesne C. A. C.	Exposition Park, Pittsburgh, PA	16	4
Oct. 16	University of Pennsylvania	Franklin Field, Philadelphia, PA	0	36
Oct. 26	Naval Academy	Worden Field, USNA, Annapolis, MD	0	34
Nov. 6	Yale University	Yale Field, New Haven, CT	0	18
Nov. 16	Bucknell University	Athletic Field, Lewisburg, PA	4	18
Nov. 17	York Y.M.C.A.	Y.M.C.A. Grounds, York, PA	42	0
Nov. 28	Manhattan Y.M.C.A.	Manhattan Field, New York, NY	16	4

Won 4; Lost 4; Tied 0

1895 Carlisle Indians

2
Playing the Best

Rules Changes for 1896:

If a runner's forward motion is stopped, the ball shall be deemed to be downed. At least five men must be on the line of scrimmage when the ball is snapped. If six men are behind the line, two of them must be at least five yards behind the line or outside the ends. Only one man may be in motion and toward his own goal when the ball is snapped. Interference with snapper disallowed.

After only two full seasons of play, Carlisle's football program had already generated considerable revenue. *The Indian Helper* of April 17, 1896 reported on one use of the proceeds: "The 28 shower baths in the gymnasium are well patronized. These are not to take the place of the tub bath, but are in addition to the weekly scrub all hands are required to take."

Students voted to accept vocal teacher Mary Bailey's recommendation for school colors at the school year's first Saturday evening meeting. Too late to obtain football uniforms in school colors for the current season, Carlisle's football players had to wait a year to be clad in Red and Old Gold. Not too late for 1896 was "Carlisle Indian School March," composed by former student and then current bandmaster, Dennison Wheelock.

The New York Sun predicted the Yale-Carlisle game would be a feature of the 1896 campaign because "They [Carlisle] were one of the best teams in the country last year, and this season they will be trained by W. O. Hickok, Yale's former guard, and by ex-Capt. McCormick of Yale." *The Philadelphia Inquirer* added, "...it is the first systematic coaching they have received." William Orville "Wild Bill" Hickok III was the scion of a family whose business was (and still is) making ruled-paper products in Harrisburg, Pennsylvania. Hickok predicted that Carlisle would have one of the strongest elevens in the country. Bemus Pierce again served as captain. This future coach ranked high in Pop Warner's estimation: "I've coached some great guards in my day. Jock Sutherland was one and Seraphim Post of Stanford was another. But I doubt if I ever coached a better one than Bemus Pierce." It was no wonder his teammates wanted him leading them.

Carlisle kicked off the season on September 26 with a 28–6 thumping of Dickinson College. Cayou scored four touchdowns. McFarland and Wheelock had one apiece, all in fifteen- and twenty-minute halves. One of the Pierce brothers, probably Hawley, made two of the kicks after touchdown; the other four failed. Dickinson scored its points on Heckman's ninety-yard fumble return and Ford's kick after.

Next up was a rematch with Duquesne Country and Athletic Club, one of the previous year's victims. The former college men fought hard and came close to scoring, but the Indians' goal-line defense stopped them two-and-a-half-yards short of paydirt. The most exciting play of the game was Seneca's eighty-yard run for a score. Seneca, Cayou, and Metoxen each notched a touchdown and Bemus Pierce made the kicks after. The final score was Carlisle 18-Duquesne C. & A. C. 0. Mr. Payne again drew a cartoon, but this time *The Pittsburg Daily Post* printed it, placing it above the game coverage. He would soon become a regular newspaper cartoonist with his own strip.

The Indians' next game started what was arguably the most difficult schedule any football team has ever faced. They played each of the Big Four on successive weeks, all on the road. First up were the Tigers of Princeton. Carlisle jumped out front early when Artie Miller picked up Bannard's fumble and raced one-hundred yards for what would be the only touchdown scored against the Tigers that year until their last game of the season, when Bass of Yale crossed their goal line. The Indians' defense stopped a Princeton drive on the five-yard line to prevent a score. The first half ended with Carlisle ahead 6-0. The tide turned in the second half when the overconfident Indians fumbled repeatedly, leading to Tiger touchdowns. Princeton 22-Carlisle 6.

The Yale contest has been written about more than most other Carlisle games because of a controversial play that changed the outcome of the game. The Indians jumped out in front early on Cayou's touchdown and Bemus Pierce's kick after. These were the first points scored against the Elis that year; they had shut out their seven previous opponents. Yale came back with two touchdowns and led 12-6 with four minutes left to play. Jamison made a run and was tackled but the ball hadn't touched the ground, so he hadn't been downed. His teammates helped him to his feet and provided interference for him to bolt across the goal line for a touchdown. However, Hickok whistled the play dead—it was common practice for coaches to officiate games in which their teams played in those days.

The crowd erupted when the play was called back and the score disallowed. Angry at the injustice, the Indians refused to play further.

Capt. Pratt jumped from his seat, leaving his daughter Nana, money-king Russell Sage and his philanthropist wife Olivia in their seats, and ran across the field to intervene. He told the team, "You must fight the battle out; if you leave you will be called quitters and probably lose us future opportunities. Listen, can't you hear that the crowd is with you? Now go back and play the game out and don't quit for any reason whatsoever."

The team started to go back but, indignant, Jamison held back. "Captain, that was as fair a touchdown as was ever made, and it belongs to us."

Pratt responded, "Jakey, it is ours. The umpire's decision will not take it from us. Go back and do your best and wait for tomorrow morning's papers, and you will find that you are a bigger man because the touchdown was denied than you would be if it was allowed."

The Indians failed to score again and lost 12–6. When the game ended, the crowd gave the Indians a tremendous ovation, lifted them up, and carried them to the "L" station, cheering as they went.

Newspapers castigated Yale and the officiating in the strongest possible terms by accusing them of cheating and stealing. In recent years, writers have vilified Hickok by accusing him of throwing the game for his alma mater. This writer disagrees. Yes, Hickok was a Yalie but, as coach of the Indians, he would have enhanced his reputation immensely by beating his old team, a perennial top-five finisher. He admitted to blowing the call but instant replay and challenging plays was more than a century in the future.

The morning of the Harvard game, *The Boston Globe* observed the general opinion at Harvard: "It was thought that the Indians would make a far better showing than against Yale, because Hickok, their coach, in his desire to win himself back into their good graces, undoubtedly has done all in his power to get them into shape to defeat Harvard." After the game, *The Times* of Philadelphia reported, "Over 12,000 people saw a magnificent contest full of hair-raising plays and dramatic incidents. There were no objectionable features but both teams played clean, hard foot-ball. It was a stubborn, desperate fight, but the red men got a fair show and a splendid reception from the immense crowd."

Harvard made a touchdown early but missed the kick after. The Indians played offense most of the game, but the Harvard line stood against their rushers whenever Carlisle got deep into their territory. Expecting to win this game from the start, because they didn't view the Crimson as strong as Princeton and Yale that year, the Indians were frustrated at the end, especially so because a single touchdown and kick after would have won it for them. Harvard 4–Carlisle 0.

Referring to the Carlisle team, *The Boston Herald* reported, "[I]f the men making up the former had scientific training added to the strength, quickness and endurance which they now possess, no college team in the country could stand against them, is a conclusion indorsed by most of the college graduates and undergraduates who are experts in football and who witnessed the game."

On November 5, the Carlisle manager cancelled the Thanksgiving Day game with Penn State and wired the New York Base Ball Club[3] to agree to play Brown at Manhattan Field. Other teams, including the Chicago Athletic Association, lobbied for games with the Indians. Post-season play had become a possibility but the regular season was far from over.

---

[3] Names had not been standardized for baseball and football at that time. Foot ball, foot-ball, base ball, and base-ball were used often.

Penn went into the game with Carlisle as underachievers in the eyes of its fans and sports writers after losing to Lafayette. Carlisle supporters thought their team sleepwalked the first forty minutes, allowing Penn to ring up twenty-one points on the scoreboard. The Indians came to life in the last ten minutes. They poured through the Quaker line like it was a sieve, giving their supporters hope, but they fell short of the goal line by a mere six inches and failed to score.

Metoxen blamed Carlisle's poor performance on the lack of sleep. Normally, the Indians arrived at the city the day before the game and slept overnight in a local hotel. This gameday, they slept in their own beds and were woken early to eat breakfast at 5:00 a.m. before catching the train to Philadelphia. After riding some hours, they were listless when they walked onto Franklin Field. Jonas finished with this: "I do not wish to detract from her glory, but admitting the fact, I must state in my judgement the Indians did not do themselves credit."

The same day, West Point Superintendent Ernest canceled the game with Carlisle that had been arranged for the 28th, with no reason given. Various newspapers echoed support for the Indians and some ridiculed the cadet brass for this decision, suggesting that they were cowards because there was good reason to believe Carlisle could have beaten Army.

For their first game west of Pittsburgh, the Indians played the University of Cincinnati on the home field of the Reds National League baseball team. Carlisle started slowly, perhaps not taking their opponent seriously enough, and only led 6-0 at the end of the first half. They woke in the second half, scoring four more touchdowns. Metoxen had three for the day, and Seneca and Cayou each had one. Cayou made four of the five conversions. Final score: Carlisle 28-Cincinnati 0.

When Carlisle canceled their Thanksgiving game with Penn State, they shifted the date to November 21. The Harrisburg location would be the closest thing to a home game Carlisle played that year, but it was far from being one because the state's capitol was Penn State territory. (The Dickinson game was played across town from Carlisle Barracks but on the opposing team's home field.) Just as they had done the two previous years, the Indians had only scheduled away games in 1896.

The high point of the Penn State game that rainy day was fullback Hayes' thirty-five-yard field goal. The Indians ran wild and their kicking improved. Final score: Carlisle 48-Penn State 5.

Five days later, on Thanksgiving Day, the Indians took on Brown in New York. Winning the coin toss, they picked the goal to defend and awaited Hall's kick. The Indians moved the ball almost at will until they turned it over on downs on Brown's five-yard line. The pre-bear Browns eschewed line bucking in favor of trick plays, passes (laterals), and double passes. They ran the ball well until they stalled out and had to punt. Cayou and McFarland made good gains but Cayou fumbled the ball away. Fultz ran around the ends, scoring Brown's first touchdown. He also made the kick after. Toward the end of the first half, Cayou scored and made the kick. At halftime, the score was tied at 6 all.

The effects of the grueling season showed up in the second half when McFarland was injured and replaced by a wounded Metoxen. Their play lacked the vim and vigor it showed in the first half. Gammons' seventy-yard sprint and Fultz's kick put Brown ahead to stay at 12-6. Soon, Fultz scored after a sixty-yard dash and made the kick. Down two touchdowns, the Indians' defense braced up and stopped Brown's offense. Cayou ran around left end for a touchdown and Bemus Pierce kicked the goal. Now down by a single touchdown, the Indians looked like they had a chance to at least tie the game. Weakened Metoxen missed a key tackle and Shefalo was injured. Having no other quarterback, Carlisle was allowed to return Hudson to action. Cayou wrenched his shoulder on an ensuing play and rebelled when he was taken out of the game. Miller was knocked out by a blow from a Brown player's knee, forcing him to the bench. After Brown recovered a fumble on their own forty-five-yard line, the center snapped the ball to Colby, who gave it to Gammons. Running shoulder-to-shoulder, the two raced past the defense, all but Metoxen. He made a valiant effort to stop the run, but he tackled the wrong man. Gammons made the last touchdown and Fultz kicked the goal. Brown won 24-12.

Reports of serious injuries and deaths to football players that year mounted, demanding that action be taken. On December 5, *The New York Sun* announced that Midwest college presidents would be meeting on December 14 to discuss abolishing football at their institutions.

Having gone toe-to-toe with the toughest teams in the East, Carlisle savored taking on the undefeated Champions of the West in what was advertised as the first West vs. East game ever played. *The Sun* also reported that Carlisle had challenged Wisconsin to a game in Chicago. It didn't report that they had also contacted the University of Chicago to set up a game with the Maroon. Chicago's faculty objected and established December 1st as the last day their football team would be allowed to play.

Four days after the college presidents meeting announcement, *The Harrisburg Patriot* declared that the Carlisle-Wisconsin contest was on and would be played under the lights in the Chicago Coliseum. The Indians' off-season of mending and recuperation would have to be delayed. Never one to miss an opportunity to promote Carlisle, Superintendent Pratt arranged for a large party numbering over fifty to make the trip. The group included administrators and spouses, the twenty-five-piece school band, nineteen football players, Disciplinarian Thompson, and Dr. Montezuma. They left for Chicago on the night of the 16th. Arriving before breakfast on 18th, they checked into the Palmer House and ate before going sightseeing.

Harness racing trainer Ike Fleming, representing the Press Club, led the team and band first to the Chicago Board of Trade wheat pit, where "The hoarse cries of excited traders rose to the rafters and men threw their hands here and there in insane fashion."

Lone Wolf hissed, "The savages!"

Metoxen shook his head, whispering, "Too bad, too bad!"

When a lull came, the traders called for music but the Carlislians hurried away to more congenial surroundings at the Stock Exchange. As they entered, a broker threw a new pigskin to them and Wheelock returned it. Footballers and brokers passed and punted the ball back and forth so rapidly the *Tribune* reporter couldn't follow the activity.

Joseph Townsend, who had boxed at the Chicago Athletic Association, was itching to test the Indians, Metoxen in particular. He found Bemus Pierce first and grabbed the big Seneca below the knees. A flick of the leg put Townsend on his back, seeing no need to further test Pierce's physical power. The band struck up "America" and all sang the hymn. On their way out, they "...gave forth one of the most remarkable college yells ever heard. The peculiar qualities of the Indian voice change the innocent syllables into the semblance of a war Hoop."

Lo-lee—Who are we!
Lo-lee—Who are we!
Lo-lee—Who are we!
Indians.
Car-l-i-s-l-e!

The next stop was the Chicago Athletic Association clubhouse, an 1893 Venetian Gothic landmark at 12 S. Michigan Avenue in the heart of the Loop, where they toured its impressive facilities. After lunch at the Palmer House, the team practiced on Marshall Field, courtesy of Chicago's coach Amos Alonzo Stagg.

That evening, the band played at the Palmer House Rotunda, the Auditorium, and the Hamilton Club. The band's program included classical pieces, popular airs, and an original work by Dennison Wheelock, "From Savagery Into Civilization." At the last stop, Thompson gave a little talk about Carlisle Indian School and its awakening to athletics.

Cayou was not yet in condition to suit up for the game with Wisconsin, so the Indians were at less than full strength. Carlisle won the toss and elected to defend the north goal. After much back and forth, the Indians pushed Metoxen over the goal line for a touchdown and Bemus Pierce made the kick. On the next possession, Carlisle's offense bogged down, forcing a punt. Bemus kicked it so high the ball wedged itself in the Coliseum's roof girders. The crowd cheered when a small boy climbed up to dislodge it. The attempt-

1896 Team

ed replay was blocked, with Wisconsin ending up with the ball on Carlisle's four-yard line. Peel was shoved over the goal line for a touchdown, but Richards missed a kick from a difficult angle. At halftime Carlisle led 6 to 4.

Both sides battled fiercely in the second half, causing their respective supporters to fill the place with cheers. In a strange play, Richards kicked but the ball landed in the seats behind the goal line. The ball must have bounced out of the seats because Wisconsin's right end Sheldon, who had been on side when the ball was kicked, pounced on it for a touchdown. Richards missed another difficult kick, making the score Wisconsin 8-Carlisle 6. Carlisle's offense then moved the ball well, culminating in a McFarland touchdown. Bemus Pierce made the kick, putting Carlisle ahead 12-8. Wisconsin tried to kick a field goal but failed. They then brought in Pat O'Day the famed Australian kicker, but he had no success, either. Later, the Indians steadily moved the ball down the field and pushed Jamison over to score Carlisle's last touchdown. Pierce again made the kick. Carlisle 18-Wisconsin 8. O'Day tried another field goal but missed. The Indians continued moving the ball until time ran out.

On Sunday morning, the Indians attended church services of their choice before taking a tour of the new University of Chicago athletic facilities. Stagg made everything available for them to see. Leading the tour, he "...spared no pains in impressing the visitors with the greatness and glory of their institution." He was equally impressed with them:

"I never saw such a fine set of men physically, and with proper coaching I believe they could whip any team in the country. They seem to be made of steel and rubber. They beat Wisconsin by main strength alone, as their interference was wretched, and at times worse than useless."

End-of-year rankings had Princeton 1st, Penn 2nd, Harvard 3rd, Yale 4th. Retrospective rankings had Brown 10th, Carlisle 11th, Wisconsin 12th, Penn State 23rd, and Dickinson 27th. What a loaded gauntlet to run! Pratt's second admonition was satisfied in whole as Carlisle had gained the reputation of playing the cleanest of any team.

A special report out of Chicago claimed that University of Chicago Coach Amos Alonzo Stagg would be training the Indians in the fall. His praise for the players could have been interpreted as a pitch to become a full-time coach for the Indians, something they hadn't had so far or, more likely, for bringing the entire Carlisle team to Chicago. Having a lifetime professorship at Chicago, a position rare for a football coach, Stagg would not likely have considered changing institutions. Other reports had Bemus Pierce and Metoxen enrolling at Chicago for the next season.

1896 Season Summary

Date	Opponent	Location	Indians	Opp.
Sep. 26	Dickinson College	Dickinson College Athletic Field, Carlisle, PA	28	6
Oct. 3	Duquesne C. A. C.	Exposition Park, Pittsburgh, PA	18	0
Oct. 14	Princeton University	University Field, Princeton, NJ	6	22
Oct. 24	Yale University	Manhattan Field, New York, NY	6	12
Oct. 31	Harvard University	Soldiers' Field, Cambridge, MA	0	4
Nov. 7	University of Pennsylvania	Franklin Field, Philadelphia, PA	0	21
Nov. 14	University of Cincinnati	League Park, Cincinnati, OH	28	0
Nov. 21	Pennsylvania State College	6th Street Grounds, Harrisburg, PA	48	5
Nov. 26	Brown University	Manhattan Field, New York, NY	12	24
Dec. 19	University of Wisconsin	Chicago Coliseum, Chicago, IL	18	8

Won 5; Lost 5; Tied 0

Winning at Last

Rule Changes for 1897:

There were no rules changes in 1897.

In January 1897, *The Philadelphia Inquirer* reported on rumors circulating around the Chicago campus: Jonas Metoxen and Frank Hudson were going to enroll at Chicago and play on their team. In February, *The Evening Bulletin* of Providence, Rhode Island predicted that Carlisle would be weakened by the loss of Metoxen to Princeton, Lone Wolf and Cayou to Chicago, and two other players to Wisconsin.

On top of this, halfback David McFarland almost didn't make it back to school. David's elderly father was the current chief of the Nez Perce tribe, many of whom wanted to replace him with his son. David wanted none of it—at least for the time being—and refused the offer. They held a pow wow and incarcerated him in a small wooden building. After five days, he saw his opportunity to escape when the guards were sleeping and took it. He finally shook those following him in Kansas City. He was determined not to return to Idaho until he graduated.

In early September, pundits were still saying that Carlisle would be short-handed this year but bringing on William T. "Billy" Bull, the celebrated Yale fullback and then head coach at Wesleyan, would improve Carlisle's kicking game. Stagg remained at Chicago. A wire service report had Cayou unable to play this year due to injuries received last season. The September 22 *Boston Journal* reported that the Carlisle starting line-up would be unchanged from the previous year except Harrison Printup would be playing center, replacing the departed Lone Wolf, who returned to his tribe instead of enrolling at Chicago. In spite of earlier stories in the press, he was the only starter from the previous year to leave.

As students and staff were trekking back from outings and vacations, *The Indian Helper* reported on the status of the new athletic field:

> The 1/4 mile running track is twenty feet wide. The foundation stones to the depth of a foot or two are laid and halfway around, medium sized stones which went through the crusher are down. There will be finer stone still put on and the whole covered with locomotive sparks, then rolled and packed according to approved methods for making the best kind of a track.
>
> Does the Government put so much expense upon your athletic field? No! The money comes from the athletic fund-money earned by the boys themselves at the various games.

The September 17th edition of the school's paper reported that Billy Bull had arrived and would remain at the school throughout the season. With Bemus Pierce again serving as captain, practice was underway. The Indians' schedule must not have been completely set yet because the September 29

Denver Post declared that the Indians would play Denver Athletic Club in December.

On October 2, the Indians traveled across town to open their season against a good Dickinson College team. Early in the game, Carlisle blocked a Dickinson punt on their own fifteen-yard line. The Indians secured the loose ball but Bemus Pierce and Dickinson's Sheetz were ejected for rough play. Peirce said, "White man hit Indian ten times. Me hit white boy once. We quits." Once was all most of his opponents could take.

Metoxen rushed the ball over for a touchdown and Hudson, who had been tutored on the fine art of kicking by Bull, made the kick. Carlisle 6-Dickinson 0. The Indians worked the ball to Dickinson's twenty-five-yard line, where they attempted, and failed, to kick a field goal. On their next possession, McFarland and Metoxen moved the ball down the field. Metoxen capped the drive with a run around right end for his second touchdown. Hudson again made the kick, raising the score to Carlisle 12-Dickinson 0.

After Jamison returned the ensuing kickoff, the team rushed the ball down the field. McFarland scored at the end of a fifteen-yard run. Hudson made the kick. Carlisle 18-Dickinson 0. A little later, Scott recovered a Dickinson fumble. After a series of long runs, Metoxen ran around left end for his third touchdown. Hudson again made the kick. At halftime, the score was Carlisle 24-Dickinson 0.

Dickinson stiffened in the second half, but Metoxen scored two more touchdowns. Final score Carlisle 36-Dickinson 0.

The Monday after the Dickinson game, *The Philadelphia Inquirer* printed a schedule of games for the major eastern schools for the season. Saturday the 9th was open for Carlisle. On Thursday, *The Sentinel* reported on Carlisle training for their game with Princeton a week and a half away. The same day, *The Bloomsburg Daily* announced a game to be played on Saturday between Bloomsburg State Normal School and Carlisle Indian School. This meeting must have been hurriedly added to both teams' schedules. No full play-by-play was found, but what is known is that Carlisle scored four touchdowns, two by McFarland and two by Jamison, in the twenty-minute first half. Bemus Pierce made two of the kicks after. One of the Pierce brothers blocked Normal's field goal attempt. Carlisle led 20-0 at halftime.

Bloomsburg's defense stiffened in the second half. The only scoring came when Cayou scooped up a blocked punt and ran it in for a touchdown. Bemus Pierce made the kick after. The final score was Carlisle 26-

Bloomsburg 0. Both sides were pleased with the clean play and Bloomsburg officials hoped to play the Indians again in the future.

Princeton and Carlisle both fought fiercely, in spite of the heat, in a game that was closer than the score would indicate. Princeton scored first on a mass play that sent Bannard over for a touchdown. Baird's kick missed. Later in the first half, Wheeler returned Hudson's punt forty-five yards. After a few short gains, Princeton's Reiter made a fifty-yard run but the Indian held the Tigers on downs deep in Carlisle territory. The Indians lost the ball immediately, allowing Bannard to score his second touchdown. This time Baird made the kick. The half ended with the score Princeton 10–Carlisle 0.

Both sides stalled in the early going in the second half, even though they played with ferocious intensity. The first score happened when Holt blocked Hudson's punt, and Reiter recovered the loose ball and ran fifty yards for a touchdown. Baird missed the kick. Princeton 14–Carlisle 0. Baird returned the ensuing kickoff twenty yards. He, Reiter, and Kelley each made large gains moving the ball down the field. Kelley went over from the five-yard line. Holt missed an easy kick. Princeton 18–Carlisle 0. The Indians never threatened to score. The game ended with the ball on their fifteen-yard line.

After the game, Carlisle disciplinarian and team manager William Thompson declared that the Indians would not play Princeton again. He said, "It was evident from the beginning that Princeton was bound to win by fair means or foul, and that was the most brutal game the Indians have ever been in."

With Jamison out and others playing injured, the Indians were lethargic at the start of the Yale game, giving up a touchdown to Benjamin and points after to Cadwalader ten minutes into the twenty-five-minute first half. Drawing first blood roused the Elis. The Indians remained indifferent, allowing Yale to move the ball down the field. Kieffer scored Yale's second touchdown and Cadwalader again made the kick after. The score remained unchanged until the end of the first half. Yale 12–Carlisle 0.

After a punt exchange that opened the second half, Yale drove the ball with small, steady gains terminated with Benjamin going over for the Elis' third touchdown. Cadwalader made the kick after. Yale 18–Carlisle 0. After another punt exchange, Hawley Pierce left the game with an injured ankle and was replaced by Thaddeus Redwater (Cheyenne). The Indians began playing with a fire not present earlier in the game. They stunned Yale when quarterback Hudson positioned himself farther back of the line. Left halfback Cayou took the snap from center and passed it to Hudson, who had aligned himself in line with the goal posts. Hudson split the uprights with a perfect drop kick, making Carlisle only the second team to score against the Elis that year. Yale 18–Carlisle 5. After a punt exchange, McBride went back to kick Yale out of danger. The Indians swarmed him, and Seneca blocked the punt. Miller recovered it for Carlisle. Yale stiffened and got the ball on downs, but Benjamin fumbled it on the first play. Metoxen and Cayou made small gains but nothing more. In what may have been an early version of a draw play, Cayou received the ball from the quarterback but didn't move. He stood still for an instant as if dazed. When the Yale linemen relaxed, Cayou dashed through them for a touchdown. Hudson missed the kick. Yale 18–Carlisle 9. Yale culminated a steady drive with a touchdown with three seconds left on the clock. Final score: Yale 24–Carlisle 9.

Carlisle got a breather in the heart of their schedule by taking on mismatched Pennsylvania College in Gettysburg. Apparently pleased with his performance against Yale, the Indians started Redwater at left guard. Everything went Carlisle's way. Line bucking, end runs, and strong interference resulted in ten touchdowns with five of the kicks after successful. The twenty-minute first half ended with Carlisle ahead 50–0.

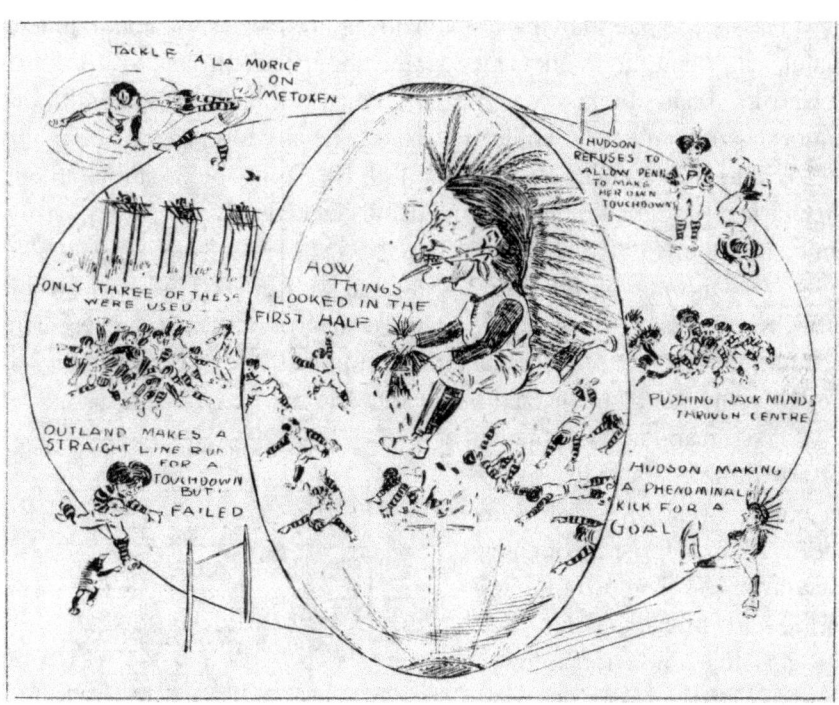

Their opponents' play improved in the second half but not enough to score. The play of the day was Metoxen's eighty-yard run on a revolving wedge play. The fifteen-minute second half ended with Carlisle further ahead, 82–0.

A large rooting section from Carlisle, including the band, entertained the sportswriters before the game. The band's impromptu concert, apparently not done before, got special attention. "That the innovation was appreciated by the crowd was amply attested in thunderclaps of applause after each measure." The game against the Quakers on Franklin Field didn't start well for the banged-up Indians. Hare made Penn's first touchdown after only five minutes had ticked off the clock. Minds' kick failed. The Indians were able to advance the ball with a close revolving wedge but were unable to push the ball across for a score. When the drive stalled on Penn's fifteen-yard line, Hudson dropped back to the twenty to drop kick a field goal to put Carlisle ahead 5–4.

Twenty-five minutes into the first half, Minds ran the ball over for another Quaker touchdown, but Weeks muffed the punt out. Penn 8–Carlisle 5. With two minutes left in the first half and the ball again on Penn's fifteen, Hudson drop kicked a second field goal, putting the Indians ahead 10–8. Penn was unable to do much before the half ended with Carlisle still ahead.

The second half started with too many punt exchanges to count. Fifteen minutes in, Penn mounted a drive Hare culminated with a ten-yard touchdown run. Again, the kick was missed. Penn 12–Carlisle 10. Several more punt exchanges followed. Hudson fumbled one and was tackled behind his own goal line for a safety. Penn 14–Carlisle 10. Shortly before time ran out, McCracken scored a touchdown and Minds kicked successfully. The game ended with the score Penn 20–Carlisle 10.

The Philadelphia Inquirer was amused with Frank Hudson's kicking prowess. "The game was a forcible argument in favor of reducing field goals to a couple of points [from five] valuation. Every point made by Pennsylvania was earned nobly, not by field goals, but by touchdowns."

The Indians' next opponent, Brown, fumbled the ball away on its own twenty-five-yard line shortly after receiving the opening kickoff. In less than two minutes of the start, McFarland slid over the goal line for a touchdown. Bemus Pierce missed the kick after. Carlisle 4–Brown 0. At the

end of a long Brown drive, a Gammon fumble rolled across Carlisle's goal line. Metoxen fell on it, giving Brown a safety and two points. Later, Miller muffed a Brown punt. Hapgood snatched it up and ran free for forty yards and a score. Richardson made the kick after. Brown 8–Carlisle 4. The Indians settled down to mass plays for steady gains and a Metoxen touchdown. Hudson made the kick. Carlisle 10–Brown 8. On a trick play, Fultz caught the Indians off guard and ran fifty yards untouched for a touchdown. He also made the kick. The first half ended at Brown 14–Carlisle 10.

The Indians played the second half with desperate vigor. Hudson eventually squirmed over the goal line, tying the score at 14 all, but his kick missed. With darkness approaching, Hapgood went around right end for a thirty-yard gain. Then Gammon was pushed over for a touchdown, but Richardson's kick failed. Brown went ahead 18–14. Just before the game ended, Wheelock's replacement, Frank Scott, collided with Brown's Hall. A grizzly bear clinch ensued. Hall freed his hand to clutch Scott's throat, while the latter swung wildly trying to hit Hall. A battle royal between the two teams exploded. The forty policemen, who had obstructed spectators' views all afternoon, separated the fighting players. After a time out, the game continued with no further scoring. Wheelock and McFarland were injured so badly during the game they were taken to the hospital.

A week later, Carlisle traveled to Chicago to play Illinois under the lights. The Illini opened with a dash, taking the opening kickoff and driving to the Indians' fifteen-yard line before giving up the ball. After a couple of possessions for each side, Illinois pushed the ball rapidly down the field with Hall making the last yard and a half for the first points of the game. Shuler made a

SCENE AT THE COLISEUM DURING THE INDIAN-ILLINOIS GAME.

difficult kick. Illinois 6–Carlisle 0. After a few punt exchanges, the Indians moved the ball to the Illinois twenty-five using Penn's guards-back formation and Princeton's tandem bucks. Then Hudson dropkicked a field goal to put Carlisle on the board. Illinois 6–Carlisle 5. Illinois ran several trick plays, all losing yardage, but their lead held until the end of the twenty-five-minute first half.

Early second-half drives stalled before the Indians moved the ball down the field with mass plays, including Metoxen shaking himself through the Illinois line for ten yards. They then pushed McFarland over the last yard for Carlisle's first touchdown. Hudson made an easy kick. Carlisle 11–Illinois 6. Bemus Pierce, Metoxen, Miller, and McFarland all carried the ball on Carlisle's next possession with McFarland going over for the score. Hudson made the kick for a score of Carlisle 17–Illinois 6. Injured Miller soldiered on but Cayou had to come in for McFarland. Metoxen made most of the yardage during the next drive and was shoved across for the touchdown. Hudson's kick was good. Carlisle 23–Illinois 6. Neither team threatened after that.

The York Gazette circulated the rumor that Carlisle would play York Y.M.C.A. a week from Saturday instead of Thanksgiving Day as they had in the past. The Thanksgiving game with Cincinnati was played in a downpour but without much wind. After a long drive four minutes into the twenty-five-minute first half, Metoxen plowed over left tackle from inside the one-yard line for Carlisle's first score. Then, on a series using the guards-back formation, he made several more carries before going over from the one, but Hudson's kick failed this time. The first half ended with Carlisle ahead 10–0.

The field got muddier as the game went on, so the officials shortened the second half to twenty minutes due to weather conditions. Hudson made a touchdown-saving tackle of Nieman, and on another play, Rendig was stopped a foot short. Carlisle won the mud bath 10–0.

Weather for the Ohio Medics on the Saturday after Thanksgiving in Columbus wasn't much better. It was cold and cloudy and the field was covered with mud. Worse yet, five Carlisle players, including their star field-goal kicker, were too beat up to play, forcing subs to be inserted in their places. In spite of all this, the pace was fast and exciting. Two minutes into the game, Cayou delighted the crowd by gathering up a fumble and racing sixty yards for Carlisle's first touchdown. Jamison soon followed with one of his own. A Pierce brother missed the kick after the touchdown. The twenty-minute first half ended with Carlisle ahead of the Medics 10–0.

WHEN THE BALL WAS ON THE INDIANS' FIVE-YARD LINE.

The Medics didn't let up in the second half, despite being behind. They scored two touchdowns, making both kicks after. But Carlisle didn't slow either. They scored two more touchdowns, missing one of the kicks. The gamed ended with Carlisle ahead 20 to 12.

A conjecture was published in the *San Francisco Chronicle* the day of the Medics game: "If it is possible to induce the directors of the Indian School to allow the aborigines to visit this Coast during the winter the San Francisco public will see this great team on one of its gridirons. This plan was almost consummated last year, but fell through at the last moment." None of the rumored post-season games materialized, quite possibly because the tough schedule had battered the team.

At 6-4-0, Carlisle had its first winning season. And those four losses were against highly ranked teams. Penn and Yale, both of whom Carlisle played, were the critics' choices for national champions. And the only points scored against Princeton, the only team to shut out Carlisle, were the six Yale scored in beating the 3rd ranked Tigers. No other team played a schedule half as tough as Carlisle's. They played three of The Big Four, all on the road, plus Brown, Illinois, Cincinnati, and a surprisingly tough Ohio Medical University team. The only team they played that had a losing record was Pennsylvania College (today's Gettysburg College). Even Dickinson College was ranked in the top 25 teams that year.

1897 Season Summary

Date	Opponent	Location	Indians	Opp.
Oct. 2	Dickinson College	Dickinson College Athletic Field, Carlisle, PA	36	0
Oct. 9	Bloomsburg State Normal School	Normal Field, Bloomsburg, PA	26	0
Oct. 16	Princeton University	University Field, Princeton, NJ	0	18
Oct. 23	Yale University	Polo Grounds, New York, NY	9	24
Oct. 30	Pennsylvania College	Nixon Field, Gettysburg, PA	82	0
Nov. 6	University of Pennsylvania	Franklin Field, Philadelphia, PA	10	20
Nov. 13	Brown University	Manhattan Field, New York, NY	14	18
Nov. 20	University of Illinois	Chicago Coliseum, Chicago, IL	23	6
Nov. 25	University of Cincinnati	League Park, Cincinnati, OH	10	0
Nov. 27	Ohio Medical University	Western League Park, Columbus, OH	20	12

Won 6; Lost 4; Tied 0

Another Winning Season

Rules Changes for 1898:

Touchdown: 5 points
Kick after touchdown: 1 points
Field goal: 5 points

The point adjustments may have been in response to complaints by those who considered scores made by kicks to be overvalued, those made by Carlisle's Frank Hudson in particular. A touchdown without the conversion was increased to equal a field goal, and the penalty for missing the kick after touchdown was cut in half.

Opponents paid Carlisle handsomely for appearing on their fields and at neutral sites. Although the $10,000 the team earned in 1897 paled in comparison to Yale's $100,000 athletic war chest, the Indians' athletic committee had accumulated a significant amount by 1898. The school, being an underfunded government institution, had ready uses for this money. However, it almost didn't get to put it to use. In January, Rep. Marcus A. Smith of Arizona moved to strike funding for Carlisle from the Indian appropriation bill. After Rep. James S. Sherman of New York informed the members that the "football eleven had placed $7,000 in the treasury of that college during the past season," the motion failed by 29 for and 65 against. Carlisle was saved.

Some of the football money was used to purchase land for athletic grounds suitable for practice fields for various sports and to build a standard-size football field with a quarter-mile track around it suitable for hosting interscholastic events. For the first time, the Indians had a respectable home field.

But they started the season with more than a new place to play. They had a new coach, a new captain, some new players, and a tough ten-game schedule. Gone were halfbacks McFarland and Jamison, important players who left large holes to be filled. Drop-kicker extraordinaire Frank Hudson was elected captain, but Bemus Pierce was still a major cog in the Carlisle machine. John A. Hall, Yale '97, a consensus All-America end, agreed to coach the Indians. He induced Arthur Wilfred Ransome, also of Yale, to work with the backs.

First up for the Indians on their ten-game schedule was the Bloomsburg Normal squad. Few outside the Indian School's students and staff saw the game because school officials closed it to the public in deference to Dickinson College, which also hosted a home game across town that day. Bloomsburg never threatened to score in this lopsided game in which the halves had been shortened to fifteen minutes because the game wasn't expected to be close. Most notable in the 43-0 blowout were Hudson's three field goals and newcomer Hazlett's long runs, including two for touchdowns.

In their first home game on their new field open to the public, the Indians thrashed Susquehanna University even worse than they had Bloomsburg Normal. Seneca, Miller, Hazlett, Hawley Pierce, and Cayou all scored touchdowns. Metoxen scored three. Hudson made all eight kicks after touchdowns. Carlisle 48-Susquehanna 0.

The warm-up games out of the way, Cornell, a team some thought in a class with the Big Four, awaited them. Carlisle received the opening kickoff and moved the ball ten yards before fumbling it away on their own twenty-five yard line. Cornell rushed the ball down the field with steady gains. Whiting made the touchdown, and Young made the kick after. Cornell 6-Carlisle 0. The Indians came to life, making large gains. Shortly before the end of the twenty-five-minute first half, Metoxen carried the ball over the goal line. Hudson made his kick, tying the score at 6 all at halftime.

Cornell changed its strategy for the twenty-minute second half. They practically abandoned mass formations. Instead, they ran trick play after trick play, confusing the Indians so badly that Whiting scored three more touchdowns. Young missed one of the kicks. A Rochester sportswriter conjectured, "Perhaps such an exciting and fast football game was never played before in Ithaca, at least never such a rough one." The Cornell partisans cheered so loudly players couldn't hear signals over the crowd noise. Cornell won 23-6.

After the game, Cornell coach Glenn S. "Pop" Warner complained that "...never before had he seen such rough playing." The explanation given was that the umpire, a Cornell man, ironically showed his impartiality by overlooking Carlisle's transgressions. Pratt responded to *The Pittsburg Press* that "...no unfair tactics will be allowed on the team, and that if any true reports come to him of the Indians slugging in a game the team will be withdrawn from the athletic world."

The game against Williams College provided little respite from the toughest part of the season. The Indians played a machine-like first half and part of the second before waking up when they realized they could lose. They scored three touchdowns in rapid succession, putting themselves back in the win column. Carlisle 17-Williams 6.

The next Saturday, Hudson's forty-five-yard first-half field goal put a scare into Yale. Changing signals and long punts turned the tide as the Eli line turned impregnable in the second half. Yale scored twice more and made both kicks for a final score of Yale 18-Carlisle 5 in a game that was much closer than expected but left the Indians the worse for wear.

Battered Carlisle made the same mistake twice against Harvard by waiting for punts—which were free balls at the time—to roll over the goal line for touchbacks. Alert Harvard men snatched the ball while Carlisle players stood flatfooted watching both times. One of Harvard's touchdowns, the difference in the game, came from one of these misplays. Carlisle's score came from a twenty-yard Hudson drop-kicked field goal from a difficult angle. Harvard scored a second touchdown but didn't convert. Cayou made several good runs, but they weren't enough. The Crimson prevailed 11 to 5, but its players were disappointed for being scored upon.

Although Dickinson College was 6-0 and scored upon only once coming into the game, Carlisle treated it as a warmup for the game with Penn the following week. They experimented with new plays and formations and rested starters in the second half. The final score was reported as 46-0, 47-0, and 48-0 by different publications, probably because the points awarded for touchdowns and extra points had changed from the year before, confusing the local sportswriters. Using the *Philadelphia Times'* scoring summary, Carlisle scored eight touchdowns: Cayou had three, Metoxen and Miller two each, and Hazlett one. Bemus Pierce kicked seven extra points, giving the Indians a total of forty-seven points (eight touchdowns @ five points each plus seven extra points @ one point each). The previous year's scoring system would have yielded only forty-six points.

    Stinging from a loss to Harvard the previous week, Penn took out its frustrations on the Indians. Carlisle received the opening kickoff but punted after failing to make the yardage necessary for a first down. Once Penn had possession, they didn't relinquish the ball until they had scored four touchdowns (Carlisle's kick offs following Penn touchdowns were not considered possessions). Only then did the Indians get the ball and a chance to score. Wheelock made a thirty-five-yard place kick with Hudson holding to put Carlisle on the scoreboard. The Quakers continued to work their guards-back formation to perfection. They gained yardage on almost every play, running up the largest score against the Indians since their second year of play. Penn won 35 to 5.

    The next Saturday, Carlisle traveled to Chicago to play Illinois again, this time outdoors. When Illinois' first possession stalled, Hawley Pierce burst through their line and blocked the punt. Wheelock picked up the loose ball and trotted across the goal line for Carlisle's first score. Hudson made the conversion. Carlisle 6–Illinois 0.

The Illini repulsed Carlisle's next drive. This time, they did something with the ball until they reached the Indians' twenty-five-yard line, where they fumbled. Carlisle retained possession for the rest of the first half.

The Indians started the second half with "a series of chopping, crippling rushes." But each drive bogged down, and punts ensued. Eventually, the Indians carried the ball seventy yards down the field with straight football, capped by Cayou's two-yard touchdown run. Wheelock's kick failed. Carlisle 11-Illinois 0. When the Indians got the ball back, they moved it down the field, five, ten, fifteen yards at a time. Cayou carried the ball over the goal line but was pushed back, as was legal at that time. With the ball on the one-inch line, the timekeeper blew his whistle, cheating Carlisle out of a third touchdown. Spectators were disappointed in seeing little of Carlisle's star players due to injuries sustained in the Penn game. Bruised Bemus Pierce limped around the field. Sore and crippled, Hudson had to be replaced, as did the other backs, except Metoxen.

The schedule had called for ten games, but who was the tenth opponent? The *1899 Spalding's Guide* had Harrisburg as a 40-0 loser to the Indians. On-line football databases include Dartmouth as Carlisle's last opponent. The November 24 *Cleveland Plain Dealer* listed the Carlisle-Cincinnati game to be played that day. The next day, *The Harrisburg Patriot* wrote that the Indians had played Cincinnati on Thanksgiving Day. Not to be left out, the *Omaha Bee* named Wisconsin as their opponent and Chicago as the location. All couldn't be true.

Wisconsin Manager J. L. Fischer wrote to *The Milwaukee Journal* on November 23, apologizing that the upcoming game with Carlisle had been called off because the Wisconsin team would likely be too banged up to play the Indians after playing a hard game on Thanksgiving. No record could be found of Dartmouth playing Carlisle that year. However, Dartmouth did play Cincinnati, and Cincinnati played Indiana on Thanksgiving. Further research into the Cincinnati game found that a Thanksgiving game between Carlisle and Cincinnati had been scheduled but was canceled due to Carlisle's financial demands. Later, the press reported on the Cincinnati Athletic Council's football debt and attempts to raise money to pay it off. They owed Carlisle a $200 debt, possibly left over from the previous year or as a penalty for breaking the current year's contract.

What about the Carlisle-Harrisburg game in *Spalding's Guide*? The November 28 edition of *The New York Sun* listed the Carlisle Indians as having beaten Harrisburg 40-0 the previous week. Nothing about that game could be found, but the November 24 *Baltimore Sun* included a write-up of a Thanksgiving game between the Carlisle Indians' second or scrub team and a Carlisle town "all-collegiate" team. The scrubs won 40-0. This had to be the mystery game. The scores were the same and the locale was close. Today's problems with the press are not new.

Not everyone was ready to close out the season. A game over the Christmas holiday between All-Kentucky college stars and Carlisle was proposed but wasn't arranged.

The Baltimore Sun reported that Bemus Pierce and Metoxen would be returning to their homes, leaving large holes in Carlisle's line-up for 1899. It also said that Hudson, Rogers, and Cayou would be attending Dickinson College and playing on its team next year. Further evidence of Carlisle having ended its season and the possible transfer of players existed in the coverage of the Dickinson College-Penn State game played on Thanksgiving. Rogers was listed at left end and Cayou at left halfback for Dickinson. They wouldn't have shifted teams if Carlisle had not ended its season.

Carlisle scored on all its opponents that year. Few others put up points against Cornell, Yale, Harvard, and Penn. At 5-4-0, Carlisle had its second straight winning season but still no win over any of the Big Four. The second half of Pratt's first stipulation had not yet been fulfilled.

John A. Hall completed his one-season head coaching career with a winning record. He assisted at Navy the next year before starting a career as a chemist. After the Williams game, *The Albany Argus* interviewed Assistant Coach Ransome:

> The Indian from one point of view is an ideal man to coach, for he does, or at least tries to do, exactly as he is told. Teach him a short, quick play, such as a dive between guard and tackle, and in a few lessons he will execute it to perfection. He has in his make-up just the amount of dash and fire which is necessary for play of this style. The question of pluck does not come up at all, for not one of them knows what fear is. There is a defect hard to overcome. The Indian is above all a stoic and it takes considerable excitement to warm him up. As soon as we see that they are really roused, we are sure that they will do their level best, but sometimes this doesn't happen until late in the game, and here lies the danger. That was the trouble with the team during the first half and part of the second Saturday afternoon. They were sure of winning and did not see any reason for not being perfect-

ly calm. Consequently, they played a rather machine-like game. Toward the end when the game was really in danger, you saw how they woke up. Very few elevens in the country could have held them during that last eight minutes.

When you know that there are not more than thirty-five braves in the Carlisle school available as football material, you can realize what a born player the Indian is. There is not a college in the country that can show such a good proportion. Out of those thirty-five, we pick twenty-one or twenty-two who compose the squad that is taken on the trips. Yet out of this number we have to depend upon twelve or 13 men. If one man is laid out, the team is severely crippled. Fortunately, the red man is not easily injured.

1898 Season Summary

Date	Opponent	Location	Indians	Opp.
Sep. 24	Bloomsburg State Normal School	Indian Field, Carlisle Barracks, PA	43	0
Oct. 1	Susquehanna University	Indian Field, Carlisle Barracks, PA	48	0
Oct. 8	Cornell University	Percy Field, Ithaca, NY	6	23
Oct. 15	Williams College	Ridgefield Grounds, Albany, NY	17	6
Oct. 22	Yale University	Yale Field, New Haven, CT	5	18
Oct. 29	Harvard University	Soldiers' Field, Cambridge, MA	10	20
Nov. 5	Dickinson College	Dickinson College Athletic Field, Carlisle, PA	47	0
Nov. 12	University of Pennsylvania	Franklin Field, Philadelphia, PA	5	35
Nov. 19	University of Illinois	Jackson Field, Chicago, IL	11	0

Won 5; Lost 4; Tied 0

3
A Coach of Their Own

Rules Changes for 1899:
If the ball should strike an official, it is still a live ball in play. If a player advances more than one step beyond the point where he makes a fair catch to heel in, the opposition is allowed to line up five yards nearer to him.

After completing a 10-2-0 season at the helm of the Cornell University football team in 1898, Glenn Scobey Warner felt secure in keeping his position. Attending college hadn't been his goal after leaving high school. Instead, he worked two years as a tinsmith and saved a little money. But he made some bad bets at a racetrack and lost it all. Away from home at the time and knowing his father wanted him to become a lawyer, Glenn sent his dad a Cornell Law School brochure. His father sent enough money for his son to enroll and live on, too, one assumes. Law studies didn't take up all of Glenn's time. He also played guard on the Cornell football team. Although he was only a couple of years older than his teammates, they nicknamed him "Pop."

After graduating, Warner coached football at both Iowa State and Georgia for two years and practiced law in the off seasons. In 1897, his alma mater offered him $600 to coach his old team. After much consideration, he accepted. Cornell went 5-3-1 that year, with the season ending on a 4-0 heartbreaker to Penn. He figured he could go about his business practicing law until the start of the 1899 season. But that wasn't to be.

Pop's assistant wanted his job and one of the two candidates for team captain supported the assistant. Rather than getting embroiled in a political fight at Cornell, he gave Carlisle a second look. Early on, commentators had observed the Indians' athleticism and vigor. Effective coaching was all they needed to become a top team. The father of American football Walter Camp had recommended the young, innovative Warner to Pratt for the Carlisle job, but he wasn't available then.

Carlisle's players had impressed Warner in their hard-fought loss to Cornell, piquing his interest. During his interview, he and Pratt hit it off, but there was a problem: Pratt had no idea how he would pay Warner's salary. Taking a leap of faith, the former tinsmiths shook hands and the deal was done. Pop Warner was Carlisle's head football coach.

At the start of practice for the 1899 season, the Indians didn't impress Warner. "My first view of Carlisle's football material was anything but favorable. The boys who reported for practice were listless and scrawny, many looking as though they had been drawn through a knothole. My heart went down into my shoes, for I was getting twelve-hundred dollars a year and felt that only an ever-victorious team could justify such an enormous salary." Pratt allayed his concerns. "They have been on farms all summer. These Pennsylvania farmers insist on getting their money's worth. The youngsters will soon begin to pick up weight, so don't worry." Although they filled out some, Carlisle's teams were usually lighter than their major opponents.

Warner coaching his Indian players

Warner inherited an experienced squad. Earlier reports of several players departing proved false, but Bemus Pierce and Cayou were gone. Pierce was coaching Buffalo, and Cayou was studying engineering and playing football at Illinois. New captain Martin Wheelock, halfback Isaac Seneca, and at quarterback, the nation's best dropkicker, Frank Hudson, returned as did several others whose names would soon loom large in Carlisle history. But getting them to work at their optimum presented a challenge.

Warner treated his new team as he had been treated as a player and as white boys were generally handled at the time: with heavy doses of profanity. Pratt's wards weren't accustomed to such language and balked. They were being trained to become Christian gentlemen and Warner's behavior didn't comport with that. Made aware of the problem, Pop apologized and cleaned up his vocabulary. The young men responded.

Warner observed that Indians learned differently from white players. "They had highly developed powers of observation handed down through many generations." He would have an experienced player demonstrate a new technique, say jumping on a fumbled ball, and the younger players, who had been reluctant to try something before seeing it demonstrated, grasped it immediately.

Warner's training regime included Wednesday scrimmages with Dickinson College. These sessions helped prepare the Indians for upcoming games, especially the early-season matchups against local colleges. That year's schedule differed from most others in that small-college games were sprinkled throughout the fall, not bunched together in September and October.

They breezed through Pennsylvania College and Susquehanna University before lining up against Penn on October 14. They racked up a 16-5 victory against the Quakers, their first win ever over a Big Four team. The victors returned home that night to a welcome not seen before in Carlisle. Led by the famed Indian School band, male students celebrated the feat by parading through the town in their nightshirts, wearing pillowcases for hats.

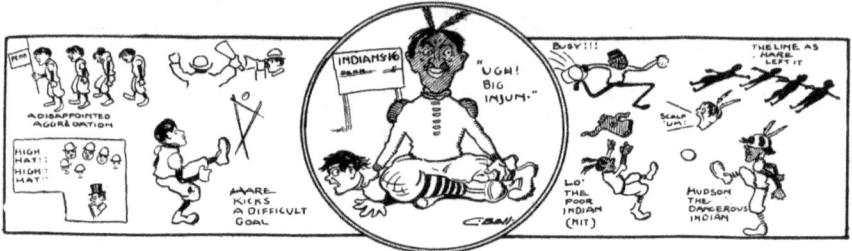

Warner's charges found Dickinson College to be more difficult than expected. It took them fifteen minutes and a failed field goal attempt to make their first score: a touchdown by Metoxen and the kick after. They scored again on their next possession but missed the extra point. They lost the ball at their own twenty on their third possession due to being offside. Dickinson failed to make a field goal but scored a safety. Carlisle 11-Dickinson 2. After a couple of fumbles, Dickinson took possession. Clippinger fumbled when attempting a drop kick but Hann got the ball and, aided by good interference, ran it around left end for a Dickinson touchdown. The twenty-minute first half ended with the Indians ahead 11-7.

At halftime, some good-natured scuffling broke out between the teams' supporters. Major Pratt (he had been promoted in July of the previous year) and Dickinson officials advised the boys to take their respective seats. They did. *The Dickinsonian* downplayed the episode; "...[I]t didn't assume the aspects of a 'scrap' as some of the papers stated."

The second half was a defensive struggle. One of Hudson's drop kicks made it over the crossbar for the final score: Carlisle 16-Dickinson 7. *The Philadelphia Evening Bulletin* sarcastically summed up the last two weeks of play: "Indians 17; U. of P. 5; Indians 16; Dickinson 7. That's all!"

The next week, Martin Wheelock was taken ill and became unavailable for the Harvard game. Carlisle jumped to a 10-0 halftime lead thanks to a thirty-five-yard field goal by Hudson and a fifty-yard fumble return by Carlisle's tallest player, guard Thaddeus Redwater. Perhaps the Crimson were looking forward to their game with Penn. Things changed in the second half. "The Crimson players quit looking bored," said Warner. Rough play in the form of a blow to the head sent fullback Jonas Metoxen to the hospital. Overpowered, the Indians gave up twenty-two points to lose 22-10.

Hamilton College was a 32-0 breather set up in Utica, New York by the congressman from that district, a former Harvard coach who refereed the game. The Indians tangled next with Princeton, their third Big Four opponent in less than a month. The Tigers hit hard and fast, scoring a touchdown on their first possession. The Indians fought fiercely but weren't able to make appreciable yardage. When an Orange-and-Black second-half drive bogged down, Hutchinson tried a Princeton[*] but it was blocked. One of Hutchinson's teammates recovered the ball to give the Tigers new life. Against a fierce Indian defense, Hodgeman made a dash to score the second touchdown. Wheeler again made the kick after to raise the Princeton lead to 12-0. The Indians got as close as the Orange's thirty-five-yard line, where Hudson's kick went wide, leaving the Indians scoreless, an infrequent outcome for them.

A scheduling snafu scratched the game with Maryland. Baltimore Medical College tried to set one up but they couldn't raise enough to cover Carlisle's guarantee. This gave the Indians a week off to convalesce and prepare for their last two games.

Pop was a tinkerer, and not just on old automobiles. He was constantly drawing up new formations and fiddling with existing ones. He tried unbalanced lines with more players on one side of the ball than the other. At times, he even put the center on the end of the line. Wanting his fast backs to get quicker starts, he tried a new stance. Rather than standing with their hands on their knees as backs did at that time, he had them put one hand on the ground, similar to a sprinter waiting for the starting gun.

Warner didn't use this new wrinkle in the upcoming game, an 81-0 slaughter of Oberlin College. He held it in reserve for the Thanksgiving game against 9-2 Columbia University. The faster start got Carlisle's backs to the

---

[*] In the mid-1890s, Otterbein developed and Princeton got credit for an improved method for placekicking. Instead of rolling, bouncing, or sliding the ball back to the holder as had always been done, the center snapped it directly back to him, similar to what is done today.

line sooner and with more force than defensive linemen expected, allowing the smaller backs to push heavier defenders back. Halfback Isaac Seneca ran through gaping holes for huge gains in Carlisle's impressive 45-0 blowout. The three-point stance soon became the standard for backs across the country.

As a cavalry officer, Pratt was able to arrange special rewards for the team. Rather than returning directly home from New York City after the Columbia game, the team toured the U.S. Army Academy at West Point and, on Saturday, attended the annual Army-Navy game in Philadelphia. Pop's work for the year finished, he left for his home in Springville, New York.

He and his players didn't get to rest on their laurels for long. An invitation to play an East-West championship game on Christmas Day ended any extended celebrations.

Jubilant after shellacking archrival Stanford 30-0 on Thanksgiving Day, the University of California at Berkeley's Manager, Irwin J. "Jerry" Muma, itched to challenge Eastern powers to post-season East-West matches in the Golden State over the holidays. He wired University of Chicago and Carlisle Indian School offering Christmas holiday games in San Francisco. Why Chicago and Carlisle? Chicago had traveled to the West Coast in December 1893 and this year's version had gone undefeated. Carlisle, already famous, had compiled its best season to date, losing only to Harvard and Princeton, Walter Camp's selections as the best two teams in the country that year.

Cal's football fortunes had been abysmal before the arrival of Princeton All-American Garrett Cochran as their new head coach in 1898. The 1897 team had gone 0-3-2 punctuated by a 28-0 drubbing by archrival Stanford. With the Spanish-American War raging in 1898, Cal's football managers added games against military teams and a second college foe. This year they handled Stanford with ease 22-0 and thumped Multnomah Athletic Club on Christmas Day in Portland, Oregon, finishing 8-0-2.

For 1899, Cochran brought Princeton All-American, Addison "King" Kelly, as his assistant. Cal played Nevada State, Oregon, State Normal School, Stanford, and League of the Cross plus Olympic Club three times, going unscored upon the entire season. Cal's players balked at extending their two-season undefeated string. On December 5, those still on campus voted eight to three against playing either Chicago or Carlisle. The reason given was that they were tired after a long season and didn't want to train more.

Chicago's season wasn't over yet. They had to play Wisconsin on December 9 for the conference championship. Carlisle, however, was eager to come out to the West Coast. Warner feared his players would be worn out after a rough season, but they voted to a man to go. He chomped at the bit to take on the challenge but accepting the offer wasn't his decision to make.

Superintendent Pratt was reluctant to allow the players to be away from school for such a long time but, after thinking about it, he agreed, reasoning, "The education they received from traveling and their contact with other college men more than offset the time they lost from their regular schoolwork." Details remained to finalize the agreement.

On December 7, Cal's manager Muma implored the players to reconsider playing Carlisle, but they turned him down by two votes. Coach Cochran talked at length with each player, ultimately persuading them to agree to the Christmas game. However, they attached stipulations to their agreement:

1. The faculty and President Wheeler must rescind their decision that team captain Whipple's suspension be lifted to allow him to play.

2. The proceeds of the game are to be used toward a training clubhouse for the university's athletic teams.

It turned out that the sticking point had been money. Cal players felt the school was exploiting them. When financial control was transferred to the athletic committee, they consented to play. Muma wired Carlisle. They wanted $4,000 to come and dispatched W. G. Thompson to Chicago to negotiate terms. Cal's coaches had said nothing would keep them in California after the Stanford game but remained in case the game with Carlisle materialized. When it did, they restarted practice and Warner returned to Carlisle.

The Carlisle contingent consisting of the starters, seven substitutes, Coach Warner, Trainer George Connors, and Team Physician Dr. Carlos Montezuma (Apache from Arizona), left for California early on December 18 in a special Pullman Sleeping Car reserved for the trip. As part of the boys' education, the team always traveled first class. In Chicago, while their car was shifted to a train making the three-day trip from there to San Francisco, the travelers dined at Palmer House and picked up Thompson. Articulate Dr. Montezuma performed as spokesman for the team.

Arriving at their ultimate destination at 9:00 p.m. on the Central Overland, the Indians completed the longest journey taken by a team to play a football game to date and were immediately ensconced in the luxurious Palace Hotel. After hearing that some Japanese people lived in the city, former scout and cavalryman Thaddeus Redwater determined to find one to take back to Carlisle for a mascot.

In an attempt to keep his men healthy, Warner only had them run signals practices. But Wheelock caught a bad cold and was questionable for the game. Cal's Cochran was injured during a practice session but was expected to be on the sideline for the game. Their quarterback Frank Ellis, who had been disqualified for the Stanford game for "professionalism," would play, but Captain James R. Whipple, suspended for "deficiencies of scholarship," would not.

Cal's fierce rivalry with Stanford stocked them well with tricks. Blaming rain, they covered Richmond Field, the grounds at 16th and Folsom, with sand, which they said would be removed before the game. Apparently suspicious, Warner dressed his players in the lightest weight uniforms and shoes he had and eschewed padding and shin guards to maximize their speed. Giving up four-

and-a-half pounds per man, this strategy exposed the Indians even more to injury.

In their playing days, California's coaches had played against both Cornell and Carlisle and had seen Warner's schemes and current players firsthand. The two surely kept abreast of Pop's season and stars as well as Hudson's drop kicking if only through newspaper coverage. Warner said that the field had been rolled for the game but was still covered with sand, and the Victor ball Cal provided for the game was larger and heavier than the standard Spalding J ball used in the Indians' other games.

Carlisle won the coin toss and kicked off at 2:15 in front of 6,000 spectators. After Cal's five-yard return, Lawrence C. "Kangaroo Pete" Kaarsburg punted. Following a series of punt exchanges, Cal found itself deep in its own territory. Kaarsburg misinterpreted the signal to be for a fake punt and in his confusion, let the pass from his quarterback sail past him. He scurried back to the four-yard line to retrieve it. Carlisle players caught him and carried him and the ball over the goal line for a safety. Carlisle led 2-0.

After another series of punt exchanges, Hudson fumbled a Cal kick on his own twenty-five-yard line, giving the home team its deepest penetration into foreign territory. After losing ten yards, possession passed to the Indians, who proceeded to fumble the ball away. Berkeley bucked for seven yards and Kaarsburg hurdled but was thrown backward. As the half was about to end, possession switched to Carlisle. Hudson attempted a forty-yard kick for a field goal out of the sand but it fell well short.

Carlisle received the second-half kickoff but was unable to move the ball and punted. Cal fumbled it back to them. After a few more failures by both teams to make first downs, Hudson attempted a field goal from the fifty-yard line. His kick was true but fell short. More punt exchanges ensued. Injured, Artie Miller was replaced by James Johnson (Stockbridge, Wisconsin). As part of yet another punt exchange, Johnson returned the kick fifteen yards. Carlisle backs hurdled and bucked Cal's line for seven more.

As the clock wound down, Carlisle gained yardage but Cal's defense stiffened in time. Hudson was hurt and replaced by Charles Roberts (Chippewa, Wisconsin). The Indians advanced the ball to Cal's thirty. With their goal kicker injured, Carlisle could only rush the ball. The game ended with the ball at the Cal twenty-five. Besides having traveled the farthest of any football team for a game, Carlisle had won the first game played between East Coast and West Coast teams.

Martin Wheelock attributed what he considered Carlisle's subpar performance not just to the long layoff since Thanksgiving. "We were handicapped by the soft ground. We have always played on sod grounds before, and I understand that the California team is used to the heavy ground. We were also unfamiliar with the style of ball used here." Carlisle's fast backs were unable to get quick starts or make sharp cuts on sand. The fourteen-ounce Victor ball would have bounced differently than the thirteen-ounce Spalding J balls Hudson had always kicked. Drop kicking on sand would also present severe challenges. Carlisle almost doubled Cal's rushing yardage and ran nineteen more plays. Cal seldom had the ball inside Carlisle's fifty-yard line and never tried to kick a field goal. They played a defensive game aimed at a scoreless tie and almost succeeded.

Upon their return to Carlisle, various team members reported on their trip to a meeting of the English Speaking Club. James Johnson started off by describing the high points of the trip west. He handed the baton in this oral relay to Charles Roberts, who covered San Francisco and the game. Joseph Scholder (Mission, California) covered the first leg of the trip home along the southern route. The first stop was at Perris Indian School, which was located in the inland desert between Los Angeles and San Diego. The campus had too little water to support the smallest of gardens. Cordial students entertained the visiting team with music provided by the school's band and mandolin club as well as a dress parade. The local boys challenged the travelers to a baseball game, which Carlisle won.

Artie Miller took the Phoenix leg. To pass time during a long wait, the boys chased jackrabbits for the fun of it. The Phoenix Indian School superintendent challenged Carlisle to a New Year's Day football game. Their coach, a Harvard man, outfitted his team in leather uniforms similar to the ones the Crimson had donned the latter part of the season. His players soon became overheated and exhausted in the hot Arizona desert sun. Carlisle added an 86 to 6 victory to its win column.

John Warren talked about Albuquerque, a place they initially thought dull but changed their minds. "The promenade party, the nice supper, the jollity of the girls and of some of the teachers who are not so old made them so sad to leave that some of the boys came near being left."

Isaac Seneca told of touring Santa Fe, the second-oldest town in the country. The boys enjoyed riding on burros. Ed Rogers told of the three-hour wait for the Utah governor's car at La Junta causing them to arrive too late at Haskell Institute in Lawrence, Kansas for a reception. However, a number of former Carlisle students then at Haskell visited with old friends. The Carlisle players received heroes' welcomes from the students at the other Indian schools. The local boys got the chance to meet face-to-face the idols familiar to them from reading the sports pages of the newspapers. Wheelock covered the leg home and summarized the trip.

W. G. Thompson expanded about the reception at Haskell: "[W]e had a royal welcome, and were entertained with a formal inspection, speeches, and music by the band." He also discussed the tour of San Francisco: "[M]ost of the boys were intensely interested and at the same time disgusted with Chinatown, which gave them, they said, their first clear idea of what a RESERVATION really meant."

Walter Camp honored Carlisle by ranking them fourth in the nation. He also placed Isaac Seneca on his All-America First Team, the first Carlisle player he named as such. He selected Martin Wheelock for his Second Team and Frank Hudson for the Third Team. Caspar Whitney ranked Carlisle fifth, behind the Penn team they had beaten. He included Martin Wheelock and Frank Hudson as substitutes on his All-America team. Where Camp had named thirty-three players altogether, Whitney only listed twenty-two.

The New York Sun prophesized, "An annual game between the Atlantic and Pacific Coasts may yet become a fixture." Some false starts, such as the 1902 New Year's game between Stanford and Michigan, were made but it took a Carlisle alum to make it a reality. On January 1, 1916, Pop Warner's protégé, Lone Star Dietz, led his unbeaten Washington State eleven to victory over Brown on a mud-soaked field to make the Rose Bowl an annual event.

1899 Season Summary

Date	Opponent	Location	Indians	Opp.
Sep. 23	Pennsylvania College	Indian Field, Carlisle Barracks, PA	21	0
Sep. 30	Susquehanna University	Indian Field, Carlisle Barracks, PA	56	0
Oct. 14	University of Pennsylvania	Franklin Field, Philadelphia, PA	16	5
Oct. 21	Dickinson College	Dickinson College Athletic Field, Carlisle, PA	16	7
Oct. 28	Harvard University	Soldiers' Field, Cambridge, MA	10	22
Nov. 4	Hamilton College	Genesee Park, Utica, NY	32	0
Nov. 11	Princeton University	Manhattan Field, New York, NY	0	12
Nov. 25	Oberlin College	Indian Field, Carlisle Barracks, PA	81	0
Nov. 30	Columbia University	Manhattan Field, New York, NY	45	0
Dec. 25	University of California	Richmond Field, San Francisco, CA	2	0
Jan. 1	Phoenix Indian School	Phoenix Park, Phoenix, AZ	83	6*

Won 9; Lost 2; Tied 0

* Other scores for the Phoenix Indian School game were reported but this one was the most reliable.

Glenn Scobey "Pop" Warner

Two days after that, Carlisle took on Maryland in Baltimore. Due to stiffness from the Virginia game and Washington water not agreeing with their digestive systems, the Indians weren't energetic. However, they got off to a good start with Palmer scoring the first touchdown eight minutes into the game. Pierce missed the kick after. After a fumble exchange, Johnson carried the ball across the Maryland goal line. This time, Pierce made the kick. Johnson made some good runs with one ending in a touchdown. Pierce made the kick after. Carlisle led at halftime 17-0. Fumbles and lack of aggressiveness would have lost the game to a stronger opponent. Their poor defensive play gave Maryland a lot of yardage but no scores. In the second half, Pierce kicked a thirty-yard field goal from placement. Later, Pierce and Baine advanced the ball down the field with Pierce carrying it over the goal line. The kick after failed. Carlisle defeated Maryland 27-0.

With twelve days to prepare for their next game, the 6-0-0 Indians may have been overconfident about 7-0, unscored-upon Harvard. Perhaps the confidence improved their play because they started strong and drew first blood ten minutes into the contest when Palmer went over for a touchdown. *The Boston Globe* described the team's reactions after making this score: "[T]hey were wild with delight, turning handsprings up the field and yelling for joy."

Harvard answered with a Daly field goal from Carlisle's twenty-five-yard line. But they missed on two attempts for field goals before the first half ended with the score tied at five all. Carlisle's offense ran out of steam early in the second half, but Harvard's got going. Kernan scored a touchdown on a long run and Lawrence converted. The Crimson were ahead for good. A blocked punt on Carlisle's ten-yard line set Harvard up for another score. Harvard 17- Carlisle 5. *The Globe* summarized the day: "Harvard had won the game, but had obviously been outplayed. That was about the size of it." One of its headlines read, "Indians Play Brilliantly." Another stated, "One of the Most Spectacular Contests Ever Seen There."

With Harvard's arch-rival Yale up next, Warner sequestered the first and second teams in the woods at Pine Grove Furnace the week leading up to the game, but the Indians must have left everything on Soldiers Field, keeping nothing for Yale. They gave up thirty-five points while getting no closer to Yale's goal line than their twenty and never threatening to score. The loss was Carlisle's worst since the 1895 Penn defeat.

Penn was the third Big Four opponent in a row, and Warner feared another lackluster performance. Ten minutes into the game, Penn's Hodge

4
Athletic Director, Too

Rule Changes for 1900:

Only five men are to be allowed to walk up and down along the sidelines. All others are to be seated. Any coaching detected by the umpire results in a ten-yard penalty. The timekeeper must now stay on the sidelines, not behind the offense. An offended team now has the right to decline a penalty assessed against its opponent. A team can only take a 20-yard loss to retain possession once per possession. The penalty for the offense being offside is now 10 yards.

A Line Up Against the Indians in 1800—What a Difference!

Coach Warner assumed he would return to his home and bride in Springville, New York after the California trip. But Major Pratt had something else in mind for him. Since graduating from law school, Warner had been coaching football in the fall and practicing law the rest of the year. After marrying an 1893 graduate of the New York State Normal School at Geneseo taking the Scientific Course, Tibb Loraine Smith, only months before the start of football season, Pop had been considering dropping football to practice law full-time. But Pratt surprised him by offering Warner the position of athletic director in charge of all Carlisle's sports for a salary of $2,500 a year. Because the position was full-time throughout the academic year, he would have to give up his law practice and could no longer coach Iowa State[5]. On the other hand, a salary greater than what he could earn as a lawyer coupled with the thrill of athletic competition weighed heavily. A few days later, he accepted Pratt's offer.

---

[5] Warner coached Iowa State, mostly from a distance, from 1895 to 1899, while he coached Georgia in 1895 and 1896, Cornell in 1897 and 1898, and Carlisle in 1899.

By taking on the job, he signed up to coach both baseball and track in the spring, a few short months in the future. Having been a star pitcher until he threw his arm out, Pop had no trouble with baseball. Track was a different matter. Knowing nothing about the sport, he read all the books on it he could find. He also picked the brains of successful track coaches Michael Murphy of the University of Pennsylvania and Jack Moakley of Cornell, and athletic trainer George Connors, also at Cornell, to get Carlisle's track team started. The baseball team had been in existence for some years. Warner observed that the players were skilled but "did not use good judgement nor put as much into their baseball as did the college boys." When these sports' seasons ended, it was time to prepare for football.

The prospects for the 1900 squad were even thinner than those who turned out in 1899. Things looked so lean that Warner scanned the Oklahoma reservations for candidates and Pratt wrote to Indian agents across the country to send him athletic boys. Their recruiting efforts yielded only John Walletsie (Umatilla, Oregon).

After the boys returned to campus from their summer outings, even the special diet fed to football players on the training table didn't put as much weight on them as it had their predecessors. To make matters worse, gone were mainstays Hudson, Redwater, Miller, Seneca, and Metoxen. Only six regulars, including last year's captain, Martin Wheelock, and three substitutes returned for new captain Ed Rogers. A number of new boys tried out for the team to fill the gaps. A younger one showing promise was Charles Albert Bender, who had run away from his home on White Earth Reservation to attend Carlisle in 1896, but he hadn't matured enough physically to crack the varsity line-up.

The outlook for another successful season wasn't good. The eleven-game schedule was published on September 14 and, unlike previous seasons, didn't change. The first game was at home against Lebanon Valley College. Jesse Palmer and Wheelock were held out due to injuries. Hawley Pierce scored two touchdowns but missed both kicks after for a 10-0 lead at the end of the twenty-minute first half. All the starters but Rogers and Pierce were replaced for the second half. Joseph Ruiz scored twice, Frank Yarlott and Nathaniel Decora once each in the second half. Pierce made all four conversions in the 24-point second half. The Indians' punting was poor and they fumbled several times but won 34-0.

Four days later, they took on Dickinson College. Pierce was too sick to play and "somewhat crippled" Charles Roberts played as well as possible, considering. Wheelock and Palmer both got in the game on a stifling h[ot day]. Palmer and Johnson each scored a touchdown. Wheelock made one [of the] kicks after. Roberts drop kicked a field goal and Wheelock kicked one [from] placement. Dickinson got no closer than thirty-five yards from the Ind[ian] goal line in the 21-0 shutout.

A light Susquehanna University team was mismatched against the I[ndi]ans. Only the wet grass and soggy ball kept the score down by making d[rop] kicks unsuccessful. Pierce, Yarlott, Ely Parker, John Baine, Decora, Whe[e]lock, and Rogers each scored a touchdown. Pierce made six points aft[er] touchdown and one field goal from placement. Carlisle 56-Susquehanna [0].

Pennsylvania College visited the next Saturday. Unfortunately for them they weren't in good condition. Kelley Lay scored first in less than a minute after the opening kickoff. Pierce, William Baine, and Lay (again) quickly followed with additional touchdowns. Pierce kicked all the extra points. The twenty-minute first half ended with Carlisle ahead 24-0. Warner made wholesale substitutions at halftime, but the scoring didn't abate. The visitors' defense strengthened, but their offense fumbled the ball away. Thomas Walker, Lum Chesowah, Decora, and Frank Beaver each scored a second-half touchdown. Redwater made only one of the kicks after. Final score: Carlisle 45-Pennsylvania College 0.

The Indians left Carlisle for their first true road trip this season on October 23 for a game against Virginia in Washington, DC. Drizzling rain made the ball slippery and footing treacherous. Fumbles and missed field goals kept Carlisle's scoring in the first half down to a single touchdown by Rogers and the extra point by Pierce. In spite of going into the wind in the second half, Palmer scored a touchdown and Pierce kicked a field goal. Virginia got the first points scored against Carlisle that year on a freak play. A kickoff bounced over Johnson's head but he touched it, making it a live ball. Palmer picked up the ball deep in his own territory but ran with it instead of downing it. At the four-yard line, a Virginia player punched it out of his hands and it bounced across the goal line. Palmer pounced on it, taking a safety to prevent a Yahoo touchdown. Final score: Carlisle 16-Virginia 2.

The Indians often played more than one game a week, especially early in the season and when on road trips. No team ever played schedules as difficult as Carlisle's. As a point of comparison, Big Four teams and the military academies traveled only to play each other. Almost all of their games were played on their home fields where all of Carlisle's important games were played on the road, putting them at a tremendous disadvantage.

KERNAN'S GREAT RUN OF 50 YARDS WITH PERFECT INTERFERENCE.
SCENES AT THE GREAT FOOTBALL GAME ON SOLDIERS FIELD.

blocked Wheelock's punt. Davidson gathered up the bouncing ball and raced forty-seven yards for a touchdown. The kick after was successful. Penn 6-Carlisle 0. Potter drop kicked a thirty-eight-yard field goal for the Quakers' three minutes later. Penn 11-Carlisle 0. The Indians picked up the pace in the second half with Wheelock scoring a touchdown and making the kick after. Penn 11-Carlisle 6. The Quakers came back to life, stalling Carlisle and edging closer to the Indians' goal with each possession. But the sun set before time was out. "...Potter carried the ball over the faint white line and a goal was kicked [but missed] which settled the score for the day." Penn 16-Carlisle 6. Pop Warner wasn't displeased with his team's efforts: "Carlisle put up a strong game today, but found Penn too much for her."

Even with the Big Four games out of the way, the sledding didn't get much easier. Washington and Jefferson College fielded a strong team that year. The mud-soaked field took away Warner's sometime-successful wing

Photo by Choate & Co. Dillon Pierce Warner (Coach) Palmer Wheelock
Williams Johnson Baine Rogers (Capt.) Smith Hare Redwater
Roberts Beaver Parker

1900 Carlisle Indians

shift and most other plays that required good footing. The W & J Presidents relied on Princeton-style mass plays on tackle. Line plunges were the order of the day, with the advantage going to the heavier W&J side. The Presidents scored a touchdown on their first possession seven minutes into the game. Although the extra point was missed, it looked as if that score was going to be enough to win the game almost to the end. With time running out, the Indians ran an end-around with Johnson carrying the ball. Knocked to the ground by Wheelock, W&J's Hayes reached up and grabbed him. Johnson fumbled while going down, and the ball bounced forward five or six yards before crossing the Presidents' goal line. The elusive, wet ball slipped away as player after player attempted to corral it. Finally, Carlisle's right end, Nelson Hare, captured it for a touchdown. W&J supporters held their breath while Wheelock attempted the kick after touchdown. They breathed a sigh of relief when the ball skipped across the ground, not even getting airborne. The result was a 5-5 tie.

Five days later, the Indians had a chance to reclaim a little glory in another Thanksgiving Day contest against a well-coached Columbia team. Before the game started, *The New York Tribune* observed major problems: "Most of the Indians looked drawn too fine while the backs, with the exception of Pierce, looked puny in comparison with last year's team. Even some of the men in the Indian line seemed small when compared to their Columbia opponents."

The Columbia line pushed the Indians around the field in the first half. After Columbia's second touchdown, the Indians' play turned ragged with their tackling especially poor. As time was running out in the first half, a drizzle started. The half ended with Columbia ahead 11-0. The Indians woke up in the second half and moved the ball well but stalled deep in Columbia territory. When Morley dropped back to fake a punt, he fumbled. William Baine chased the loose ball across the goal line and pounced on it for a Carlisle touchdown. Johnson made the kick after. Columbia 11-Carlisle 6. The drizzle got heavier, making playing more difficult, more so for the lighter Indians. Most of the crowd departed. The darker it got, the more aggressive Columbia became. They backed Carlisle down the field, eventually pushing Austin over for a touchdown. Bruce made the kick for the final score of Columbia 17-Carlisle 6.

The 6-4-1 season was a far cry from the previous year's results. To put things into perspective, Carlisle competed against every player on Walter Camp's All-America Team First Eleven and all but one of his Second Eleven, not having an All-American at any level on its squad. Would 1901 be better?

1900 Season Summary

Date	Opponent	Location	Indians	Opp.
Sep. 22	Lebanon Valley College	Indian Field, Carlisle Barracks, PA	34	0
Sep. 26	Dickinson College	Indian Field, Carlisle Barracks, PA	21	0
Sep. 29	Susquehanna University	Indian Field, Carlisle Barracks, PA	46	0
Oct. 6	Pennsylvania College	Indian Field, Carlisle Barracks, PA	45	0
Oct. 13	University of Virginia	National Park, Washington, DC	16	2
Oct. 15	University of Maryland	Union Park, Baltimore, MD	27	0
Oct. 27	Harvard University	Soldiers' Field, Cambridge, MA	5	17
Nov. 10	Yale University	Yale Field, New Haven, CT	0	35
Nov. 17	University of Pennsylvania	Franklin Field, Philadelphia, PA	6	16
Nov. 24	Washington & Jefferson College	Exposition Park, Pittsburgh, PA	5	5
Nov. 29	Columbia University	Manhattan Field, New York, NY	6	17

Won 6; Lost 4; Tied 1

AN ESQUIMAU WHO PROMISES TO BE A GREAT FOOTBALL PLAYER.

Nekifer Schouchuck, the Esquimau boy that plays on the Carlisle Indian School football eleven, is the only player of his race. Schouchuck is not plays like Lone Wolf, the greatest centre Carlisle ever had.

Pleasures of English Traveling.

A new terror has been added to railway traveling. A friend of mine (writes a correspondent) was journeying the other day with his wife from Lancashire by the Midland. Three men got into the same compartment, the one in the middle without his boots being apparently a prisoner. One of

SCHOUCHUCK, FIRST ESQUIMAU TO PLAY FOOTBALL.

5
A Search for Talent

Rule Changes for 1901:

There were no significant rule changes this year, only clarifications of existing rules.

1901 Carlisle Indians

Warner must have thought he was reliving Ground Hog Day when he reviewed the material for the 1901 team. With only four starters returning, he again found size and talent lacking. Bender wasn't big enough to take one of the empty spots but he was doing well pitching for the baseball team. Last year's football captain, Ed Rogers, was now attending law school and playing football for Minnesota.

Starting the season earlier than other schools wasn't unusual for Carlisle, but this year their schedule opened on September 14 against Steelton Y. M. C. A. Due to President McKinley's assassination, the game was postponed until September 25. Even with that delay, Carlisle's September 21 contest with Lebanon Valley College was the earliest game played in the East that season. Warner's focus on the LVC warm-up was on evaluating players. He started the second string in the short game of seventeen-minute halves. The first string got their chance in the second half. Substituting liberally, twenty-seven men got the chance to perform in the 28-0 cakewalk.

The rescheduled Steelton Y. M. C. A. match was played four days later. Palmer kicked the opening kickoff out of bounds. Steelton captain and right halfback Metzenthin ran the rekick back one-hundred yards for a touchdown. This was unusual because the Indians rarely had kicks returned for scores. Burton missed the kick after. With only twenty-five seconds expired off the clock, Carlisle trailed 5-0. The game became a defensive struggle with no further scoring in the first half. Five minutes into the second half, culminating a series of short line plunges, Decora ran the ball over for Carlisle's score. Palmer's extra point attempt was blocked by players who appeared to be offside, but it wasn't called. Late in the second half, the Indians moved the ball within inches of a score but lost the ball on downs. Final score: Carlisle 5-Steelton Y. M. C. A. 5.

Three days later, Carlisle played the deaf students of Gallaudet College in a game of twenty-minute halves. Carlisle scored early when halfback Peter Chatfield[6] went over for a touchdown. Hare missed the extra point. The tide turned quickly when Hare fumbled the ensuing kickoff and Gallaudet recovered it on Carlisle's twenty-yard line. Steady gains, aided by penalties, put Captain Waters over. Geilfuss kicked the extra point for a 6-5 Gallaudet lead at halftime. The Indians picked up the pace in the second half and sent in several substitutes. Beaver (accounts vary) scored two touchdowns, and Hare made both kicks after. Carlisle's final two points were made on a safety when Mathers was downed behind his goal line. Final score: Carlisle 19-Gallaudet 6. Warner had succeeded in getting three games under his young players' belts before most teams had played one, but would it be enough experience to fuel a better outcome than the Indians had the previous year?

He got his answer four days later in the game with Pennsylvania College, a team Carlisle had pummeled in the two previous meetings. Anticipating a large turnout (as well as a lucrative gate), the Harrisburg Athletic Club arranged for the game to be played on Island Park on a Wednesday afternoon when it would have little competition for fans of football. Pop Warner may have underestimated his opponent because he kept four stars out of the game, including Captain Wheelock. He might have been resting them for Dickinson College three days later.

Although raining, the game didn't start badly. Carlisle moved the ball down the field with line plunges, punctuated by two good runs by Hudson, and Palmer put the ball over for a 5-0 Carlisle lead. The Indians challenged

---

[6] No first name was provided but Peter Chatfield was the only Chatfield at Carlisle at that time and he played on the baseball team.

once more in the first half but couldn't quite get the ball across the goal line. The rain picked up for the second twenty-minute half. Pennsylvania College moved the ball well in their first possession. Speer scored after a series of successful end plays and James kicked the extra point. Carlisle now trailed 6-5. They moved the ball to their opponents' five-yard line twice but the lighter Indians couldn't push the ball over the goal. They lost 6-5.

The Patriot opined about the state of Carlisle football: "Two things were demonstrated in yesterday's game. First, that the Indians are not nearly so strong as in former years. Second, that they can be rounded out into a credible team with careful attention from the coach and some good work on the gridiron. There is some promising material among the Redmen and next season should see the Carlisle eleven well up in the football world."

It was a long time before the next season. Carlisle had ten more games to play, of which only one or two might be easy wins. The immediate future looked bleak for Warner and the Indians. Even Dickinson College was a problem.

Three days after the unexpected loss at Island Park, the Indians "traveled" to their crosstown rivals' field. Confident of winning this time, Dickinson fought fiercely in a battle royal with the Indians. The game was played cleanly but hard, so hard Carlisle center Scrogg sustained game-ending injuries in the opening seconds. The team awoke from the lethargy it had shown earlier in the week and scored two touchdowns in the first half but missed both kicks. Dickinson inserted four new men for the second twenty-five-minute half and pushed the Indians back. Stanton went over for a touchdown. A little later, Shiffer recovered a Carlisle fumble and ran fifty yards for a second Dickinson touchdown. Core's extra point put them ahead of the Indians 11-10.

Being behind incited the Indians into even fiercer play, producing another touchdown. Johnson's kick put them ahead 16-11. Dickinson later tried to tie the game with a field goal, but Cannon's place kick failed. Carlisle escaped with a hard-fought win. Boys attending the game marched through the Dickinson campus, down Main Street (now High Street) to the square, and out Hanover Street to Carlisle Barracks, singing and cheering as they went.

Carlisle and Bucknell renewed their rivalry the next Saturday in Williamsport rather than on either school's home field to attract more spectators. In the most exciting game witnessed at that site, other than fumbling too often, both teams played well. Johnson eventually scored a touchdown on a reverse around his right end, and Wheelock made the kick. When the first twenty-minute half ended, Wheelock's teammates carried him off the field with a badly wrenched right knee. Weakened without their star, Carlisle gave up yardage until McMahon was shoved over the goal line for a touchdown not long before time was out. Smith's kick failed, allowing Carlisle to escape with a 6-5 win.

Haverford was probably scheduled as a midweek warmup to prepare for the tough game expected from Cornell on Saturday. Before that game, the scrubs played Dickinson Prep School, likely to help prepare the backups in case they were needed on Saturday. Line-ups weren't published for the 23-0 victory but Fielder and Ruiz were identified as having played well. Carlisle scored its first touchdown against Haverford within the first minute of the twenty-minute first half. The Indians were off to the races, scoring early and often while their defense was not being fooled by Haverford's trick plays. Warner substituted liberally with Ruiz getting some playing time at quarterback. Carlisle breezed to a 29-0 win.

Off-field incompetency reigned supreme on Buffalo Day at the Pan-American Exposition Stadium in Buffalo, the site of the Carlisle-Cornell game. Although the fair was selected to attract the largest audience possible, stadium management wasn't aware of or ignored the likelihood of a large crowd coming to the game. Fully 16,000 people descended on the stadium but only one of the four entrances was open and the ticket office was closed. The entire turnout was funneled to the one open gate, creating a bottleneck. Thousands tired of waiting became violent. Their rush swept the ticket takers away and the gate with it. Others crashed the east entrance, tore down the barriers, and swarmed into the seats, tearing clothing and trampling women and children in their way. Guards brutally billy clubbed some at the head of the throng swarming in regardless of age or gender, but they couldn't stop the mob. Those who paid for reserved seats couldn't get near them.

The crush of the crowd caused several women to faint. Mr. and Mrs. W. Caryl Ely after being denied admission were knocked down and trampled. Mrs. Ely fainted but, when revived, refused to leave, saying that she came to see the game. Exposition President John G. Milburn and his wife worked their way to a gate but were turned away by a handsomely uniformed officious guard. Thousands were turned away disappointed. Many a deserved curse was heaped on the heads of those who were to blame for this gross mismanagement.

Facing his alma mater—whose team he formerly coached—couldn't have been easy for Pop, especially when he had a weak squad. His undersized Carlisle linemen were no match for the heavier Ithacans, one of whom was

Pop Warner's younger brother, Bill. Like his older sibling, he played guard for Cornell and was quite good at it. So good that Walter Camp named him to his All-America First Team for 1901 at the end of the season.

Perhaps his extra preparations helped because twenty minutes out of the twenty-two-and-a-half-minute half passed before Cornell forced Hunt over Carlisle's goal line. Coffin made the extra point. Cornell used their size advantage to wear down the Indians in the second half. Ten minutes in, deep in Cornell territory, the ball popped into the air and Hunt snagged it. He ran ninety yards for their second touchdown. Coffin again made the kick. Cornell led 12-0. After a punt exchange, Coffin circled Carlisle's right end and dashed seventy yards for the final score. An Indian tackled him so hard he was wobbly and missed the kick. Cornell continued to batter away at the center of Carlisle's line until time expired. Final score: Cornell 17-Carlisle 0.

Desperate, Warner scanned recently arrived students for prospects. Among the newest was an Aleut, Nekifer Shouchuk. He had arrived in July from Woody Island Baptist Orphanage, two-point-six miles east of Kodiak, Alaska. A lack of English skills limited his progress. Aware he was on the team, although not yet playing in games, *The Buffalo Times* reporter must have noticed him on the Carlisle bench at the Cornell game. His racist reporting mocked Shouchuk: "Nikifer's [sic] training methods when at home are said to include such trivial maneuvers as iceberg juggling and walrus dodging. He wrestles an hour or two before breakfast every morning with a polar bear and holds all records for long distance, unpaced blubber eating." He might have had to eat those words if he ever met the sturdy Shouchuk, who was as solid as an oak and just as unmovable, face to face.

Pop needed to look no farther than across town to find a guard to bolster his undersized line. James Phillips (Cherokee, North Carolina) and his brother Theophilis had graduated with B.A. degrees from Lincoln University in Philadelphia in 1900 courtesy of a rich aunt. Theophilis returned home to teach and preach. James enrolled at Dickinson School of Law and played on the Dickinson College football team. While the 1901 season was underway, he changed jerseys. He continued taking law courses but he joined the Indian School squad. Exactly how and why this shift took place is lost to history.

Soon, Warner was not happy with his new prospect's development as a player and pulled him out of his place at a practice. He told James that he was not playing nearly aggressively enough and said, "Now get down there and show me how it should be done."

Warner lined up opposite Phillips as he often did when trying to demonstrate a technique to a player. When the signal was given, Phillips charged so hard that he knocked Pop unconscious. When he came to and cleared his head, Warner just said, "Now, that's the way it's done!"

Next up on the gauntlet was Harvard. Warner complained that the Indians tackled too high, a fatal move against a competitor with a twenty-five-pound weight advantage per man. They rallied toward the end of the first half, already down by two touchdowns, but time ran out before they could score. Another advantage Harvard had was enough depth to substitute for players who were only slightly injured. Wheelock nursed his bad knee through the entire first half and much of the second before it gave out. Phillips replaced him in the new player's first appearance in a Carlisle uniform. Harvard won 29-0. After the game, Warner said, "Harvard was too much for us. Her team was the heaviest we have played against this year, and we were completely outclassed." The day after the Harvard game, James Phillips enrolled at Carlisle Indian School but didn't take courses there.

With Wheelock out of commission and so many other players banged up, Warner saw no way to beat the tough Michigan squad they were scheduled to meet on November 2. So, he decided to rest injured players with the hope they'd be up to par for the last four games of the season. He left the starting halfbacks at home to recover and brought Louis Leroy and Edward DeMarr to play in their places. If the situation wasn't bad enough, these two, who had histories of running away, disappeared from their hotel the morning of the game. Lacking halfbacks, Warner tried to negotiate a shorter game with Michigan Coach Fielding Yost but, according to Warner, he would have none of that. Press reports indicated 27 ½ minute halves were played.

Warner patched together a starting line-up that included Phillips at left guard and Shouchuk at center. Circumstances put both new players in the starting line-up for this game, if not a few more. Although Shouchuk was bright and motivated to learn, Pop was concerned about his progress with the English language, since he spoke almost none when he arrived on campus. So, Pop decided to test his pupil's understanding of the signals.

"Nik, what do you do on 15-25-36?"

Shouchuk responded with a smile, "Me run. Yes sirree, Mister Pop. Me run most fast."

Putting him in a game, especially at center, was a huge risk but Warner was short of options. Nine minutes into the first half after fumble and punt exchanges, Carlisle was penalized ten yards twice for being offsides, giving

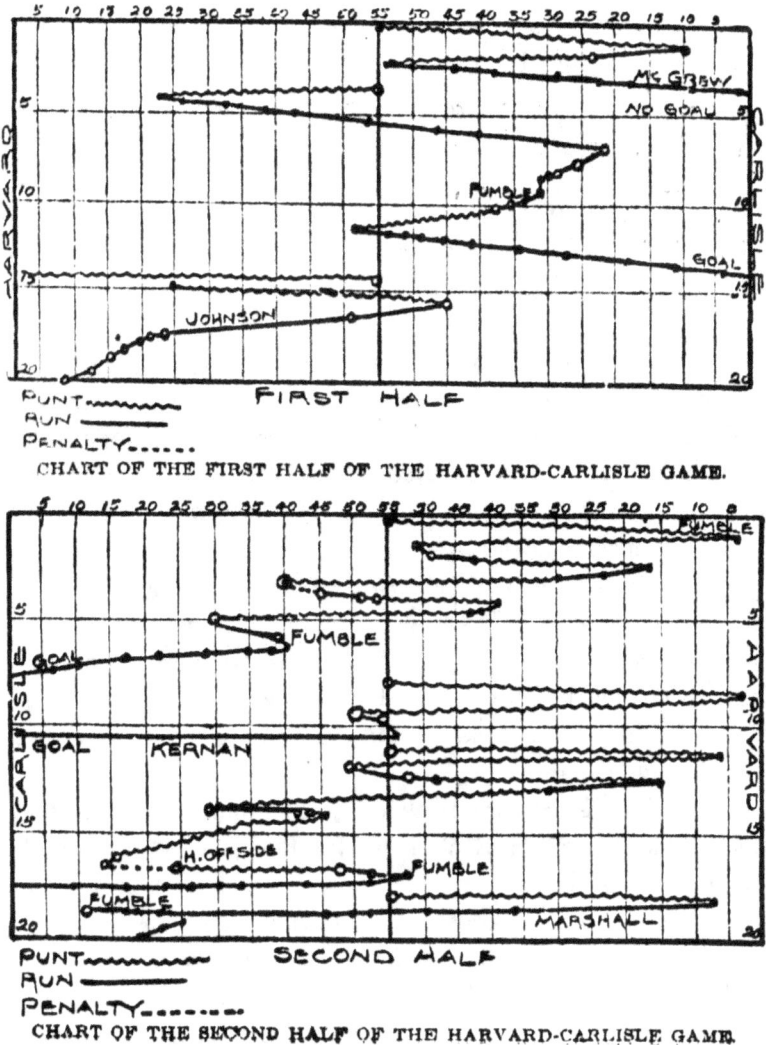

CHART OF THE FIRST HALF OF THE HARVARD-CARLISLE GAME.

CHART OF THE SECOND HALF OF THE HARVARD-CARLISLE GAME.

Michigan good field position. Future hall-of-famer Willie Heston broke free for thirty yards. Then Michigan pounded the Indians' right tackle until Wilson was pushed over for the first score. Shorts missed the kick from a difficult angle. Michigan retained possession until Heston ran for the second touchdown. Shorts again kicked the extra point.

After a punt exchange, Weeks made a fair catch and Short kicked a twenty-yard field goal. Michigan 16–Carlisle 0. Michigan moved the ball again after receiving the kickoff but had to turn over the ball for holding on the

Carlisle fifteen-yard line. When they got the ball back, they quickly moved it to Carlisle's ten but fumbled it away. Carlisle had some success with the "wing shift," but the half ended before they could score.

The second half consisted of a series of punt exchanges until the Wolverines repeatedly pounded the lighter Carlisle line with Shorts, Heston, and Snow. Sweeley then went around end for twenty yards and Shorts was pushed over for the touchdown. He also kicked the extra point. Final score: Michigan 22–Carlisle 0. The only serious injury was Bradley's dislocated collarbone. He would have to stay in Harper Hospital in Detroit for at least two days.

In an attempt to make the argument that Michigan's team was as good as Harvard's, *The Detroit Free Press* argued that Warner had fielded as good a line-up against Michigan as it had against Harvard. It considered Phillips as a regular starter because he had played in the Harvard game. No mention was made of Shouchuk not having appeared in a previous game. Other than Wheelock being in the hospital, Carlisle's deteriorated condition wasn't considered and the runaway halfbacks were listed as having played. The headlines, "Warner Used His Best Team" and "Carlisle Indians Were As Strong As When They Met Harvard," were misleading. Warner put the best team he had available on the field, but several of his best players weren't available. Without Wheelock, the Indians were definitely not as strong as when they met Harvard.

The Navy game started well for Carlisle when Johnson ran the opening kickoff back twenty yards. Williams and Phillips each made good gains, moving the ball to the Navy forty-yard line. Johnson took it the rest of the way on a double pass. The kick after was missed. When the Middies' opening possession of the second half stalled, they punted. Disaster struck when the ball rolled to the edge of a high bank behind the goal. Johnson tried to fall on it, but a scramble developed and one of the players knocked the ball over the edge. Read fell on it for a Navy touchdown. Strassberger made the kick. Energized, the Midshipmen scored two more touchdowns to put the game on ice. Final Score: Navy 16–Carlisle 5.

Warner complained about Navy's rough play, saying that they never lost an opportunity to "twist legs and otherwise intentionally injure his men" and their language was "most profane and ungentlemanly." He cited instances where Navy players urged each other to violence. After the Navy game, Cornell athletic trainer George Connors returned to Carlisle, presumably to help injured Indians heal as he had done previously with the track team.

The game Warner had been planning on for weeks finally arrived and he had his players ready for the Quakers—except for trick plays. Carlisle started well. After a series of punt exchanges, the Indians smashed Penn's line several times, with Wheelock eventually shoved over for the touchdown. He also made the kick, putting Carlisle ahead 6-0. When the Quakers' drive stalled, a quarterback kick[7] was caught by Snook and advanced to the Carlisle fifteen-yard line. Another quarterback kick again fooled the Indians and the ball went over the goal line. Snook corralled it for a Penn touchdown. The kick after failed. Carlisle still led 6-5.

The Indians then moved the ball four and five yards at a clip down to Penn's eight-yard line. A signal mix up caused them to lose the ball. The Quakers weren't able to do much with it and punted. This time, Johnson, following magnificent interference, ran the kick back sixty-five yards for a touchdown. Wheelock made an easy kick. Carlisle 12-Penn 5.

After a few punt exchanges opening the second half, Penn scored, again via a quarterback kick. The extra point failed. Carlisle's lead shrunk to one point, 12 to 11. Penn's next and last touchdown came via a drive half the length of the field, with Teas going over on a two-yard run. The kick after failed but Penn led 16-12.

With the sun setting and time running short, Penn stalled deep in its own territory. Rather than risk giving Johnson the chance to run back a punt

---

[7] The rules at that time allowed the quarterback or any player behind him to retrieve a punt kicked by the quarterback.

for a touchdown, Penn took a safety, narrowing the margin to Penn 16-Carlisle 14. The Indians had the ball after the free kick but too little time remained to score. *The Philadelphia Times* headline read, "Pennsylvania, Although Outplayed, Won from Indians by Two Points."

The next Saturday, the Indians fought the Washington and Jefferson Presidents to a scoreless tie in a mud bath in what in effect had become a shallow lake. Ten minutes into the game on this cold, rainy day, observers could no longer tell one player from another due to being covered with mud. Players' faces had to be sponged off every few minutes to enable them to see the ball. Rampant fumbling of the slippery ball was the order of the day, and footing was impossible.

Five days later, the Indians faced a good Columbia team again on Thanksgiving Day. Pop Warner had complained earlier in the season about how hard it was to prepare good ends, and Columbia's head coach George Sanford took heed of what he said. He designed a formation to exploit Carlisle's weak ends by shifting a tackle to the backfield. That location got him around the end to lead the blocking faster than pulling out of the line when the ball was snapped. As cold winds howled across Coogan's Bluff, Smith and Weekes, Columbia's halfbacks, took turns making long runs and scoring touchdowns. Carlisle was helpless to stop them until they'd run up a score of forty to nothing. But something changed in the last ten minutes of the game. The Indians came to life. Spectators who had given up to the cold and were heading to the exits turned around and returned to their seats to see what was happening. Using Warner's wing shift play, Carlisle carried their heavier opponents down the field by storm, pushing Wilson Charles over Columbia's goal line twice. Wheelock made both extra points. Final score: Columbia 40-Carlisle 12.

The 5-7-2 season was worse than the year before, a far cry from the results Pop wanted. The only bright spots were Wheelock being named to Walter Camp's All-America Second Team and Johnson being named to the Third Team. 1902 had to be better. At the football banquet that winter, Warner looked forward to the next season, pointing to good material being in sight and the spirit of the upcoming team was manifest in the last half of the Columbia game.

1901 Season Summary

Date	Opponent	Location	Indians	Opp.
Sep. 21	Lebanon Valley College	Indian Field, Carlisle Barracks, PA	28	0
Sep. 25	Steelton Y.M.C.A.	Steelton Athletic Field, Steelton, PA	5	5*
Sep. 28	Gallaudet College	Indian Field, Carlisle Barracks, PA	19	6
Oct. 2	Pennsylvania College	Island Park, Harrisburg, PA	5	6
Oct. 5	Dickinson College	Dickinson College Athletic Field, Carlisle, PA	16	11
Oct. 12	Bucknell University	Athletic Park, Williamsport, PA	6	5
Oct. 16	Haverford College	Indian Field, Carlisle Barracks, PA	29	0
Oct. 19	Cornell University	Pan-American Stadium, Buffalo, NY	0	17
Oct. 26	Harvard University	Soldiers' Field, Cambridge, MA	0	29
Nov. 2	University of Michigan	Bennett Park, Detroit, MI	0	22
Nov. 9	Navy	Worden Field, Annapolis, MD	6	16
Nov. 16	University of Pennsylvania	Franklin Field, Philadelphia, PA	14	16
Nov. 23	Washington & Jefferson College	Exposition Park, Pittsburgh, PA	0	0
Nov. 28	Columbia University	Polo Grounds, New York, NY	12	40

Won 5; Lost 7; Tied 2

*Originally scheduled for September 14 but rescheduled due to President McKinley's assassination.

When the Crown Prince of Siam Comes to Boston

The experiences of Prince Somdetch Chowfa Maha Vagiravudh during the next few days are likely to be such as to make his visit to this city one of the memorable events of his American tour. He will make his Boston debut tomorrow afternoon.

6

The Walking Wounded

Rule Changes for 1902:

The sides will change goals after each extra point attempt and each successful field goal.

Forward passes and players in motion before the snap are now penalized five yards instead of loss of possession. When a penalty is declined, yardage made from the spot of the infringement is limited to twenty-five yards.

No one other than the 22 players in the game at that time may step onto the field, even during time outs, except in the case of injury. Coaching during the game is not allowed. Plays may not be sent in with substitutes or the water boy. The penalty for infringement of this rule is the loss of five yards. (Pop Warner was frequently criticized for getting on the field, and his behavior may have instigated this rule change.)

The timekeeper is instructed to start his clock when the ball is put in play, not when the official blows his whistle.

1902 Carlisle Indians

Warner planned on taking the twenty-five most promising candidates to camp at Pine Grove Furnace the first week of September, but this doesn't seem to have happened. Something else that didn't happen was Charles Albert Bender maturing as a football player. Just before the season started, Connie Mack signed him to a contract to pitch for the Philadelphia Athletics. Soon, "Chief" Bender became a household name as Mack's most reliable hurler.

Warner's younger brother and Walter Camp 1901 All-America First Team guard Bill arrived about that time and assisted his older brother. He was nicknamed "Little Pop" by his Cornell teammates, even though he towered over his decade-older brother. Although Cornell captain, he must not have considered his helping a team he would be playing against later in the season as a conflict of interest, but things were different in those days.

The same paragraph in *The Red Man & His Helper* that announced Little Pop's arrival and purpose provided further evidence of the Pine Grove Furnace camp not happening: "While other teams go off to expensive places for preliminary practice—the Pennsylvania University team at Eagle's Mere, for instance—our boys remain at home and take only the time out of school and work hours."

Charles Williams was elected captain and many of last year's starters, including former captain Wheelock and star quarterback Johnson, returned. This year's prospects, like those of recent years, were lean when they came back to campus. Bender wasn't among them. He had graduated in the spring and spoke about how government programs on the reservations were holding Indians back. He enrolled at the Dickinson College prep school and began pitching for the Dickinson College nine. Carlisle expelled him for "Treachery to baseball team. (Was Captain)." On Decoration Day, he pitched his first game for the semi-pro Harrisburg Athletic Club and before football season started, he signed with the Philadelphia Athletics.

Warner monitored the squad to see if the training table was putting weight on them. Sometimes he and Bill ate with the boys, but the reason wasn't given. It could have been for team cohesion or to evaluate the quality of the food. Warner was encouraged about their progress, saying:

> If harmony can be maintained and the players each strive for self-control, other difficulties will soon be conquered. To bring best results, all jealousy must be banished and each man must be willing to play his best in any position he is placed. We notice that the new

coach on the University of Pennsylvania team changes his men to new positions frequently. It is the only way to find the best men for the best places, and certainly that is what must be to succeed. Men, obey your Captain and Coaches, and do what you are told instantly and without a word back, and we will have a successful season.

Carlisle opened against Lebanon Valley College for the third straight year. Pop was upbeat going into the game. Returning starters had improved and the previous year's subs were competing well for positions in the line-up. He also found players' attitudes much improved. Not expecting much of a challenge from LVC, Warner held Wheelock and Johnson out of the game. The Indians weren't tested, winning 48-0. He played thirteen other players in the second half, all different from the starters, except for Wilson Charles who played quarterback in the first half and fullback in the second. Charles had a red-letter day, scoring a touchdown, six extra points, a thirty-yard field goal, and a safety!

In spite of the large margin of victory, Coach Warner identified several things that needed improvement. A major problem was that some linemen continued playing high instead of getting low where they would have more leverage. The second-half bunch played too far back from the ball and didn't watch the ball while it was being snapped. Not seeing it snapped hindered them from charging quickly. Another problem was using their hands when blocking. They failed to put the opposing ends and halfbacks out of the play far too often.

Carlisle took on Pennsylvania College on an unseasonably hot day on a soft, slippery field, a combination that sapped the combatants' energy. Phillips and Shouchuk were again in the starting line-up along with some other new men, but Carlisle still won 25-0.

Lubo returned from his home in California in time to play Dickinson College, but the game was canceled. Dickinson's Captain Stanton and Carlisle's Captain Williams and Coach Warner could not reach agreement on the lengths of the halves to be played. Warner wanted them to be thirty minutes where Dickinson wanted them to be shorter. Each side compromised until only a five-minute difference remained, but they were unable to reach agreement. The Dickinson team, which had waited in a drizzle for the game to start, departed Carlisle Barracks unhappy not to have played the game.

On the following Saturday, heavier Bucknell took full advantage of the water and mud to defeat the lighter Indians. Fumbles plagued Carlisle but they only trailed 10–0 near the end of the game when they finally came to life. The Indians ripped through Bucknell's line for big gains, moving the ball all the way down to the five-yard line. Then Charles fumbled it away. Anderson picked it up and ran the distance of the field for a Bucknell touchdown. McCormick kicked the extra point. Final Score: Bucknell 16–Carlisle 0.

Warner scheduled a mid-week warm up with Bloomsburg Normal to get his team ready for Cornell on Saturday. It was as much a test of Warner's appliances[8] designed to protect Lubo's and Wheelock's injuries as well as their abilities to tolerate serious pain as anything else. Johnson sat out the 50–0 rout.

The Indians had plenty of incentive to win in Ithaca after their two previous poor showings against Cornell. Warner had even more to prove after losing badly to his alma mater, former team, and younger brother the year before. Cornell was missing two of its stars but Wheelock and Lubo went AWOL from the hospital ward to make the game. Patched up with homemade protective devices, they buckled up as best they could. After a missed field goal attempt by Cornell, the Indians moved the ball deep into enemy territory. The Cornell defense rose to stop them at the two-yard line and took over on downs. Brewster punted immediately. A Cornell player interfered with Johnson after he called for a fair catch. Wheelock took advantage of the improvement in field position resulting from the penalty and made a thirty-yard field goal via place kick to put Carlisle ahead 5–0.

Later in the first half, Williams punted from his own twenty-yard line but Brewster misplayed it, allowing the ball to roll deep in Cornell territory where it touched Tydeman, making it a free ball. A Carlisle player pounced on it to give the Indians possession of the pigskin. At the end of a series of rushes, Williams ran it in on a third-down play for a Carlisle touchdown. The kick after failed. Carlisle 10–Cornell 0.

Still in the first half, Bill Warner blocked a Carlisle punt. Cornell's Smith recovered it behind the goal line for an Ithaca touchdown. Coffin made the kick after. The first half ended with Carlisle ahead 10–6.

The Indians moved the ball at will throughout the second half but turned it over several times by fumbling, thwarting them from scoring again. Cornell Captain Warner repeatedly chided Coach Warner about getting onto the field illegally. The umpire, Nathan Stauffer, recalled a Cornellian's remorse about not scoring in the second half:

---

[8] Warner tinkered with football formations, automobiles, and protective devices for players. Details for the ones he created for Wheelock and Lubo are discussed at length in chapter 8.

Indians everywhere. Why, when a Cornell player was falling on the ball an Indian would dive under him and grab it. It would be the Indian's ball and first down. It was a magnificent victory for the Indians. Clear cut and fully earned. No flukes, but good, hard, fast football. The Indians never ceased trying to score more and only their terrible fumbling kept them from it....The consensus of opinion on all sides seemed to be that the Indians could have beaten any team on Saturday. The game was replete with brilliant runs. Several tries for field goals added to the interest.

Only the older boys (large boys in Carlisle jargon) met the football players' train with it arriving late at 11:00 p.m. Sunday night. They cheered as they marched from their quarters to Carlisle Junction and back. The following Saturday, the team got a respite from tough opposition. The heavy Medico-Chi team from Philadelphia lacked training and were no match for the Indians. Even with Wheelock and Johnson sitting out, presumably to save them for Harvard, the Indians won 63-0.

After defeating Cornell, the Indians thought they had a good shot at whipping Harvard for once. But they immediately got off on the wrong foot by fumbling on their own twenty-five-yard line. The Crimson pounded Carlisle's weaker front until they caried the ball over for a score, early in the first half. They again moved the ball well after receiving Carlisle's kickoff. This time Kernan made two long end runs, bringing the ball to Carlisle's fifteen. A holding penalty turned the ball over to the Indians, who immediately fumbled it back. This time, Carlisle's defense held and took the ball over on downs. After Carlisle punted, Harvard employed end runs and tackles-back plays for their second touchdown.

Using a variety of plays and formations not seen before, the Indians confused spectators and Harvard players alike. They moved the ball well but eventually fumbled it away. Later, after carrying a Carlisle player on his back the last eight yards of a long punt return, Marshall attempted to kick a field goal. It barely missed.

Harvard scored two more touchdowns in the second half before resting its starters. They played a dozen substitutes in this half. The game became a free-for-all mix up between the fresh Crimson men and the game, but tired, Indians. Carlisle made some long runs but couldn't escape a last defender to score a touchdown. Losing 23-0 was a huge disappointment.

Martin Wheelock retired from football after the game to return to his home where he would recuperate from the pleurisy that had plagued him all fall. Not only was he an important part of the team, he also served as an assistant coach, teaching younger players how to play the game.

Next up was a much weaker Susquehanna University team. Warner held out Lubo, Exendine, and Johnson, probably saving them for Penn the week after. In spite of fumbling several times, the Indians had the game in hand from the start. Sheldon scored three touchdowns and Phillips one. Wilson Charles attempted two field goals but both were blocked. He did make all four extra-point kicks in the 24-0 Carlisle romp.

Pop Warner wasn't at the Susquehanna game. He was in Cambridge, sizing up the next opponent, Penn, while they played Harvard. He may have taken Johnson, Lubo, and Exendine with him because he sometimes took star players along to scout future opponents when his team wasn't playing or was sure of winning without him. He wasn't supposed to coach the team during the game, anyway.

Winning the coin toss, Carlisle chose to receive Penn's opening kickoff, but they couldn't do anything with it. Plays that previously worked for them, end runs in particular, didn't gain yardage. It wasn't clear if Johnson's knee was already wrenched or if it happened during the game. Carlisle's best end-run threat couldn't make the sharp cuts he was known for. Unable to figure out the Quaker defense, they played most of the scoreless first half on defense. Line bucks proved more successful in the second half, so successful

INDIANS DEFEAT PENN 5 TO 0 IN SLOW GAME

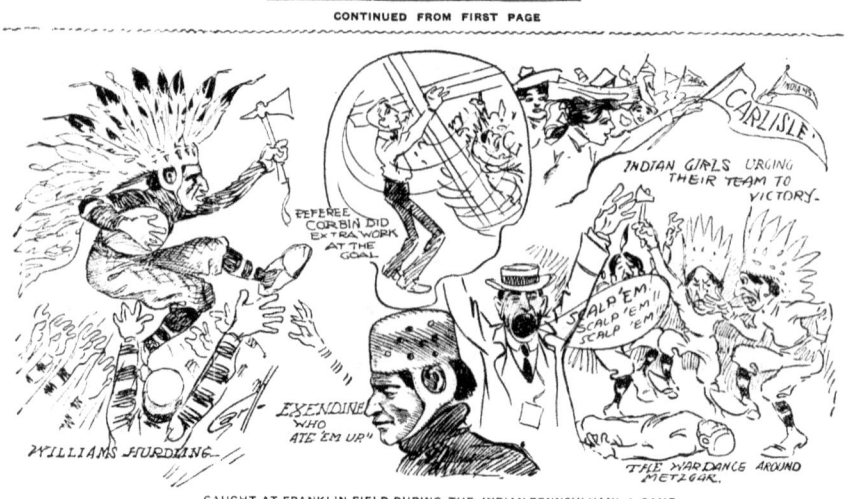

CAUGHT AT FRANKLIN FIELD DURING THE INDIAN-PENNSYLVANIA GAME

that the Indians pushed the Quakers all over the field. Their defense stiffened, keeping Penn far from their goal the entire second half.

Receiving a kick on their own fifteen, Phillips, Exendine, and Charles Williams threw themselves at, through, or over Penn's heavier line for steady gains. Carlisle interspersed these line-smashing plays with fakes that allowed Sheldon, Williams, and Parker to skirt around the tackles for five- and ten-yard gains. Their play sequence kept Penn's defense guessing, often wrongly. The closer the Indians got to Penn's goal line, the stiffer was Penn's defense. On the twenty-fourth play of the drive, Phillips attempted to carry the ball across Penn's goal line but he ran smack dab into the goal post so hard the crossbar fell, striking him on the head. When the mass of bodies was untangled after the play ended, the ball was placed on the one-foot line. Phillips had time to recover because it took some time for a carpenter to replace the crossbar. Captain Williams carried it over on the next play for a touchdown. Beaver's kick failed. Carlisle 5–Penn 0.

Girls from the Indian School sitting in the north stand livened up the frequent stoppages of play by singing, "Play Ball! Play Ball!" to the tune of an old Methodist hymn. Bored Penn students sitting across the field opposite them joined in.

Carlisle again moved the ball well on their next possession and quickly progressed to Penn's twenty-yard line. There, a holding penalty gave the ball to the Quakers. They then gave the ball to Mitchell, the largest man on the field. He broke tackles and rambled down the field until the diminutive Johnson sat him down, ending Penn's longest gain of the day. Choosing to play defense, every time the Indians got the ball, they punted it away, even those times they were close enough to try field goals. A blocked kick could be returned for a touchdown, so they played it safe and punted. Williams' punts kept the Quakers in their own territory and Johnson didn't muff any of theirs. The fumbleitis that had plagued the team the last few years had vanished. Carlisle had the ball on the Penn twenty-five when the game ended. They had beaten Penn for only the second time.

When word of the win hit the Indian School, the horns, Indian yells, and the band could be heard nearly a mile away. Soon a night-shirt parade formed and took possession of the town for an hour or more. Students did war dances in large circles accompanied by genuine Indian yells on Hanover and East Main Streets, then marched quietly back to campus.

Overconfident, the Indians didn't play their hardest against Virginia, ranked first in the South that year by J. L. de Saulles. The Wahoos made repeated gains through the guards and drew first blood when Council went over for a touchdown. Harris made a successful kick after. The Indians sprang to life in the second half, keeping Virginia on defense most of the time. After several attempts to cross the goal line, Wilson Charles, who had replaced Williams when he was knocked unconscious, succeeded. His kick after would have tied the score, but it hit the upright and failed. Johnson, Lubo, and Bowen, who were out with injuries, were sorely missed. The final score was Virginia 6–Carlisle 5.

Five days later, Thanksgiving Day, found the Carlisle team in the nation's capital playing on Georgetown University's campus. Sluggish at the start of the game, the Indian defenders rallied when their goal line was threatened. Their ragged offense did little with the ball. Lucky for the game to be a scoreless tie when the first half ended, a different team—or so it seemed—emerged for the second half. One wonders what Warner had to say in the locker room because nothing is said about it in his biographies.

The team was energized and moved the ball well. They made touchdowns at five-minute intervals with Ely Parker scoring three of them and William White one. Johnson succeeded with one kick after touchdown. The game was called for darkness with thirteen minutes to play. Final score: Carlisle 21–Georgetown 0.

The next day, the Indians met with President Theodore Roosevelt, a football fan and Harvard man, in the White house. Disciplinarian Thompson introduced the boys to the President.

"Delighted," exclaimed the President, grasping Johnson's hand. "You play quarterback. The mass play of your team was splendid. I am delighted."

Roosevelt moved to the next man, halfback Parker. "Delighted. Your play was brilliant. You made three touchdowns, didn't you? How in the world did you do it?"

When he came to a bandaged player, he said, "You're a football player. That's self-evident." To another, he said, "I see without asking that you played yesterday and it didn't improve your beauty."

At the end of the line stood Shouchuk, the Inuit *The New York Sun* incorrectly identified as Exendine. The President took his hand, saying, "Delighted to meet you. I congratulate you on coming to this country to get an education. So you are an Esquimau. I don't suppose the coal famine worries you a bit."

The crowd roared at the humor and passed out of the President's office.

At season's end, Nathan Stauffer announced his selections for All-Americans and All-University teams, including Carlisle players Charles Williams, Martin Wheelock, and James Johnson, all of whom Walter Camp and Caspar Whitney overlooked. Stauffer placed Williams as fullback on his All-America squad by comparing him with Graydon of Harvard: "Both are good kickers, fine line plungers and fast runners, but Williams, the Indian, is the strongest defensive back in the country today...I have seen Williams stop a three-man tandem tackle coming between guard and tackle so quickly and so hard that it knocked two of the three for a complete loss...."

He placed Wheelock as center on his All-University team and Johnson as quarterback. Stauffer also placed Bill Warner on his All-America team at guard as did Caspar Whitney. Walter Camp demoted him to his Second Team.

The 1902 season was Carlisle's best since 1899 but Pop expected bigger things for 1903.

1902 Season Summary

Date	Opponent	Location	Indians	Opp.
Sep. 20	Lebanon Valley College	Indian Field, Carlisle Barracks, PA	48	0
Sep. 27	Pennsylvania College	Indian Field, Carlisle Barracks, PA	25	0
Oct. 4	Dickinson College*			
Oct. 11	Bucknell University	Athletic Park, Williamsport, PA	0	16
Oct. 15	Bloomsburg State Normal School	Indian Field, Carlisle Barracks, PA	50	0
Oct. 18	Cornell University	Percy Field, Ithaca, NY	10	6
Oct. 25	Medico-Chirurgical College	Indian Field, Carlisle Barracks, PA	63	0
Nov. 1	Harvard University	Soldiers' Field, Cambridge, MA	0	23
Nov. 8	Susquehanna University	Indian Field, Carlisle Barracks, PA	24	0
Nov. 15	University of Pennsylvania	Franklin Field, Philadelphia, PA	5	0
Nov. 22	University of Virginia	Lafayette Field, Norfolk, VA	5	6
Nov. 27	Georgetown University	Varsity Field, Washington, DC	21	0

Won 8; Lost 3; Tied 0

*Canceled due to a pouring rain and captains not coming to agreement on the length of the halves. Cessation of Dickinson College-Carlisle Indian School games resulted.

James Phillips in Carlisle uniform

Coast to Coast

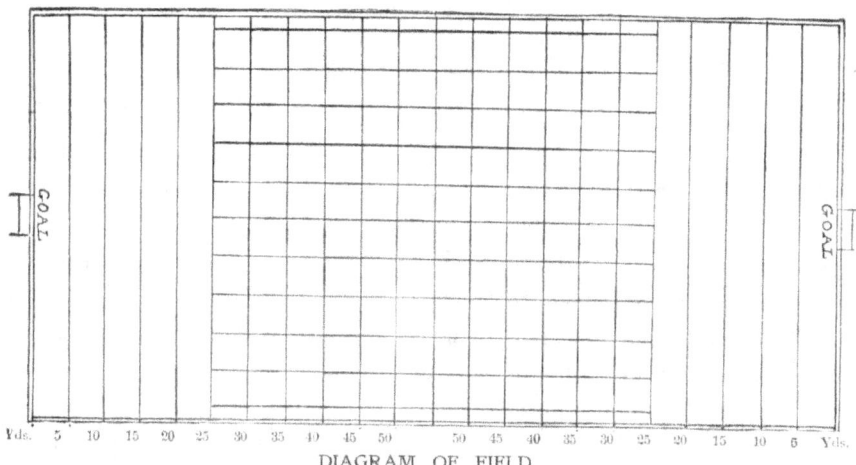

DIAGRAM OF FIELD.

A certain alteration in the foot ball rules for the season of 1903 provides that when the ball is put in play in the scrimmage at any point within the centre section of the field, that is, the portion bounded by the two twenty-five and the two side lines, that at least seven of the players of the side having the ball must be on the line of scrimmage and also that the player who first receives the ball, commonly known as the quarter back, within the above mentioned territory, may carry it forward beyond the line of scrimmage, provided in so doing he crosses such line at least five yards from the point where the snapper-back put the ball in play. As it was feared that the referee, under whose province this run by the quarter-back is placed, would have some difficulty in telling at a glance whether the distance out from the centre was five yards, it was determined to suggest certain changes in marking. As the field is now marked off with white lines every five yards, parallel to the goal line, for measuring the five yards to be gained in three downs, under the new rules it is proposed that through the middle section of the field, that is, between the two twenty-five yard lines, additional white lines five yards apart, parallel to the side lines, should be marked in order to assist the referee in thus determining whether the quarter-back runs under the rules or not. Thus, while the foot ball field still remains a gridiron, the central section of it now resembles a checkerboard, and the appended diagram shows exactly how the field should be marked. As the field does not divide into five yard spaces evenly, it is wise to run the first line through the middle point of the field, and then mark off the five yards on each side from that middle line.

Rule Changes for 1903:

The person receiving the center snap (usually the quarterback) may now carry the ball across the scrimmage line, but must be at least five yards laterally of the center snap. Prior to 1903, the person receiving the snap was required to give the ball to another player to advance it downfield. Double pass plays allowed quarterbacks to advance the ball after getting it back from another player.

Traditionalists resisted this rule change and achieved the compromise of having it in effect only between the twenty-five-yard lines. The old mass-play rules, including the number of men required to be on the line of scrimmage, were in effect between the twenty-five-yard lines and the goal lines closest to them. Enforcing the rule required placing lines perpendicular to the yard lines five yards apart.

At least seven men of the team possessing the ball must be on the line of scrimmage.

The team being scored upon now has the choice of receiving or kicking off after a score.

A penalty for roughing the punter was also instituted.

When Tom O'Rourke, an old fight promotor, offered Pop Warner's brother Bill $300 to play in the World Series of Football over the 1902/1903 New Year's holiday in Madison Square Garden, Pop recommended that he take it. He had always opposed professionalism in football, primarily because he saw no future in it. But when O'Rourke offered him the same deal, Pop accepted. That he would be playing alongside Bill and former Carlisle stars Bemus and Hawley Pierce surely affected his decision. He overestimated his ability to perform on the field after being on the sidelines seven or eight years. He missed the extra point attempt and three (maybe more) field goal attempts. Perhaps the gash on his head he received early in the game had a little to do with that. He finished the game but the next morning he was so stiff and sore he needed his brother to help him dress. Pop Warner's professional career ended after that one game. The affair was a financial loss, and he got paid twenty-three instead of the $300 he was promised. Bill was smarter—he got his money upfront.

Later in January, a Chicago newspaper published an article based on interviews with Drs. Carlos Montezuma and Charles Eastman, both of whom had been associated with Carlisle Indian School. They stated that Carlisle would no longer be the force in the football world it had become because Superintendent Pratt did not believe in strenuous athletic competitions. This falsehood was soon refuted when the schedule for 1903 was released.

Richard Henry Pratt was promoted to the rank of colonel on January 30. Within a week, he offered to retire immediately, instead of December 1904 when he would reach the retirement age of sixty-five, if he were promoted to brigadier general upon retirement. Apparently not amused by Pratt's assertion that he was due this promotion, President Roosevelt wasted no time in retiring him—as a colonel. Pratt complained that he was being treated unfairly to no avail. The Army had no problem with him being retired because it opened up a colonel billet in which to promote a younger officer. It was also happy to allow Pratt to remain at Carlisle; his serving as superintendent freed an active-duty cavalry officer for regular duty.

In April in an apparent attempt to limit who could wear the C, *The Red Man & Helper* announced that only those who had earned letters in football, baseball, or track would be allowed to wear Cs on their sweaters. Letters would be awarded to: 1) those who play in any of the three most important football games; 2) the ten best baseball players; and 3) those who win first place in the class contest, win points in any of the dual meets, and the winner of the annual cross-country run. Others would not be allowed to wear the Carlisle C on their sweaters.

Some experts thought the rule change allowing the quarterback to carry the ball across the line of scrimmage between the twenty-five-yard lines would necessitate a change in the physique of that player. Not having many boys of age and size to pick from, Warner had to stay with the diminutive (5'7" tall, 138 pounds) player who was the best they had. That was James Johnson, son of a mixed-blood father from Tennessee and a full-blood Stockbridge mother, from Gresham, Wisconsin.

Later in April, *The Red Man & Helper* announced a thirteen-game schedule terminating with a Thanksgiving Day meeting with Northwestern University in Chicago. The schedule was arranged to keep the toughest contests two weeks apart with lesser opponents interspersed between them. Bemus Pierce was engaged to assist Warner in coaching the team. Prospects for a successful season looked good in spite of fielding the lightest team of any prominence. Because of the leadership he had shown, the team voted James Johnson as their captain. He had finished his Carlisle and Conway Hall coursework, although taking courses at Dickinson College, and remained active in the Invincible Debating Society at the Indian School. Last year's captain who had played extremely well, Charles Williams, remained on the team.

Football practice started on September 2nd under the direction of Coach Warner, his brother Bill, and Bemus Pierce. Young Warner left on the 11th to lead his old Cornell team. The illness of Minnie L. Ferree, the domestic science teacher who had managed the training table the previous year, delayed the start of the training table until a satisfactory cook could be found.

Carlisle's 28-0 win over Lebanon Valley College was a warmup in which Warner inserted a different line-up for the second half to look over more players in game situations. He complained of fumbling and linemen being slow getting started.

In their second game, the Indians played unusually well for that early in the season despite it being unseasonably hot. The Gettysburgians had hopes of scoring this year but two minutes of play showed them they were no match for the Indians. After the 46-0 drubbing, Bemus Pierce left for California to coach the Sherman Institute team at a salary increase.

No reason was given for canceling the mid-week game against Mt. St. Mary's. Perhaps Warner wanted to focus on Bucknell, the Indians' opponent on Saturday. The boys were concerned because of past losses and that they would be without Nicolas Bowen, who had been injured crashing into the goalpost in the last game. They played well against Bucknell, but the Indians seemed to lose heart after Johnson fumbled twice. Bucknell made some long gains but time ran out, ending the first half in a scoreless tie.

Near the end of the second half, the Indians came alive. Taking advantage of the new rules, quarterback Johnson made long run after long run around the ends. Wilson Charles dashed the last ten yards for the touchdown and Johnson made the kick. As the clock was running down, an Indian blocked a Bucknell punt and Johnson fell on the ball for the second touchdown. He also made the kick. It took their best efforts but Carlisle won 12-0.

Bloomsburg cancelled the mid-week game, so the light Franklin & Marshall Nevonians were next. Carlisle's weight, "magnificent interference and swift play" overwhelmed the overmatched diplomats so badly, the Indians ran only straight plays. Warner withheld his tricks for their next contest. The only negative was that F&M gained more ground in the 30-0 shellacking than had previous opponents.

On the road again, Carlisle visited highly rated and unscored-upon Princeton. The lighter Indians couldn't get any footing in the rain. In spite of that, they gave Princeton the best fight of any team the Tigers had played up to that point. Princeton scored twice in the first half, missing the first extra point. Carlisle held them scoreless in the second but couldn't score themselves. Princeton shut them out 11-0.

Swarthmore came to visit the next Saturday for Carlisle's third and last home game of this long season. Despite the Little Quakers holding mighty Columbia to five points, Warner kept several starters out of the game to rest them for Harvard. In a hard-fought battle, Swarthmore's men played clean football. It took all Carlisle could do to defeat them. A fumble by quarterback Joseph Baker set up Swarthmore's only score, a forty-yard drop kick for a field goal. Arthur Sheldon scored both Carlisle touchdowns and Charles made the kicks after in Carlisle's 12-5 win.

It is a shame that the 1903 Carlisle-Harvard game is best known for a trick rather than the overall quality of play and the suspense at the end. *The Boston Post* coverage opened with hyperbole: "With a team outweighed nearly forty pounds to the man, crippled, bruised and battered from other contests, and on a foreign field, the Indians gave an exhibition of football that has no parallel in the annals of Harvard football."

Johnson kicked a field goal from the twenty-five-yard line for the first and only score of the first half. In the week leading up to the game, Warner directed Mose Blumenthal, operator of the school's tailoring shop and proprietor of The Capital men's store, to have elastic strips sewed into the tails of several jerseys as part of a trick play. Pop had run it against Penn State some years earlier and was going to try it against the Crimson. Johnson corralled Marshall's second-half kickoff on his own five-yard line. The rest of the team bunched around him so Harvard players couldn't see him slip the ball under the back of Charles Dillon's enhanced jersey. The team scattered, with the usual ballcarriers acting as if they had the ball. Dillon, a guard with footspeed, walked toward the distant goal line. When he passed the last defender, he broke into a run and was across the goal line before anyone noticed he had the ball. Johnson raced to him to remove the spheroid from his jersey and touch it down for the score. Since Warner had apprised the officials before he ran the hidden-ball play, it was allowed. Johnson kicked the extra point for a 12-0 lead early in the second half.

Although outplayed most of the game, Harvard didn't give up. They pounded Carlisle's front, moving the ball slowly but surely to Carlisle's two-foot line. But the Indians held like a stone wall and got the ball on its own two-inch line. They punted to the forty where Harvard took over again. The bruised, battered, and exhausted Indians couldn't stop the onslaught this time. Even in that condition, Harvard had to have the chain brought out to measure twice. Eventually, Meier crashed through Carlisle's weak right side.

Harvard brought in three fresh substitutes and used them to tear though the fatigued but resolute Indians. Gains became longer. When Harvard made the touchdown, it was across the extreme right edge of the goal line, a difficult place for a punt out. So, Marshall raced across the field to make a free catch on a dead run. He jerked to a dead spot facing the goal post and managed to heel the ball. The kick from this spot was easy. Harvard now led 12-11.

The Indians fought back. They got the ball on a fumble on Harvard's forty-yard line and forged a lightning-like attack. They moved to the fifteen but had to make two more yards for a first down. Instead of kicking a field goal for the win, Johnson chose a run play and one of the halfbacks, Sheldon or Fritz Hendricks, fumbled. Harvard won 12-11. This was the last game to be played on Soldiers' Field. Demolition started the next day for construction of Harvard Stadium, the U-shaped structure still in use in the twenty-first century.

Five minutes into the next game, it became apparent to spectators—the sportswriters at least—in the stands that Carlisle fielded the better team despite Georgetown being seven or eight pounds heavier per man. Little Johnson was everywhere and ran like an eel. On their second possession, Carlisle moved the ball well with Sheldon carrying it across the line. Johnson's kick after failed. Four minutes later, following line plunge after line plunge, Sheldon scored again. Johnson's kick was successful. The half ended with Carlisle ahead 11-0.

Early in the second half, Edmondson blocked the Indians' punt from their twenty-yard line and fell on it after it rolled across the goal line. Carroll kicked the goal-after touchdown, making the score Indians 11-Georgetown 6. Johnson returned the ensuing kickoff twenty yards. On this drive down the field, he handed the ball off to Hendricks and Sheldon on most of the plays. Charles Williams ran the ball in and Johnson made the kick after. The Indians made their fourth and last touchdown in a similar way. And Frank Jude kicked a field goal shortly before time ran out to raise the score to Carlisle 28-Georgetown 6. Carlisle's management considered Georgetown's play unnecessarily rough and did not schedule games with them for some years.

The Indians had been looking forward to playing Penn all season and they were ready. Quaker Captain Sol Metzger summed up the game: "Our defeat yesterday is due to the fact that Carlisle outclassed us completely until the second half, when with a few changes things took on a brighter outlook and, for a while, we had a good chance to pull out a tie game, but slow playing and poor judgement at a critical point lost us a second chance to score...Johnson, their captain and quarterback, is the best man in that position that we have ever faced." Given that Penn routinely played against numerous Walter Camp All-Americans, Metzger's was high praise indeed.

Warner saw things differently: "While the victory was decisive, it is nevertheless a fact that the Carlisle team did not play as well as it has in most of the other games and, but for fumbles and penalties, the score would have been much larger. There is no doubt that each man in the team did his best, but somehow there was not as much life and spirit in the team's play as was exhibited in the game against Harvard."

Johnson and Charles scored touchdowns and Johnson kicked an extra point in addition to a field goal. Torrey scored Penn's touchdown and Bennett kicked their extra point. Carlisle won 16-6.

The day of the Penn game, a press report announced that Carlisle would be traveling to the West Coast for a New Year's game in California and that other games would be played on the trip. No specifics were given. The win over Penn may have made this trip possible. However, two games on the regular schedule remained to be played.

The next Saturday, Virginia, a team that beat Carlisle the previous year and was again the best team in the South, faced them. The Indians had to play desperately to prevent defeat by the heavy Yahoos, for whom this was the most important game on their schedule. Neither team scored in the first half, although both sides had chances. Johnson saved the day when a Virginian broke free with the rest of his team arrayed to interfere for him. The petite quarterback knifed through the blockers to make the touchdown-saving tackle from behind.

Virginia made an on-side kick that probably caused a rule change because it only traveled eight yards before being snared by one of the kicker's teammates. The kicker might as well have handed him the ball, the way the rules were written. The Yahoos moved the ball down the field until Council went over for the score. He also kicked the extra point.

The Indians got stronger and responded with a drive of their own capped with a touchdown by Bowen. Johnson kicked the extra point, tying the game at 6-all. Bowen was injured on the play and replaced by a new sub, Moore. Williams was also injured and replaced by Charles. Hendricks later replaced Charles and another new man, Wright, was substituted for Walter "Tex" Mathews. Carlisle's ability to replace wounded players made the difference. They held off the Virginians' rushes and were threatening to score when the game ended with the score tied Carlisle 6-Virginia 6.

Unbeaten Northwestern University was Carlisle's Thanksgiving opponent that year. After Haskell Institute lost to Chicago, its Superintendent H. B. Peairs threw down a gauntlet: "We hope now to see Northwestern beat Carlisle, as Carlisle has refused for three years to give us a game, saying that we were not in their class. If Northwestern beats them they might come down a peg or two."

In spite of blinding snow, the Indians made four touchdowns, three extra points, and a field goal. The Chicago papers admitted that the Indians outplayed the Methodists man for man. One Northwestern player didn't participate. James Phillips had played at guard for Carlisle the year before but was then studying law at Northwestern. He refused to play against his old teammates. Watching from the stands, he opined that Carlisle's speedy backs would have doubled the score had the field been clear of snow. Carlisle 28-Northwestern 0.

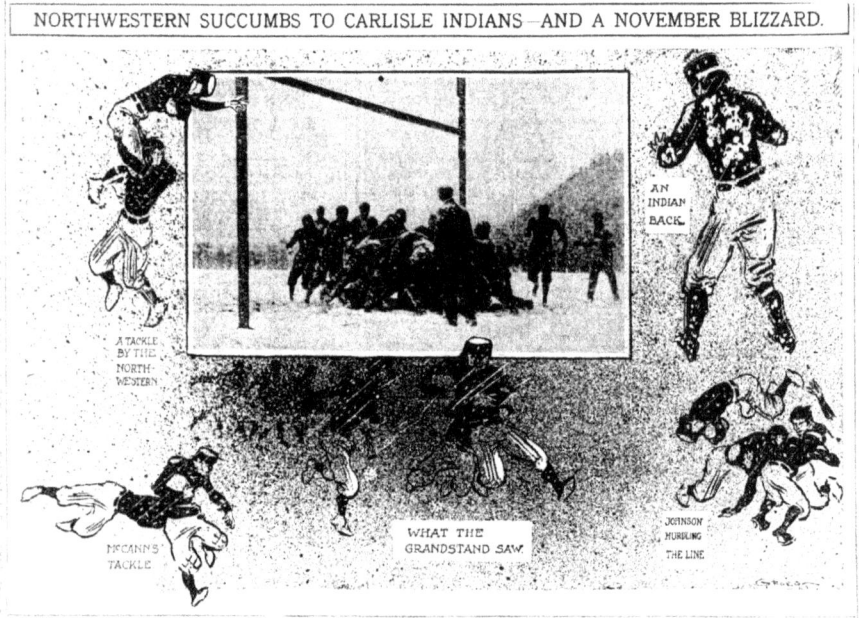

Carlisle students may not have been collegians but they celebrated the victory and the successful football season like they were—but with their own special touches. As night fell, a weird collection of human forms assembled in front of the large boys' quarters. Soon the band began to play and the night-robed and blanket-wrapped spectators moved in mass to the flagpole. Turkey feathers peeped out of some blankets and satanic horns appeared on some. Carrying colored lights, they danced, jumped, and got entangled. Those in night robes led a zigzag dance across the campus, holding hands to create a worm-fence line. Dynamite firecrackers, Roman candles, sky-rockets, megaphones, class yells, songs, and shouts created a racket that mingled with the band's music. Off-campus on the road leading from town to the school, they burned a huge bonfire. Boys danced around the flames and set off fireworks of every description. When they tired of this, the school band played a concert. Later, a musical company performed in the chapel, ending the festivities.

In mid-November, Carlisle alum Frank Cayou arranged to be in Arcola, Illinois, where he had worked the previous summer. There, he and Anna Snyder, the eighteen-year-old daughter of a prosperous farmer, eloped to Tuscola, Illinois, where they secured a marriage license and a Methodist minister to officiate the ceremony. Afterward, they took a train to Champaign, Illinois, where he was working as a coach. News of their wedding soon hit the wire services: "His bride is regarded as one of the most handsome young women of Douglas County, a county famous for fair women."

Carlisle's regular season was over but several western teams yearned to play them. However, arranging post-season schedules was a messy business with deals constantly in states of flux. An article in the December 1 edition of the *Los Angeles Times* about a contract between Pomona College and Sherman Institute, an Indian school located in Riverside, California, for a football game divulged that a New Year's Day game between Carlisle and the Sherman Institute was planned. The same day, *The San Francisco Call* reported that Bucknell, Columbia, and Carlisle had requested post-season games with unbeaten Stanford, but no game was scheduled.

If that wasn't enough news for the day, *The Washington Times* made known that Cornell students were demanding that Pop Warner be brought back to coach their team. This position was supported by the local Ithaca press as well as *Alumni News*.

The next day, *The San Francisco Call* announced that the Associated Students of the University of California had decided to play a New Year's Day game with an eastern team. Michigan, Minnesota, and Carlisle were the likely opponents. Two other possible games were declined: a match game with the University of Washington and a game against Stanford at the Carnival of Roses.

On December 4, Carlisle wired the manager of the Reliance Athletic Club that the Indians would not be able to play them on New Year's Day as proposed. Carlisle had intended to play Sherman Institute on Christmas Day but that game was changed to the University of Nevada in Salt Lake City. On December 12, negotiations finally settled on December 19 for a game with the University of Utah in Salt Lake City. The same day, the *San Francisco Chronicle* announced a Christmas Day game was to be played between Carlisle and Reliance Athletic Club. The R. A. C. team would be bolstered by Cal and Stanford varsity players. Carlisle was to play a New Year's game with U. S. C. or Pomona College or the University of Colorado. A second piece on the same page stated that Carlisle would play Sherman Institute on New Year's Day. The schedule for the western trip was set, sort of.

Wallace Denny

The team, accompanied by Mr. & Mrs. Warner and Wallace Denny, departed on Monday the 14th for Utah. Denny, an excellent track man and tennis player but small for football, had begun his career as Pop Warner's trainer.

Local pundits had little enthusiasm for Utah's game with Carlisle after completing a 2-4 season, even though some grads would be bolstering the line-up. The home team's performance didn't surprise them. That the Utes gained but three yards during the game would suggest an astronomically high score in Carlisle's favor. But snow and a slippery field hindered the Indians' high-powered offense. Warner claimed to have benched Johnson for an undisclosed rule infraction. This kerfuffle must have happened sometime after the opening kickoff because Johnson was mentioned in write ups of the game. In spite of that, they won handily, 22-0, even though they only played twenty-minute halves. The only injury was to Baker, the back-up quarterback playing in Johnson's place, who was knocked unconscious toward the end of the game. Charles replaced him, not Johnson.

In San Francisco an hour before the start of the game against the Reliance Athletic Club's All-California team, Warner huddled with Johnson and Baker in a corner of the locker room. When Pop informed Johnson that he would be the starting quarterback, Johnson, who was still angry at being benched at Utah, shouted, "Listen, Pop. I don't care if I never play in one of your ball games!" Warner didn't know if it was because of his kudos for Baker or Walter Camp's praise Johnson had been reading in the papers that incited him.

Pop turned to Baker and told him he would be starting. The other players couldn't help but overhear what had transpired. They came over and pleaded with Warner to let Johnson play. Pop responded, "Baker really did a fine job for us against Utah. And besides, I couldn't play a player whose heart wouldn't be in the game."

Apparently feeling the emotional weight from his teammates, Johnson spoke. "Well, Coach. If the other boys want me to play, I will." He went out and played the best game of his life.

The all-star team Reliance Athletic Club had assembled by augmenting its regulars with Cal and Stanford players had the upper hand at first by using their sixteen-pounds per man weight advantage. But it didn't last long. One Californian couldn't take Johnson down by himself. It sometimes took as many as four to get the little guy on the ground. The rest of the team played well, too, and fumbled only one time. Later, the Indians invoked a seldom-used provision in the rules to retain possession of the ball. They moved back twenty yards instead of punting the ball away after failing to make the yardage necessary for a first down. They were simply too fast for their opponents. Johnson capped a drive late in the first half by keeping the ball on a fake and circling his right end for a touchdown. He missed the kick after. The half ended with Carlisle ahead of Reliance All-California 5-0.

The home team's poor conditioning began to show. Charles capped a long drive early in the second half by running the last three yards for a second touchdown. Johnson made the kick. On a later possession, Johnson was thrown down hard by a defender. When he regained consciousness, his right hand hurt. He played even better with the bandaged hand. On a later drive, Johnson's twenty-yard run set up Sheldon to make the third Carlisle touchdown. James again made the kick. In the next series, he made two twenty-five-yard end runs setting up the Indians for another score. Williams scored after a fake and Johnson kicked the goal, putting. Carlisle ahead 23-0.

The Californians stiffened and repeatedly threw their heavy men against the lighter Carlisle line. But the rapid pace tired them more than the Indians. With the win assured, Johnson left the game to a loud ovation. At the end, a group of spectators surged onto the field and carried him off on their shoulders. A number of women were carried away by their enthusiasm and embraced him. It was Johnson's day.

New Year's Day found the Indians in Los Angeles playing Sherman Institute. In addition to coaching the team, Bemus Pierce played fullback against Carlisle. Some other former Carlisle students were also on the team.

Fumbleitis returned to haunt Carlisle but most were made at the end of hard tackles, not when handling the ball. An expert wrote, "The Carlisle-Sherman game was by far the fastest, most brilliant and exciting football contest ever held in Southern California." The game would likely have ended as a 6-6 tie except for an unfortunate call by an official. Sherman players claimed they heard a whistle blow and stopped because the play was over. Carlisle players claimed they didn't hear it and continued the play with the ball carrier running unmolested for a touchdown. The official said he didn't blow his whistle and awarded Carlisle the winning touchdown. Final score: Carlisle 12-Sherman Institute 6. Warner thought his squad hadn't taken this team seriously and played just well enough to win. They were more interested in seeing if they could pull off gadget plays or hocus-pocus, as Warner called it. He let it ride because they had played such a long season.

Walter Camp placed Johnson on his All-America First Team at quarterback. Caspar Whitney selected him as a substitute on his All-America team. James Phillips was named to the All-Western team as a guard. A reason for Phillips transferring to Carlisle from the Dickinson College team may have been something other than football, academics, or finances. On December 29, he married Carlisle grad Ernestine "Earney" Wilber in a Catholic church near her home on the Menominee Reservation near Neopit, Wisconsin and left for Seattle to make their fortune.

The 1903 season was Carlisle's best since 1899. George Orton of Penn evaluated Carlisle highly: "[T]he Indians would be given high rank against all the big colleges both of the East and West…No team in the country deserves more credit for their season's work and no coach merits higher praise than

Warner, whose work and brains were responsible for much of the success of the season."

What would the future hold?

1903 Season Summary

Date	Opponent	Location	Indians	Opp.
Sep. 19	Lebanon Valley College	Indian Field, Carlisle Barracks, PA	28	0
Sep. 26	Pennsylvania College	Indian Field, Carlisle Barracks, PA	46	0
Sep. 30	Mt. St. Mary's College*			
Oct. 3	Bucknell University	Athletic Park, Williamsport, PA	12	0
Oct. 7	Bloomsburg State Normal School†			
Oct. 10	Franklin & Marshall College	Williamson Field, Lancaster, PA	30	0
Oct. 17	Princeton University	University Field, Princeton, NJ	0	11
Oct. 24	Swarthmore College	Indian Field, Carlisle Barracks, PA	12	5
Oct. 31	Harvard University	Soldiers' Field, Cambridge, MA	11	12
Nov. 7	Georgetown University	Varsity Field, Washington, DC	28	6
Nov. 14	University of Pennsylvania	Franklin Field, Philadelphia, PA	16	6
Nov. 21	University of Virginia	Lafayette Field, Norfolk, VA	6	6
Nov. 26	Northwestern University	South Side Park III, Chicago, IL	28	0
Dec. 19	University of Utah	Cummings Field, Salt Lake City, UT	22	0
Dec. 25	Reliance Athletic Association	Richmond Field, San Francisco, CA	23	0
Jan. 1	Sherman Institute	Prager Park, Los Angeles, CA	12	6

Won 11; Lost 2; Tied 1

*Reason for cancelation not given.
†Canceled for unknown reason.

Shops Warner Used to Make Protective Devices

Shoe Shop

Tin Shop

8
Captain Leadership

In 1924, J. P. Glass and George Byrnes interviewed Pop Warner for a syndicated column that was distributed nationally by the North American Newspaper Alliance (NANA). In this interview, Warner told of the heroic efforts in 1902 of several past, present, and future Carlisle captains: Martin Wheelock, Antonio Lubo, Charles Williams, James Johnson, and Albert Exendine, in a big game with Warner's alma mater. This is the story in Warner's own words:

"Two men who were dallying with death and should have been in hospital; a third who would have looked well in an invalid's chair; two pieces of leather, which, joined together, closely resembled a puttee; and, finally, a brace of aluminum plate that resembled nothing so much as the rubbing portion of a washboard — these were the chief factors in making possible a strategy that decided one of the most sensational football battles I ever saw.

"It was way back in 1902, during my first term of coaching the famous Carlisle Indian team. In those days our annual game with Cornell was one of the biggest events of the season, notwithstanding that during the course of the hectic schedule which the Indians always played we were apt to engage almost every important team in the country. We set a lot of store on winning from the Ithacans, but this year, as the game approached, it looked as if victory was going to be impossible. In earlier games hard luck gave us a kick that sent us reeling, and Saturday, October 18, the day set for our engagement with Cornell, didn't promise to be an occasion for jubilation.

..."To begin with, my brother Bill had been a big help. Bill was guard at Cornell and one of the best in the game. This year he was captain of the team and mighty anxious to have it make a good showing. Cornell didn't start its training season until September 15 while the Indians got into action on September 1....

"I could picture the rest of my brother's thoughts. He stood over six-feet-one himself and weighed 220 pounds. The Cornell center, Davitt, and the left guard, Hunt, were built in the same proportions. Nobody ever had punctured the Ithacans' lines while those lads were holding forth, but they had done a lot of damage to the other fellows' defense.

"So I knew Bill was going back to Cornell to tell his comrades just what he was thinking then: namely, that the Ithacans must keep possession of the

Martin Wheelock

ball when they met us a month later and batter our line to pieces. And I had a hunch that the formation he would have in mind for accomplishing this purpose would be their famous guards-back play. In that, you know, one guard got back of the other to carry the ball, with the whole backfield in tandem formation helping them to plow through the enemy's line....

"Just then everything went wrong. First, after the initial game of the season, Wheelock, our star left tackle, probably the best man in the position that year and the leading drop and place kicker who did all our booting, was taken sick and sent to the school infirmary. He was thought to have pneumonia, but that was averted and then he had a recurrence of pleurisy from which he had suffered the previous year. His pain was so great that he couldn't bear even to have the bedclothes touch him, and the hospital attendants had to rig up a special apparatus that suspended his sheet above him an inch away that they protected him without coming in contact with his body.

"Second, Exendine, our great right end, wrenched his ankle so badly in a succeeding game he could scarcely run.

"Third, Shouchuk, who played at center and was as good as there was in the country, was so badly hurt the week before the Cornell game he had to be placed in the hospital.

"There I was, with the big battle less than a week away, with a line that my brother Bill had called only 'pretty good' completely shot to pieces. What could I do? Exendine partly solved my troubles. He insisted he would play despite his bad ankle. It was out of the question for him to take his end assignment. We bound his crippled limb with tape so tightly that he couldn't move his foot and shifted him to right tackle, sending Whitely, who played the position regularly, to fill the left tackle place vacated by Wheelock's illness.

"But I still had no center and no right end. I could throw in a center that might fill Shouchuk's shoes acceptably, but I could not replace Wheelock, whose kicking would be sadly missed. He was my best offensive weapon, having made at least one field goal in every game he played.

"It was at this time that I was given two demonstrations of the red man's courage which fully upheld all the legends of their stoical indifference to suffering ever told. In 1901, when he played the Navy at Annapolis, Lubo, our left tackle, a thin, wiry fellow, who made up in bravery and football brains what he lacked in size—he only weighed 160 pounds — had his left wrist smashed and cut open. The injury was slow to heal. We didn't tell him at the time, but the school physician thought he had a tubercular infection. The superintendent of the academy positively refused to let him play any

Antonio Lubo

more football. His arm was placed in a sling and he was instructed to indulge in no exercise except walking, and even then he must conserve his strength.

"Lubo couldn't play, but there was nothing to prevent his watching his teammates during practice. Throughout my brother Bill's sojourn, he trudged up and down the field, observing everything that was done, listening to everything that was said. He was a true Indian, talking little but retaining every scrap of information that came his way, although in this case it could be of no value to him.

"He was really a pathetic figure. In form, he would have been a tower of strength for us, for despite his size he could hold his own against the huskiest of opponents. But he had been carrying his arm in the sling for a year now and it was shriveled away almost to mere bone.

"All the time, though, he was hoping against hope that luck would turn his way. At the start of the season, he applied for permission to play, but the superintendent's only reply was an order to me.

"'Don't even give him a uniform,' he said. 'His health means more to the school than winning a couple of football games.'

"Nevertheless he continued his appeals. And when the injury to Shouchuk capped the climax of our troubles he decided to make one more try.

"Four nights preceding the Cornell game a knock brought me to my door. There stood Lubo.

"'Coach,' he said without any preliminary, 'I'd give anything if I could play against Cornell. I know how Shouchuk and Wheelock can't play. I'd like to go up there for you and for Carlisle.'

"I brought him inside and explained as gently as I could that it wasn't possible.

"'Not with that arm,' I said.

"'But that wouldn't make any difference,' he protested.

"'I've been exercising and have kept in good shape in every other way. Besides, coach, I think I can do as much with my right arm as with two arms. I can protect my left so it won't get hurt.'

"I asked where he thought he could play.

"'Tackle, in Wheelock's place.'

"'No, that's out of the question. A tackle must have both arms.'

"'Well, then, center.'

"'No, a center must use both hands to pass the ball.'

"'Well,' he declared. 'I know I could play somewhere on the team.'

"I had to tell him it was impossible, although I appreciated his spirit. But when he left, after two hours of argument, he insisted. 'Somehow, I'm going to play.'

"As to when he saw the superintendent I don't know, for it was half past ten o'clock when he left my house. But the next morning the chief telephoned me to come to his office. Lubo had been to see him again, he said, and had asked to be allowed to face Cornell.

"'I told him, no,' he added, 'but the boy said he must play—he owed it to Carlisle. He's so fine I'm inclined to be lenient, if you and the doctor think it is possible.'

"I didn't because I believed Lubo would be performing merely on his ambition. But when the physician told me that, except for his left arm, the Indian was in fine condition, I began to change my mind. We could at least let him practice a bit. I told him so the next day, which was the Wednesday preceding the date at Ithaca on Saturday.

"He was on hand promptly. It didn't take him long to convince me that, handicapped though he was, he was better than any substitute I could use. If only he hadn't had that withered arm.

"That night he came around to see me again.

"'Coach,' he said, 'there must be some way to fix my arm.'

"I thought hard. I've always been handy at repairing injured players and finally hit on a scheme. I dug up two strips of leather. These I sewed around his bad wrist, extending from the tips of his finger to his elbow. We stuffed the inside with cotton and bound the whole in tape. It seemed to offer adequate protection.

"'Lubo, it looks like you were going to get into that game,' I said. He just stood there smiling and saying over and over, 'Thank you, Coach, thank you.'

"I don't mind telling you I felt pretty weepy.

"Of course Lubo couldn't play end or tackle. I decided to switch Beaver, the right guard, who had done some playing at end, to Exendine's old position and use Lubo in his place.

"News of this decision soon got me into trouble. All the cripples around the place asked for harness that would enable them to play. But the biggest shock I got came when [Martin] Wheelock showed up at my house. He had been in the infirmary three weeks but in the last few days had been allowed out in the air a bit. Still he was in such pain he couldn't bear to have anyone lay a hand on him.

"'Now look here, Coach,' he said, 'if you can fix Lubo you can fix me. There's nothing wrong with my arms or legs; all I've got is pleurisy.'

"I didn't argue with him. Arguments didn't seem to count much with those Indians. We went up to the engineering school and asked for help. Someone dug up two wide sheets of aluminum, resembling, as I said before, the metal portion of a washboard.

"'That's the stuff!' said Wheelock. 'First I'll put on a heavy shirt. Then you can fix these on me, one in front and one in back. Bind them with tape, so they won't slip. Put my jersey on over all and I'll be absolutely all right.'

"There was left but one vacancy on the team. That was center. Fortunately this would be the one position where Wheelock would suffer a minimum of pain, although he was bound to have plenty of it no matter where he was placed. I assigned him to it.

[Warner then discussed some strategy and the events of the game's first half that put Cornell ahead, 6–5.]

"The second half got under way with Cornell rushing us off our feet. And yet, just when it seemed that she was about to score, an Indian would appear from nowhere and throw the man carrying the ball for a loss on third down. Mostly it was Lubo and Wheelock. How Lubo did it with his lame arm I don't know. And time after time Wheelock winced in pain as he came in contact with his opponents. But always they are on the job diving over or under interference and bringing down the man with the ball. Williams backed up both. Johnson was wonderful in running back punts. The lame Exendine, at tackle, more than held his own. Well into the second half we got a break which repaid our cripples for their devotion to the team. Williams, standing on Carlisle's thirty-yard line, delivered the best punt of the day. It was a wonderful kick that carried the ball a full fifty yards before it touched on Cornell's thirty-yard line.

"Brewster, the Cornell quarter [back], apparently figured that the ball would roll clear to the line. He decided to let it pass, so that it could be brought out again on the twenty-yard line. But after one high bound, the ball took a backward instead of forward leap, and struck the leg of Tydeman, right end, who had run back to give Brewster interference. This made a free ball of it and Bradley, Carlisle right end, who had charged down the field, grabbed it.

"It was Carlisle's ball on Cornell's 13-yard line, and Quarterback Johnson immediately proceeded to the most brilliant strategy of the game. This consisted in using the same formation, with variations, four times in succession."

[Warner described an early incarnation of his single-wingback formation, which was designed to protect his crippled players. Johnson's brilliant strategy used fakes, deception, and speed to confuse the defense as to where the ball was going and who was carrying it. On the fourth play of the series, Willliams dove over the middle of the line for the go ahead touchdown.]

"Lubo was able to continue after this play, but Wheelock's outraged body could endure no more. He fell in an agony of pain and had to be taken from the field. This necessitated the only substitution of the game. We missed the goal after touchdown and the score was Carlisle 10; Cornell, 6.

"But the game was won. Williams played center on defense and we held the Ithacans until the whistle blew.

"Was Lubo happy? Was he! And that reminds me. After the game that night I talked again with Bill, my brother.

"'How did Lubo impress you, Bill?' I asked.

"'Say, Glenn, was that fellow in uniform when I was down at Carlisle?'

"'No, he's the one who followed you around with his arm in a sling watching you at practice.'

"'Well, if that fellow can play like that when he's crippled,' replied Bill, 'I'd hate to tackle him when he was in good condition.'

"In view of the fact that Bill was placed on the All-American that year by Walter Camp and all the other critics, his performance in the Carlisle game being praised particularly, I consider he paid Lubo a fine tribute. But the boy deserved everything good that could be said about him.

"And Wheelock, too. The strategy by which Johnson won the game was fine; but never so wonderful as the splendid feat of these two boys in playing that day. When you get down to facts, it was their devotion to their school and their team that beat Cornell. There's a lesson in it for every lad that aspires to play the game."

Fact or Fiction

A review of the record shows that Warner's memory of a set of extraordinary events that took place over two decades earlier appears to have been fairly accurate. Carlisle played Cornell on Saturday, October 18, 1902 at Ithaca, New York and won 10-6. Game accounts list Exendine, Lubo, and Wheelock in the line-up at tackle, guard, and center, respectively. However, the *Syracuse Post-Standard* has the Indians at full strength and

Cornell crippled. Two days later that paper described Cornell's claims of being crippled as a "lame excuse." The game account discusses Bradley's recovery of the punt that hit Tydeman's leg. On the Wednesday preceding the Cornell game, Carlisle played Bloomsburg Normal (today's Bloomsburg University) at Carlisle. Warner would very likely have viewed the mid-week 50-0 thrashing of a teachers college as little more than a scrimmage. Newspaper reports of the game indicate that both Lubo and Wheelock played in part of it. It is probable that Warner tested the protective gear for them in this fortuitously timed scrimmage. He wouldn't have needed his star players to beat such a weak opponent, but they provided an opportunity to test and improve the gear, if necessary. That Martin Wheelock left Carlisle to convalesce from the pleurisy after the Harvard game provides further evidence of the story being essentially true.

A diagram of the special formation Warner used to protect Lubo and Wheelock and which James Johnson used brilliantly to score the winning touchdown was included with the 1924 article. This is an early use of a wingback in football, but the development of the single-wing is a story for another time and place.

Carlisle Strategy Which Gave Crippled Lubo Reward

Glenn Warner and the story he tells illustrated by a diagram prepared by George Byrnes of the Colgate football department. Key to the Play: A (Johnson, Carlisle quarter) received ball from center and, taking end run, sped to right. B (Williams, Carlisle fullback) who on previous formations had taked line plunge, took ball from Johnson. C (Carlisle right halfback) and D (Carlisle left halfback) ran to right as though to protect A (Quarterback Johnson). With latter drawing attention of Cornell backs, B (Williams) made flying dive over Cornell line, just too quick for a Cornell back to stop him, and scored the winning touchdown.

9

Major Changes

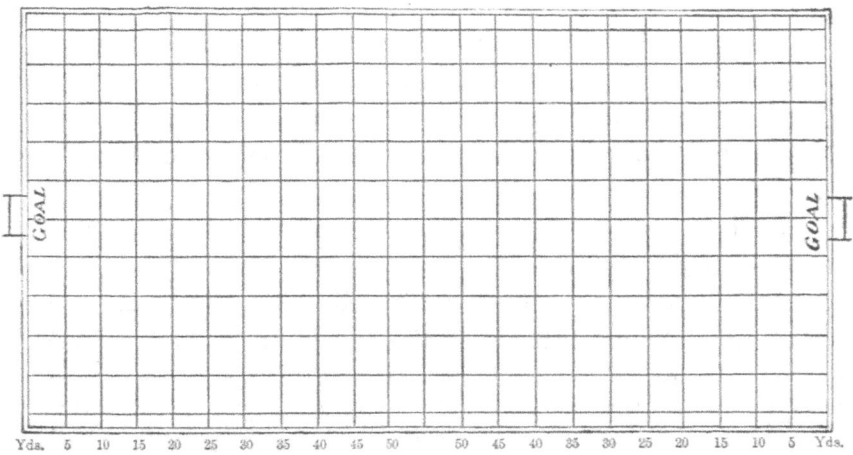

Rule Changes for 1904:

As of 1903, the person receiving the center snap (usually the quarterback) could carry the ball across the scrimmage line, but not within five yards of the center snap. Another 1903 rule limited the above rule change to between the twenty-five-yard lines. These restrictions were eliminated for 1904, expanding the checkerboard marking to the entire field.

At least six men of the team possessing the ball must now be on the line of scrimmage. If only six are there, one of the men behind the line must be outside the man on the end of the line.

Points for a field goal are reduced from five to four. The umpire is to use a bell or horn. His signal does not stop the play, only the referee's whistle.

Kickoffs over the goal line were touchbacks the forced the receiving team to kick out from behind its goal.

The new Commissioner of Indian Affairs came in the form of Francis Ellington Leupp, a newspaper man and personal friend of President Roosevelt. At the time the vacancy opened, the correspondent for the *New York Post* and former editor of the *Syracuse Herald* was investigating unspecified Indian affairs for the president. He had a long-time interest in the plight of the Indians and had published a pamphlet about his experiences,

"Notes of a summer tour among the Indians of the Southwest." Leupp agreed to take office on January 1, 1905, not exactly the start of Roosevelt's second term, but close enough.

In late January, three Cornell officials visited Warner to offer him the head coaching jobs for football and baseball. This offer presented difficulties for him because his brother, Bill, was Cornell's head football coach at the time and had posted a respectable 6-3-1 season. Pop thought it over for a couple of weeks before deciding to take the job. Sensing that Pratt was on thin ice and would likely be replaced within a year or two due to his age if nothing else may have figured into his decision.

In April 1904, both houses of Congress passed legislation that promoted Army officers who had served in the Civil War one grade upon retirement, effective retroactively. Working as a retired officer as superintendent of Carlisle Indian School, Pratt was made brigadier general. Criticizing government policy was nothing new for him, but what he said to a conference of Baptist ministers about the Bureau of Indian Affairs raised hackles inside the Bureau. When challenged, Pratt didn't deny saying, "It is a barnacle to be knocked off sometimes. Better, far better, for the Indians had there never been a Bureau. Then self-preservation would have led the Individual Indian to find his true place and his real emancipation would have been speedily consummated." He then doubled down by publishing his speech in the school newspaper.

Pratt on Horseback

A rumor circulated that, in retaliation to Pratt, the government was moving Carlisle Indian School to Helena, Montana. Assistant Secretary of the Interior Thomas Ryan denied that there was any truth to the rumor.

Commissioner of Indian Affairs William Arthur Jones had tolerated Pratt's criticisms in the past, but this time he wasn't given the chance. Jones's boss, Secretary of the Interior Ethan Allen Hitchcock, was far from amused. He demanded that President Roosevelt fire Pratt over Jones' objections. A breach over Pratt's removal opened so wide between Jones and Hitchcock that Jones submitted his letter of resignation in mid-July, effective whenever a suitable replacement could be in place. He then spent the next three months working in the field rather than returning to his office in Washington.

Carlisle citizens complained of the "curt order" that dismissed Pratt from the position he had held for twenty-five years and would have held a public meeting as a show of support if he had consented. They resented what they deemed as a slight and injustice to Pratt, whom they held in high esteem, both in the tenor and text of the order. Pratt's supporters claimed that the school had received donations of $140,000 from friends of Indian education who had confidence in his methods. This money was used to enlarge the school's buildings, to purchase a farm, and to outfit the various industrial shops.

The July 29 edition of *The Red Man and Helper* announced that this would be its last. It was being replaced by *The Arrow*, the first issue of which was expected to be released in two or three weeks. No reason was cited for the change. In fact, "...the size will remain the same, that being best adapted to one Babcock cylinder press." It is possible, due to the relationship of Leupp and the President, that the publication's name change may have been ordered by Leupp before his name was released to the public as Jones' successor.

Secretary of War William Howard Taft detailed Captain William Allen Mercer of the 7th Cavalry to replace Pratt at Carlisle.

The August 25, 1904 edition of *The Arrow*, the first of the new school newspaper, announced the arrival of Head Coach Ed Rogers and the expected arrivals of his assistants, former players Bemus Pierce and Frank Hudson. Carlisle alum Ed Rogers had just completed his law degree at Minnesota, where he had

Major William A. Mercer

also captained the football team, and Frank Hudson took three weeks of leave from his banking job in Pittsburgh to coach their old team. Pierce coming back to Carlisle, opening up the job at Sherman Institute, may have been the last part of a Warner 3-D chess move to take over at Cornell. Last year's captain, James Johnson, didn't return. Instead, he chose to take up dentistry at Northwestern University and play for them. Arthur Sheldon would captain the 1904 team.

Football practice started on September 1st. The paper also contained an eleven-game schedule for the varsity. "Dr." Wallace Denny spruced up the football field prior to the start of practice. Soon, most of the prior year's players returned and were joined by new men wanting to make the team. The forty-five candidates who turned out were winnowed down to thirty-three making the varsity squad.

BEMUS PIERCE

The first game of the season turned out to be tougher than expected. For starters, it was so warm that Lebanon Valley objected to playing halves longer than fifteen minutes. Their squad was fifteen to twenty pounds heavier per man than their Carlisle counterparts and they played like veterans. Due to fumbling, the Indians scored only a single touchdown in the first half, but they did better in the second. Frank Jude made two fifty-yard runs and he, Charles Dillon, Antonio Lubo, and Nicholas Bowen each scored a touchdown. Jude also kicked three extra points. Carlisle won 28–0.

The F&M game didn't materialize because the future diplomats changed their minds about coming to Carlisle to play as had been arranged the year before. The Indians were off until October 1st because they weren't able to fill the September 24 open date. The lighter boys from Gettysburg didn't stand a chance and Carlisle controlled the ball most of the game. Scoring twenty-eight unanswered points in the first half allowed Coach Rogers to try new men at several positions in the second. The final score was Carlisle 41–Pennsylvania College 0.

Four days later, the Indians hosted Susquehanna University. Despite losing players to injury, Carlisle led 41-0 at halftime. A set of substitutes were put in for the shortened second half, scoring only twelve points. Carlisle won 53-0.

Three days after that, they traveled to Williamsport to play a much-tougher foe. Bucknell played the roughest game the Indians had experienced in over a decade. Even the Williamsport paper, *Grit,* took them to task.

> Once a Bucknell player tackled an Indian who was carrying the ball. He threw one arm around his neck and with his free arm deliberately struck him several times in the face. Time and again Carlisle players were struck while on the ground. The metal nose guards were used as clubs on several occasions. The Indians apparently wanted to play fairly. They remonstrated and warned, but to no avail.

The Wellsboro Gazette told of its hometown boy's antics on behalf of Bucknell: "'Buster' Morris...gave a good account of himself. In fact so strenuous was his play that the Indians protested against his 'slugging,' which was said to have been of the swiftest and hardest order." The police arrested Bucknell's Captain Cockrill and several of his team's rooters for assaulting the Indians. Carlisle won 10-4. Surprised by the Bisons' slugging, Carlisle management took Lewisburg off the next year's schedule.

Carlisle's next opponent, Albright College, was perhaps their worst mismatch ever, even though the Indians were shorthanded with Jude and Nekifer Shouchuk recovering from injuries. Hawley Pierce rejoined his old team to play fullback. Arthur Sheldon scored a touchdown thirty seconds into the 59-point first half. Albright's coach stopped the game in the abbreviated second half when the score reached 100-0.

Before the Harvard game, *The Boston Globe* reported that the Indians hadn't completely recovered from the Bucknell melee, the worst they'd ever experienced. The scoreless first half with the Crimson was a defensive struggle. Neither team could penetrate the other's line. Any gains made were around the ends. It was a story of punt and fumble exchanges. Carlisle got the ball to start the second half but didn't make the yardage needed for a first down. Instead of punting, Charles Kennedy, the center filling in for injured Shouchuk, kicked the ball forward on a trick play. Because the Indians were behind the ball when it was kicked, they were all onside, making them eligible to possess the ball if they could corral it. None did.

Using the stiff arm, Harvard's Nichols and Hurley repelled Indian tacklers to make long runs. Hurley scored the first touchdown and Kernan kicked the extra point. Harvard scored again on their next possession after a long, grinding drive. Carlisle was unable to counter this. Harvard won 12-0.

The University of Virginia, always a challenge for the Indians, played true to form in the first half. Carlisle's offense could do nothing but Virginia's Council broke through the middle of the Indian line on a fifty-five-yard dash for a touchdown. Yancy made the kick for a 6-0 Virginia lead at halftime. After a series of fumbles and penalties by both sides, Archie Libby made a thirty-yard field goal by place kick for Carlisle's first four points. Later, on a botched punt attempt, Carlisle recovered the ball on Virginia's three-yard line. Two fast, furious plays later, Sheldon carried the ball over the goal line for Carlisle's touchdown and Libby made the kick after putting Carlisle ahead 10-6. With little time remaining, Libby kicked another field goal, this one from forty-five yards out to increase the final margin of victory to 14-6.

The next Saturday, Carlisle met Ursinus College for the only time the schools would meet on a football field. The plucky Pennsylvania Germans held the sluggish and fumble-prone Indians to a single touchdown in the first half. Carlisle roused in the second and played their usual snappy game. Wilson Charles came in at right halfback and made runs of fifty and sixty yards, helping to put Carlisle over 28-0.

Hoping to make it three in a row over the Quakers, or at least be the first to cross their goal line this year, Carlisle sent the largest contingent, 500 strong, from the school it had ever brought to the game. Their famous band played often and the girls, resplendent in their blue suits and hats, filled the air with

PENN PIERCING THE INDIAN LINE.

cheers and parodies of popular songs. They sang their favorite, "I Was Only Teasing You," whenever something went their team's way. Before the game, the musicians in bright-red uniforms paraded around the field twice, then settled into a cheering section to watch the game.

The Indians had a couple of chances to score in the first half but Stevenson, the only man between the runner and the goal line, made touchdown-saving tackles for Penn. Stevenson also refused to stay down when returning a punt. He caught the ball at his twenty-yard line and raced down the field. Every time he was tackled, he rolled to his feet and kept going. It took several Indians to finally hold him down at their thirty-five. Several plays later, Lamson touched the ball down barely past the goal line. Reynolds made the extra point. Penn 6–Carlisle 0. Later in the half, Penn got the ball on the Carlisle forty-five-yard line. After hammering away at the lighter Indian line, Reynolds made twenty yards on a fake kick, getting to the five-yard line. Pounding away again, Ziegler carried the ball over for the score. Reynolds again made the kick, putting Penn ahead 12-0 at halftime.

Tomahawk replaced Kennedy at center and Charles came in for Libby at quarterback to start the second half. Left end Jude had been injured earlier in the game and was replaced by Frank Mt. Pleasant. Early in the half, Penn got the ball on the Indian forty-five. The Quakers banged away at the Carlisle line until Lamson scored. Reynold made his third extra point of the game for a commanding Penn 18-0 lead. The Indians strengthened and moved the ball better than they had earlier. Twice they were in position to kick field goals, but their kicker, Libby, was on the bench injured. Penn won 18-0. The only consolation was that no other team scored a touchdown on Penn the entire season either.

Ohio State had been scheduled to close out the 1904 season on Thanksgiving Day, but this wasn't a normal year. St. Louis World's Fair organizers wanted to host a big game for President Roosevelt to see when he visited in late November. Their first choice, the military academies, wouldn't shift the location of their annual game to the Fair. So, the Fair did the next best thing: they invited the two flagship government Indian schools to play the Saturday after Thanksgiving. This arrangement made the two teams' previously scheduled Thanksgiving games sideshows. Haskell Institute used its scrubs to drub Washington University of St. Louis 47-0. Carlisle fielded its second team at Columbus, disappointing Buckeye fans.

The Ohio State school newspaper, *The Lantern*, claimed that they didn't actually face the second team because a number of Carlisle players had been in the Harvard game. The reason they were in the game was because first stringers had been injured. Shouchuk, Lubo, and Libby got into the Ohio State game late, probably to give them a little practice after being out of commission for some time. The scoring tells the story. Touchdowns were scored by Doxtator and William Gardner (three) and extra points were kicked by Charles (three), not by varsity regulars. The final score 23-0 score wasn't close.

The Carlisle-Haskell game was intended to give St. Louis fans a look at first-rate football as both teams were among the leaders in their respective regions. To say Carlisle played its first team against Haskell would be an understatement. Head Coach Rogers suited up at left end, Assistant Coach Bemus Pierce (then twenty-nine) at right halfback, and Hawley Pierce at fullback. Haskell brought in some old players, too, but didn't have the abundance of talent to choose from that Carlisle had.

The game started well enough for Haskell when Hawley Pierce fumbled on his twenty-five-yard line, leading to a field goal attempt from the twenty. Pete Hauser's kick split the uprights, putting Haskell ahead 4-0. The Lawrence, Kansas team continued to play hard but didn't have the strength and talent to stop the coming Carlisle onslaught. Before the game was over, Albert Exendine, Bemus Pierce, Dillon (two), Bowen, and Fritz Hendricks had all scored touchdowns. Libby kicked six extra points. Chauncey Archiquette prevented another Carlisle touchdown when he jumped onto the ball for a safety after Exendine blocked a punt and it caromed across the Haskell goal line. The final score was Carlisle 38–Haskell 4.

The coda for the game was the eventual transfer of nine Haskell players to Carlisle. Of these, the Hauser brothers (Pete & Emil/Wauseka), Guyon brothers (Charles & Joe), Chauncey Archiquette and Scott Porter (Little Boy) became prominent in Carlisle history.

George Orton of Penn ranked Carlisle, as he often did, behind Penn and Princeton for the Middle States. He considered their defense strong in spite of the players' lack of weight. He gave Athletic Director W. G. Thompson credit for the team's success rather than the coaches—former Indian stars Ed Rogers and Bemus Pierce. No Carlisle player received All-America honors from any pundit or newspaper.

1904 Season Summary

Date	Opponent	Location	Indians	Opp.
Sep. 17	Lebanon Valley College	Indian Field, Carlisle Barracks, PA	28	0
Sep. 21	Franklin & Marshall College*			
Oct. 1	Pennsylvania College	Indian Field, Carlisle Barracks, PA	41	0
Oct. 5	Susquehanna University	Indian Field, Carlisle Barracks, PA	53	0
Oct. 8	Bucknell University	Athletic Park, Williamsport, PA	10	4
Oct. 15	Albright College	Indian Field, Carlisle Barracks, PA	100	0
Oct. 22	Harvard University	Harvard Stadium, Cambridge, MA	0	12
Oct. 29	University of Virginia	Lafayette Field, Norfolk, VA	14	6
Nov. 5	Ursinus College	Indian Field, Carlisle Barracks, PA	28	0
Nov. 12	University of Pennsylvania	Franklin Field, Philadelphia, PA	0	18
Nov. 24	The Ohio State University	University Field, Columbus, OH	23	0
Nov. 26	Haskell Institute	World's Fair Stadium, St. Louis, MO	38	4

Won 9; Lost 2; Tied 0

*Canceled because F&M didn't want to play at Carlisle.

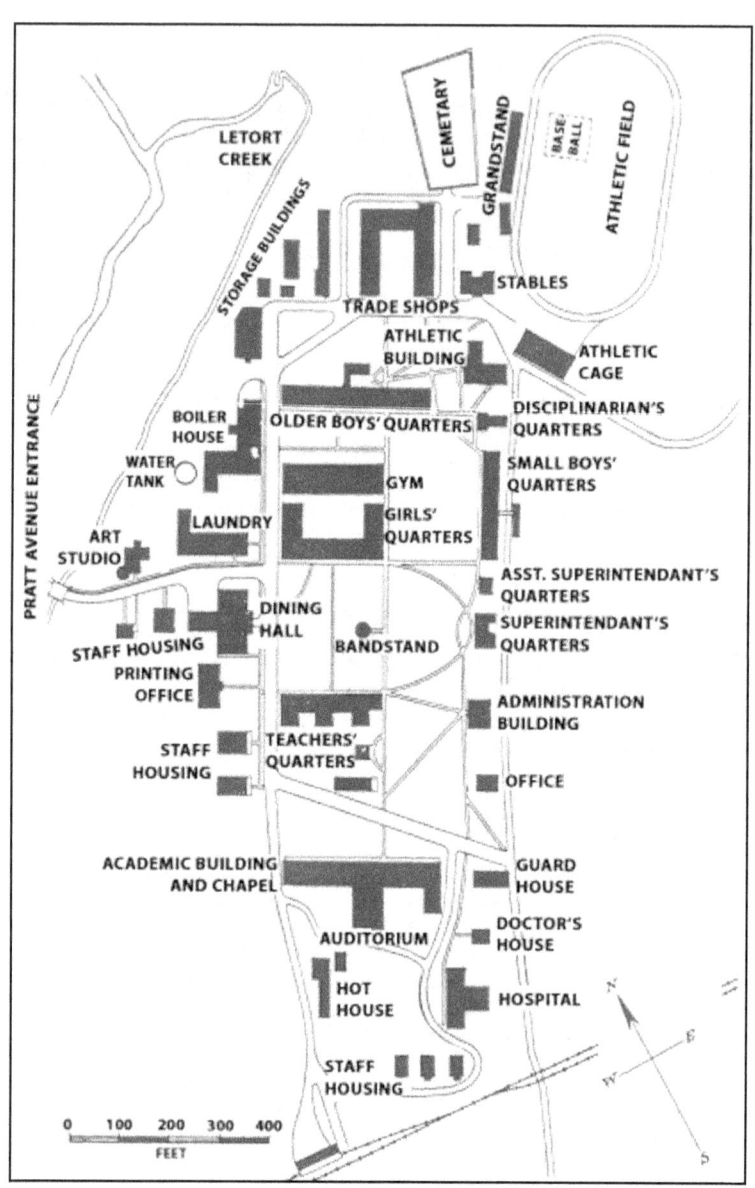

Map of Carlisle Barracks that included the basketball cage

10

Hoo-ah!

Rule Changes or 1905:

The rule changes for 1905 were mostly interpretative in nature.
If the snapper makes a motion as if to snap it or not, the ball is considered to have been snapped.
Players may not be out of bounds when the ball is put in play, except for a player holding for a place kick.
The referee is to blow his whistle immediately when forward progress is stopped.
Substitutes must report to the referee before taking part in the game.
The penalty for coaching from the side lines is increased to ten yards.

Commissioner of Indian Affairs Francis Leupp's first initiative at Carlisle was to convert the school into a sort of West Point to prepare young Indians to enter the Army as enlisted men. Along with that, he intended to establish a hospital to train Indian girls to become nurses. President Roosevelt whole-heartedly supported the military school aspect but Congress wouldn't appropriate the $20,000 needed for the hospital. Pratt had already dressed the boys in military uniforms and organized them in military-like units. So, Leupp's first goal was reached in good measure before he started because it wasn't unusual for boys to join the Army or Navy after leaving Carlisle.

Quakers, however, opposed militarizing the school further and, likely, cut back on the generous donations they had given during the Pratt years. A large portion of donations during the Pratt years came from Quaker donors. In his 1905 Commencement address at Carlisle on March 16, Leupp suggested "to organize also an Amazon corps" of militarized girls similar to the boys' units.

Negotiations with Ed Rogers to coach the Indians that year fell apart. He severed relations with his old school and would not be returning. Purdue made him an offer, but he turned it down and returned to Minnesota to practice law and coach the local St. Thomas team. The August 25, 1905 edition of *The Arrow*, the first edition of the new school year, released a football schedule that included eleven games and two open dates. George Woodruff, the long-time Penn mentor, arrived in September to serve as

Ed Rogers in his playing days

advisory coach. Bemus Pierce and Frank Hudson would be in charge of the line and backs, respectively. Nicolas Bowen (Seneca) was elected captain.

Training tables were set up in the dining hall to put some weight on the football players. During the first four or five weeks of eating the rich diet on the training table in previous years, players suffered greatly from boils, "...which are in some cases numerous and extremely painful. The school physician, Dr. Shoemaker, has been able to relieve the pigskin chasers from any serious handicaps this year from those afflictions."

James Johnson recruited last year's captain Arthur Sheldon to join him at Northwestern, but after learning he could only play on the freshman team that year, Sheldon returned to Carlisle. William White, Jr. was one who didn't return. He wasn't allowed to might be more accurate. In January, Superintendent Mercer wrote the Commissioner of Indian Affairs requesting approval of dismissing White and Josephine Williams "...from the school for immoral conduct of a grave character." Left to the imagination was what exactly they did. They apparently eloped at some point because records show them as a married couple.

New that year was Wahoo, aka Charles Guyon, an end who formerly played for Haskell Institute. Not only did he start the flow of players from

Lawrence, Kansas to Carlisle, his adoption of a nickname started a trend. The press listed Kicked-on-the-Jaw, Two-Dogs-in-the-Snow, Strong Arm, Long Horn, Man-Who-Forgets, and Little Old Man as players on the squad.

Practice started the first week of September with Captain Bowen, but some other last year's starters were slow to come back from the summer:

KICKED-ON-THE-JAW

...thinking perhaps that the usual round of track running would be indulged in for several weeks; but George C. Woodruff, ... Immediately jumped the candidates for football laurels into the hardest kind of fundamentals. Woodruff expended a vast amount of energy in his work at Carlisle, and evolved numerous tricks, which the Indians introduced with considerable success. They brought out this year the 'diamond-back' formation. Which may be destined to play a considerable part in the game of football as the future will know it.

Trainer Wallace Denny enlisted a staff of "rubbers" to work out players' charley horses this year as Advisory Coach Woodruff's enthusiasm was becoming contagious.

The September 23 open date was filled by a game with Pennsylvania Railroad Y. M. C. A. Woodruff tried two or three men at every position, scoring thirty-six points on six touchdowns and extra points in the twenty-minute very hot first half and thirty-five points on six touchdowns and five extra points in the fifteen-minute second half. Even Charles Kennedy, a center, scored one.

Carlisle took advantage of the extra practices made available by the mid-week open date when Walter Camp All-America First Team guard Ralph Kinney, Yale '05, arrived to assist Woodruff. Albright College canceled and

George W. Woodruff

scheduled a game with Lebanon High School instead. They were quickly replaced by Villanova for the September 30 spot. The temperature wasn't the only thing that was hot during the first meeting ever of these two schools. After Carlisle scored twice early on long runs by Archie Libby and Mt. Pleasant and line bucking of Paul LaRoque (often spelled LaRocque) and Sheldon, some of the visitors' tempers flared. When four of their players were disqualified for slugging, the entire team left the field. After some negotiations, the disqualified players were allowed to play again and the game continued. Villanova put up a scrappy defense but its offense couldn't make a single first down in the 35-0 beatdown.

On Wednesday, the Indians hosted Susquehanna for another warm-up game. The first string scored thirty-five points in the first half before turning the game over to the second string. Third stringers were gradually substituted in until thirty-five players had been in the 47-0 game.

Next up was Penn State, an improving team the Indians hadn't played in a decade. This affair was played at a neutral site, an island in the middle of the Susquehanna River adjacent to the city of Harrisburg. It was quite a spectacle. Before the game, the schools' bands led their rooters as they marched across the half-mile-long spans to meet in the middle of the river at the park. There, the two sides' supporters sat in stands across the field from each other. The Indian School band played "Tammany" and students sang "Ken Ne Dee" to it in honor of their center Kennedy, telling State what he intended to do.

State supporters sang back, "We've come here to meet the Indians at the capital of the state; we'll do them brown and paint the town; oh, won't that be great."

Indians: "You'll have to show us."

State: "We have the goods."

Indians: "Then trot them out."

The crowd cheered loudly.

Familiar faces lined the sidelines: Previous years' coaches Vance McCormick and Orville Hickock, and George Woodruff. Penn Professor Stauffer served as referee, Dr. Sharpe of Yale as umpire, and Sen. Fred Godcharles as linesman. Stauffer gave the players some fatherly advice before the game started: he would stand for no roughness or trickery. Both sides promised to be good.

Exendine drew first blood when he rushed the ball across the goal line following an eighty-yard run by Mt. Pleasant, line bucks by Stephen Albanez and Lubo, an end run by Jude, and Archiquette hurdling tacklers. The rest of the first half was a scoreless defensive struggle. The second half wasn't much different except for Bowen pushing through for a touchdown. Dillon kicked the extra point to cap the Indians' 11-0 shutout of Penn State. Players on both sides kept their promises to play cleanly except when the referee's back was turned.

The next game took them to Richmond, Virginia. Unable to dent Carlisle's line, the Virginians were forced to play on defense the entire game. They played hard and well, but the Indians broke through occasionally. In the first half, Bowen scored the first touchdown at the end of a long drive. Libby made the kick after. In the second half, Carlisle pounded Virginia's line for small but steady gains but stalled at the six-yard line. Twice the Indians hammered Virginia's forwards and twice they held. But with only forty seconds left on the clock, the Indians pushed Sheldon across the goal line. Dillon kicked the extra point. Time ran out during the ensuing kickoff, ensuring Carlisle's 12-0 victory.

Carlisle and Dickinson renewed football and track competitions in 1905. This year the game was played at Harrisburg's Island Park, site of the earlier Penn State game. Both teams, their bands, and supporters traveled together on a special train that left from the school's siding, but few others turned out to see it. *The Sentinel* declared Harrisburg to be a poor football town and that the turnout would have been larger had the contest been held in Carlisle. It reported:

Spirits were reported to be high for supporters of both teams:

> Before [the game] started a couple of Dickinson students dressed as a cowboy and an Indian rushed on the field where the Indian was cap-

tured by the cowboy and scalped. This piece of side play was met by one from the Indians.

A colored boy wheeled around an invalid chair in which a dummy representing a Dickinson student and as each touchdown was made, an additional arrow was shot into the emaciated Dickinsonian.

This side play was taken good naturedly by both sides. Both teams played hard.

It is to be regretted that there was much unnecessary roughness for which the Indians were not responsible.

In one instance Dickinson's Captain Davis was hurt badly enough to have to leave the game after a fight with Alfred Dubois. A fight between the teams ensued but no one was seriously injured. The Indians prevailed with Sheldon, Archiquette, Lubo, Albanez (two), and Exendine scoring touchdowns. Dillon kicked three extra points. Mt. Pleasant kicked the other three. Carlisle overwhelmed their crosstown rivals 36-0. What might the score have been had the field not been "a trifle soggy" and without a strong northwest wind?

The Indians failed to threaten Penn's goal the entire first half. Before halftime on a fake-kick play, Penn's Greene broke loose for a thirty-nine-yard gain to Carlisle's one-yard line. Lamson then bulled over for a touchdown. Sheble kicked the extra point. The half ended Penn 6–Carlisle 0. Both sides battled mightily in the second half but neither side threatened to score.

Fortunately Carlisle escaped serious injuries in the Pennsylvania game because Harvard was next on their schedule. Early in the week, Woodruff had four strings out working against each other. He saved the first string physical damage by having them run signals drills. The Indians were overeager against the Crimson, resulting in six penalties for being offside. On offense, they were able to breach Harvard's line, but not often enough. Paul capped the first Harvard possession with a short run for the Crimson's first touchdown. Burr kicked the goal after, putting Harvard ahead 6–0.

When the Indians finally got the ball, they steadily moved it downfield. Dubois tore through and broke over the line. Mt. Pleasant's punt out was no good, eliminating any chance at making the extra point. Harvard still led 6–5. Later in the first half, a hole opened in the Carlisle line and Hurley ran through it for Harvard's second touchdown. Burr again made the kick. There was no further scoring in the first half. It ended with Harvard leading 12–5. On Harvard's first possession of the second half, Guild made several good runs before carrying the ball across for Harvard's third touchdown. The punt out wasn't caught, eliminating the extra point attempt. Carlisle wasn't able to move the ball so punted. Harvard advanced the ball down the field until Leonard ran the ball over for another Crimson touchdown. White kicked the extra point. Harvard pulled further ahead 23–5. Later, Mt. Pleasant made a brilliant run returning a punt but was tackled and carried out of bounds by the Harvard safety at the Crimson thirteen-yard line. Several plays later, Sheldon put it across the goal line. Mt. Pleasant punted the ball out and kicked the extra point. The game ended without further scoring: Harvard 23–Carlisle 11.

One recent author criticized Woodruff for less-exciting play than that of previous Carlisle teams. A factor that slowed play was that the new signal caller, Mt. Pleasant, took much longer to decide which plays to call than had his predecessors. Some who have read certain early twenty-first-century books about Jim Thorpe may be surprised to see that Carlisle's 1905 season didn't end with the Harvard game. Many will be shocked when reading the name of the team Carlisle faced next.

Some years earlier the then West Point commandant had rejected the offer of a game with Carlisle. Not clear was whether the current commandant

> **REDSKINS SCALP WEST POINT, 6-5**
>
> Indians Keep Cadets Guessing With Their Numerous Trick Plays
>
> Army Makes Its Touchdown by Good Straight and Hard Football—Soldiers' Defense Is Good

approved of a game with Carlisle, or Major Mercer (he had been promoted) had political connections that made it happen or if it was Woodruff's relationship with President Roosevelt. The day of the game with Army coincided with the visit to West Point of Prince Louis of Battenberg, plus several British and American naval officers. The packed stands at The Plain groaned under the weight of the brass and other officials for the Indians' first game against the future soldiers.

The Cadets seemed to get the best of the action in the first half but didn't score. The Indians were alive throughout the game. Almost every time the ball got loose, an Indian corralled it. After several punt exchanges, Army had the ball on their own fifty-yard line (there were two of them in those days). When Christy fumbled, right end Frank Jude snared the ball and ran it in for a touchdown. Mt. Pleasant kicked the extra point, putting the Indians ahead 6-0. Play remained in the middle of the field most of the rest of the half. However, Carlisle did get close enough to attempt a field goal. But it was blocked.

On Army's second possession of the second half, they marched down the field, sending Weeks over for a touchdown. But Frank Beavers' kick went wide by a hair, leaving Carlisle still ahead by the slimmest of margins, 6-5. The Cadets never threatened to score again. Whenever they got close, Mt. Pleasant boomed a punt, moving them way back. West Point weakened toward the end of the game, allowing the Indians to get down to the six-yard line. But no more scores were made. Carlisle beat Army in their first meeting ever and in front of numerous dignitaries!

George Woodruff left the team after the game to take a job in Washington as the Acting Secretary of the Interior under President Theodore Roosevelt, leaving his three assistants in charge of the team. Late that night, Major Mercer treated the team to something they considered to be a delicacy and they coined a new yell: "Rah! Rah! Rah! Half a dozen oysters!" The boys returned to Carlisle the next morning, remaining there only until Monday evening when they boarded a train for their "western" trip. Because of the digestive problems experienced with the food and water on a trip the previous year, they hired a special dining car in addition to their Pullman car. They stocked it with enough food to last the entire trip. Water would be shipped to points near where the team would play to refresh their drinking supply.

Two games with the country's arguably best professional teams had been inserted into the schedule earlier in the season. The Canton Athletic Club was added with the stipulation that the Indians wouldn't play another game in Stark County, Ohio. This restriction was an attempt to prevent Canton's archrival, Massillon, also located in Stark County, from booking a game with Carlisle. Wily Massillon management arranged for their game with the Indians to be held out of Stark County, at Case School of Applied Science in Cleveland where more people might turn out. And they scheduled it a week ahead of Canton's game with Carlisle, on the Wednesday after the Army game.

Professional players were older and heavier than the college boys but not as well coached. The inch of snow on Case Field melted as the game progressed, turning it into a muddy and treacherous mess. This, and a miscalculation by Coach Kinney, put the forty-pounds-per-man lighter (per a newspaper report) Indians at a severe disadvantage to the massive Massillon Tigers. Kinney expected them to play a line-bucking game and kept his fastest players on the bench. Massillon unexpectedly ran around the ends. With eligibility not an issue when playing a professional team, Hudson and Pierce suited up for the game. The only score in the first half came on a safety after Libby was tackled behind his goal line when trying to run back a Massillon punt. He had replaced Hudson after the latter was knocked unconscious and had his nose broken when tackling Riley.

Former Carlisle and Washington & Jefferson player "Tex" Mathews replaced Riley for the second half and scored the game's only touchdown at the end of a short drive following a fumble recovery. Schrontz kicked the extra point. Score: Massillon 8–Carlisle 0. Mt. Pleasant replaced Libby at quarterback and ran a flurry of fast plays. At the Massillon twenty-yard line, he kicked a field goal. Exendine pleaded with his coach to go in, and he did, nursing two broken ribs. On their next possession, the Tigers moved the ball down the field until time expired. Final score: Massillon 8–Carlisle 4.

On Saturday, they played the University of Cincinnati on its home field. The local fans considered scoring on the Indians a small victory. The Indians played fast and furious. On their first possession, they quickly advanced the ball to Cincinnati's five-yard line, then pushed Exendine over for their first score. Charles kicked the extra point. When they got the ball back again, they marched down the field to the fifteen. From there, Scott Porter, aka Little Boy, carried it over on a "sharp skin tackle play." Charles again made the kick.

Charles made a touchdown-saving tackle resulting in the Indians getting the ball at their own twenty when Cincinnati couldn't move the ball further. Charles skirted the end and ran ninety yards for Carlisle's third touchdown. He also kicked their third extra point. When Carlisle got the ball again late in the first half, they rushed down the field as fast as they could. With the ball inside the thirty-five and time running out, Charles kicked a field goal. The first half ended with the score Carlisle 22–Cincinnati 0.

Several substitutions were made for the second half with Mt. Pleasant for Libby and Hendricks for Charles the most notable. Carlisle moved the ball almost at will but fumbled it away several times. After Hendricks returned a punt to Cincinnati's twenty-two-yard line, the Indians ground out three yards at a time, moving the ball to the five. Cincinnati held twice but Titus Whitecrow was pushed over on third down for Carlisle's fourth touchdown. Mt. Pleasant kicked the extra point. After receiving a kickoff deep in their territory and failing to move it past the fifteen, Du Bois, who had replaced Porter at fullback, dropped back to punt from the goal line. Cincinnati's Sexton broke through the Indian line and blocked the kick. Capt. Foley gathered in the loose ball for the Cincinnati touchdown. Caldwell's kick hit the crossbar and didn't go over.

Later in the half, Archiquette, who had replaced Hendricks at halfback, made runs of twenty and twenty-five yards. Then Albanez, who had replaced Sheldon, raced fifty-five yards for Carlisle's last touchdown. Jude kicked the extra point to make the final score Carlisle 34–Cincinnati 5.

The team took in the sights in Cincinnati before going to Canton for a Wednesday game with the professional former college players or thirty-five-pounds-heavier-per-man giants, as described by the press. The field was muddier even than the one a week earlier in Cleveland. After a few back and forths in the first half, Canton moved the ball to the Carlisle one-foot line. The Indians held off the first onslaught but, on the second, Ozersky shot through Pierce for a touchdown. Sutter kicked the extra point to put Canton ahead 6–0. Both sides fought furiously, but neither threatened the other's goal. After a Carlisle punt was blocked, Rayl tackled Bowen behind the goal line for a safety. Final score: Canton 8–Carlisle 0.

Three days after the Canton loss, the Indians took on Washington & Jefferson College in Pittsburgh. Getting the ball first, the Red & Black of W&J

rushed the Indians with line bucks and end runs, succeeding in getting the ball to Carlisle's twenty-yard line. That would be the closest they got to scoring all day. The play on both sides was clean and hard with neither side able to score in the first half. A punt by W&J fullback Wright went awry, going out of bounds inside his own twenty-five-yard line, giving the Indians great field position. Sheldon skirted the opponents' right end with little interference to help him, picked his way through enemy tacklers, and raced across the goal line for a touchdown. Bridges spoiled the Indians' chance for the extra point on the punt out. Carlisle 5–W&J 0. Later, Albanez returned a punt twenty-five yards after receiving it at midfield. Frantic to score again, the Indians ran play after play, moving the ball closer and closer to the goal, until Porter carried it over for a touchdown. Libby kicked the extra point. The Indians ran the ball after receiving the kickoff but turned it over on their own forty-five-yard line. Seamon tried but failed to kick a field goal for W&J. The Indians had the ball in the middle of the field when the game ended. They won 11–0.

Five days later, on Thanksgiving, the Indians played Georgetown in the nation's capital. The home team never had a chance. The Indians scored twelve touchdowns and Charles kicked a thirty-five-yard field goal. The Indians were never forced to punt but let loose with one every now and then. Mt. Pleasant even booted a seventy-yard spiral. Jude kicked the seven first-half extra points and, after the scrubs were put in in the second half, kicked the last five. Carlisle put on the greatest diversified demonstration of football Washington had ever seen in the 76–0 wipe out. The same day, Carlisle's Third Team defeated Shamokin High School 11–0 with Mike Balenti and Whitecrow scoring the touchdowns. Meanwhile, the JV (younger boys) defeated Chambersburg Academy 12–0. Joseph Libby, Archie's brother, served as linesman for that game. All three games were played on the opponents' fields. The Second Team didn't schedule a game, probably because too many of them were needed as substitutes for the varsity squad.

Major Mercer and the football manager, Wm. Thompson, accompanied the team to the Georgetown game. On Friday, they must have done some sightseeing in the nation's capital because they attended the Army-Navy game at Princeton on Saturday. One can imagine the taunting the Middies gave the Cadets upon seeing their rival's conquerors in the stands, especially since the Indians had failed to beat the sailors in three tries.

Also present at the annual military brawl was President Roosevelt. Afterward, he said, "By George! It's a great game, but it should be materially amended so as to avoid such injuries as have occurred in this game. It is deplorable."

A Carlisle press release reported, "It is notable along this line that with all the hard games played by the fifty-four members of this year's football team not a single one bears to-day an injury worth notice." It announced, W. G. Thompson will be introducing soccer to younger boys to prepare them "...to make football players of the American type who do not get injured."

The *Washington Evening Star* ranked Carlisle as the eighth best team in the country. Caspar Whitney ranked them tenth and placed Mt. Pleasant as quarterback on his Substitutes for his All-America Eleven. The *New York Evening Sun* placed him on its All-America team. Coaches also listed All-America choices. George Woodruff picked Wahoo (Charles Guyon), Dillon, and Mt. Pleasant. Dr. N. P. Stauffer picked Dillon.

Among the offerings at Carlisle's annual football banquet were oyster soup and oysterettes.

1905 Season Summary

Date	Opponent	Location	Indians	Opp.
Sep. 23	Pennsylvania R. R. Y. M. C. A.	Indian Field, Carlisle Barracks, PA	71	0
Sep. 27	Open			
Sep. 30	Villanova College	Indian Field, Carlisle Barracks, PA	35	0
Oct. 4	Susquehanna University	Indian Field, Carlisle Barracks, PA	47	0
Oct. 7	Penn State College	Island Park, Harrisburg, PA	11	0
Oct. 14	University of Virginia	Broad Street Park, Richmond, VA	12	0
Oct. 21	Dickinson College	Island Park, Harrisburg, PA	36	0
Oct. 28	University of Pennsylvania	Franklin Field, Philadelphia, PA	0	6
Nov. 4	Harvard University	Harvard Stadium, Cambridge, MA	11	23
Nov. 11	U. S. Military Academy	The Plain, West Point, NY	6	5†
Nov. 15	Massillon Tigers	Case Field, Cleveland, OH	4	8
Nov. 18	University of Cincinnati	Carson Field, Cincinnati, OH	34	5
Nov. 22	Canton Athletic Club	Mahaffey Park, Canton, OH	0	8
Nov. 25	Washington & Jefferson College	Exposition Park, Pittsburgh, PA	11	0
Nov. 30	Georgetown University	Boundary Field*, Washington, DC	76	0

Won 10; Lost 4; Tied 0

*Also known as American League Park II.
†George Woodruff's last game as a coach.

FOOTBALL IS TACKLED HARD BY COLUMBIA.

11

Football goes Airborne

Rule Changes for 1906:

The forward pass is legal under limited conditions.

Ten yards are now necessary to obtain a first down instead of five as it had been previously.

Each side has its own line of scrimmage, parallel to the goal lines and passing through the nearest end of the football. This rule established a neutral zone the length of the ball.

Six men must be on the line of scrimmage when the ball is snapped. If an interior lineman positions himself behind the line of scrimmage, he must drop back at least five yards and another player must take his place on the line.

The ball is now down whenever any part of the player with possession of the ball touches the ground with any part of his body besides feet and hands while in the grasp of an opponent. Forward progress applies to the entire field.

Hurdling is forbidden and tripping, already illegal, is defined more clearly.

A fair catch is to be signaled for by the player attempting to catch the ball by raising his hand clearly above his head.

The officials shall be a referee, two umpires and a linesman. The second umpire can be dispensed with at the discretion of both teams.

Halves are shortened to thirty minutes in length. Each team can call time out three times during a half. Additional calls for time outs are penalized two yards.

Severe injuries and deaths had become commonplace in football and President Roosevelt, a supporter of the game and proponent of "The Vigorous Life," was disgusted by the brutality that caused them. He "invited" the athletic directors of Harvard, Princeton, and Yale to lunch on October 9, 1905 to discuss changing the rules of the game. Nothing was decided but a conversation was started.

"Only" eighteen players died in 1905—a significant decrease from the twenty-five fatalities in 1903—but the newspapers were filled with ghoulish cartoons and statistics of players injuring, killing, and maiming each other, mostly high school boys. College faculties railed against football and several schools, including Columbia, Northwestern, and Stanford, dropped the sport. In spite of this, college football was poised to continue with little changed until the wrong player was injured.

Too slow for the backfield and just two pounds heavier than the lightest man on the team, Theodore Roosevelt, Jr. played left end for the Harvard freshman team. In spite of his small size, he held his own most of the season. He even played well against archrival Yale although the Eli deemed him a weakness and directed their offense at him. Time after time, he'd make the tackle against the heavier Yalies and get back into position for the next assault. He fought gamely until he staggered from exhaustion. TR Jr. even got knocked out but came to and remained in the game.

> Finally a play came around his end that proved too much for the little 145-pounder. When the whistle blew and the men were pulled off the heap, there, down underneath everyone else, lay young Roosevelt, cut, bruised, and bleeding, unable to stir.
> This time he did not protest, but allowed himself to be carried to the locker building, where he was patched up under the doctor's care.
> The son of the President had put up a game that brought roars of applause from friends and foes alike, and it was a bitter disappointment to him when he was taken out.

Later reports catalogued Teddy Jr.'s injuries: "The hero of all Cambridge is Theodore Roosevelt, Jr., with battered head, discolored eye, swollen cheek, two stiff fingers, a pair of barked shins, and a badly shaken up body as the result of a plucky fight he made in the Yale-Harvard freshman football game." Within two weeks, he underwent surgery to repair his broken nose. The surgeon claimed: "...his patient looks better than even before it was broken. The slight natural crook that was noticeable has been eliminated." Initially blamed on the football game, the broken nose was soon reported to have been a relic of an earlier boxing match.

President Roosevelt was appalled by what happened to his son. His former criticisms were taken to mean he would ban football if the rules were not changed to eliminate the brutality from the game. Several on the rules committee balked at making radical changes, so a new one was formed in competition with the old one. In mid-January when it became clear that serious changes had to be made to avoid Roosevelt banning football, the old and new committees merged. While the President probably didn't have the authority to ban the game, no one wanted to test him. After much haggling, the committee released a set of new rules at the end of January.

NEXT!
A president who "does" things.

Several coaches and athletic directors criticized the proposed rules, which were designed to open up the game. The committee reviewed the comments and revised the rules, releasing a new set in April. These rules included making the forward pass legal within certain prescribed parameters. After reading the changes over the previous year's rules, pundits opined that they would benefit Carlisle more than any other team in the country because bulk could now be offset by speed to a significant extent. By making these changes, the game of football escaped Roosevelt's wrath and survived.

In response to Roosevelt's rant, Major Mercer ordered the creation of the Athletic Committee, consisting of three faculty members and the captains of the football, baseball, and track teams. One of the faculty members on the committee, Alfred Venne, was designated as Athletics Manager under the graduate manager system that was adopted.

In February 1906, Commissioner of Indian Affairs Leupp made an unusual move to change the philosophy of Carlisle Indian School when he hired Angel DeCora, an accomplished, classically trained Winnebago artist, to head the new Native Art Department. Normally, faculty was hired by the superintendent. This time Leupp asserted his authority. His goal was for the students to build on and improve their native culture, particularly in the area of art, rather than to abandon it. The Native Art Department was housed in the newly constructed masonry building that was paid for with funds from the football program. The labor was provided by students learning the various building trades. Prior to Leupp's decision this building was to be a photographic studio.

DeCora was the granddaughter of the hereditary chief who, at an early age was tricked into attending Hampton Normal and Agricultural Institute, a school that was established shortly after the Civil War to educate freed slaves and, later, American Indians. After finishing her term of enrollment, she returned home to find her father and grandfather dead and her mother remarried. Not seeing a place for herself on the reservation, she was unhappy with her new situation. When a representative from Hampton saw her situation, she arranged for Angel to return to the school. DeCora didn't exactly run away from home like Bender did, but it would have been an option if she had no other option to return to Hampton.

Frank Hudson

In his 1906 commencement address, in response to some rumors Leupp stated, "We have no intention of moving the school West. It is the intention to make this more of a military school, for the training of soldiers for the army." He also discussed his hope of acquiring fifty or more horses to use in introducing cavalry drills at the school.

On September 1, Carlisle management announced several things. The first was that school officials "have decided to place the coaching work entirely in the hands of full-blooded Indians of intelligence." The reason cited was that "the Indian will work harder for an Indian coach than for the expert trainer. Coach Glenn S. Warner is undoubtedly the only white man who has been able to hold fast the attention of the redskinned footballist and teach him better things." Bemus Pierce would serve as head coach and Frank Hudson, who was then an employee of the school and treasurer of the athletic committee, would assist him. Hudson had already been working with kickers for eight or ten days. Archie Libby and George Thomas were showing the most promise. Hudson's focus had a purpose. Pundits expected kicking, especially punting, to be a more valuable skill under the new rules. The requirement to make ten yards, instead of five, in three downs was expected to stop many nascent drives and drastically cut scores.

A newspaper article circulated stating that Business manager Alfred Venne, Chippewa class of '04, "…is fitting out his squad, which will probably number about thirty-five. The Indian coaches have decided that it is not good policy to turn out as large a football squad as that of last year, which numbered fifty-one, as it is too difficult for them to give the needed attention to all."

Major Mercer and Coach Pierce reached out to the most famous coaches in the East for assistance. Pop Warner responded and came to Carlisle to spend a week in early September preparing coaches Pierce and Hudson for the new rules and showing them a rudimentary version of what would evolve into his single-wing formation. The harness shop made a bucking strap to aid in instructing players on both the line and in the backfield the finer points of line bucking. It helped ball carriers to start quickly, run low and fast, learn the correct form and position to take when bucking, spot an opening and take it, buck hard and low, and keep strong on their feet. Backs used it to practice how to receive the ball and carry it without fumbling. Linemen used it to develop leg power. This leather device may have been one of Warner's best inventions. The establishment of the neutral zone was intended to keep linemen from standing toe-to-toe in easy range to punch each. It did that but it also made possible having linemen use Warner's three-point stance.

Most of last year's players returned. Among those who didn't due to their periods of enrollment being completed were: Lloyd Nephew, Sheldon, Jude, Charles Roy, and Guyton. Carlisle students were jubilant over the prospects

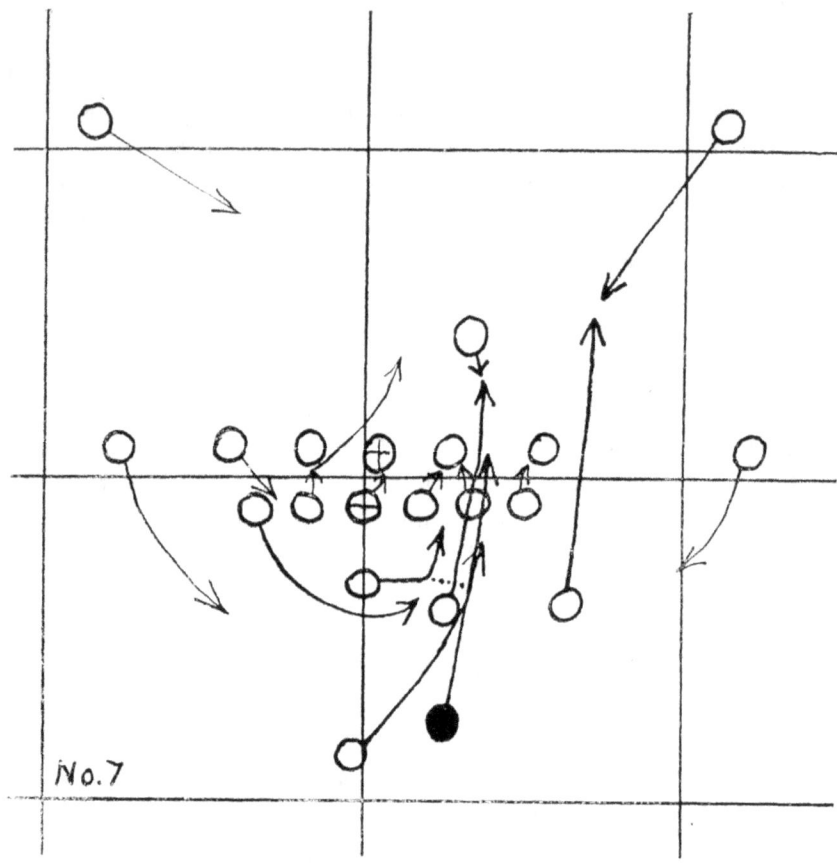

An early incarnation of the single-wing formation.

for a strong team and Warner thought the new rules favored the open style of play the Indians preferred. Some considered the rule changes to be an abomination. Fielding Yost reputedly said, "Michigan will never throw a forward pass."

Carlisle scheduled a game with Villanova on the Wednesday before the Saturday season start to demonstrate playing under the new rules. Football coaches and officials from all over the East along with local players were invited to attend the first important game played under the new rules. A wooden grandstand was constructed to accommodate the anticipated crowd. Attendees constituted the largest crowd assembled on Indian Field to watch a football game to date. The 2,000 in attendance overflowed the seating and numerous cars and carriages lined the track that surrounded the field.

Frank Mt. Pleasant throwing a forward pass.

At 3:00 p.m., Captain Exendine led his warriors onto the field for the opening kickoff. The game was criticized for the numerous fumbles and penalties but praised for the more exciting play. The passes thrown by both sides were described as being basketball-like. Unfortunately, no play by play was included in the game coverage in the newspapers. About all that was revealed about scoring was that Libby tried to dropkick a field goal and failed and that Little Boy scored a touchdown somehow and Mt. Pleasant made the extra point. Carlisle substituted liberally in the second half and came close to scoring again, but didn't. They still won 6-0.

Albright College and Susquehanna University were dealt with summarily, 82-0 and 24-0, respectively. Concerns about lack of scoring under the new rules weren't realized. Next up was Penn State at Williamsport, Carlisle's first road game of the season. Rain prevented the Indians from taking much advantage of the new rules in what became a game of punt exchanges. A combination of the need to make ten yards in three downs, poor footing, and a slippery ball made gaining yardage difficult. In the second half, Penn State's Vorhis attempted drop kicks from distances and angles but the wet ball always went awry. Libby tried one for Carlisle but it, too, went wild. Late in the second half, Mt. Pleasant ran a Penn State punt back to the Indian thirty-five-yard line but fumbled out of bounds when tackled. Penn State recovered the ball but netted only four yards in their first two downs.[9] When McCleary lined up to kick a field goal from placement, the Indians attempted to block it. One potential blocker jumped into the air, but the ball went under him. A second

---

[9] Out-of-bounds fumbles were free balls at that time.

potential blocker tipped the ball as it sailed over his head, deflecting it enough to clear the crossbar. Penn State won on a fluke 4-0.

Beginning with the Penn State game, the weekly school newspaper *The Arrow* promoted coverage of football games to the front page from interior pages. This shift to such a prominent position might have reflected Superintendent Mercer's commitment to the football program.

With the heart of the Indians' season approaching, C. L. Flanders, Yale '06, Walter Camp All-America Second Eleven center arrived at Carlisle to assist the Indian coaches. His line-coaching over the two-week break between games may have made the difference. Western University of Pennsylvania only got into Indian territory one time

HOW THE INDIANS LINE UP TODAY

The eleven players to the left were Carlisle's starters against Penn. Starting from the top left-to-right: Little Boy, fullback; A. Libby, quarterback; Mt. Pleasant, left halfback; below them: Hendricks, right halfback; from the bottom up: Exendine, right end; Lubo, right tackle; LaRocque, right guard; Hunt, center; Dillon, left guard; Wauseka, left tackle; Gardner, right end.

and that was by a single yard. Gardner, Wauseka (Emil Hauser), and Little Boy (Scott Porter) scored touchdowns. Mt. Pleasant kicked three extra points. Libby kicked one field goal and missed one. Carlisle won 22-0.

Against Penn, the Indians got off to a bad start. Exendine fumbled the kickoff out of bounds at his own twenty-yard line and a Quaker recovered it. Carlisle's defense held, causing Penn to try a field goal. Mt. Pleasant blocked it, recovered the ball, and ran out to his twenty-five before being tackled. A couple of possessions later, Oscar Hunt, Little Boy, and LaRoque gained enough to put the ball in field goal position. Libby's dropkick split the uprights for the first four points of the game. A couple of possessions later, Penn's Levene blocked Mt. Pleasant's punt. Draper scooped it up and ran it over for a touchdown. Hollenbach kicked the point after, putting Penn ahead 6–4.

Later in the half, Mt. Pleasant punted from midfield but the ball landed untouched on Penn's twenty-five-yard line. Gardner rushed down the field, picked up the loose ball, and scored Carlisle's first touchdown. Mt. Pleasant kicked the extra point to give Carlisle the lead at 10–6. Later, Sheble muffed a Mt. Pleasant punt on his own fifty-yard line. LaRoque snared the ball and raced to a touchdown. Mt. Pleasant made the kick after, increasing Carlisle's lead to 16–6. Late in the half, Mt. Pleasant punted over Longwell's head. The Penn back scurried to recover the ball on his own two-yard line but Carlisle defenders caught him and threw him over the goal line for a safety. The half ended with the score Carlisle 18–Penn 6. There was a lot of back and forth in the second half with both teams missing field goals. Late in the game, Greene punted out of bounds and Mt. Pleasant kicked it out to his thirty. Folwell raced down the field to get the ball but missed it. Exendine picked it up and sprinted eighty yards for a touchdown in the most exciting play of the game. Mt. Pleasant made the kick for the final score of Carlisle 24–Penn 6.

After the game, the Indians were entertained at the Hotel Normandie, a luxury hotel in center-city Philadelphia. Management said that they had never entertained a more gentlemanly team.

A week later and ankle deep in the Buffalo mud, heavier Syracuse relied on mass plays where light Carlisle utilized the new rules. The Indians kept the ball in Syracuse territory the entire first half, during which Little Boy was pushed over for a touchdown and Libby kicked a field goal. Mt. Pleasant missed the extra point. Syracuse redoubled their efforts in the second half but Carlisle stiffened near their goal line, forcing Stein to kick a field goal. Mt. Pleasant received a loud ovation from the partisan Syracuse crowd when he left the game with an injured leg. The Indians held without him to keep the final score at Carlisle 9–Syracuse 4.

The soggy Harvard field offset Mt. Pleasant's sprinter speed—he ran the one-hundred-yard dash in nine-point-eight seconds—and the Crimson's ten-pounds per man weight advantage were too much for Carlisle to overcome. In front of their largest crowd to date, Harvard made the only score, a single touchdown, but missed the extra point. Had the ball bounced differently on one play or had a Carlisle player interfered with the opposition instead of his own man on two others, Carlisle would have evened the score or possibly won. When Exendine covered Mt. Pleasant's sixty-three-yard punt into the end zone, it bounced toward a Harvard man for a touchback. Had it come to Ex' it would have been a Carlisle touchdown. Twice, Mt. Pleasant intercepted passes in the end zone with a clear field in front of him. On both plays, one of his own men got in his way. Harvard won 5-0.

Stinging from the Harvard loss, Carlisle left on its long road trip to Minneapolis to challenge the Champions of the West. Seasonably cool weather kept spectators away until game time. Warner tried another of his innovations against the Gophers. He gave his receivers white headgear to better identify them to his passers. Unfortunately, conditions worked against the Indians' passing attack.

Playing on yet another muddy field, the Indians outplayed their heavier foes. Carlisle tended to gain on the frequent punt exchanges due largely to Minnesota's inability to catch them cleanly. The two teams' kickers, Libby and Marshall, both attempted field goals in the first half. Libby succeeded on an eighteen-yarder for Carlisle's first score. Near the end of the half, his drop kick for another one failed. Early in the second half, Minnesota's Larkin misplayed one of Mt. Pleasant's punts, letting it roll past him down to the fifteen where an Indian recovered it. Libby's dropkick for a field goal struck the upright and bounced back. In the next series, Minnesota turned the ball over after a failed forward pass. Libby soon tried another dropkick. This one went through the uprights for his second field goal of the day. A few possessions later, Carlisle took over on Minnesota's twelve-yard line. From there, Libby dropkicked an easy third field goal. Later, a Minnesota punt was blocked and the ball rolled across the goal line where Mt. Pleasant pounced on it for a touchdown. The catch on the punt out was ruled illegal, denying Carlisle the opportunity to kick the point after touchdown. There was no more scoring. Final score: Carlisle 17-Minnesota 0. While Carlisle whipped Minnesota on the road, Penn skinned the Michigan Wolverines at Franklin Field by the same score, further reinforcing the East's dominance over the West.

Instead of proceeding directly to Cincinnati as had been previously scheduled, the Indians traveled to Nashville, Tennessee for a recently arranged game with the Champions of the South, Vanderbilt. In front of the largest crowd ever assembled at a football game south of the Ohio River, Vanderbilt outplayed the sluggish Indians. The only score was a Commodore field goal kicked by Bob Blake late in the first half. Vanderbilt won 4-0.

Other than a brief mention in *The Arrow* following the discussion of the Minnesota game, the Vanderbilt game wasn't mentioned, even later in the season. It was covered briefly in *The Sentinel,* and the *1907 Spalding's Guide*

VANDY HANDS A LEMON TO THE INDIANS.

listed it. Perhaps this trip wasn't sanctioned by the Department of the Interior. Carlisle realized $3,000 from the gate receipts, Vanderbilt $2,000.

Two days later, the Indians played a team of All-Stars supporting the University of Cincinnati. Left out of the coverage was that most of Carlisle's starters were kept out of the game after playing a hard one two days before to rest them for the Thanksgiving game coming up in five days. Despite that, Gardner, Joe Libby, and Little Boy scored touchdowns. Wilson Charles kicked all three extra points. Each team attempted a field goal. Both failed. Carlisle won 18-0.

On Thanksgiving in Norfolk, both Virginia and Carlisle were tentative during the first ten minutes, until Little Boy fumbled a punt. Johnson of Virginia scooped up the ball and ran thirty yards for a touchdown. Randolph missed the extra point. The Indians responded by playing with determination. Line bucks and end runs secured several first downs and Little Boy was pushed over for a Carlisle touchdown. Mt. Pleasant kicked the extra point to put Carlisle ahead 6-5. The Indians continued their line smashing and sent Little Boy over again. Mt Pleasant again kicked the extra point. Less than a minute later, the Yahoo's Johnson received the ball on a double pass and dashed eighty yards for his second touchdown. This time, Randolph succeeded in kicking the extra point. The earlier missed extra point kept Carlisle ahead 12-11.

The Indians wasted no time in responding. Mt. Pleasant received the ball on a double pass and sprinted around right end for fifty yards with virtually no interference to clear a path for him. He kicked his third extra point of the day. After twenty minutes of fast and furious play, Virginia's Hornicker emerged from the scrimmage and raced through a broken field eighty yards for a touchdown. Randolph kicked the extra point. The game ended five minutes later with the score: Carlisle 18-Virginia 17.

Walter Camp placed Albert Exendine at end and Oscar Hunt at center on his All-America Third Team. He also placed J. Owsley Manier of Vanderbilt on that team. He was the first Southern player to get this level of recognition. Caspar Whitney ranked Carlisle as fifth in the nation behind Yale, Princeton, Harvard, and Navy, and right ahead of Penn, Cornell, and Brown. He gave honorable mention to Archie Libby as quarterback, Frank Mt. Pleasant as halfback, plus Albert Exendine and Charles Dillon at no particular positions. Pop Warner named Exendine and Libby to his All-Eastern Eleven along with four of his Cornell players.

On December 14, *The Arrow* reported, "A delightful reception in honor of Mrs. Warner and Mrs. Snyder (formerly our teacher, Miss Cochrane) was given by the '500 Club.'...We all wished that 'Pop' Warner could come too and complete the surprise." Was this presaging something that was about to happen?

1906 Season Summary

Date	Opponent	Location	Indians	Opp.
Sep. 26	Villanova College	Indian Field, Carlisle Barracks, PA	6	0
Sep. 29	Albright College	Indian Field, Carlisle Barracks, PA	82	0
Oct. 3	Susquehanna University	Indian Field, Carlisle Barracks, PA	48	0
Oct. 6	Penn State College	Seminary Athletic Field, Williamsport, PA	0	4
Oct. 20	Western University of Pennsylvania	Exposition Park, Pittsburgh, PA	22	0
Oct. 27	University of Pennsylvania	Franklin Field, Philadelphia, PA	24	6
Nov. 3	Syracuse University	Olympic Park, Buffalo, NY	9	4
Nov. 10	Harvard University	Harvard Stadium, Cambridge, MA	0	5
Nov. 17	University of Minnesota	Northrup Field, Minneapolis, MN	17	0
Nov. 22	Vanderbilt University	Dudley Field, Nashville, TN	0	4
Nov. 24	University of Cincinnati	Carson Field, Cincinnati, OH	18	0
Nov. 29	University of Virginia	Lafayette Field, Norfolk, VA	18	17

Won 9; Lost 3; Tied 0

Carlisle received an early Christmas present shortly after the close of the 1906 season: Pop Warner was available again. Three years earlier, 2,000 Cornellians had greeted him when he arrived at Ithaca to negotiate a contract that would bring him back to coach at his alma mater a second time. Two short years later, he was at the center of controversy for dismissing popular back-up quarterback and former halfback Lawrence J. Rice from the team for "insubordination and stirring up dissensions that seriously threatened the welfare of the team." Alumni and students alike protested the move and continued to simmer, even following Cornell's successful 8-1-2 1906 campaign under Warner. With his season over and his three-year contract at Cornell completed, Warner searched for other opportunities. He had to look no farther than Carlisle. His attending the Army-Navy game two days after his season ended and encountering Carlisle end Albert Exendine in the crowd was probably not a coincidence. Carlisle Superintendent Major Mercer, who promoted sports more than had his predecessor, would surely be there.

When Exendine asked Warner if he was considering a return to Carlisle, Warner responded, "You have coaches."

Exendine disagreed. "They aren't coaches." He directed Pop to talk with Mercer that very afternoon.

Angel DeCora, the Winnebago artist hired directly by Leupp

12

Warner Returns to His Favorite Players

Rule Changes for 1907:

Only a few modifications were made to the major rule changes of 1906.

The game was lengthened ten minutes by adding five minutes to each half.

The side throwing an incomplete forward pass now retains possession of the ball, except for third-down plays, after which the ball is turned over to the other team at the same line of scrimmage from which the third-down play commenced.

A lineman may carry the ball provided he doesn't leave his position in the line before the ball is put in play.

If a player signals for a fair catch but a teammate catches the ball, the ball is dead at the place it is caught but the person catching the ball does not get the protections of a person who calls for a fair catch.

Clarifies that back is eligible receiver only if he is at least one yard behind LOS when the ball is snapped and a forward pass bounding or rolling in end zone results in touchback.

Unemployed, Carlisle wasn't the only possibility Warner considered. The University of Minnesota was also looking for a head coach, and Pop applied for the open position. Lucky for Carlisle, their contract arrived in Warner's mailbox before Minnesota's did (although it had been mailed first), and he immediately accepted it. Had Minnesota's letter arrived first, he would have become a Gopher.

Three weeks after the Army-Navy game in the December 21, 1906 issue, the Christmas edition, *The Arrow* announced Warner's return as athletic director and head coach. The article, possibly written by Major Mercer, described the Indian coaches' work in glowing terms but said a year-round athletic director was needed where the Indian coaches were only available for football season. The Cornell administration lauded Warner's achievements in improving their team but made no effort to keep him. Years later, Warner stated that he had enjoyed each of his coaching assignments except the ones at his alma mater.

In less than a year, Commissioner Leupp's position had changed. He then wanted to eliminate Carlisle and some other off-reservation schools. The previous fall, Leupp omitted the appropriation for off-reservation schools in the upcoming year's budget (July 1 to June 30 in those days), but two Pennsylvania politicians pled their case so successfully when lobbying senators that Carlisle wasn't abolished. They had a difficult fight against Secretary of the Interior Hitchcock, Indian Affairs Commissioner Leupp, and politicians from some western states who wanted to shift the funding to their states.

Carlisle's excellent 1906 football season, with wins over Penn State, Pitt, Syracuse, Penn, Minnesota, Cincinnati, and Virginia had come at a good time. Newspapers cited the Indians' success as a reason to keep the school: "In this exigency, the Carlisle School's football record may stand it in good stead. It is a heroic episode, proving the pluck and adaptability of the Indian race. The American people may not like to see a school that can make such a record wiped out for the sake of purely local interests or to wreak a personal spite."

Carlisle Superintendent Major Mercer, who was "worn down by the nervous wear and tear" by being in a vise squeezed between the Leupp and Pratt factions, submitted a request to be relieved of command. It was turned down.

On January 11, several of Carlisle's leading citizens circulated petitions to have Pratt reinstated as superintendent of the school. The next day, newspapers reported that Leupp had again submitted a budget request recommending that all non-reservation schools be abandoned. The day after that, Pratt had an op-ed piece on saving Carlisle published. In late-January, apparently unaware of the ownership of the various campuses, Leupp inserted a clause into his appropriations request to turn the buildings and grounds of non-reservation schools to the states in which they were located.

Then, Carlisle alum Albert Nash challenged the Bureau of Indian Affairs, which he described as "a nest for grafters," in an op-ed piece chiding the bureau for not hiring qualified Indians. In February, Rep. Olmsted argued to senators that educating Indian students cost fifty dollars more on Arizona reservations than at Carlisle. He presented the facts so well that he convinced Arizona Delegate Marcus A. Smith to agree when Committee on Indian Affairs Chair James Schoolcraft Sherman proposed to both restore all appropriations for non-reservation schools and to include one for a new school. Thwarted from shuttering the schools, Leupp was still free to investigate the terms on which Indian schools could be turned over to state governments.

In his mid-February letter to President Roosevelt, Carlisle graduate, former halfback on the football team, and leading cattleman as half-owner of

Hazlehurst Stock Farm, State Senator William Hazlett of Fort Cobb, Oklahoma asserted that "...schools like Carlisle, located in the midst of the business and oldest communities, offer advantages and opportunities to students that can never be had where the Indians are herded together and live the old life that the government has been trying to do away with for years." Hazlett's letter impressed President Roosevelt so much he forwarded it to Leupp.

Leupp didn't attend the 1907 graduation exercises. Rep. Olmsted did the honors instead. Later that year, the commissioner renewed his efforts to close off-reservation boarding schools, Carlisle and Chilocco in particular.

In June, Pop Warner gave rides in his automobile (possibly a Chalmers) to any girl wanting to hop in. He was known for buying older cars and tinkering with them.

An August 31 piece datelined Carlisle claimed that Carlisle's 1907 schedule was "the most difficult schedule that has ever been tried by an American team." The schedule was definitely more difficult than any other team played, but it wasn't all that different from typical Carlisle schedules. In fact, it was weaker than some other years in that the Indians only scheduled three games in ten days one time. Other powers considered Carlisle's schedules suicidal but wouldn't admit that in print.

The article also announced that Warner was back at Carlisle and he would be assisted by James Johnson, who had just graduated from Northwestern University's dental school. Bill Newman, Cornell '07, would be in charge of the second team and would, at times, assist with the varsity. Antonio Lubo was captain for 1907. Lost from last year's team leaving large shoes to fill were Charles Dillon, Oscar Hunt, Paul LaRocque, and Archie Libby.

Hunt was a particularly sad loss. The reputed millionaire through inheritance from Mathias Splitlog had returned home to Oklahoma for a visit after the season ended. While there, he was arrested for killing Joe Wolfenberger during a drunken binge. The witnesses were all so inebriated, none could remember the details of the chaotic fight. While awaiting trial, he went insane and was allowed to return home. There, he contracted pneumonia and, after four days of delirium, died. Probably trying to stir up trouble, W. G. Thompson, who Mercer had reorganized out of a job, wrote Dr. Carlos Montezuma that Hunt had committed suicide while awaiting trial.

Major Mercer complained that he had fourteen football teams to outfit each year. The varsity would get new uniforms and their old ones would get handed down to other teams. The bulk of these teams were shop and club teams that played in intramural leagues. These teams were sometimes coached by experienced varsity players. Promising prospects were sometimes promoted to the second team. In some years, games were scheduled for the third team. The JV team at Carlisle was for young boys, not underclassmen just entering the football pipeline. They required several years of growth to be ready for interscholastic football.

Warner wouldn't let just anyone join his teams. That spring, a skinny Sac and Fox boy from Oklahoma happened by the high jump pit on his way back from his job. Although he was dressed in overalls, a hickory shirt, and borrowed gym shoes, he asked the boys practicing there if he could give it a try. Not expecting much, they let him. After he broke the school record wearing work clothes, Pop put him on the track team. He flourished but, when the boy asked to join the football team, Warner demurred. He didn't want his most valuable track man hurt playing football. When the boy wouldn't take no for an answer, the coach slammed a ball into the boy's gut and told him to give the varsity some tackling practice. Having a real football in his hands for the first time, the wannabe halfback ran through the tacklers as if they were cardboard cutouts, causing Warner to fume so badly his ever-present Turkish Trophy cigarette fell out of his mouth.

"You're supposed to give the first team tackling practice, not run through them!"

The boy's huge grin faded before he responded, "Nobody is going to tackle Jim."

Young Jim Thorpe was now on Pop's football team whether the Old Fox wanted him or not. Not having played before, the young man spent most of the season learning the rules and rudiments of the game while watching Albert Payne play left halfback. Thorpe was far from unusual for a Carlisle footballer in that he had lost a parent, his mother, before coming to the school.

The author's previous research found that the majority of Carlisle footballers had lost at least one parent. Quite a few had lost both. Life was hard and short in those days and worse on the reservations. Life expectancy in the United States at birth in 1900 for white males was 48.23 years and 32.54 for males of other races. Jim had lost his mother in 1900 to blood poisoning and his twin brother Charlie to pneumonia when they were only eight years old. His father, Hiram Thorpe, picked Carlisle because it was too far from home in Oklahoma for the boy to run away as Jim had taken off from other schools closer to home. He much preferred being outdoors on the allotment hunting, fishing, or breaking horses to sitting in a classroom. A few months after Jim arrived in 1904, Hiram was stricken with septicemia on a hunting trip and died, leaving Jim a twinless-twin orphan who didn't have a home to run away to anymore.

The Indians' first victim that year was usual warm-up foe, Lebanon Valley College. Despite playing in a downpour on a field that was a sea of mud, the Indians outclassed their rivals 40 to 0 while not allowing them a single first down. Pete Hauser scored four touchdowns and Albert Payne one. Frank Mt. Pleasant kicked three extra points and Louis Island two. Warner substituted liberally in the second half, so liberally that, although Thorpe's name didn't appear in the write-up for the game, he was credited with scoring two touchdowns.

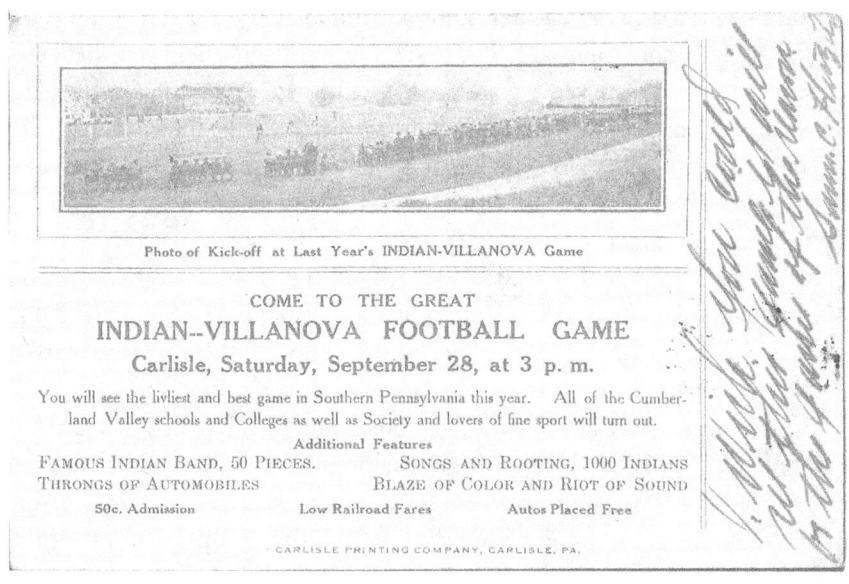

The Villanova game recap was the first to adorn the front page of *The Arrow* that year. The earlier minor games were relegated to the inner pages. Villanova put up a fight as usual. Mt. Pleasant returned the opening kickoff twenty-five yards then engineered a drive of line plunges and end runs, terminated by Hauser scoring a touchdown. Mt. Pleasant made the kick after. Later in the first half, Hauser kicked a thirty-yard field goal from placement for a 10 to 0 Carlisle lead. Villanova gained yardage with forward passes but never threatened Carlisle's goal. They did hold Carlisle for downs at the two-yard line to prevent another score. The final score was a respectable 10-0 loss for Villanova.

The Wednesday game against Susquehanna University was no contest. Carlisle scored two touchdowns in the first two minutes of the game. Warner rested the first team, giving Thorpe his first start as the Old Fox gave the second team and the scrubs game experience. Thorpe scored four touchdowns before he was replaced. Theodore Owl also scored four, Libby and George Thomas scored one each, William White scored three, and William Little Wolf scored two. Island kicked six extra points, Two Hearts kicked four, and Mike Balenti two. Island also kicked a field goal. The Indians scored two and a quarter points per minute in the 91-0 blowout, more than doubling Fielding Yost's point-a-minute rate in this one game.

Saturday's game against Penn State at Williamsport was more of a challenge. Mt. Pleasant's punts, coupled with downfield coverage by ends Albert Exendine and William Gardner, kept the Indians out of bad field position. His passes also gained yardage. The first score was from a field goal kicked by Hauser. On Penn State's first possession after that score, McCleary skirted his left end and ran sixty-five yards for a touchdown, crossing the goal line at the extreme corner of the field. The difficult punt out was not caught, eliminating a kick for the extra point. The score put Penn State ahead 5-4. Two possessions later, the Indian offensive bogged down at the State thirty-yard line and Hauser's kick for a field goal was blocked. On the Indians' next possession, Mt. Pleasant completed a pass to Exendine who ran thirty yards after catching it for a touchdown. Mt. Pleasant kicked the extra point for a Carlisle 10-5 lead.

Penn State's McCleary made occasional long gains, but their drives always petered out. Carlisle's drives were also stopped but were within Hauser's range. He kicked two more field goals of ten and fifteen yards, respectively. Three plays later, the game ended with the final score of Carlisle 18-Penn State 5.

The *Buffalo Courier* praised the Indians' play against Syracuse the next Saturday. "While the work of Hauser, Fritz Hendricks, Exendine and Mt. Pleasant was perhaps the best exhibition of football ever seen in Buffalo, their teammates came in for a great share of glory which was honestly won. For every man in the Syracuse line-up played for all he was worth." Hauser was responsible for all of Carlisle's scores. He kicked two field goals and plunged the last five yards needed for their touchdown.

Early in the game, Mt. Pleasant tricked the Orange by faking a punt and hitting Gardner with a pass for a gain of thirty yards. A few plays after that the Indians tried another trick but the Orangemen weren't fooled and intercepted his pass. Some possessions later, Hauser split the uprights from twenty-eight yards out for Carlisle's first score. Shortly after that the Indians marched down the field using a mix of line plunges, end runs, and forward passes to both ends. From a half-yard out, his teammates hurled Hauser over the Orange line for a touchdown. Mt. Pleasant made the extra point kick for a Carlisle lead of 10–0. Four minutes later, Syracuse bounced back when Banks ran through the entire Carlisle team for a forty-five-yard touchdown. Stein made the kick, cutting Carlisle's lead to 10–6.

Both coaches made moves at halftime. Warner adjusted his defense to counter Syracuse's "Big Shift" in which all but two men positioned themselves on one side of the center. He shifted Little Boy to left tackle, put Shouchuk in at center, and replaced Payne at left halfback with Thorpe. Syracuse's onside kickoff attempt was recovered by Lubo on Carlisle's forty-five-yard line. Several possessions later, Carlisle moved the ball to Syracuse's half-yard line. Syracuse's goal-line defense held and took over the ball on downs. Stein's punt was tipped to Mt. Pleasant by Pete Hauser's brother Emil, aka Wauseka. This time the Orange stopped Carlisle at their one-yard line. Stein's punt was blocked and recovered by Hauser who later kicked a fifteen-yard field goal. Mt. Pleasant and Hauser made some good runs, but the Indians didn't score again. The final score was Carlisle 14–Syracuse 6.

A number of Indians from Canada and New York's Cattaraugus Reservation attended the game. Not mentioned but likely present were members of Mt. Pleasant's family and friends from the nearby Tuscarora Reservation. Several bet on Carlisle. One won $200 and, smiling broadly, said, "Ugh, Mount Pleasant heap fast. Hauser too big for palefaces."

Bruised and battered, several Carlisle players were not in good enough condition to take the field against Bucknell for the last home game of the season. Neither Mt. Pleasant nor Hauser played, Lyon didn't last long, and Thorpe got the start over Payne. Warner wasn't at the game. He must have been scouting the next opponent, Penn, which was playing Brown in Philadelphia. Coach Johnson was in charge of the team that day. For once, field conditions were perfect and a large crowd was present.

Five minutes into the sloppily played game, Thorpe scored Carlisle's first touchdown at the end of a drive with all the yardage made on the ground. Quarterback Louis Island kicked the extra point. During Carlisle's next possession, Thorpe ran around end for fifteen yards but fumbled when tackled. The loose ball bounced ahead and into Owl's arms. He ran it across for the Indians' second touchdown. Island missed the kick. A couple of possessions later, Island dropkicked a thirty-yard field goal. He almost didn't make it because the ball struck an upright on its way through. The first half ended with Carlisle ahead 15-0. Johnson brought in the second string for the second half. The teams played evenly and neither scored. Carlisle beat Bucknell 15-0.

Next up for the Indians was Penn, undefeated in seven straight games. Early in the first half of the Penn game, the Indians put on a dazzling display of what they could do using a developing version of what was later called the single-wing formation. Mt. Pleasant skirted the ends and passed for long yardage. Fullback Hauser pounded the line and passed to end Exendine and Gardner. Halfbacks Hendricks and Payne ran through the line and caught passes. With four yards to make on third down at the Penn twenty-five, Hauser booted a field goal with Mt. Pleasant holding to put four points for Carlisle on the scoreboard. Later in the half, Mt. Pleasant fumbled on his own fifteen-yard line. Penn recovered it, but Hollenbaugh dropped it when smashing Carlisle's line. Hendricks dashed forward from the secondary to pick up the ball and took off on a dead run with two teammates running interference for him. He scored a sensational touchdown, and Mt. Pleasant made the kick after to increase Carlisle's lead to 10-0. When Penn took possession of the ball, they moved it down to Carlisle's 28-yard line. When their drive stalled, Penn's Regan hooked a dropkick.

Late in the first half, the Indians ran and passed the ball steadily down the field. With the ball on Penn's five-yard line and one yard to go for a first down, Mt. Pleasant sent Payne around Penn's left end for a touchdown and made the kick after. The first half ended with Carlisle leading 16-0.

The second half featured punt exchanges, fumbles, and intercepted passes until Little Boy blocked Hollenbaugh's punt on the Penn twelve-yard line and ran it across for a touchdown. Mt. Pleasant made the kick. With that lead, Island and Thorpe came in for Mt. Pleasant and Payne. A Hauser-to-Gardner twenty-five-yard pass and a twenty-yard run by Thorpe set Island up for a field goal try from the twenty-eight-yard line. He missed. After a few intercepted pass exchanges, Penn had the ball but their short drive stalled. Hollenbaugh's punt sailed over Hauser's head. Dwyer picked it up and dashed ten yards for Penn's touchdown. Scarlet kicked the extra point. After a short Penn punt, the Indians had the ball on Penn's thirty-yard line. Penalties negated their gains, so Hauser kicked a field goal for a final score of Carlisle 26-Penn 6.

Not only did the win extend the Indians' unbeaten string to nine games—the first two of which were at the end of the 1906 season—it also signified their first win over a Big Four team that year. The *Philadelphia Ledger* described their play: "A sturdy set of fearless, unscrupulous braves, who took no chances with Fate and played the game boldly, spectacularly, as football has rarely been played in Philadelphia." The Quakers would go on to win their remaining games, giving up only a total of fourteen points to their opponents other than Carlisle.

The school made arrangement for students and townspeople unable to travel to New York for the Princeton game to follow it at the school. Information obtained from telegraph messages were posted on a large blackboard in the gymnasium with the position of the ball indicated to help people follow the plays. Cheering continued from the kickoff to the final gun. After the game was over, the students sang "Old Carlisle" as they marched to their quarters.

The students who stayed home were wise because the game was played in anything between a drizzle and a downpour. As it turned out, they were wise to pass on the trip for other reasons, too:

"It seems strange to say that Carlisle was overconfident of beating Princeton, but such was the case." The Indians' heads were swelled after their overwhelming defeat of Penn and from reading newspaper accounts of their

INDIAN MAIDENS VIEWING THE GAME

great victory. "Princeton, on the other hand, was keyed up to their best efforts and played with such speed and dash and fierceness that Carlisle was surprised, dazed, and demoralized, just as Penn was when Carlisle went at them the same way the Saturday previous."

Treacherous footing prevented Carlisle from taking advantage of the host of plays made possible by the new rules. Line plunging was about all they could do under the circumstances. That put the lighter Indians at a severe disadvantage. Princeton's first score came as the result of a muffed twisting punt. McCormick pushed the ball over and Harlan kicked an easy extra point. Their second score came from a field goal kicked from a fake line-plunge play. Spectators even missed what they had done. The second half brought harder rainfall and Princeton's second touchdown. Tibbott followed his well-organized interference fifty yards for the score. Harlan kicked the extra point. Thorpe played the entire game at left halfback but didn't have much chance to shine in the mud. The final score was Princeton 16–Carlisle 0. Little Boy explained why the Indians always had difficulties in inclement weather: "Football no good fun in mud and snow." The write-up of this game was demoted to the inner pages of *The Arrow*.

The Indians had lost ten straight times to their next opponent, Harvard, the school Carlisle students considered to be the pinnacle of excellence. Mealtime provided numerous opportunities for mimicry. (Using Harvard beets as model, they labeled various dishes as being prepared "Harvard style.") Beating the Crimson was uppermost in the players' minds. On this perfect football Saturday afternoon, upward of 30,000 spectators overflowed Harvard Stadium, the vast majority cheering for the Indians in black jerseys with red and old gold stripes below the elbows.

Carlisle started in a fury. Mt. Pleasant yelled, "Remember last Saturday," before he'd put the ball in play. Only a fumble prevented them from scoring. On their second possession, they couldn't be stopped. Two rushes up the middle and a run around end earned the Indians a first down. On the next play, Hauser dropped back as if to kick. Instead he launched the ball in a high arc to Gardner, who fumbled but quickly recovered possession inside the Crimson five-yard line. Hauser then carried it across for a touchdown. Mt. Pleasant kicked the extra point. On defense, the normally stoic Indians unnerved the Crimson players with their chatter:

Capt. Lubo: Who got that last man?
Hauser: I did, Captain.

Capt. Lubo: Good. Who'll get this man?
Exendine: I will, Captain. I'll get him.
After the play was over, the conversation picked up again:
Exendine: I got my man, Captain.
Capt. Lubo: Good. Gardner, you get this man.
Gardner: I'll get him, Captain.
After the play was run, the conversation continued:
Capt. Lubo: Did you get him, Gardner?
Gardner: I got him, Captain.
Capt. Lubo: I'll get this man.
Hauser: I'll help you, Captain.
Chorus: We'll help you, Captain. We'll get him, Captain.

Harvard's "buck up" and "cheer up, old boy" were lost against Carlisle's machine-gun peppering "We'll get him, Captain."

A short time after making their first score, Mt. Pleasant and Payne couldn't corral Newell's onside kick. In the scrum that followed, Harvard lineman Grant snared it within feet of Carlisle's goal line. Apollonio ran it over on the next play. Capt. Parker kicked the extra point to tie the score 6–6. The Indians took possession of the ball and didn't relinquish it for fifteen fiercely played minutes. Harvard then broke up two plays on its thirty-yard line before Hauser's kick from placement fell short by a few feet. Mt. Pleasant ran Burr's kick back to the Harvard thirty-five to start Carlisle's next possession. The entire team carried Payne forward for fifteen yards.

The Crimson defense held for two plays but were caught off guard by Hauser who, when about to be tackled, raised his hands over his head and lobbed to ball to Lubo, who stood alone by the sideline. The Carlisle captain ran unmolested over the goal line. Mt. Pleasant kicked the extra point, but Johnny Harvard still had some life in him. Newell made a fair catch of Hauser's short kick on the Carlisle twenty-eight. Parker kicked a field goal to bring the score at halftime to Carlisle 12–Harvard 10. Warner made no personnel changes for the second half.

After a missed field goal attempt early in the second half, Mt. Pleasant caught a kick at his own thirty-five with no defender near him. His interference formed and convoyed him into Harvard territory. There, the diminutive runner left his blockers behind as he stiff-armed two tacklers and sidestepped Newell, the last man between him and paydirt. Frank still had to run as fast as he could because Lockwood, Harvard's fastest man, had an angle on him.

POOR JOHN! POOR JOHN!!

Lockwood tackled him from behind but he had already crossed the goal line, completing his seventy-five-yard touchdown run. Frank also made the extra point. A later fumble gave Harvard the ball on the Indian fifty-yard line. Line plunges, followed by end runs and an errant forward pass that Harvard recovered, put the ball on Carlisle's five-yard line. Lockwood's teammates lifted him over the goal line for a Harvard touchdown. Lockwood missed the kick, making the score Carlisle 18–Harvard 15.

But the Indians weren't done. Hauser later tried a field goal, but the ball hit the crossbar and bounced back. Shortly after that, Mt. Pleasant caught

Harvard's punt on their thirty-eight-yard line. From there, Hauser hit William Winnie with a pass, putting the ball at the five-yard line. Two plays later, Hauser carried the ball over the goal line. Pop made some substitutions but didn't put Thorpe into the game. Carlisle continued to gain yardage and Harvard fought back. The game ended with Carlisle winning 23-15.

Thousands of fans poured over the walls and onto the field and surrounded the Carlisle players. *The Boston Globe* observed, "It was a game in which the Indians, playing the best football they ever have played, showed the wonderful possibilities of the new game, and gave an exhibition of old football, too, which was a revelation. It was not so much that Harvard was merely beaten, but she was outclassed individually and as a team, ripped and torn throughout the line, and shown up in pitiable weakness almost on the eve of the season's all-important game—that with Yale."

At 7:00 p.m., Indian School boys celebrated the great victory by donning their nightshirts, using their pillowcases for hats, and parading through the town. Two boys carried a stretcher bearing a beat-up dummy, wearing an H on its red sweater, at the head of the procession immediately in front of the school's band. Hundreds of the town's residents watched them making snake dances as they went. While students and players reveled over the team's greatest victory to date, Warner looked forward to one he wanted even more.

The players had little time to rejoice and recuperate because their next game was played all the way out in Minneapolis against the University of Minnesota. They were soon back on a train for a few days. Meanwhile, the 2-1 Gophers had two weeks off since their last game, a loss to Chicago, to prepare.

The warm sun melted the frost, making the field slippery at first. Otherwise, conditions were perfect. Minnesota started strong while Carlisle floundered with its passing and fumbled the ball away. Minnesota shot out in front by kicking a thirty-five-yard field goal. Carlisle shifted to straight football, eschewing forward passes and trick plays. Both teams made short gains back and forth. When a Carlisle drive stalled at the Minnesota thirty, Mt. Pleasant dropkicked for a tying field goal but missed. His attempt from the forty-five also went wide. The Indians finally got their offense working, passing and running the ball down the field. Stalled at the Minnesota five-yard line, the Indians lined up as to kick a field goal. Instead, Mt. Pleasant tossed the ball downfield to Lubo who scampered in for the touchdown. Hauser kicked the extra point to put Carlisle ahead 6-4. Later, the Indians moved the ball to the Minnesota twenty-two using a combination of line bucks and passes. Mt.

Pleasant hit Gardner with a pass and he carried the ball across the goal line. Hauser kicked the extra point. The first half ended with the score: Carlisle 12–Minnesota 4.

At halftime, Mt. Pleasant discovered that he had a broken thumb. Warner made several substitutions, including Island for Mt. Pleasant and Payne for Thorpe. Minnesota fought hard but Carlisle continued to gain ground. They got as close to scoring as Minnesota's nine-yard line but fumbled. Chestnut picked up the ball and outran all the defenders the length of the field to score Minnesota's touchdown. The final score was Carlisle 12–Minnesota 10.

Minnesota's center Kjeiland caused quite a ruckus when he tried to abscond with the game ball. Warner grabbed him and some angry Carlisle players surrounded the culprit, swinging their fists at him. Unaware that time had expired on the clock held by an official on the sideline, a throng descended from the stands after hearing a rumor that Carlisle had forfeited with three minutes left to play. It took several policemen to clear the field long after both teams had left.

While all of this was going on, Penn beat Michigan again, further cementing the superiority of Eastern football over the Western variety. This time the score was 6-0, which was better than the previous year's 17-0 loss. Oklahoma was celebrating its becoming a state and Charles Curtis, a Kaw, taking office as a senator. A student from Oklahoma wrote a small piece for *The Arrow* about his or her home state being granted statehood and that Carlisle's motto, "Labor conquers all things," was adopted for the state motto. A short bio of Curtis told of how he was orphaned at an early age, made money selling fruit and newspapers at the Topeka train depot and, later, riding horses in the summer. In the early 1870s he worked for an attorney with his pay being tutored to become a lawyer. His first public office was being elected county attorney when he was twenty-four and gained a reputation for hard work.

Rather than return to Carlisle after the game, Warner took his team to Lake Forest, Illinois to rest and prepare for the game with unbeaten and untied Chicago, 1907's Champions of the West. While there, Warner wrote *The Arrow* to inform Carlisle's followers of the team's status. Not only did Mt. Pleasant have a broken bone in his thumb, the undersized star's hip also hurt too badly for him to play. Pop had to rearrange his offense and defense because Mt. Pleasant was an integral part of both. Exendine's injured side wasn't expected to get him out of the Chicago game. Warner warned of a let up at the end of the year as had happened other times.

Warner had long wanted to beat Amos Alonzo Stagg head to head, and he was finally getting his chance. Making the prospect more delicious was that Stagg considered the 1907 Chicago team his best ever. Perfect weather brought out more fans than the stands could hold, so standing-room platforms were built to augment the seating. Netting was hung along the sidelines to keep players and spectators apart.

Keeping the ball in Chicago territory eighty percent of the time, Carlisle drew first blood on a Hauser place kick with Gardner holding. He missed another one a little later. After a series of punt exchanges, Lubo blocked Chicago quarterback Steffen's punt, giving the Indians the ball on the Maroons' fifteen-yard line. A fumble spoiled what should have been a touchdown run, but Hauser was able to kick a second field goal. A timekeeper error caused the first half to be cut short by five minutes. When the issue was resolved, the teams returned to the field of play. Successful forward passes got Hauser two more tries for field goals but he missed both of them. At the end of the first half Carlisle led 8–0.

Chicago stiffened in the second half until Samuel McLean, aka Afraid-of-a-Bear, broke through the Maroon line and blocked another Steffen punt at midfield. After a series of plays moved the ball closer to Chicago's goal, Hauser tried another field goal and missed. A minute later, Carlisle had the ball back and was ready to strike. In Exendine and Gardner, Warner had what he, and others, considered the best pair of ends in the country. On defense, they stifled Chicago's shifty Steffen, and on offense they were excellent pass catchers. Well aware of them, Stagg had his defenders hammer each of them one, two, three times on every pass play. On this possession, Exendine let the defender push him off the field. He then slipped behind the Chicago bench and ran downfield parallel to the sideline. Deep in Chicago's secondary, he emerged back onto the field miles from a defender and waved his arms wildly. With Mt. Pleasant injured, aerial duties fell to Hauser, who was also an excellent passer. Hauser hung onto the ball as long as he could before heaving it downfield. The ball made a high, long arch before settling into Exendine's hands. The lonesome end trotted across the goal line for Carlisle's only touchdown that day. Hauser kicked the extra point.

Not wanting this trick play to beat them, Chicago players claimed that Little Boy, who as the Carlisle center was an ineligible receiver, had caught the ball, not Exendine. Referee McCormack didn't believe them. Completely legal but unforeseen by the rules writers, the Rules Committee soon made this type of play illegal.

Steffen later muffed one of Balenti's punts and Carlisle took possession. The ensuing drive fizzled before they could score another touchdown, so Hauser kicked his third field goal. Chicago then showed its first flash of speed in the game, but that petered out outside the Carlisle forty-yard line. Steffen broke the shutout by making his field goal try from that distance. Substituting fresh men, the Maroons battered Carlisle's line for small gains that gave them no chance of winning the game. Perhaps Steffen didn't want to risk turning the ball over to Carlisle to keep them from scoring again. The final score was Carlisle 18–Chicago 4.

Warner considered the win over Stagg one of his signature wins as a coach. And this game was Jim Thorpe's last as a benchwarmer.

St. Vincent's College of Los Angeles (today's Loyola Marymount University) and the University of Washington in Seattle invited the Indians to postseason games to be played on Christmas and New Year's Day, respectively. Warner supported the trip, "...feeling that Carlisle had drawn much of its strongest material from the sections in which these cities lay." Disinclined to take the boys away from their studies anymore that season, the administration saw it differently: "Carlisle has already made two transcontinental trips to play football, and will hardly be able to give the Pacific coast games until next year."

Walter Camp placed Exendine on his All-America Second Eleven and Hauser on his Third Eleven. He backhanded Mt. Pleasant: "Mt. Pleasant of the Indians is one of the best quarters of the year, but less rugged in physique than the others mentioned. He is brilliant, and up to the time of the Princeton game had made more out of the team than any of the other quarters, but Dillon proved more successful in that game, and he and Jones lasted out the season better." Camp made no mention of the much more difficult schedule Carlisle had played.

Caspar Whitney ranked Carlisle third in the nation behind Yale and Princeton, just ahead of Penn and Harvard. He placed Hauser at fullback and Exendine at end on his All-America Eleven. He gave Honorable Mention status to Mt. Pleasant at quarterback.

GROUP OF CARLISLE FOOTBALL STARS.
[No. 1 is Little Old Man; No. 2 is Exendine; No. 3 is Hendricks; No. 4 is Captain Lubo.]

A report of the receipts for the Harvard-Yale game and each school's share was circulated around the country. *The Lewisburg Journal* expanded the report to include a couple of annual totals. Yale took in $80,000 that year, a near record for that school. Carlisle Indian School collected over $100,000, of which $75,000 was expected to be profit, after playing "an exceedingly hard" schedule. Some of the football money was used toward building the Leupp Indian Art Studio, which also included a photography lab.

At odds with the shift in the school's direction after Pratt's departure, Dr. Carlos Montezuma's letter critical of Carlisle Indian School was published adjacent to the Chicago game coverage in *The Chicago Tribune*. He claimed that most of Carlisle's players were employees and not students enrolled at Carlisle.

Major Mercer submitted his resignation as superintendent: "Though in good personal health, I find the daily annoying responsibilities all more than I can stand, and I am advised that a few months leave of absence would be of benefit. Such a course, followed by a change back to the out-of-door military life, I am convinced is a necessity and that relief as above will best suit the conditions."

1907 Season Summary

Date	Opponent	Location	Indians	Opp.
Sep. 21	Lebanon Valley College	Indian Field, Carlisle Barracks, PA	40	0
Sep. 28	Villanova College	Indian Field, Carlisle Barracks, PA	10	0
Oct. 2	Susquehanna University	Indian Field, Carlisle Barracks, PA	91	0
Oct. 5	Penn State College	Seminary Athletic Field, Williamsport, PA	18	5
Oct. 12	Syracuse University	Olympic Park, Buffalo, NY	14	6
Oct. 19	Bucknell University	Indian Field, Carlisle Barracks, PA	15	0
Oct. 26	University of Pennsylvania	Franklin Field, Philadelphia, PA	26	6
Nov. 2	Princeton University	Polo Grounds, New York, NY	0	16
Nov. 9	Harvard University	Harvard Stadium, Cambridge, MA	23	15
Nov. 16	University of Minnesota	Northrup Field, Minneapolis, MN	12	10
Nov. 23	University of Chicago	Marshall Field, Chicago, IL	18	4

Won 10; Lost 1; Tied 0

13

Go West Young Men

Rule changes for 1908:
Penalties could now be refused by the offended team
Pass interference rules were instituted. The defense may only push an offensive player to allow him to intercept the pass.
Field Judge was made the timekeeper
The use of four officials is strongly advised
Time stopped for enforcement of incomplete pass penalty
If the ball strikes an official, the play must be done over

A January 2, 1908 news article out of Washington, DC opined, "The perculiar [sic] situation is presented that the grand work of the Carlisle football team on the gridiron during the past season may be the means of preventing interference. The fact that the redmen proved such worthy foes with the pigskin won for them unbounded admiration. According to the Americans' love of sport, it is hardly possible that they would allow much interference without uttering a howling protest."

The previous fall, Carlisle had its best football season to date, with just a single loss and wins over Harvard, Penn, Syracuse, Minnesota, and Chicago. The positive publicity the team and its stars generated may have made the difference in thwarting Commissioner Leupp and keeping Carlisle open.

Major Mercer resubmitted his request to return to active cavalry duty. This time it was accepted and he was relieved of command effective February 1, 1908. He performed the required daylong horse riding test with flying colors before being allowed to join the Eleventh Cavalry, which was stationed in Cuba at that time. Mercer recommended Principal Teacher John Whitwell as his replacement but Charles H. Dickson was appointed temporary superintendent. The government then searched for what they considered a suitable permanent superintendent.

When Leupp arrived for the 1908 Commencement exercises held the first week of April, he declared that he was much pleased and endorsed Carlisle's outing system. In his graduation talk, he addressed reports that he had tried to destroy the school. He informed those present that his position concerning Carlisle had been misunderstood. "I wish to be judged by what I have done, and when I do attack the Carlisle school, I will attack it in a way

that everybody will know it." Leupp opposed having a military man in charge of the school and succeeded in having Mercer permanently replaced by a professional educator, Moses Friedman. Not wanting a military man seemed to conflict with his goal of making Carlisle a mini-West Point. Noticing that the new superintendent was a civilian, *The Carlisle Sentinel* asked, "Is this another link in the chain for hastening the consummation of Commissioner Leupp's plan for the disbandonment [sic] of the school?"

The Philadelphia Inquirer challenged Leupp: "[I]t would be interesting to know what it was that was so misunderstood that Congress had to pass a particular act to see that the school was not abandoned."

Superintendent Friedman waited until graduation was over before making an appearance. At the end of Commencement Week, he signed receipts for the government property and formally received command from Charles Dickson. Friedman was then officially Superintendent of Carlisle Indian School.

Lewis Tewanima had arrived at Carlisle in January 1907 as one of a dozen hostile Hopis taken as prisoners of war who were sent there against their wishes. Initially, they refused to have their hair cut and participate in campus activities. After a period of essentially being ignored, the Hopis changed their minds. A year later, when Tewanima asked Warner if he could be on the track team, the coach gave the short, scrawny guy a skeptical look and said, "What can you do?" Tewanima replied, "I run good fast. All Hopi run good fast." It didn't take long for the diminutive 110-pound athlete to become America's best long-distance runner and a candidate for the 1908 U. S. Olympic team.

A scant year after first putting on track shoes, Tewanima placed ninth in the marathon in the London Olympics in spite of his sore feet and hurting knees. Former Carlisle student Frank Mt. Pleasant, hindered by an injured ligament in his knee, finished sixth in the triple jump and seventh in the long jump. On July 31 in a special meet on the outskirts of Paris, when both were in better condition, with a leap of twenty-two feet and six inches, Mt. Pleasant beat both the Olympic and the American intercollegiate champions in the long jump. Tewanima came in second in the three-mile handicap race to a runner who was given a 125 meters head start. Their feats were overshadowed in the American press by the arrival in the City of Lights of the Thomas automobile in the New York-to-Paris automobile race made famous in the 1965 Blake Edwards movie *The Great Race.*

In early 1908, Stacy Matlock, the student whose broken leg caused Pratt to ban off-campus football in 1890, was selected to fill the leadership void that had opened up when the principal chief of the Pawnees died. He returned to Carlisle as part of a delegation visiting Washington and for personal reasons. The previous fall, his wife Ellie had contracted typhoid fever and died, leaving him a widower with children. Pawnee customs dictated who would replace deceased young wives. Often it was an unmarried sister of the departed. While on campus, Stacy married Blanche Bill, who was the next relative in line when his wife died. Although this marriage was recorded in the official files, it wasn't mentioned in school publications, probably because of the twenty-year age difference between bride and groom. Stacy's visits became more frequent when his daughter Cecelia attended the school.

Lone Star Dietz had arrived on campus in September of 1907 to no fanfare. He tried out for the football team but didn't crack the varsity line-up. After the season was over, it was time for his outing period. Rather than living and working with a white family, he enrolled at the School of Industrial Art in Philadelphia where he, although an artist, studied mechanical drawing. Over the Christmas break he and Angel DeCora, whom he had met at the Model Government Indian School exhibit at the 1904 St. Louis World's Fair, slipped away to New Jersey, where they eloped. A department head marrying a student would have caused a scandal, so the marriage was kept quiet until after commencement. Without any fanfare, Miss DeCora then became Mrs. Dietz or Mrs. DeCora-Dietz and he became an assistant instructor in the Native Art Department. He also remained on the football team, though not yet cracking the varsity line-up.

Several Carlisle veterans had reached the four-season eligibility limit and had to leave the team. Al Exendine, then a student at Dickinson School of Law, assisted Warner. Regulars Antonio Lubo, William Gardner, and Fritz Hendricks departed. These vacancies created opportunities for other talented young men. The most prominent was the Sac and Fox track star who had seen just enough action in 1907 to also letter in football.

James Johnson, Carlisle's 1903 Walter Camp First Team All-America quarterback and practicing dentist, returned in September 1908 to assist Pop with the coaching. Former Cornell end Bunny Larkin again spent two weeks of the preseason working with the ends before going to Ithaca to coach Cornell. He reputedly advised the players, "Boys, football is like this: When white man has ball, knock down white man. When Indian has ball, knock down white man." With Emil Hauser, aka Wauseka, as captain, the team looked forward to another good season but couldn't expect to duplicate the 1907 results.

James Johnson

The 1908 football schedule, printed in the September 25 edition of *The Carlisle Arrow,* differed little from the schedule published in the spring. The game against St. Mary's (probably Mt. St. Mary's in Emmitsburg, Maryland) scheduled for September 30 was dropped and was not replaced. The rest of the games remained the same, including away games with Minnesota and St. Louis to end the season.

Football practice started on September 1st with light workouts, having only one of last year's regulars present. Each week during the month, *The Carlisle Arrow* announced the return to campus of coaches, lettermen, and potential replacements as they trickled back from summer baseball, vacations, or outings. The first game on the schedule was with Albright College of Reading, PA on Saturday the 19th, but Albright telegraphed earlier in the week that they wouldn't be fielding a team that year. A practice game with Dickinson College's prep school, Conway Hall, was hurriedly arranged as a replacement.

The plucky Conway Hall boys put up a good fight in the mismatch, losing 53 to 0 in a game of two fifteen-minute halves. The Indian varsity play was ragged as many players hadn't had time to learn the new plays and signals. Those not in football condition yet sat out the game. The following Wednesday, Carlisle was an inhospitable host to the Lebanon Valley College Dutchmen, beating them 35-0. Because the visitors were so light and the temperature so hot, fifteen-minute halves were played. Virtually the entire Carlisle squad got into the game for a few minutes each.

Villanova was up next, on Saturday the 26th. The Indians were victorious, 10-0, in a fiercely fought game. On the following Friday, *The Carlisle Arrow* reported, "...there was a great deal more unnecessary roughness than is usually seen in a game...our team should learn to hold their tempers and not be drawn into any ungentlemanly behavior....Several of the football boys are nursing severe injuries and the team will not be in condition for tomorrow's game with State College at Wilkesbarre [sic]."

Gov. Edwin Stuart desired the neutral-site contest with Penn State to be a major event, "...the greatest game in the history of these two colleges." Senator Boies Penrose even used his influence to secure the Indian school band's attendance. This game proved to be a coming-out party of sorts for Jim Thorpe. But before he could show his stuff, Weaver blocked Mike Balenti's punt and ran it in for a touchdown, putting State ahead 5-0. Hirschman missed the extra point. Thorpe soon kicked a field goal from placement, bringing Carlisle close at 5-4. Later in the half he made a good run: "Breaking through the line and escaping several wicked tackles the big halfback wiggled through for thirty yards, bringing the crowd to its feet." In the second half, he

FORWARD PASS HAS RELEGATED MASS PLAY

ACCOMPANYING ILLUSTRATION SHOWS HOW FORWARD PASS IS MADE.

kicked two forty-five-yard field goals and missed a fourth attempt, but Carlisle's victory was assured at Indians 12–Penn State 5.

Syracuse provided the next week's opposition, but not at home. For the second Saturday in a row, Carlisle played at a somewhat neutral site, this time in Buffalo, New York. The previous week, the Orangemen had outgained highly rated Yale but couldn't push the ball across the goal line. Ted Coy scored a touchdown for the Eli for the only points in the game. After giving Yale such a hard time, Carlisle expected a good fight. Big Bill Horr had Syracuse's best gain when he skirted right end and sprinted across the field to avoid tacklers. But Albert Payne raced over and grabbed a fistful of Horr's jersey and tore it off him. The Indians improvised a changing room with blankets to allow the opposing player to don another jersey. Thorpe starred again by kicking three field goals and missing two by mere inches for a 12–0 Carlisle victory. A Buffalo newspaper observed, "Carlisle came here with stories of a weakened team but the men who were sent in to defend the Carlisle goal were in the pink of condition and they were trained to the hour."

After Susquehanna canceled the October 17 game, probably because the previous year's game had been a grotesque mismatch, Pop Warner put the open date to good use. He took the varsity to Franklin Field in Philadelphia to scout Carlisle's next opponent, Penn, in action against Brown. His assistants took other football boys across town to observe the Dickinson-Ursinus game.

A report out of Winslow Junction, NJ stated that Penn had been thwarted in its attempt to hold a secret practice in preparation for the upcoming game with Carlisle. Two suspicious men loitered around the inn at which the Quakers were staying. They claimed to be Penn law school alums interested in watching their team workout. Penn coaches restrained players from thrashing the pair and they left—supposedly to catch the train to Atlantic City. But they weren't on it. The men's identities were never discovered and several possibilities exist: 1) They could have been spying for Carlisle, 2) They could have been working for a future opponent. Carnegie Tech, Lafayette, Michigan, and Cornell remained on their schedule. Of these, Michigan would have been the least familiar with Penn's players and formations, or 3) Gamblers, the most likely in the author's opinion.

The day's news report from Carlisle stated that several players would not suit up for the game with Penn: left guard John Aiken for breaking training; fullback Pete Hauser and linemen Fritz Hendricks and Napoleon Barrel would still be hospitalized; and quarterback Mike Balenti had wrenched his back badly. Much-bruised Afraid-of-a-Bear would fill in for Aiken, who had been expelled from the school. The *Philadelphia Inquirer* headline read "Thorpe, [David] Little Old Man and Afraid-of-a-Bear Are All in Fine Shape." Warner brought his men to the city the night before the game. The only pre-game workout his players would get was a "...long walk in the morning just to limber them up for the afternoon's work." When asked about the recent spying incident, Warner responded, "In the first place I want to deny the published statement that Indian spies were sent to Winslow Junction to gather information about Penn's team. None were sent from Carlisle, and I do not know of any being there."

Almost 400 Carlisle students and employees took the special chartered train to Philadelphia. Their first stop after arriving was Gimbels department store. After a two-hour tour of the various departments, the contingent was taken by elevator to the seventh floor. There they sang football songs and the band played a few selections. They then marched to another room for a dinner consisting of vegetable soup a la Warner, browned potatoes touchdown fashion, fried oysters Mt. Pleasant style, and Wauseka pie with ice cream for dessert. Jim Thorpe hadn't earned himself a place on the menu yet. After eating, Gimbel Brothers then paid for their trolly ride to Franklin Field. During the game, the students were glad they brought their blankets, which provided a bit of shelter from the rain.

Philadelphia newspapers overcame their bias for the home team and were objective in their coverage. *The Inquirer* opined, "...but if the Indians break up this defense Penn will be helpless and the massacres of the last two years will be repeated." (Carlisle defeated Penn 24-6 and 26-6 in 1906 and 1907, respectively.) Its headlines after the game summed it up:

They Outplay Red and Blue, Which Team Is Lucky Not To Be Defeated
Thorpe Makes Grand Run of 43 Yards for Carlisle's Score
25,000 Cheer
Touchdowns Made and Goals Missed

Afterward, *The Inquirer* made no bones about the Quakers being outplayed, even allowing that Thorpe's grand forty-five-yard run was the highlight of the game. They acknowledged Penn's first-half touchdown to be the result of luck on an onside kick. They also attributed the normally reliable Thorpe's missed kicks to the muddy field and wet ball. Otherwise, the Indians would have run up a large score. This game put a belief about the Indians to the lie: "...the same crowd later saw the Indians, dispelling all belief in the tradition that once beaten they stay beaten, come back so strong and playing so fiercely that Penn was swept off the field." Penn was lucky to get away with the 6-6 tie.

In other news that day, Lehigh canceled their game with Dickinson College, protesting Frank Mt. Pleasant's eligibility due to the four-year rule and that he was a member of the Dickinson faculty. The latter charge seemed ridiculous on its face because Mt. Pleasant was still an undergrad at the college. Dickinson

FIVE CARLISLE STARS

From left to right—Little Old Man, left end; James Thorpe, left half; George Gardner, right end; Afraid-of-a-Bear, left guard; Little Boy, right tackle.

countered, "The plucky little quarterback has gone to Dickinson three years and prepared for college with two years at Conway Hall." Not mentioned was that Frank played for Carlisle at least some of those years.

Meanwhile, a dispatch from Portland, Oregon announced that Carlisle had called off its post-season trip to the Pacific Northwest. Games with Multnomah Athletic Club of Portland and Washington State College of Pullman would not be held. No reason was given for the cancellations.

A week after the tie with Penn came highly regarded Navy. Heavy on the coaches' minds was developing punters to approximate Mt. Pleasant's kicks. Warner cut scrimmages after Wednesday to keep the team in top physical condition for what was expected to be a tough game with a team they hadn't beaten the three times they had previously met.

In spite of fumbling several times in the first half, the Indians had the ball at the Navy thirty-yard line after a short Navy punt. Unable to make a first down, Balenti kicked a field goal from placement. This caught Navy off guard because they expected Thorpe to dropkick Carlisle's field goal attempts. Not stated was the reason for the change. It might have been the strong wind that day, Thorpe's difficulty the previous week, or using Thorpe as a decoy. Regardless, Carlisle won 16-6 on the strength of Balenti's four goals in spite of numerous penalties being called against the Indians. The Middies' touchdown came from recovering a punt Thorpe fumbled on his own twelve-yard line.

THE INDIANS COMMITTED HIGH TREASON ON THAT NAVY BUNCH

The next Thursday, twenty-five students, the first team, the substitutes, Coach Warner, Mrs. Warner, school physician Dr. Ferdinand Shoemaker, and financial clerk William H. Miller left for Boston in a special train car. They dined on a catered meal at Broad Street Station in Philadelphia while waiting for their connection. Harvard would be Carlisle's third undefeated opponent in a row. After eating, Afraid-of-a-Bear and William Winnie left to check into a hospital for a few days of treatments for unstated injuries. The rest of the group spent the time waiting for the train window-shopping. On board Victor Kelley led the group in singing a few songs.

When they reached Jersey City, New Jersey, their train car was put on a ferry. The boys enjoyed a moonlight cruise around Manhattan and up the East River to Holland, where their car was put back on railroad tracks. They arrived at Back Bay Station at 7:10 a.m. Friday morning and immediately checked into Copley Square Hotel. After breakfast, they took a bus tour of Boston's numerous historic sites. Pop Warner had the team run signals practice after lunch. That evening the famous Indians received a round of applause from the audience in Keith's Theatre when they entered to see the Vaudeville show playing there. On Saturday morning, they rested.

Before the opening kickoff, Warner noticed crimson football-shaped patches affixed to the fronts of Harvard's jerseys, and the game ball had been dyed to match. Earlier in the season, Warner had similar patches the color of normal footballs sewn on his players' jerseys to make it difficult for opponents to determine who had the ball. Harvard Coach Percy Haughton had outmaneuvered him. To settle the matter, Pop had the patches removed and Haughton replaced a normal ball for the crimson one.

Carlisle's players underestimated Harvard because the Crimson had only tied Navy where the Indians had moved the ball at will against the Middies. Overconfidence struck again. Carlisle had chances to score from inside the five-yard line but failed. They allowed Harvard to score on an on-side kick play that their backs should have covered. They seemed to lack their usual speed, aggressiveness, and teamwork. The result was a 17–0 shellacking. One bright spot was that Jim Thorpe's kick off went over the goal posts.

Cold weather struck for the Western University of Pennsylvania (renamed the University of Pittsburgh that year) game. The *Inquirer's* coverage said the October 24th game was played in a blizzard. That was surely hyperbole but it wasn't too far off. "There was an inch of snow before the game started and the fall was so heavy during the game that at times it was impossible to see the teams at all. However, after the first scrimmage in the snow and mud, it made no difference as Indian and 'Pitt' players looked alike after that." Field markings were covered with snow, so yard lines had to be marked with flags. This environment made passing impossible and kicking treacherous. The teams ground out little yardage. An altercation involving Pete Hauser occurred in the first half after an official accused him of being "peevish" at what he considered biased officiating.

Football at the University of Pittsburgh began in 1889. In 1908, the team became known as the "Panthers." This photograph showing the team in action was taken by Frank Bingaman. (Courtesy Carnegie Library of Pittsburgh.)

The fullback reacted by punting the ball to the far end of the field. When he refused to retrieve it, the official threatened to penalize the team if anyone other than Pete touched the ball. After considerable palaver, he relented. Warner must have lit a fire under his players at halftime because they started the second half with a purpose. The only score in the game was a touchdown by Little Old Man and the kick after by Thorpe. An interesting feature of this game was that players on both teams wore numbers painted or embroidered on large squares of cloth sewn onto the backs of their jerseys, an innovation Pitt had initiated that season.

The team returned home badly bruised, so Pop Warner kept them indoors and gave them light workouts to prepare for their upcoming road trip. Light workouts included a four-mile run on the elevated gymnasium track and running plays in the basketball cage[10]. Meanwhile, newspapers boosted Pop for the open Penn head-coaching position.

On November 17, Carlisle had informed the University of Denver that the game was off because a leave of absence could not be obtained for such a long journey. As soon as he learned of this, former senator and owner of *Rocky Mountain News* and *The Denver Times* Thomas M. Patterson wired President Theodore Roosevelt to grant the Carlisle Indians a leave of absence to allow them to play the game as scheduled on December 5th. The next day, Leupp wired Patterson, "Have sent your statement concerning Carlisle football

---

[10] Early basketball games were played inside a wire or rope mesh twelve feet high that surrounded the court. Its purpose was to prevent injury to players and spectators. The rules in place then gave possession of out-of-bounds balls to the first player who touched it.

team to the Superintendent [Friedman], with directions that the team should carry out its contract if possible, and to notify you of action taken." To Friedman, he added, "...although the office doesn't understand what the trouble is." He also telegraphed the University that he had directed the Indian team to fulfill the contract, if possible.

Friedman responded to Leupp that the western games had been scheduled before he took charge at Carlisle and that he was opposed to the students being away from campus for such a long time. He added that the boys did not care to play because the high altitude would put them at a disadvantage and "...it would be a terrible humiliation to be defeated by Denver University after they had played successfully against the greatest Universities in the East, and had defeated Annapolis." Friedman wired Denver officials that the game would be played and he informed Carlisle players and coaches that he would not consent to more than two games per year in the West and none west of the Mississippi.

Days later, Carlisle embarked on the western trip, starting with Minnesota in Minneapolis. The Gophers had played a soft schedule that year, playing five games and losing both Western Conference (later Big Ten) games they played. Having two weeks resting at home allowed Minnesota to prepare well for Carlisle. Prior to the game, Carlisle rooters considered the Gophers the easiest team on the western schedule based on their record coming into the game. Unfortunately, Mike Balenti, Afraid-of-a-Bear, and Sampson Bird were too banged-up to dress for the game.

The day before the game, members of Red Lake Indian Agency gave the Carlisle team a mascot in the form of a long-necked partridge, a fowl that frequents northern swamps and catches fish around the shores of lakes and rivers. This bird was intended to instill fright into the Minnesota players. It didn't.

Minnesota played its best game of the year, beating Carlisle 11 to 6. Plankers, Johnson, and Pettijohn played sensational football for Minnesota while Hauser, who left the game in the second half with blood streaming down his face, Little Old Man, and Thorpe starred for Carlisle. Warner considered this the most unfortunate event of the season, "...since there can be absolutely no doubt but that Carlisle had the better team, but was beaten because of the demoralized and crippled condition of her men and by the poor work of the officials." This was the Indians' tenth game, the last seven of which were played on the road against strong opponents. Warner denied the rumor that Minnesota had severed relations with Carlisle and added, "I regret to say that

Wauseka did momentarily lose his temper and strike the referee but the statement that the Indian players used such language as to drive ladies from the boxes is wholly untrue."

A November 24 article in *The Daily Sentinel* of Grand Junction, Colorado reported that President Roosevelt ordered Indian Commissioner Leupp to investigate why Carlisle was demurring from playing Denver. An excuse given was that the team couldn't stay away from school long enough to play the game. Another reason was that they were afraid playing in the high altitude could rupture the players' lungs. When they learned that the President wanted them to play, they agreed to honor the contract.

Against St. Louis University on Thanksgiving Day, the Indians started slowly but overwhelmed the Billikens 17-0. Hauser, Payne, and Little Boy (aka Scott Porter) scored touchdowns. St. Louis tried, and missed, three field goal attempts. Thorpe missed one of the three extra-point kicks.

The same day, November 26, *Lawrence Weekly World* ran an article discussing the possibility of Carlisle playing Haskell Institute while on the western trip. Harvey Meyer of Carlisle and Hervey B. Peairs of Haskell were negotiating details. The winner would be considered the champion of the Indian Schools. December 8th was the date desired for the game. This article also mentioned games with Nebraska and Denver that had been added to Carlisle's schedule, although not having been mentioned in Carlisle's press. The Haskell game was arranged for November 30, probably because Lawrence, Kansas was on the way from St. Louis to Lincoln, Nebraska. Due to having already played a heavy schedule and with Nebraska on tap in two days, Warner may have viewed this stop more as a scrimmage and recruiting event than as a game. Their 1904 contest at the St. Louis World's Fair had resulted in a flood of Haskell stars transferring to Carlisle. Several of the former Haskell students played for Carlisle on this trip. Mike Bynum listed a 12-0 win for Carlisle in his biography of Warner. The only newspaper accounts found for this game, short ones at that, were published the day after the game in the *Carlisle Evening Herald* and *The Sentinel.* They gave the same score.

Ahead of the game with Carlisle, Nebraska pundits opined that the Cornhuskers were a better team on paper than the Indians. They based this on comparative scores with Minnesota and St. Louis. Nebraska faculty members and media claimed that Carlisle was a professional team because Little Boy and Wauseka had played baseball for money before coming to Carlisle. But football fans bought tickets and the game went on.

Both teams were greeted by a temperature near zero and a rock-hard Antelope Park field. At first, things went Nebraska's way. Thorpe's punt went straight up into the air and Nebraska recovered the ball on Carlisle's ten-yard line. Three line plunges later, Ernest Kroger scored a touchdown and James Harvey kicked the extra point to give Nebraska an early 6-0 lead. Again showing that they could come back from behind, Carlisle moved the ball into field goal range. Hauser's kick went through the uprights to tighten the score to Nebraska 6-Carlisle 4. The Indians' next possession started on the home team's twenty-eight-yard line. Thorpe, Little-Old-Man, and Payne pounded the ball down to the two. Payne muscled it in through left tackle for Carlisle's first touchdown. Hauser missed the extra point. Carlisle went ahead 9-6. Hauser drop-kicked another field goal. Then Thorpe recovered Payne's punt and raced forty-five yards for a touchdown. And Hauser kicked the extra point to put Carlisle ahead at halftime 19 to 6. The Indians shifted into high gear in the second half with Payne, Kelley, and Wauseka scoring touchdowns. Hauser kicked three more extra points. The final score was Carlisle 37-Nebraska 6. Afterward, Nebraska players said they had never met a team that played cleaner.

The December 4 edition of *The Carlisle Arrow* contained the first mention in a Carlisle publication of the two added games, only including the score of the Nebraska contest. A wire report revealed that the bone of contention regarding the Denver game had been Carlisle's demand of a $3,000 guarantee. Eventually, the westerners agreed to pay this amount.

When the team arrived in Denver on Friday the 4th, a committee from the Colorado Traffic Club met them at Union Station. That contingent, accompanied by the 21st Infantry Band, escorted them to a luncheon at the club. Warner roused his charges early the morning of the game and ran them four blocks in the crisp Denver air. After breakfast in luxurious Brown Palace Hotel, he took them on a walking tour of the city.

Just three days after the Nebraska game, the Indians took the field against 7-0 University of Denver in the mile-high city's thin air. The Ministers never left the state that year. Their only away games were in Colorado Springs and Golden. The Indians, on the other hand, had played a grueling thirteen-game schedule, were 1,600 miles from home, and a mile above sea level. Amos Alonzo Stagg and Walter Eckersall were brought in from Chicago to officiate the most important game to be played in the region up to this time. The field was mostly playable as snow and sawdust covering the field were removed by game time. Standing water was limited to one sideline and a corner of the field. The soft field and mud made getting traction difficult.

The Indians had the best of the first half with Pete Hauser kicking two field goals for an 8-0 lead. Denver received the second-half kickoff on its eight-yard line. Using a series of end runs, trick plays, and line bucks, the Ministers advanced the ball down the field to Carlisle's one-foot line, where they turned the ball over on downs. They had a second chance after Carlisle punted, but Archie Brusse's field goal was all the scoring Denver could muster. Carlisle's offense tired in the second half but their defense held. Clem Crowley and Lieber played strong defensive games for the Skyline Conference Champions. Thorpe, Hendricks, Hauser, and Balenti starred for the Indians. The final score was Carlisle 8-Denver 4.

In the evening, the players of both teams were entertained by seeing the play, *Brewster's Millions*, at Broadway Theatre, which was decorated with pennants from both schools. After that, it was time to catch the train home. The team arrived just in time to be restricted to campus to avoid the town's measles epidemic.

About the school's future with football, *The Carlisle Arrow* reported: "The plans for next year are to considerably shorten the schedule and materially curtail the number of out-of-town games. It is probable that no western trip will be attempted, unless perhaps a game is arranged with Michigan, and there will be some good games at home. The season will undoubtedly end before Thanksgiving." The 12-0 win over 3-5-1 Haskell wasn't mentioned, possibly because Pop wasn't authorized to make the stop and it may have been little more than a scrimmage.

Walter Camp, Caspar Whitney, and numerous others released their selections for All-America players. Placing Jim Thorpe on his Third Team, Walter Camp observed, "Thorpe of Carlisle was a powerful runner, was in fact the man who could gain ground around Harvard's tackle [Hamilton Fish], and fought well on defense, besides being a good kicker from placement." *The Philadelphia Inquirer* chose him for their left halfback. Warner didn't place any of his players on his eleven-man All-America team. The *New York Herald* had Mike Balenti as its quarterback as did the *Washington Star*.

Parke Davis selected 11-0-1 Penn over 9-0-1 Harvard as national champions. Various pundits ranked Carlisle from third to fifth best team in the East. Penn's George Orton summarized the season "in the Middle States" in the *Spalding's Guide,* naming Carlisle the best team in the region behind Penn. He opined:

The new style of football is much to the liking of the Indians and they played a very up-to-date game. They made more ground than any other team in the country by the quick place kick, this reaching its highest development in the Indians' play. In field goal kicking, the Indians also stood first, as they scored about half their goals by this means. In Thorpe and Balenti, Carlisle had probably two of the best men playing back of the line last season. They proved wonderfully clever in running with the ball, getting off place-kicks, and in securing the ball on forward passes and on short place-kicks. Both are speedy and great dodgers. Thorpe's record as a foot ball player and track and field athlete shows that he is one of the greatest all-round athletes in the world to-day.

Gate receipts weren't nearly as lucrative as that had been in 1907 because the Indians played in neither New York City nor Chicago this year. Little Boy was elected captain for the 1909 season but couldn't serve because he had already played four seasons. Fritz Hendricks also couldn't play again for the same reason. Even without them, Carlisle appeared to still have a shot at having a good 1909 season but something again happened in the off-season to impact their prospects.

1908 Season Summary

Date	Opponent	Location	Indians	Opp.
Sept. 19	Conway Hall	Biddle Field, Carlisle, PA	53	0
Sept. 23	Lebanon Valley College	Indian Field, Carlisle Barracks, PA	35	0
Sept. 26	Villanova College	Indian Field, Carlisle Barracks, PA	10	0
Oct. 3	Pennsylvania State College	Driving Park, Wilkes-Barre, PA	12	5
Oct. 10	Syracuse University	Baseball Park, Buffalo, NY	12	0
Oct. 17	Susquehanna University	*Canceled*		
Oct. 24	University of Pennsylvania	Franklin Field, Philadelphia, PA	6	6
Oct. 31	Navy	Worden Field, Annapolis, MD	16	6
Nov. 7	Harvard University	Harvard Stadium, Boston, MA	0	17
Nov. 14	Western University of PA	Exposition Park, Pittsburgh, PA	6	0
Nov. 21	University of Minnesota	Northrop Field, Minneapolis, MN	6	11
Nov. 26	St. Louis University	Sportsman's Park, St. Louis, MO	17	0
Nov. 30	Haskell Institute	Haskell Field, Lawrence, KS	12	0
Dec. 2	University of Nebraska	Antelope Park, Lincoln, NE	37	6
Dec. 5	University of Denver	Varsity Park, Denver, CO	8	4

Won 11; Lost 2; Tied 1

14
Thorpe Bolts

Rule changes for 1909:

To clarify which players are eligible to receive forward passes, an end is not eligible if he stands between one foot and one yard of the line of scrimmage.

A field goal is reduced from four points to three points.

On a touchback, the team can either kick out, as had been the rule, or put the ball in play as a first down on their twenty-five-yard line.

Warner disagreed with the field-goal point change. He thought the kicking game was neglected by many and the points for field goals should be increased.

In November 1908, William Howard Taft was elected President. As was common practice, he wanted to appoint men aligned with his thinking in leadership positions. On December 8 in a report to the House of Representatives, Leupp abandoned his plan to abolish the Indian School at Carlisle. In late-December, he submitted his resignation, effective Inauguration Day, March 4, 1909. On January 2, he recommended that his position be abolished. He had apparently come to Pratt's position that the Bureau of Indian Affairs should be abolished. President Taft did not agree and appointed Robert G. Valentine to replace him. *The Daily Oklahoman* opined that Leupp's departure "...will not be the occasion of much regret among friends of the Indian. Mr. Leupp's abilities lie in the line of picturesque interviews or entertaining stories rather than in the solution of practical problems."

With Leupp out of the picture, Carlisle Indian School was no longer imperiled—at least for the time being.

In January, Jim Thorpe was elected captain of the track team as indoor practice had already started. He also joined the basketball team. The Warners moved into the new four-square house that was constructed using football funds. It was located near the front gate diagonally across the street from the Native Arts building.[11]

---

[11] Both buildings still stand as of this writing and the house serves as the quarters for the base Sergeant Major.

Lewis Tewanima

Lewis Tewanima kept Carlisle's name in the papers this winter by winning long-distance runs around the country. Joe Libby was elected captain because Little Boy could no longer play on the team due to the four-year eligibility rule. The twelve-game 1909 football schedule was published in the March 26 edition of *The Carlisle Arrow*. It featured five home games, more than they usually scheduled, and fewer hard games than before. Pop Warner complained that the big teams didn't want to play the Indians once they got to be a good team.

With a most successful track season concluded, Jim Thorpe waited at the train station to go to work on a farm for the summer under the school's outing program. Had it been a job to break horses on a ranch, Jim would have looked forward to it. But it was just to do ordinary dirt farming in which he had little interest. When Joe Libby and Jesse Youngdeer, who were also waiting for a train, told him they were going to North Carolina to play summer baseball, he decided to tag along. Soon, he was playing for Rocky Mount in the East Carolina League. While school officials may not have authorized this, they surely were aware of it.

Awaiting athletes upon their return from the summer were new athletics quarters. Joe Libby came back for football season but Thorpe, seeing little future playing football as a profession, and Youngdeer didn't. Having accompanied Thorpe on his departure, some blamed Joe for the star's absence. Without Thorpe, Little Boy, and some other regulars from last year, as captain, Joe had his work cut out for him. LSU coach Edgar R Wingard, on leave from his duties during the football season to observe eastern and northern football, assisted Warner with the team. He would also scout opponents for Warner. On September 10, *The Harrisburg Telegraph* claimed that Thorpe and Pete Hauser would be the only starters to return from the previous year's team. Apparently, Warner didn't broadcast Thorpe's departure.

The Indians opened against East End Athletic Club of Steelton with numerous new faces in the line-up. Dietz and Hendricks didn't suit up. They served as Timekeeper and Head Linesman, possibly to give Warner a better look at the new players in game situations. Carlisle won easily 35-0. On Wednesday, in spite of sloppy play with overly plentiful fumbles and poor forward passing, the Indians still swamped Lebanon Valley 36-0. On Saturday, Hauser scored a touchdown on a thirty-five-yard run and kicked a field goal to defeat Villanova in a hard-fought battle. A week later, the Indians overwhelmed Bucknell 48-6 in the last warm-up game and introduced more new players. Although crippled and playing limited minutes, Hauser made some sensational runs to demonstrate what determination and fierceness of play could accomplish.

An improving Penn State provided Carlisle the toughest opposition they had faced to this point in the season. Carlisle scored first when Hauser broke free up the middle, throwing off tacklers along his forty-yard long way to Penn State's goal line. He hurled himself over for the touchdown. Libby kicked the extra point. The first half ended with Carlisle leading 6-0. Penn State came out of the locker room to start the second half with renewed vigor. In three minutes, they had their own touchdown when Smith carried the ball over after making several long runs. Vorhis's dropkick for the extra point swerved into the goal post and bounced back, making the score Carlisle 6-Penn State 5. On their next possession, Vorhis kicked a thirty-yard field goal to put Penn State up 8 to 6. Carlisle then focused on the kicking game. Every time they got within range they attempted a field goal. They all missed but Penn State had to field the errant kicks. Vorhis caught one in front of his goal line but failed to run with it or punt it. Instead, he wandered back behind his goal line where Wauseka tackled him for a safety to tie the game.

Warner accused Penn State of rough play after two Penn State players were ejected from the game for slugging. After the game ended in an 8-8 tie, a Penn State player knocked the ball out of Hauser's hand. Wauseka jumped on the player who did the knocking. Indian subs and Penn State players fought so fiercely to get the ball that police had to separate them. The ball was Carlisle's because they had defeated Penn State the previous year. Newspapers warned of Carlisle possibly suspending play with Penn State.

The Indians outclassed Syracuse in the game played on the New York Giants' baseball diamond, but committed numerous inexcusable errors. Fumbles, misplayed punts, and frequent penalties for being offside, incomplete forward passes, and illegal use of hands put them in a precarious position. Carlisle scored first early in the game when Hauser carried the ball over at the end of a drive that featured his runs and Libby's passes. Libby kicked the extra point. After a few punt exchanges, a hard rain started to fall,

making both the ball and footing slippery. Darby's punt sailed over the heads of the Carlisle backs. Scully caught the ball on a bounce and scurried over the line for a Syracuse touchdown. Hartman made an easy kick to tie the game at 6-all. With the wind at their backs, the Indians used fake kick formations to disguise pass plays as they moved the ball down the field. Hauser ran the ball over from the one, but the punt out put the kick after goal at a bad angle. Libby missed it. Leading 11-6, the Indians moved the ball but repeatedly lost it on fumbles and penalties. Libby's misplay of a long Scully punt was disastrous. Joe touched the ball several times as it headed toward his goal but he couldn't corral it. Scully raced past him and grabbed the elusive pigskin on the three-yard line. Syracuse had no problems pushing the ball over, but Hartman missed an easy extra point. This tied the score at 11-all. It seemed the game was going to end this way until Carlisle mustered another drive. Battered, bruised, and limping badly, Hauser used onside kicks to make forward progress. On the last one, Jerome Kennerly recovered for Carlisle after Ainsley fumbled, setting up the Indians in good field position. Hauser made a few small gains through the line to move to the twelve-yard line. Libby knelt, caught the snap, and held the ball for Hauser's place kick. It sailed through the uprights for three points and a 14-11 Carlisle victory.

The evening after the game, the team plus one-hundred other Indians attended a performance of the musical comedy *Bright Eyes* at the Hippodrome. They also watched Maori dancers from New Zealand perform. The male Maoris challenged the Indians to a scrimmage at the Polo Grounds. No record of that ever happening was found. With a tough game ahead of them the next Saturday, it was unlikely Warner would have disrupted his training regime for this.

In ankle-deep mud and rain seven days later, the Indians battled Pitt. It took the heavier Iron City bunch fifteen minutes but they scored first when Roe fielded Hauser's punt on his own fifty-eight-yard line, ran around left end, and outdistanced the entire Carlisle team. Galvin kicked an easy extra point for a 6-0 Pitt lead. Hauser then missed a thirty-yard field goal. On the Indians' next possession, Libby's attempt hit the upright and bounced away. After recovering a Pitt fumble on their own sixteen-yard line, Hauser kicked a fifteen-yard field goal. The first half ended with the score Pitt 6-Carlisle 3.

Early in the second half, Galvin kicked a field goal from the thirty-three-yard line extending Pitt's lead to 9-3. When an Indian fumbled a punt on his ten-yard line, Roe recovered the ball for Pitt. Richards was pushed over for Pitt's second touchdown. Roe was unable to catch Galvin's punt out, so no extra point could be kicked. Warner made some unusual substitutions to shore up his team: Lone Star for Libby, Yankee Joe for LeClair (Shoshone from Wyoming), and Stansill "Possum" Powell for Kennerly. Having the substitutes play unfamiliar positions showed how versatile the Indians were. The final score was Pitt 14-Carlisle 3. Warner was disappointed with his team's play and the officiating. He thought the outcome would have been different on a dry field.

CARTOONIST WINNER'S IDEA OF YESTERDAY'S FOOTBALL GAME.

CAPT. ROE BOWLS OVER THE WHOLE INDIAN TEAM AND SCORES PITT'S FIRST TOUCHDOWN

THE ENTIRE PITT TEAM GET THE SECOND ONE OVER

Penn's management made a major mistake before their game with the Indians even started by seating the bands and rooters for both teams next to each other. Their discourteous behaviors soon spilled out onto the field. Right off the bat and aided by serious interference, Penn's Miller made a brilliant sixty-yard run for a touchdown. Braddock made the kick after. Soon after that, Scott punted over Libby's head. While chasing after it, the Carlisle quarterback grabbed hold of the ball but fumbled it. Cozens recovered it to set up Penn's second touchdown. A quarterback kick put Heilman in position to cross the goal line. Braddock again kicked the extra point.

With Penn in possession of the ball again, Miller made a twenty-yard run and was tackled hard by Wauseka as he was going out of bounds. Fretz came to Miller's assistance. Wauseka took exception to Fretz's action, and the two came to blows. Umpire Edwards intervened. Finding himself the target of a punch, he immediately ejected Wauseka from the game. Then, Warner took exception to one of Edwards' decisions. Seething with anger, Edwards escorted Warner to the sideline. When Warner objected, Edwards called a policeman to enforce his command. Meanwhile, Penn's Fretz said something about taking a club to Referee Okeson. That official ejected him from the game. The Penn faithful expressed their disapproval, but the referee wasn't moved and sent Fretz to the locker room. Not long after that, Edwards took offense to something an unnamed Carlisle official seated next to the bandmaster said, and with the assistance of a policeman, chased him back from the sideline.

Down two touchdowns, the Indians fought back. Deep in his own territory, Libby launched a forward pass to William Newashe, catching Penn defenders flat footed. He cradled the ball cleanly and rambled eighty yards down the field. Cozens raced after him, catching the Carlisle end just as he crossed the goal line. Libby kicked the extra point. Miller duplicated his first touchdown run for Penn's third touchdown. Braddock again made the kick after. Miller later tried a place kick from the forty-three-yard line but failed. The first half ended with Penn comfortably ahead 18–6.

Early in the second half, Penn moved the ball in steady, if not long, gains toward Carlisle's goal line. A fumbled forward pass caused a scramble that Braddock ended by grabbing the loose pigskin on the five-yard line. Heilman took it over on the next play. Braddock made his fourth extra point. Penn soon got the ball back at midfield after a Hauser punt. A penalty and a couple of runs moved the ball to the forty-five. Ramsdell ran it in from there but didn't make the kick. The final score was Penn 29–Carlisle 6.

After the game, *The Carlisle Arrow* attributed Carlisle's erratic play to inexperience and to stage fright for the several new players in their first big game.

George Washington University was supposed to be a change of pace but the Hatchetites put up a great fight in front of 2,500 fans, their largest crowd of the season. Perhaps as a hangover from the Penn game, the Indians sleepwalked through the first half. Some regulars sat out the game due to injuries, but Hauser played in spite of them. Ten minutes in, Hauser dropped back from GWU's twenty-two-yard line and kicked a field goal with Libby holding. Later with the ball on the Indian forty, GWU's Morse tried a drop kick but it fell ten yards short into Libby's arms. A few plays later, Morse tried again, this time from the Carlisle thirty-six. His kick went wide. He got a third shot after William Garlow dropped a forward pass, but it sailed six inches outside the post. The first half ended with Carlisle leading 3–0.

On GWU's first possession of the second half, Crafts returned Libby's punt with only Morse running interference for him. Crafts eluded all the Indian tacklers until Libby caught him on the Indian eighteen-yard line. When Morse circled Garlow's end for twelve yards, the partisan crowd put out a deafening yell: "Touchdown, George Washington! Put her over!" Morse then slipped the ball to his stocky halfback Ellis on a delayed pass. Ellis bulled his way through Peter Jordan and Lone Star for a touchdown and the lead, but missed an easy extra point. Two and a half minutes into the second half, the score was GWU 5-Carlisle 3.

The next four minutes, the ball seesawed in midfield. The Indians finally got into gear when Morse punted to Libby on his own thirty-eight-yard line. A line plunge by Hauser followed by an end run by Libby and a couple of forward passes advanced the ball within three yards of glory. Hauser slashed over off tackle for Carlisle's touchdown and Libby kicked the point after. With but two minutes left to play and the ball on GW's twenty-five, Hauser dropped back to kick another field goal. Defenders breached Carlisle's line and blocked the kick, but there was no other scoring and Carlisle won 9-5.

CAPTAIN LIBBY.
Quarterback on the Carlisle Indian football team. Libby is a fitting successor to the long line of star quarterbacks that have played on the Carlisle team in past years.

A home game against Pennsylvania College gave the Indians a much-needed easy victory. Having played Penn closer than Carlisle did, the battlefield boys thought they had a chance at beating the Indians. The unseasonably hot weather wore on both teams, but Warner wasn't able to substitute as freely as he would have liked in this blow out because some injured starters had to sit out the game, Hauser most notably. His replacement, Louis Dupuis, played a great game, including a fifty-yard kickoff return. The Indians scored almost at will in the first half when they built an insurmountable lead. They kept the battlefield boys on defense most of the game in the 35-0 blow out.

That *The Carlisle Arrow* included no coverage of the Brown game after touting it as the Indians' second most-important game of the year said something about the administration's reaction to the team's play. Brown was favored but Carlisle hoped to pull off an upset. The Indians got off to a good start when Hauser kicked a field goal from the thirty-yard line to give them a three-point lead. Then a Carlisle offside penalty gave Brown good field position. Several line plunges moved the ball to the Indians' ten-yard line and Regnier made six on a delayed pass play. From there Sprackling tossed the ball to Regnier on an end-over formation for a touchdown. Regnier kicked an easy extra point to put Brown ahead 6 to 3. Hauser later tried another field goal from the twenty-two but it was blocked. The Indians kept the ball in Brown territory the rest of the half. They got as close to scoring as the Brown two-yard line but the Brunonians held. The first half ended with the score Brown 6–Carlisle 3.

Sprackling returned the opening kickoff for a touchdown to start the second half. Regnier made the kick after. After several punt exchanges, Sampson Bird intercepted a pass on the Brown thirty-yard line. Hauser made three runs, ending with a touchdown. Libby missed an easy kick. Brown still led, now 12 to 8. Seeing an opportunity to win, the Indians played fiercely but penalties kept their offense far from the goal. After Regnier returned a punt to the Carlisle forty, Mackay broke through for a touchdown on a split-tackle play. Regnier kicked an easy extra point. Brown didn't let up and moved the ball to Carlisle's eighteen-yard line where Sprackling drop kicked a field goal. Poor tackling doomed the Indians to defeat. The final score was Brown 21–Carlisle 8.

With the Thanksgiving game five days away and in St. Louis, the Indians probably didn't return to campus but took a train straight to Mound City, so called because of the Indian mounds in the area. This was the first time Pop and younger brother Bill squared off against each other as coaches. His Indians had played against Bill when he was a player at Cornell but not when he was their coach.

St. Louis had its best chance to score when David Solomon fumbled the opening kickoff and St. Louis's Snyder recovered it on Carlisle's ten-yard line. Arens fumbled it back to the Indians on the next play. The Blue and White never threatened Carlisle's goal again. The *St. Louis Globe-Democrat* described the onslaught in stark terms:

> Hoodwinked and hypnotized by the native trickery and masterful strategy of the aborigines from faraway Carlisle, St. Louis University went down to an ignominious defeat on the gridiron at National League Park yesterday afternoon in a game that rang down the curtain

on a season of mediocrity in local football. The ultimate count was 32 to 0, which in its decisiveness does not tell how hopeless was the fight of the paleface against the redman. It was an unmerciful slaughter that lasted seventy-seven minutes and became all but unendurable at the close. Eventually it palled on the spectators.

Libby relied on the forward pass but mixed in criss-cross plays masking his intentions with fake and punt formations. The Indians' interference cut down defenders like wheat to the scythe. When he misjudged a punt, the ball rolled back to his goal line, where he regained it and ran eighty yards through St. Louis's feeble tacklers. Libby wasn't the only one having a good day. Hauser scored three touchdowns and kicked two extra points. Solomon, Yankee Joe and Newashe each scored one. The Hauser brothers, Pete and Emil, and Thomas "Ted" St. Germain were a stonewall combination swatting away the weak St. Louis attacks.

The young team's 8-3-1 finish wasn't terribly impressive but several players gained valuable experience that would bear fruit in the years to come. No player received All-America status after the season, and the team wasn't ranked.

The baseball season long over and having nothing pressing to do, Jim Thorpe visited Carlisle in December. He brought several new students from Oklahoma with him and hinted about reentering the school in time for track season. How he got there is unknown. A good guess is that the school paid his train fare for escorting the new students from Oklahoma.

1909 Season Summary

Date	Opponent	Location	Indians	Opp.
Sept. 18	East End Athletic Club of Steelton	Indian Field, Carlisle Barracks, PA	35	0
Sept. 22	Lebanon Valley College	Indian Field, Carlisle Barracks, PA	36	0
Sept. 25	Villanova College	Indian Field, Carlisle Barracks, PA	9	0
Oct. 2	Bucknell University	Indian Field, Carlisle Barracks, PA	48	6
Oct. 9	Pennsylvania State College	Driving Park, Wilkes-Barre, PA	8	8
Oct. 16	Syracuse University	Polo Grounds, New York, NY	14	11
Oct. 23	University of Pittsburgh	Forbes Field, Pittsburgh, PA	3	14
Oct. 30	University of Pennsylvania	Franklin Field, Philadelphia, PA	6	29
Nov. 6	George Washington University	National League Park, Washington, DC	9	5
Nov. 13	Pennsylvania College	Indian Field, Carlisle Barracks, PA	35	0
Nov. 20	Brown University	Polo Grounds, New York, NY	8	21
Nov. 25	St. Louis University	League Park, St. Louis, MO	32	0

Won 8; Lost 3; Tied 1

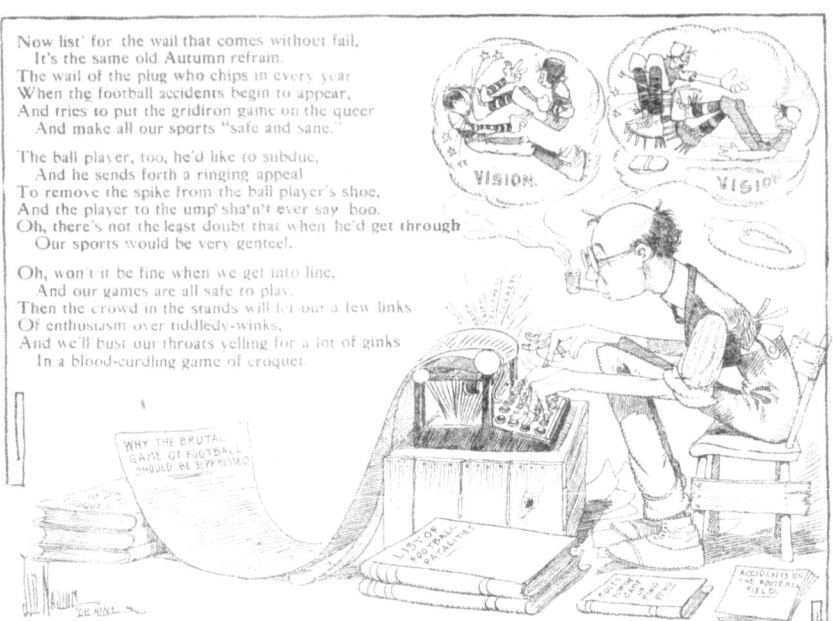

READY FOR THE OPERATION

From the Philadelphia Inquirer.

15

Major Rule Changes

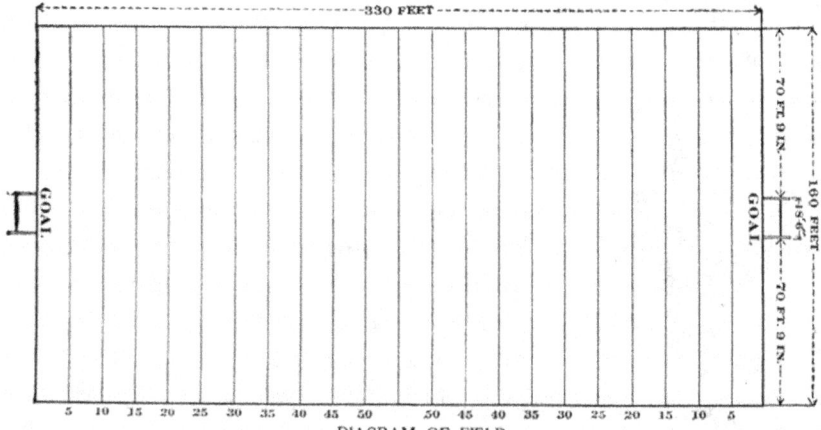

DIAGRAM OF FIELD.

The foot ball rules formerly provided that when the ball was put in play in a scrimmage, the first man who received the ball, commonly known as the quarter-back, might carry it forward beyond the line of scrimmage, provided in so doing he crossed such line at least 5 yards from the point where the snapper-back put the ball in play, and furthermore, that a forward pass might be made provided the ball passed over the line of scrimmage at least 5 yards from the point at which the ball is put in play. The rules now no longer place this 5 yard restriction upon either play, hence the longitudinal lines are omitted as unnecessary. The field is marked off at intervals of 5 yards with white lines parallel to the goal line, for convenience in penalizing fouls and for measuring the 10 yards to be gained in three downs. Thus the foot ball field comes back to the gridiron appearance as in 1902.

Rule changes for 1910:

The player receiving the center snap may now cross the line of scrimmage at any point. This rule change allows quarterback sneaks to be run, passes to be thrown anywhere at least five yards behind the line of scrimmage, and eliminates the need for lines five yards apart parallel to the sidelines.

The game is now divided into four quarters. Players previously removed from the game, except those ejected, can be returned to the game once, at the beginning of a later period.

No player can leave the field of play during the short intermissions between quarters. No one can come on the field except for one who looks after the physical condition of the players.

Crawling to advance the ball is now penalized. Seven players must now be on the line of scrimmage. A passer or kicker must be at least five yards behind the line of scrimmage and forward passes cannot travel more than 20 yards past the line of scrimmage.

The ball carrier can no longer be pushed or pulled by his teammates.

On January 1, 1910, the Indian Service announced that the federal government is "apt to abolish football at the government Indian schools." The troubles in the Carlisle-Penn game and the injuries received by a Haskell player in a different game had something to do with the rumor. Thorpe did not return to Carlisle for track, or any other season, that year, probably because he saw baseball as the only sport at which an athlete could support himself.

Edward Bracklin with lacrosse stick

Athletic Director Warner announced in the January 14, 1910 edition of *The Carlisle Arrow* that interscholastic baseball was being discontinued at Carlisle. That sport was being replaced by lacrosse. The loss of good athletes, Thorpe in particular, to professional baseball likely had a lot to do with the change. The 1910 football schedule was published on April 15 with the comment: "all the games will be played in the East and practically all will be played on college grounds." Princeton requested a game now that Carlisle was weaker and Penn State was dropped "on account of the latter team's unsportsmanlike and ungentlemanly conduct in the game at Wilkesbarre [sic] last year." Anonymous reports from Carlisle said that Warner had received requests for games from schools they didn't play in 1909: Cornell, Harvard, Princeton, and Yale. Of these, only Princeton ended up on the schedule.

In June, Frank Mt. Pleasant graduated from Dickinson College with a Bachelor of Philosophy degree, the first Indian to do so in the college's 127-year history and the first Carlisle student in its thirty-one years of existence. Several others had graduated from Dickinson School of Law but not Dickinson College.

Sampson Bird (often misspelled in Carlisle records as Burd) and Margaret Blackwood left Carlisle at the end of the school year to live and work on one of Bird's family's ranches near Browning, Montana. Marrying in July, his bride was struck with spinal meningitis on their honeymoon. Within a month she was dead. Sam returned to Carlisle and rejoined the football team. William Gardner assisted Pop for several days before leaving for Kentucky to coach Louisville Manual High School. Joe Libby coached the third team in addition to playing on the varsity and Wauseka trained the second team.

Warner was optimistic the rule changes would benefit the Indians and his system. Allowing the player who received the center snap to cross the line of scrimmage at any point made possible for Warner's single-wing formation to come to full fruition. Pop eliminated the traditional quarterback role, repositioned as the blocking back behind a tackle. The center snap would come directly to the left halfback (tailback in Warner's scheme) or the fullback. That player would run with the ball, pass it, kick it, or hand it off to another player. With the quarterback as the blocking back, the single-wing could concentrate the most force at the point of attack of any football formation. The right halfback was positioned outside an end and renamed wingback. A weakness of the single-wing was its dependence on a triple-threat player at tailback because really good ones didn't come around often. Frank Mt. Pleasant was gone, as was Jim Thorpe. Team captain Hauser, a fullback, was the closest thing they had this year.

Carlisle kicked off its season with a Wednesday warmup at home against Lebanon Valley College. Curiosity about the effect the new rules would have on the game brought out a huge crowd at the Indian School, particularly from Harrisburg. Dickinson College's coach shifted his team's practice to an earlier time to avoid the blistering heat and to let his boys attend the Indian School game. Newspaper coverage of the game didn't include a play by play, so summary information was all that was published. The Carlisle line-up included

1910 Carlisle Indians

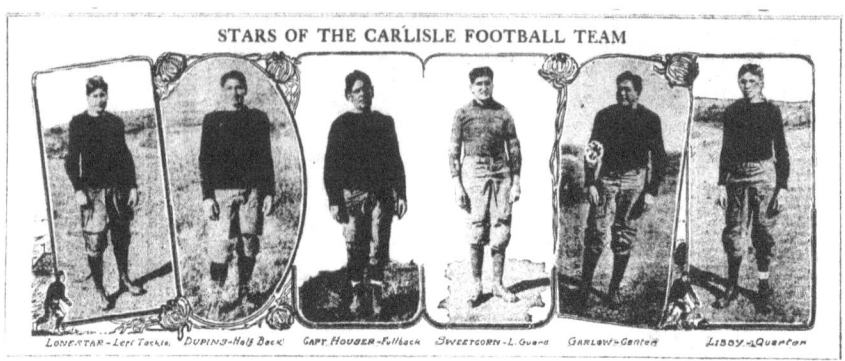
STARS OF THE CARLISLE FOOTBALL TEAM
LONE STAR - Left Tackle, DUPUIS - Half Back, CAPT. HOUSER - Fullback, SWEETCORN - L. Guard, GARLOW - Center, LIBBY - Quarter

several new names for both starters and substitutes. Joel Wheelock, Dupuis, Hauser, and Alex Arcasa each scored two touchdowns. Peter Gaddy scored one. Libby kicked four extra points, Hauser two. The details weren't provided for the safety that accounted for the Indians' other two points in this 53-0 thrashing of a smaller team. After the game, Warner congratulated the LVC team for their plucky play after the four eight-minute quarters were finished: "This is the best team you ever sent down from Lebanon Valley. You played a pluckier game than I thought you would, and under the new rules, 53-0 is a better score than 35-0 last year."

Three days later on Tuesday, the Indians played Villanova in "the first important game played under the new rules" as it was advertised. And advertised it was. Carlisle artist and right tackle Lone Star Dietz made signed sketches of his team's players to promote the game. Special trains were scheduled to bring spectators to Harrisburg for the game, and the rates on regular runs were reduced to entice more to come. A game between Harrisburg High and Conway Hall was scheduled for the field before the big game. Other local teams shifted their game times to allow their teams to attend. The George W. Bogar Seven-Mile Handicap Marathon, which featured America's top distance runner Lewis Tewanima and two of his Carlisle Indian School teammates, Mitchell Arquette and John Goslin, was scheduled to finish well ahead of the start of the football game. Haberdasher H. Marks and Son displayed in their window the silver, gold-lined loving cup adorned with both schools' colors that sat on an ebony base. The fourteen-inch high trophy was to be awarded to the winning team on the field or later at the Majestic. The management had reserved box seats for both teams to see the play *The Beauty Spot* at that theater.

The Carlisle contingent's train arrived about 1:15 p.m. They marched to Market Square where their band played several selections, after which they walked to Island Park over the Market Street bridge. The Carlisle band set up in an empty area in front of the stands and struck up "Hail to the Conquering Heroes" when the Indians took the field. The veritable army of cheerers kept up their Indian yells for five minutes. Villanova rooters and glee clubs made some noise for their team as well.

All expected a close, hard-fought game as the two teams usually played, but this time Villanova had a weight advantage. Their starters averaged 193 pounds per man where Carlisle's only weighed 165. The scoreless first half, in which only two first downs were made, was a series of punts, penalties, incomplete passes, and injuries. At one time, seven players were down at once. Warner attributed the frequent knockouts to the beastly heat too hot for football.

At halftime, the Carlisle band marched over the field and played several songs to loud applause. The crowd gave Tewanima a huge ovation when he walked onto the field carrying the trophy he won and wearing the medal from the seven-mile marathon that day.

Early in the second half, Dupuis intercepted a Villanova pass on his fifty-yard line. Wheelock then ran for twenty yards and Dupuis made shorter runs off tackle before going for twelve around his right end. Wheelock was held for no gain, then Dupuis made three through right tackle and followed it around right end for a touchdown. Hauser kicked the extra point. After that, it was a series of stalled drives, punts, and penalties. Carlisle won 6-0.

On Saturday, the Muhlenberg Cardinal and Gray gave the Indians a good game for the first seven minutes, advancing the ball as far as the Carlisle four-yard line. After that, it was all Indians. Muhlenberg had no answer for the Indians' passing attack and line bucks. Lone Star, Wheelock, Dupuis, Hauser, Edward Bracklin, and Bird stood out. Wheelock scored two touchdowns. Garlow, Hauser, Dupuis, and Gaddy each had one. Island kicked an extra point. Hauser kicked the other five plus a field goal to top off Carlisle's 39-0 win.

Western Maryland College canceled their game with Carlisle because of injuries they had sustained in their defeat of Dickinson College. This gave Warner a week to prepare for Carlisle's game with Dickinson. Pop renewed competition against the Red and White after a five-year hiatus. Both teams showed improvement since their earlier games, but the collegians were no match for the Indians. Carlisle scored a touchdown in each quarter with Wheelock and Dupuis making two each. Hauser kicked the extra points. He even tried a fifty-five-yard field goal but missed. The final score was Carlisle 24–Dickinson 0.

Bucknell didn't put up its usual tough game against the Indians. Instead, Hauser had a red-letter day, making hair-raising runs and kicking goals. Late in the game, he kicked a forty-five-yard field goal and, seconds later, followed it with a fifty-yard touchdown run for the final score of the day. Pete, Wheelock, and Dupuis had three touchdowns apiece for the game. Hauser kicked all six extra points and made the field goal. The final score was Carlisle 39–Bucknell 8.

With Hauser and several others too injured to play, substitutes and men put in unfamiliar positions took the field against Pennsylvania College. The Indians played an understandably ragged game but prevailed 29–3. The Gettysburg quarterback attempted three field goals, making one. Wheelock scored two touchdowns for Carlisle. Newashe, Wheeler, and Arcasa each had one and Newashe kicked four extra points.

Forest E. Craver, Dickinson College Advisory Coach, who was officiating the game, warned undersized guard Asa Sweetcorn, aka Esau Fastbear, twice about rough play. The third time he saw it, he ejected Warner's wildest and most unpredictable warrior. When Sweetcorn asked what he had done, Craver replied, "Slugging."

"Dyah see me?" Sweetcorn challenged.

"Out."

"Dyah see blood?"

"Out!"

"When I slugs 'em you see blood," said Sweetcorn as he stomped off the field.

An early field goal was all Syracuse needed to defeat a battered Carlisle squad. They later scored two touchdowns on long runs of fifty and seventy yards. Syracuse won 14 to 0. Things didn't get better the next week.

Princeton always had a muddy field when Carlisle came calling, and 1910 was no different. This time the game was played in a driving rain. The dash and sensational plays that would have been prevalent under dry conditions weren't possible in the mud. Unbeaten and unscored upon Princeton's greatest advantage was Ballou's punting. The weather conditions didn't impede him as his punts were "all low spirals that were difficult to catch and always took a long low bound on striking the ground." As a result the game was almost entirely played in Carlisle's territory. After a scoreless first half, the Tigers' Pendleton caught one of Hauser's punts at midfield and dashed twenty yards along the sideline. He then ran for eighteen yards off tackle, putting the ball on the Indians' twenty-three-yard line. Sparks took it from there, and in the course of three plays, he ran, dodged, and squirmed away every time he appeared to be stopped for certain until he crossed the Indians' goal line. Pendleton kicked the extra point. Neither side was able to score after that. Princeton won 6-0.

CARLISLE INDIANS LINED UP IN BATTLE ARRAY

The next Saturday the Indians played the Penn Quakers in better weather conditions. In the opinion of Penn's hometown newspaper, Carlisle outplayed Penn, but the Indians' miscues and the Quakers' kicking game saved the day for the home team. After several punt exchanges, Hauser's kick into the wind went out of bounds on the Carlisle twenty-eight-yard line. Penn lost no time in taking advantage of the opportunity. A forward pass to Jourdet moved the ball to the three-yard line. Two plays later, Mercer plunged over for a touchdown. Cozens kicked the extra point. After a missed Penn field goal attempt, Carlisle elected to rush the ball rather than punt it away. On one play, Hauser uncorked a pass that unfortunately landed in Cozen's waiting arms. He raced the interception twenty-five yards for Penn's second touchdown. Ramsdell kicked the extra point for a 9-0 Penn lead. In the third quarter, Hauser attempted a field goal from the Penn eighteen-yard line. Cozens broke through the Carlisle line and blocked the kick with his face. After the bleeding stopped, the game continued. Shortly, Mercer misplayed Hauser's straight and high punt and Wheelock took possession for the Indians but an unnecessary roughness penalty on the tackle of Mercer gave the Quakers fifteen yards and the ball. He then electrified the crowd by making a sixty-yard run for a touchdown. However, an official cited an infraction and called it back. Late in the third quarter, the Indians got going when Wheelock caught Hauser's onside kick on the Penn thirty-four. Powell and Wheelock advanced the ball to the ten using sliding tackle plays. Hauser then hit Wheelock with a pass for an Indian touchdown. The punt out didn't work so no extra point could be kicked. Penn led 12 to 5. Penn scored their final touchdown in a similar way when Scott hit Kaufman with a forward pass. The Indians blocked Cozens' extra point kick. Penn won 17 to 5.

For once, Carlisle had the advantage on a soft field when they played Virginia because the Indians were heavier on average than the Wahoos. Hauser and Libby were out nursing injuries, so new players were tried and others again were put in positions other than the ones they normally played. Most noteworthy was Newashe, who, filling in for Hauser at fullback, scored all four Carlisle touchdowns. The Indians made most of their yardage from fake punt plays and crossbucks. Their interference continued to improve, increasing the length of their runs. They only tried four forward passes and all four failed. The Cavaliers started strong, but by the end of the first quarter were running out of steam.

Early in the second quarter, Newashe dropped back as if to punt, but even though the Virginians expected a fake, the big fullback ripped off a twenty-yard gain. Wheelock hit the line for gains of twelve and five yards before Bracklin shot through left tackle for eight. With the ball now on the Virginia ten-yard line, Newashe crashed into the line for six yards. On his next carry, he put the ball over the line for Carlisle's first touchdown. His extra point kick missed. When the Indians got the ball back, a penalty put them in an obvious punting situation. Newashe dropped back and Garlow snapped the ball to him. Before the Cavaliers knew what happened, he was off on his way to a thirty-five-yard gain for one of the more spectacular plays of the game. Bracklin made another first down and Newashe circled the end for twenty-two more. On a lateral to Powell, the Indians made another first down. Wheelock then hit the line for five and Newashe made five more, putting the ball on Virginia's two-yard line. Newashe ran it over on a split play for Carlisle's second touchdown. Powell's kick was good. The first half ended with Carlisle leading 11 to 0.

A refreshed Indian team started the second half with a hurricane offense, bowling over Virginia's line until the ball rested on the ten-yard line. Wheelock knifed through the defense, but his touchdown was called back for holding. Newashe faked a kick and threw a pass that Virginian Bowen intercepted but bobbled. Lone Star recovered it on the fifteen. That play ended the third quarter. Lone Star and Sweetcorn opened a large hole for Newashe to begin the fourth quarter. That was all Newashe needed. Powell kicked the extra point. Carlisle now led 17-0. Later, Wheeler returned a punt thirty-five yards, setting up Carlisle in a pretty position. Runs by Bracklin and Wheelock moved the ball to Virginia's four-yard line. Newashe bulled it over but Powell missed the kick. Carlisle then lead 22-0. It looked like that was where the game would stay until, with the sun lowering, Newashe tried another forward pass. Jordan, his target, got tied up in Virginia's interference, allowing Honaker to make the interception. He dodged the three Indians nearest him and raced down the field. Newashe raced after him and made a desperate dive to tackle him but he missed. Honaker completed his eighty-five-yard touchdown run unmolested but Todd missed the kick by inches. The game ended with Carlisle ahead 22 to 5.

The Indians next challenged the unbeaten, unscored-upon Midshipmen in one of the most stubbornly contested games seen on the Annapolis gridiron in several years. Both teams moved the ball but failed to score in the first three quarters. Navy tried, and missed, five field goal attempts where Carlisle tried none, preferring, but failing, to score touchdowns instead. Officials assessed penalties frequently throughout the game. Five minutes into the fourth fourteen-minute quarter, Navy mounted a fifty-yard drive in which halfback Dalton broke loose for a thirty-yard run. Two plays later with the ball on the Carlisle three-yard line, Dalton carried the ball over but fumbled. The big guard Brown pounced on it for a Navy touchdown and then kicked the extra point for the only scoring in the game. Navy won 6-0. The Middies finished their season two weeks later, still unbeaten and unscored upon. A highlight of the trip was touring Commodore Dewey's flagship, made famous in the Battle of Manila Bay in the Spanish-American War, the *Olympia*.

Sometime after November 4, a game against Harvard Law School All Stars was slipped into the schedule during the week between the Navy and Johns Hopkins games. Former Harvard star Hamilton Fish, then enrolled at Harvard Law School, yearned to get back out onto a football field. Surrounded by football-playing alums of six other colleges, he put together a team of former stars and scheduled a few games. The first was against the Harvard varsity, which beat them 6-0 on two field goals. A game with Carlisle was touch and go because so many of the Indian starters had been injured.

Eventually, the game was scheduled for November 16, the Wednesday between the Navy and Johns Hopkins Saturday games.

Capt. Fish recruited seven well-known former players from Harvard, four from Yale, four from Princeton, and one each from Michigan, Nebraska, and Holy Cross. Since they weren't long out of college, they were still in playing condition. Carlisle players, on the other hand, after having played eleven games, were beat-up. Libby, Hauser, and Newashe weren't in the line-up, but several substitutes were. Warner patched together an eleven from those well enough to play. That they did as well as they did was a miracle. The only score was Philbin's first-quarter dropkick field goal for Harvard Law. The game was played mostly on Carlisle's end of the field. The Indians got no closer to Harvard's goal than the thirty-yard line. The final score was Harvard Law 3–Carlisle 0.

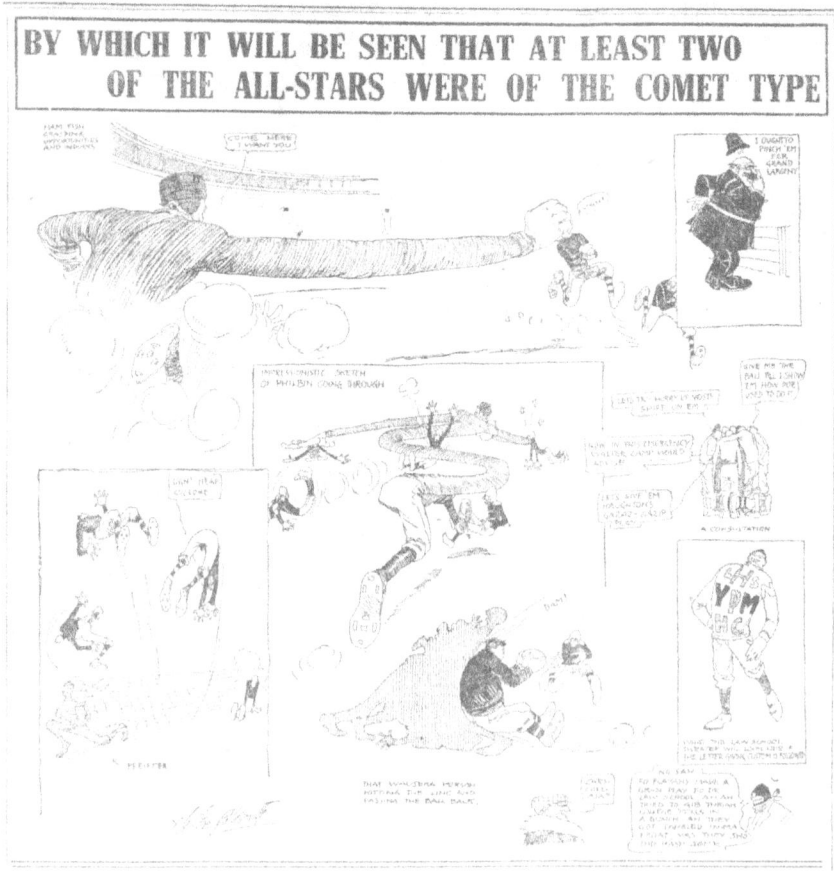

Libby, Hauser, and Newashe weren't healed enough to play against Johns Hopkins on Saturday, so Warner had to again patch together a line-up by using backups and shifting starters out of position. Joel Wheelock must not have been able to play because he served as assistant linesman. The Black and Blue fought the Indians for every inch of ground and almost scored when Stollenwerck's dropkick from the fifty-yard line hit an upright and bounced back. Dupuis scored both Carlisle touchdowns and Powell kicked both extra points. On the first play of the second quarter, Dupuis burst through left tackle and eluded three potential tacklers on his fifty-three-yard touchdown run. Powell made a difficult kick for the extra point. Going into the last minute of the game, Carlisle's 6-0 lead still held. The Indians hurriedly moved the ball by a series of forward passes and line plunges until Dupuis got the ball on the Hopkins' eight. He momentarily fumbled it before carrying it across. Powell again made the kick for a 12-0 Carlisle victory.

JUST AS THE HOPKINS INTERFERENCE IS STARTING

This snapshot shows the Indians breaking through the locals, awaiting an opportunity to diagnose the play.

Five days later on Thanksgiving Day, Carlisle took on Brown, on the Brunonians' home field this time. That the Indians had no trouble moving the ball was evidenced by their not having to punt a single time that day. The Indians had the ball on the Brown eight-yard line in the first quarter but turned the ball over on downs. Later in the quarter, Spradling dropkicked a field goal from the Carlisle forty-yard line for a 3-0 Brown lead. Brown scored its first touchdown in the second quarter after a long drive. Smith kicked the extra point for a 9-0 Brown lead at halftime. The Indians made the game more interesting in the third quarter when Hauser scored a touchdown at the end of an eighty-five-yard long drive and kicked the extra point to narrow Brown's lead to 9 to 6. It looked like the Indians were going to duplicate the feat on their next possession but they fumbled the ball away at the Brown twenty-yard line. In the fourth quarter, Hauser attempted a field goal that would have tied the game, but his kick came up short. A Carlisle fumble on their own thirty-five-yard line set them up to lose. Two successful forward passes netted the Brunonians their second touchdown. Smith made the kick to seal the 15-6 Brown win.

The team's 8-6-0 record was far from impressive, but several players gained valuable experience. No player received All-America status after the season and the team wasn't ranked. Warner had thought the new rules would benefit the Indians but it would take something special to make that happen.

1910 Season Summary

Date	Opponent	Location	Indians	Opp.
Sept. 21	Lebanon Valley College	Indian Field, Carlisle Barracks, PA	53	0
Sept. 24	Villanova College	Island Park, Harrisburg, PA	6	0
Sep. 28	Muhlenberg College	Indian Field, Carlisle Barracks, PA	39	0
Oct. 1	Western Maryland College	Canceled		
Oct. 5	Dickinson College	Biddle Field, Carlisle, PA	24	0
Oct. 8	Bucknell University	Driving Park, Wilkes-Barre, PA	39	0
Oct. 11	Pennsylvania College	Indian Field, Carlisle Barracks, PA	29	3
Oct. 15	Syracuse University	Archbold Stadium, Syracuse, NY	0	14
Oct. 22	Princeton University	University Field, Princeton, NJ	0	6
Oct. 29	University of Pennsylvania	Franklin Field, Philadelphia, PA	5	17
Nov. 5	University of Virginia	American League Park, Washington, DC	22	5
Nov. 12	Navy	Worden Field, Annapolis, MD	0	6
Nov. 16	Harvard Law School	Harvard Stadium, Cambridge, MA	0	3
Nov. 19	Johns Hopkins University	Homewood Field, Baltimore, MD	12	0
Nov. 24	Brown University	Andrews Field, Providence, RI	6	15

Won 8; Lost 6; Tied 0

16
Carlisle's Best

Rule changes for 1911:

To assist in measuring the progress of the ball, it is desirable to provide two lightweight poles about six feet in length, connected at their lower ends by a stout cord or chain ten yards in length. (Chains had been in use for decades.)

A player turning to catch a forward pass must not be tackled until he has caught the ball.

If the ball, while in play, hits an official, it shall not be declared dead, but play shall continue.

Throwing a player to the ground after the ball has been declared dead is unnecessary roughness.

1911 Team Photo
Top row, l-to-r: Powell, Hugh Wheelock, Lone Star, Warner, Jordan, Busch.
Middle row, l-to-r: Roberts, Bergie, Newashe, Bird, Thorpe, Joel Wheelock, Garlow.
Bottom row, l-to-r: Arcasa, Sousa, Welch.

Carlisle's prospects for 1911 didn't look good early on. Pete Hauser was gone. He was working for a sporting goods company and assisting Coach John Heisman at Georgia Tech. His brother Emil, aka Wauseka, Louis Dupuis, Asa Sweetcorn, Jerome Kennerly, Edward Bracklin, and Joe Libby were also gone, leaving Pop with big holes to fill in the line-up.

A chance meeting on a dusty Anadarko, Oklahoma street changed Carlisle's fortunes. Carlisle alum Albert Exendine, who was visiting there for a few weeks, unexpectedly ran into a no-longer-skinny Jim Thorpe. In his two years out of football, Thorpe had filled out, giving him a perfect athletic physique, but his minor league baseball experience hadn't gone well. Bankrupt, the East Carolina League had folded in midseason, leaving Thorpe with nothing to do. An orphan without a home, he was wandering aimlessly around Oklahoma.

Exendine immediately phoned Warner to let him know of Jim's availability. Thorpe was hesitant at first, thinking the Indian School wouldn't want him back. To sweeten the pot, Pop offered Jim the possibility of an opportunity to compete in the 1912 Olympic Games if he came back. But he didn't need that enticement. Jim returned to Carlisle in time for football camp and moved into the athletic quarters with another orphan, quarterback Gus Welch, as his roommate.

Assisting Warner that year were Charles "Pat" O'Brien, formerly a student at Dickinson and Bucknell and a coach of Conway Hall, and Albert Exendine, who was there for a few weeks before he started his season as head coach at Otterbein College in Ohio. Captain Sampson Bird returned from his summer in Montana with five new students.

Football camp started well with thirty-five boys wanting to make the team. Veterans from the previous year's team, including Garlow, Hugh and Joel Wheelock, Lone Star, Powell, Jordan, and Acasa, dribbled in. Thorpe's return encouraged them all. If nothing else, Jim would shore up the kicking game, which had been a weak spot the year before. The team's improvement stimulated the players to work harder to compete for spots on the roster. Soon, Pop thought he might have something at last.

On September 15, Vanderbilt University announced that they had filled a gap in their schedule that was created by Carlisle reneging on playing them. The university claimed that Carlisle had signed a contract with them but canceled when Harvard became available. If this happened, it had to have been months earlier because the schedule Carlisle released in March included the Harvard game on November 11. Harvard had dropped Carlisle two years earlier to make room for Cornell.

As usual, Carlisle opened its season a week earlier than other teams, this time against Lebanon Valley College. Just forty seconds after the start, "Possum" Powell crossed LVC's goal line for the Indians' first touchdown for 1911. He soon had two more as did Thorpe. Joel Wheelock, Eloy Sousa, James Crane, Henry Broker, and Albert Lorentz had one each. Although the Dutchmen didn't challenge the Indians, they gave Warner the opportunity to try men in new positions in game situations. That the Indians only made three of the ten extra points concerned Warner because the kickers had used poor judgement and seemed careless. The final score was Carlisle 53-LVC 0.

Four days later, on Wednesday, the Indians hosted one of the strongest teams Muhlenberg College had fielded up to that time. The game started slowly with the visitors' defense holding strong for five minutes. Then Thorpe, apparently adjusting to the slippery, wet footing, broke loose for a sensational ninety-yard run in which he dodged or brushed off every defender for a Carlisle touchdown. He missed the kick after touchdown. The first ten-minute quarter ended with the score Carlisle 5-Muhlenberg 0. Thorpe scored three touchdowns in the second quarter and made one of the extra points. Lone Star "made one of the most brilliant runs ever seen on the local field at the close of the half," in the opinion of *The Philadelphia Inquirer,* but he didn't score. The sixteen points scored in this quarter brought the score to Carlisle 21-Muhlenberg 0 at halftime. Warner substituted liberally in the second half. Welch and Arcasa came off the bench to score two touchdowns and kick one extra point, respectively. The final score was Carlisle 32-Muhlenberg 0.

Three days later, on Saturday, Dickinson College "traveled" across town for their first game of the season. In spite of great runs by Thorpe and Hyman Goldstein for their respective sides, neither team scored in the first quarter. Powell scored twice in the second quarter thanks to the tricky sidestepping of Welch and Arcasa. Thorpe made one of the kicks, putting Carlisle ahead 11-0. In the third quarter, he made a touchdown and kicked the extra point to end the scoring for the game played in eleven and ten minute quarters. Thorpe, Arcasa, Powell, Bird, Joel Wheelock, Henry Roberts, Lone Star, and Newashe were constantly active and effective in the 17-0 Carlisle win. However, Warner wasn't satisfied with his team's play, especially the line. The Dickinson line had outcharged his men and had broken up the Indians' interference around end. Thorpe's punts were disappointing due to the line failing to give him enough protection, and the center snaps were too slow to get punts off when being rushed. Warner put some old men at their prior positions, others at new ones, and new men at old men's positions. He needed to find the right combination. They only ran signals and practiced kicking the day before the next game. Pop held injured Gus Welch out and put Bird at the unfamiliar position of quarterback (blocking back in the single-wing formation) while Welch scouted Georgetown, the following week's opponent.

Nineteen husky men from the Mt. St. Mary's College team drove to Carlisle in automobiles on Saturday morning, probably because there was no direct train service between Emmitsburg, Maryland and Carlisle. The Indians were waiting for them. Loughran fumbled Thorpe's kickoff and the big Indian recovered it. A few short plays later, Thorpe was thrown across the goal line for Carlisle's first score. After a series of punt exchanges and fumbles, the Indians pulled off some onside kicks and end runs for the second score. Three touchdowns later, the first half ended with the score Carlisle 30-Mt. St. Mary's 0.

Liberal substitution in the second half slowed the scoring but, after Sousa and Fred Broker gained confidence, the Indians made three more touchdowns. A Carlisle player's careless fumble in the fourth quarter allowed the Indians' goal line to be crossed for the first time this season when alert end Malloy picked up the ball and ran sixty yards for the Mt. St. Mary's touchdown, the first scored against the Indians this year. The final score was Carlisle 46-Mt. St. Mary's 5.

A number of government officials attended Carlisle's game with Georgetown in Washington, including a large delegation from the Indian office. Welch must not have healed completely because Arcasa played quarterback against the Blue and Gray. "As they ran off signals, the whole team pivoted to protect one man—the man with the ball—and the most enthusiastic of old Georgetown suddenly awakened to the fact that the home team's ends had work, and plenty of it, cut out for them." Although they had a heavy, fast team, they were powerless against Carlisle's attack.

> Thorpe, the greatest left halfback of the Redskins, played one of the best games ever witnessed on the Hilltop, while Newashe, the chunky tackle, fooled the entire Georgetown team time and again by taking the ball on a double pass and going ten and fifteen yards at a clip. Powell, the dashing fullback of the braves, hit the Hilltoppers' line for substantial gains time and again, while little Arcasa passed the ball in fine style. Arcasa also ran punts back in fine style, often dodging three and four tackles before being downed.

The outstanding play of the day happened in the third quarter when Thorpe faked a forward pass and Bird took the ball out of his hands before racing twenty-five yards through the entire Georgetown team for a touchdown. This description sounded like a version of the old Statue of Liberty play. The Hilltoppers got on the board in the third quarter when Hart ran in a blocked Carlisle punt. The final score was Carlisle 28-Georgetown 5 for the Blue and Gray's only loss that season.

The next week, Pitt partisans were thankful for only one thing: "The attendance broke all records for a Carlisle Indian game in Pittsburg as the Redmen have usually brought miserable weather with them." The Indians put the Panthers on the defensive from the beginning by ripping off five to fifteen yards on every plunge. But Pitt braced and stopped them on its five-yard line, turning them over on downs.

CARLISLE INDIANS OUTPLAY PITT TEAM, WINNING BY 17 TO 0

Redskins Prove Too Speedy for Gold and Blue Eleven. Thorpe the Star.

TRICK PLAYS USED OFTEN BY VISITORS—BIG CROWD OUT

Unable to move the ball themselves, Pitt's Galvin punted immediately. Not caught off guard, Thorpe called for a fair catch, then heeled the ball for a free kick from the thirty-seven-yard line. Luckily for Pitt, the ball sailed wide of the upright. The Panthers moved the ball well enough for a try of their own from the Carlisle forty, but Galvin's kick failed. The second quarter started with Pitt punting the ball out of danger from its fifteen. Thorpe pulled off a clever onside kick that skipped away from the Panthers' Dewar to Wheelock, who carried Dewar on his back across the goal line for the first touchdown scored against Pitt that season. Thorpe kicked the goal after. The first half ended with Carlisle ahead 6-0.

Pitt optimists hoped for a tie game but these hopes were soon dashed. After several punt exchanges in which Carlisle always gained yardage, Thorpe picked up an Arcasa quick kick on the Pitt fifteen and ran it over the goal line. The punt out wasn't caught, eliminating an extra point try increasing Carlisle's lead to 11-0. In the fourth quarter, Pitt faked a field goal attempt to move the ball to the Indian eight-yard line. Two incomplete passes later, the Indians had the ball on their own twenty-five. Some plays later, Galvin punched Arcasa's replacement, Welch, in the face and was ejected from the game. The penalty put the ball on the Pitt twenty-seven, from where Powell forced it over. Thorpe made the kick after.

The 17-0 final score was Pitt's worst loss of the season. Afterward Coach Joe Thompson said, "We were fairly beaten by a better team, and give the Indians credit for their victory. It was certainly a wonderful aggregation that we faced and, mark my word, they will be heard from before the season ends."

The Pittsburg Press raved about Thorpe's play: "The star of the game was Thorpe, the big half back of the Indian eleven, and one of America's greatest all around athletes. It is doubtful if Pittsburgers have ever seen such an exhibition as this big giant put up. Speedy as the wind, a wonderful dodger, and one of the best kickers on the gridiron today, he was half the Carlisle team himself." They went on to talk about his punts, which averaged over fifty yards for the game, his precise onside kicks, and his runs which were sure to net ten to fifteen yards every time he touched the ball.

The undefeated and only once scored-upon Maroon and White of Lafayette College hosted the Indians next on a crisp, cool football day. The early going favored Lafayette, but fortunes switched when a Carlisle player recovered Roop's fumble on the Indian twenty-five-yard line. Lafayette's defense kept Carlisle off the scoreboard early in the second quarter when they stopped the Indians three times in a row and took possession on their six-inch line. But the game didn't remain scoreless for long. After Welch was downed upon catching a punt on the forty-yard line, the Indians got going. They ran a variety of plays and, with tight interference, moved the pigskin into scoring range. Thorpe took the ball from there and squirmed across the goal line for Carlisle's first touchdown. His extra point attempt failed. The Indians didn't sit on their lead; that wasn't their style. The second score came more easily. Wheelock carried the ball over after a string of short gains had positioned the ball under the shadow of the Lafayette goal post. Thorpe's kick failed again, giving Carlisle a 10-0 lead at halftime. In the third quarter, Thorpe, whose right ankle had been twisted badly earlier in the game, kicked a field goal and was replaced by Sousa. After a punt exchange, the Maroons advanced the ball to the Carlisle twenty-five but the Indians braced, stopping the drive. Dannehower's dropkick fell short, giving the Indians the ball. Wheelock scored another touchdown in the fourth quarter, and Bird kicked the extra point for the final score of Carlisle 19-Lafayette 0. Thorpe, Bird, Wheelock, and Lone Star were the shining lights and Powell was becoming a good replacement for Hauser at fullback.

The Indians aimed to avenge the previous year's loss to the Quakers, even with Thorpe too injured from the Lafayette game to play. Penn's captain, Mercer, was also kept out of the game. Thorpe's absence was hardly missed.

Carlisle struck early after Arcasa, Welch, Wheelock, and Powell pounded against the Penn line like battering rams, moving the ball down to Penn's twenty-yard line. Right tackle Lone Star got the ball on a deceptive double-pass play and, seeing a hole in his vacated position, ran twenty yards through it for the Indians' first score. Newashe kicked the extra point. A punt exchange and a fumble gave Carlisle the ball deep in their own territory. Welch called his own number and "twisted, dodged, squirmed and ducked around ends, through a broken field behind interference which equaled anything heretofore given on Franklin Field this year…Time and again he was grasped, and time again he wiggled away from the clutching fingers before he was downed." But not before his eighty-five-yard dash brought him across Penn's goal line for Carlisle's second touchdown. Newashe's kick was unsuccessful. The first quarter ended with Carlisle ahead 11 to 0.

In the second quarter, Carlisle left end Roberts was ejected from the game for tackling Thayer too roughly. Keeping the Indians from scoring in this period gave Penn resolve for the rest of the game. Early in the third quarter, the Indians got the ball on the Penn twenty-five-yard line when Jordan intercepted a pass. Newashe and Powell gained twenty yards on line crashes; then Powell hit for two more. With the ball on their three-yard line, Penn braced and stopped Powell for no gain. But Arcasa caught the Quakers sleeping and scampered around left end untouched for Carlisle's third touchdown. In spite of Powell missing the kick, Carlisle led 16–0 at the end of the third quarter. Neither team scored after that. The Quakers never got closer than Carlisle's twenty-five-yard line, and their stay there was brief.

Carlisle had a victory over Penn in another sport that day: a dual cross country run between the two schools. Lewis Tewanima came in first, Tala Yamptewa came in second, and Mitchell Arquette came in fifth in the five-and-a-half-mile race held at Fairmont Park.

Jim Thorpe wasn't healed enough to discard his crutches, let alone play Carlisle's next opponent, Harvard, but he couldn't be kept on the bench. Wearing a cast Warner improvised for his injured leg wasn't enough because his swollen ankle wouldn't allow him to make the cuts and runs he was accustomed to making. So, Warner revised the game plan to use his star as a decoy and blocker. The Old Fox could do this because the Penn game demonstrated that Carlisle had plenty of other thunderbolts besides Thorpe to carry the ball. The Crimson, still wincing from their 8–6 loss to Princeton the week before, wanted to be sure of beating the Indians. Harvard Coach Percy Haughton started his second string—which in Warner's opinion was almost as good as his regulars—to wear down the Indians, who only dressed sixteen men for the game, and bring in his fresh first team later to finish off the tired Carlisle eleven.

Ignoring the pain, Thorpe opened up the scoring midway in the first quarter by kicking a thirteen-yard field goal. Harvard countered with one by Hollister to tie them. In the second quarter, Thorpe kicked a forty-three-

yarder to put the Indians ahead again. Hollister then recovered a Thorpe fumble in Carlisle territory. Harvard's first play gained five yards, but Reynolds then broke through Carlisle's left wing. Welch was the only defender with a shot at catching him, and Gus tackled him but couldn't keep him down. Reynolds bounced to his feet and scrambled the last thirty yards for a touchdown. Hollister kicked the goal to put Harvard ahead 9–6. Harvard had a chance to perhaps put away Carlisle on a later possession when their entire right wing blocked Thorpe's punt, sending the ball skimming toward the Indians' goal line. Lone Star outran everyone else to pounce on the ball on his own fifteen-yard line, preventing a Crimson touchdown. The first half ended with Harvard maintaining its three-point lead.

Early in the third quarter, Wheelock blocked Reynold's punt, causing the ball to bound toward Harvard's goal line. Wheelock and Lone Star raced after it with Wheelock getting to it first. When he tried to pick up the ball, it struck his knee, which launched it away from him and toward the Harvard goal line. Hollister threw his body into Wheelock, stopping his pursuit. Lone Star raced after the ball but, when his fingers touched it, they drove it over the goal line where Harvard's Parmenter dived on it to secure a touchback.

On a seventy-yard drive in the middle of the third quarter, Acasa and Powell made consistent gains with those on Warner's new reverse play the

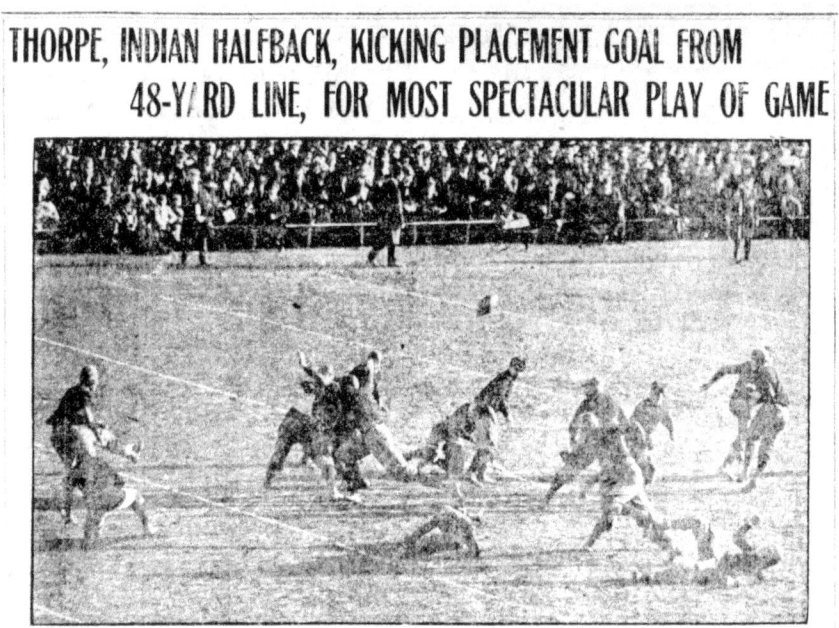

THORPE, INDIAN HALFBACK, KICKING PLACEMENT GOAL FROM 48-YARD LINE, FOR MOST SPECTACULAR PLAY OF GAME

longest. (Warner had adjusted his formation to have a player neutralize the defensive end, who had previously destroyed criss-cross plays.) Powell finished the drive with a short plunge. The kick after was successful. Carlisle now led 12–9 but they weren't finished. Injured Thorpe started carrying the ball. His end run moved the ball twenty-five yards closer to Harvard's goal. When the Crimson defense stiffened, Big Jim kicked his third field goal, a thirty-seven yarder, putting Carlisle farther ahead, 15–9.

Harvard made wholesale personnel changes to start the fourth quarter by putting their fresh first team on the field. The Crimson made gains at first, but the tired Indians stiffened and stopped their drive. The Indians couldn't penetrate Harvard territory very far, so Thorpe attempted, and made, a forty-eight-yard field goal, the fourth that day on a bum leg. With a nine-point lead, the Indians breathed a little more easily. Four minutes later, Storer blocked Thorpe's punt and caught it on a bounce, allowing him to dash over the goal line for another Harvard touchdown. Fischer kicked the extra point. The gassed Indians kept Harvard far enough from their goal to prevent further scoring. The final score was Carlisle 18–Harvard 15.

The game over, the stunned Haughton said, "I realized that here was the theoretical superplayer in flesh." Teammate Victor "Choc" Kelley described Thorpe's play:

> Jim was a terrific runner, passer, and kicker. He weighed around 190 and had tremendous leg drive. Often you could see him knock out would-be tacklers simply by running right over the top of them. He didn't try to overpower you if he didn't have to, for Jim was a snaky ball carrier in a broken field. He gave you the leg and then took it away....He was a good-natured, easygoing guy. When you're talking about Big Jim's football ability you can't exaggerate. He was just the greatest, that's all.

That evening in Carlisle, Indian School students carried a stretcher holding a beat-up Harvard dummy in a nightshirt parade that entertained the people of the town. Warner later recalled another success on that day: "The Harvard game also brought in $10,400 to Carlisle as our share of the contest's gate receipts—the largest amount that Carlisle had received for a single game up to that time." With the last two victories, the Indians were having their greatest season ever.

Mother Nature defeated Napoleon in Russia, and she defeated Carlisle in Syracuse. Playing in mud, slush, and ankle-deep water put the Indians at a distinct disadvantage. They started well, taking only eight plays before Thorpe carried the ball over for Carlisle's first touchdown. His missed kick after proved to be disastrous. Then, a Syracuse punt sailed over Thorpe's head and was recovered by Kallett on Carlisle's fifteen-yard line. Two plays later, Captain Fogg took the ball over the line to tie the game. Day kicked the extra point, putting Syracuse ahead by one. With only a minute left in the half, Castle returned a Thorpe punt, running through the entire Carlisle team for a second Orange touchdown. Day again kicked the extra point to put Syracuse ahead 12-5 at halftime.

Welch was in no condition to play, having been in sick bed for two weeks with a back injury, but came into the game as quarterback anyway. Thorpe's bad ankle bothered him enough to prevent him from kicking or carrying the ball. The third quarter was a scoreless punting duel with the Orange getting the better of it. *The Philadelphia Inquirer* considered "The last quarter to be the greatest fifteen minutes of football that was ever seen in the stadium." Twice, the Indians drove down to the Orange five-yard line where the staunch defenders stopped their advances. With time running out, Welch hit Roberts on three short passes before Thorpe had Welch call his number, and he carried the ball across the goal line. He made this extra point. Time ran out with Syracuse ahead 12-11. Warner blamed the players for the defeat: "The game would be lost by the Indians because they underrated their opponent, and lost through overconfidence."

Johns Hopkins had the misfortune of playing the Indians seven days after the upset loss. Getting the ball on the Hopkins fifty, Thorpe shot through the right side of the Black and Blue line and ran down the sideline, stiff-arming would-be tacklers on his way to Carlisle's first touchdown. He missed the extra point. Sousa came in for Thorpe because his ailing ankle was probably still too sore to play well on. In the second quarter, Powell was shoved over at the end of a drive for Carlisle's second touchdown. Joe Bergie kicked the extra point. The Carlisle center then blocked a Hopkins punt from in front of their goal line. The ball bounced off the goalpost back of the goal line. Charles Williams (Caddo)[12] pounced on it for the Indians' third touchdown. Bergie again kicked the goal-after touchdown for a 17-0 Carlisle lead at halftime. The Indians didn't coast in the third quarter. After advancing the ball down the field to the Hopkins ten-yard line, Welch went back as if to pass and waited with the ball raised. Just as defenders were about to sack him, right end George Vedernack snatched the ball from Welch's hand and raced around the opposite end for a touchdown as another example of the classic Statue of Liberty play. Joe kicked his third extra point. Carlisle's fifth and last touchdown of the day was made on an end run by Powell's replacement, Fred Broker, from the Hopkins forty. He raced around the left end and never looked back until he crossed the goal line. Bergie kicked his fourth extra point for the day. Late in the fourth quarter, Morton picked up a Carlisle fumble on their fifty-yard line and ran it across for the Hopkins touchdown. La Motte kicked the extra point. The final score was Carlisle 29-Johns Hopkins 6.

The Indians wanted to settle the score with Brown for several Thanksgiving Day defeats and had the team to do just that. All the scoring happened in the second quarter of that mud game. First, Thorpe kicked a twenty-seven-

---

[12] An earlier player by the same name was from the Stockbridge tribe.

yard field goal. Shortly after that, he kicked one from thirty-three yards out. "Handicapped by a wet shoe, a slippery ball and treacherous footing," he failed on three other attempts. Welch made five runs of over twenty yards each. The one for sixty-two yards netted him a touchdown. Thorpe kicked the extra point. Although most of the game was played on Brown's end of the field, they got a touchdown when Ashbaugh blocked Thorpe's punt, raced down the field to recover the ball on Carlisle's twenty, ran it across the goal line, and kicked the extra point. *The Boston Globe* headline read: "Only the Good Nature of the Indians Keeps Them From Running Up Bigger Score." Carlisle won 12 to 6.

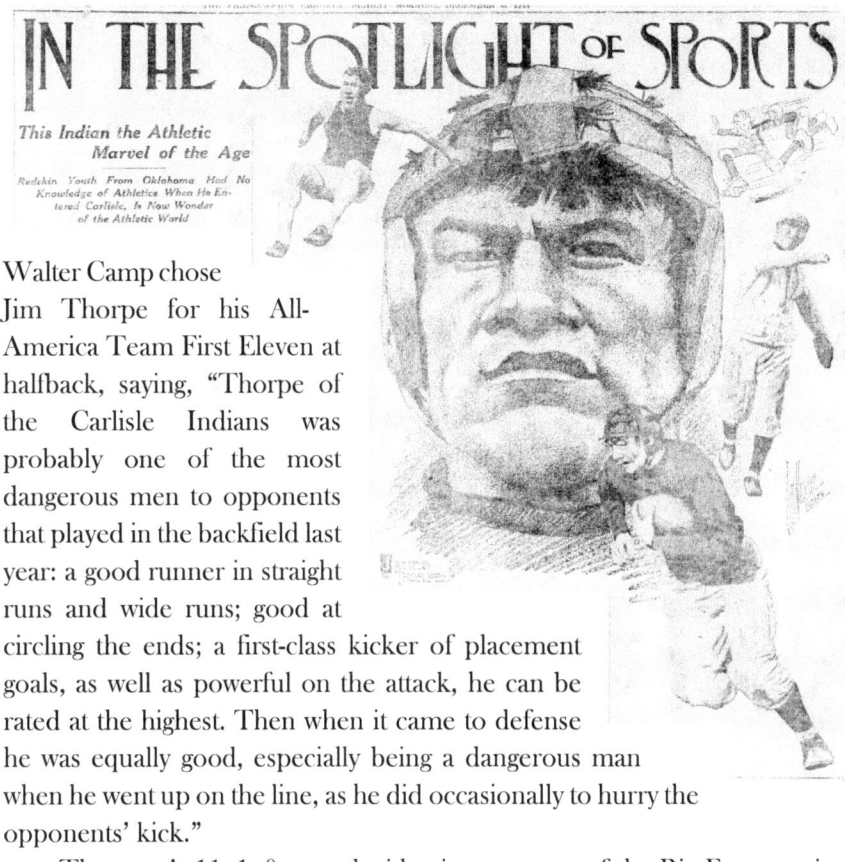

Walter Camp chose Jim Thorpe for his All-America Team First Eleven at halfback, saying, "Thorpe of the Carlisle Indians was probably one of the most dangerous men to opponents that played in the backfield last year: a good runner in straight runs and wide runs; good at circling the ends; a first-class kicker of placement goals, as well as powerful on the attack, he can be rated at the highest. Then when it came to defense he was equally good, especially being a dangerous man when he went up on the line, as he did occasionally to hurry the opponents' kick."

The team's 11-1-0 record with wins over two of the Big Four was impressive. 8-0-2 Princeton and 8-0-1 Penn State were generally ranked ahead of Carlisle this year, putting the Indians third in the nation. However, a recent analysis considers Princeton's two ties to be similar to a loss and Carlisle's one-point defeat was on the road as were all its important games. Princeton only played Navy (the scoreless tie) and Yale (a 6-3 victory) away from home. Penn State's tie was also a scoreless tie with Navy. The Lions only played four away games, one of which was the tie. Penn State and Carlisle had two opponents in common: Penn and Pitt. Their point differences against Penn were similar, but Carlisle shut them out. Both schools shut out Pitt but Penn State's margin of victory was only three points where Carlisle's was 17!

1911 Season Summary

Date	Opponent	Location	Indians	Opp.
Sept. 23	Lebanon Valley College	Indian Field, Carlisle Barracks, PA	53	0
Sep. 27	Muhlenberg College	Indian Field, Carlisle Barracks, PA	32	0
Sep. 30	Dickinson College	Indian Field, Carlisle Barracks, PA	17	0
Oct. 7	Mt. St. Mary's College	Indian Field, Carlisle Barracks, PA	46	5
Oct. 14	Georgetown University	Georgetown Field, Washington, DC	28	5
Oct. 21	University of Pittsburgh	Forbes Field, Pittsburgh, PA	17	0
Oct. 28	Lafayette College	March Field, Easton, PA	19	0
Nov. 4	University of Pennsylvania	Franklin Field, Philadelphia, PA	16	0
Nov. 11	Harvard University	Harvard Stadium, Cambridge, MA	18	15
Nov. 18	Syracuse University	Archbold Stadium, Syracuse, NY	11	12
Nov. 25	Johns Hopkins University	Homewood Field, Baltimore, MD	29	6
Nov. 30	Brown University	Andrews Field, Providence, RI	12	6

Won 11; Lost 1; Tied 0

17

An Olympic Year

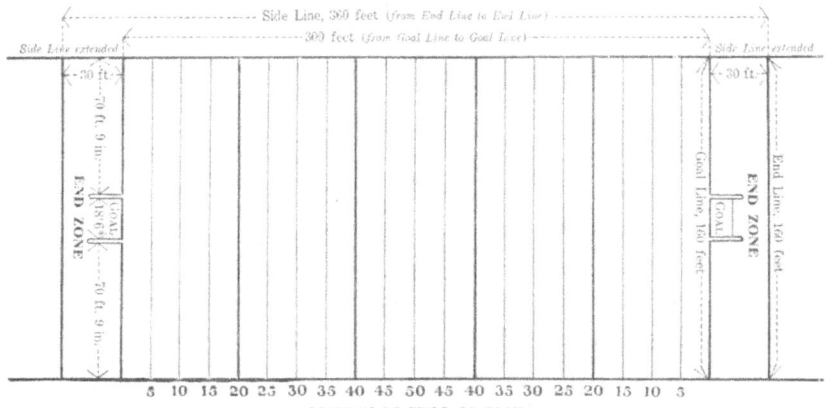

DIAGRAM OF FIELD OF PLAY.
The Field of Play is a Parallelogram bounded by the side lines and goal lines and thus measuring 300 feet by 160 feet.

Rule changes for 1912:

The points scored for a touchdown were increased from five to six.

The number of downs a team has to make ten yards was increased from three to four.

The distance from goal line to goal line was decreased from 110 yards to 100 yards and an area (end zone) ten yards deep was added behind each goal line to allow a player to legally receive a forward pass beyond the goal line.

Kick offs were repositioned to be from the kicking team's 40-yard line.

Only one person from each team was allowed to walk up and down the sidelines.

Forward passes were then allowed to be for any distance, eliminating the 20-yard limit.

Onside kicks/punts from scrimmage were eliminated.

The field couldn't be widened because Harvard Stadium wouldn't accommodate a wider playing field.

Pop Warner and Jim Thorpe didn't get to take much time off after the football season ended because Pop was preparing Thorpe and Lewis Tewanima to compete in the Olympic Games being held in Sweden that summer. He signed them up for indoor meets through the winter of 1912.

Jim trained for the shotput, high jump, broad jump, and low hurdles. When the spring outdoor season arrived, he added the pole vault, javelin, discus, and hammer throw. Thorpe dominated eastern track meets and Tewanima set records for distance runs. Two real events happened during this period that spawned legends.

The first of these was that Warner arrived at Lafayette with only Thorpe and Tewanima as his team and won the meet. What actually happened was that Warner took seven boys: Thorpe, Tewanima, Welch, Bird, Bruce Goesback, George Earth, and John Squirrel. When Lafayette Coach Harold Anson Bruce saw Warner's small contingent, he suggested that they cancel the dual meet. The Old Fox told him Carlisle couldn't afford the train fare to send the full squad but would do the best they could do with the seven. Thorpe won six events, Tewanima two, and Welch two in the 71-41 Carlisle win.

Another legend about Carlisle was spawned that spring at the annual Pennsylvania Intercollegiate Athletic Association meet on Harrisburg's Hargest's Island (City Island today). That one is that the Carlisle football team would run to games in Harrisburg, play the game, and run back to Carlisle afterward. What really happened is that while training for the Olympic marathon, Tewanima ran eighteen miles to the meet and circled the track to the cheers of the girls watching the event.

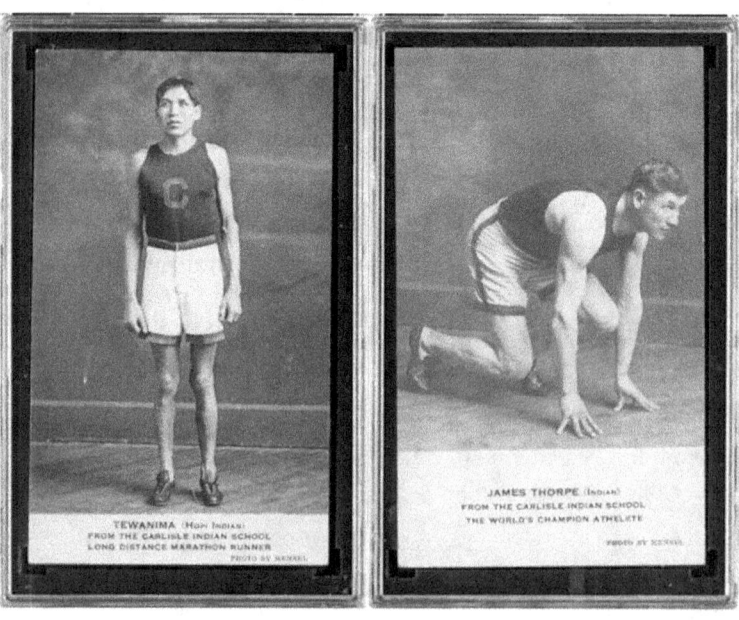

The U. S. Olympic Committee held no formal trials in 1912. They chose Tewanima by virtue of his having demonstrated he was America's best distance man by winning numerous races. The USOC chose Thorpe for the decathlon and pentathlon because of his record of winning so many different events. Warner coached the pair from Carlisle and traveled with them to Stockholm aboard the SS *Finland*. Tewanima was seasick for the entire voyage, a factor that may have affected his performance.

Tewanima had been in Europe before—for games in London and Paris in 1908—but Thorpe had never been abroad. Accommodations and meals on the luxury liner were probably akin to those in the first-class hotels and restaurants the football team slept and ate in on road trips. But the U. S. O. C. didn't provide accommodations for the Carlisle members of the team. In spite of Tewanima's sickness and Thorpe's track shoes being stolen, Carlisle's two-man team scored more points at the Stockholm Olympics than any American college team did. Thorpe won gold medals in both pentathlon and decathlon while Tewanima won a silver medal in the 10,000 meter run and came in sixteenth (out of sixty-eight) in the marathon.

At the end of the games, King Gustav V said to Thorpe, "Sir, you are the greatest athlete in the world." To which Jim replied, "Thanks, King."

Thorpe and Tewanima received a hero's welcome when they returned to Carlisle. The town held a parade through the main streets them and hosted a celebration at Dickinson College's Biddle Field that 7,000 attended. They were invited as guests to numerous other festivities.

Soon, it was time to train for the football season. Jim had been elected captain to replace Sam Bird, who along with tackles Lone Star Dietz and William Newashe, had all used up their four years of eligibility and had to be replaced. Sam continued his education at the Dickinson College prep school but did not play football for Dickinson College. In the spring, he married another former Carlisle student, Margaret Burgess, and returned to Browning, Montana to ranch. He returned to the ranch house one day early in his marriage to find his Haida/Tlinget bride in tears. Sam's mother and sister had shunned her because she was not Piegan. Sam immediately moved to another of the family's holdings, the old Aubrey Ranch, never to return. He continued to work and manage the family ranches but never lived with them again.

Reserve lineman Hugh Wheelock eloped with a girl from Mt. Union, Pennsylvania while playing in the band there over the summer. Married, he didn't return to Carlisle but took a job in a brick yard and continued to play in the town band. His brother Joel remained at school, active in the band and on the team.

Two new athletes, Joe Guyon and Pete Calac, weren't needed in the set backfield, so would be put to work on the line. Joe quickly took to wrestling the other boys on the team. Guyon later related his introduction to Thorpe:

> Jim wanted to see who in the hell that damn Chippewa was that had come off the reservation and was flipping all these guys. So we wrestled. I couldn't throw him because he was quick and fast himself. We wrestled to a standoff and we became buddies right away.
>
> Jim hated the training table, because it never had enough on it to eat. He loved steaks. Pop Warner, our coach at Carlisle, would ration off steaks to us, and Jim would buy them off the other players. He could do that. Oklahoma Indians had money.

In May, Warner released a twelve-game schedule that differed significantly from 1911's in that Albright College replaced Muhlenberg, Washington & Jefferson replaced Mt. St. Mary's, Lehigh took Lafayette's place, Army instead of Harvard, and International YMCA College replaced Johns Hopkins. With only one Big Four team on the schedule and the powerful backfield returning intact, this year's team was expected to do even better than the 1911 version. Warner had his hands full. He had new rules to adapt his offensive scheme to

1912 Line, L-to-r: Charles Williams, Pete Calac, Elmer Busch, Joe Bergie, William Garlow, Joe Guyon, Roy Large

and a line to rebuild. He put Dietz to work as his assistant working with the younger boys.

Carlisle's first foe that year, Albright College, had a team for the first time in six years and was no match for the Indians even though Carlisle fielded no more than six lettermen at any one time and Thorpe didn't play due to a sore shoulder. Needing to evaluate prospects for filling holes in his line-up, Warner substituted liberally. The bright spot for the visitors was when Light recovered a fumble in the second quarter and ran it in for only the second touchdown ever scored against the Indians on their home field. Warner considered the team's play ragged and careless at times. Six different players scored Carlisle's eight touchdowns in this 50-7 victory. Scheduled a week ahead of the official start of the season, this game gave coaches and players the opportunity to see a game played under the revised rules. As expected, first downs were easier to make and there were considerably fewer punts.

The day of the Albright game, Hugh Miller negotiated the arrangements for a game against Villanova to be squeezed into the schedule on Wednesday, October 9. Because the teams had become bitter rivals, a neutral site, Harrisburg's Island Park, was selected for the match.

Two Lebanon Valley College players fearful of being scalped by the Indians, had their heads shaved before catching the train for the Wednesday game in Carlisle. Expecting to win without them, Warner held Thorpe and Powell out of the game, probably to give their injuries more time to heal. He again gave a number of players the opportunity to convince him they belonged in the starting line-up. Welch was the star of the 45-0 blowout. His spectacular seventy-five-yard end run showed off his speed. Six players scored Carlisle's seven touchdowns. Bergie kicked two extra points and Garlow tallied one.

The next Saturday, Thorpe finally got a chance to show his stuff when he snagged an errant pass and ripped, tore, side-stepped, and plunged through the entire Dickinson College eleven on his way to a sixty-yard touchdown run. Warner again tried numerous players as the starters weren't needed. The Indians' last game for the year in their hometown ended with the score: Carlisle 34-Dickinson 0.

The start of Wednesday's game against Villanova was held up for a few minutes when Miss Belle Story ran out onto the field to present Thorpe with her lucky rabbit's foot. She was a vaudeville actress and singer of whom composer Richard Rogers said, "[She] had a lovely coloratura voice and made a big hit wherever we played." Thorpe accepted the good-luck token and the game was soon underway.

It took all of five minutes for the Indians to make their first score at the end of a fifty-seven-yard drive. Arcasa went for twenty yards around right end and Thorpe kicked the extra point. With that, they were off to the races. Almost all of the damage was done in the first half when Carlisle scored fifty-eight points on eight touchdowns and extra points plus a safety. Substitutes went in for the second half and only scored once. The final score was Carlisle 65-Villanova 0. Thorpe was the star of the game, but Arcasa, Welch, and Powell also played well.

The Indians had played Washington and Jefferson twice before, the most recent in 1905. Both games had been tight, so a tough game was expected again. The combatants fought each other to a standstill in the first half. The Presidents brought in fresh substitutes for the second half, but Carlisle kept its injured starters on the field. The Indians tore through the W&J line defense to move the ball down to the one-yard line, where they frittered a touchdown away with a fumble. In the fourth quarter, Thorpe tried to put Carlisle on the scoreboard with his toe but failed thrice. A kick from the twenty-seven sailed wide, one from the forty was partially blocked, and the one from the forty-five fell short. The Indians' fifth game in fifteen days ended in frustration.

Wash-Jeff Eleven Holds the Carl'sle Indians to a Scoreless Tie

ALEXANDER STOPS ARCASA ON W. & J. GOAL LINE; CRITICAL POINT IN CARLISLE GAME.

The Indians could not have forgotten how the Orangemen had spoiled their perfect season the year before and the loss the year before that. Playing in a sea of muck, neither team could mount an attack during the first half. When the rain stopped at the start of the third quarter, the Indians went to work. Thorpe was the star of the day, making all the long runs, scoring three touchdowns, and kicking three of four field goals. Carlisle avenged the two previous losses 33-0.

A rumor circulated around the University of Michigan campus that Carlisle would be playing in Ann Arbor on November 2, the day of Carlisle's game with Lehigh. The reporter remarked, "Such a piece of good fortune at the eleventh hour is too good to be true, but it is the only thing that can save an otherwise poor schedule."

Pitt was Carlisle's opponent the next Saturday. Florent Gibson of the *Pittsburgh Daily Post* observed, "A puzzling shift formation that allowed every copperskin to get into the play on end runs overwhelmed Pitt ends time after time. Five of six touchdowns registered were made on long runs from this formation. One was bucked over by Arcasa from the Pitt one-yard line." Thorpe, Welch, and Arcasa each scored two touchdowns. Thorpe kicked five extra points and a field goal. The downside was that Pitt scored a touchdown in the third quarter, followed by a safety when Thorpe was tackled in his end zone while retrieving Bergie's off-target center snap. The final score was Carlisle 45–Pittsburgh 8.

Cheers of "Hoya! Hoya! Saxa!" thundered from the cheering section on the hill when the unbeaten Blue and Gray of Georgetown trotted onto the field the next Saturday. Avenging the defeat by the Indians the previous year reigned uppermost in the players' minds. An early Georgetown fumble, followed by a Carlisle march for a touchdown, silenced the cheerers. Four more Carlisle possessions yielded four more touchdowns. The Indians looked unbeatable when the first half ended with them ahead 34–0.

The second half was a completely different story. The Hilltoppers played with a ferocity not present earlier. After a couple of Carlisle penalties and some short gains, Georgetown had the ball in field goal range. Harry Costello dropkicked a twenty-five-yard field goal to break up the shutout. Later in the third quarter, Costello kicked another one, this time from the twenty-yard line. Early in the fourth quarter, Thorpe attempted, and missed, a field goal from the forty-five. Georgetown's runners couldn't be stopped without making gains and scored a touchdown. After ten minutes of back and forth in the middle of the field, Thorpe fumbled when tackled hard. "Tug" Fury picked up the ball and ran thirty-five yards for a touchdown. A punting duel ensued until time expired. The final score was Carlisle 34–Georgetown 20.

Immediately after the game, the Carlisle team took cabs to Union Station to catch the express train to Toronto. Warner had inserted a game into their schedule against University of Toronto Old Boys to be played on Monday, October 28, Canadian Thanksgiving Day. It was also a celebration of the 100th anniversary of the end of the War of 1812. The Old Boys were varsity rugby stars who had graduated. The first half was played under American rules, with which the Canadians were unfamiliar, and the second under Canadian rugby

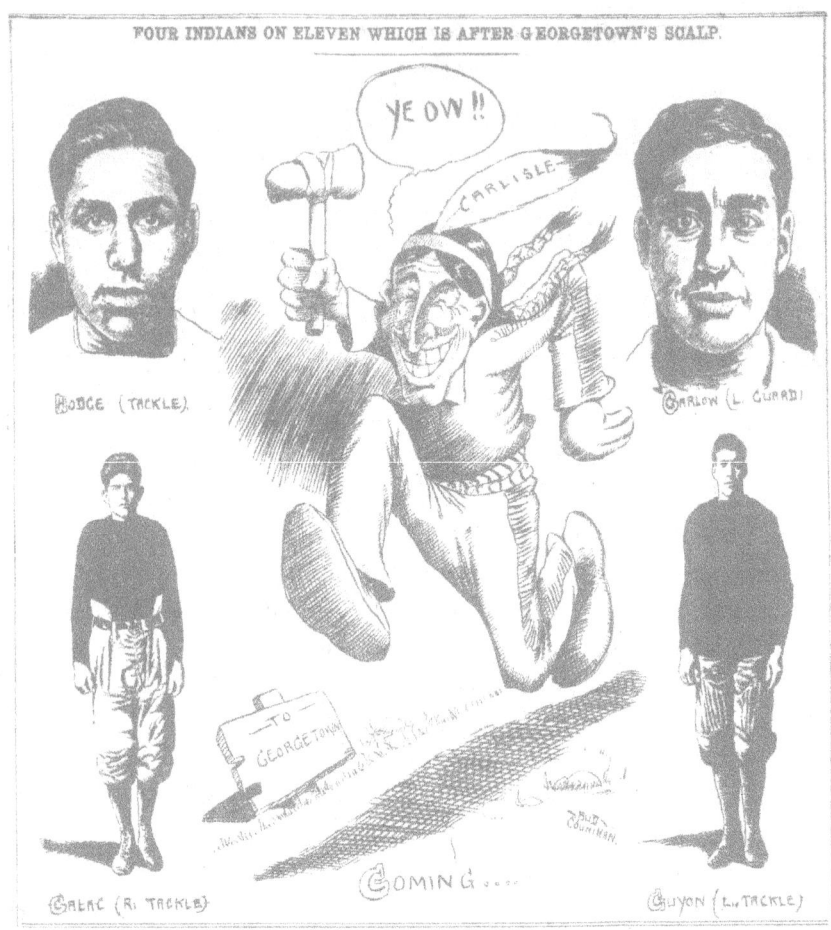

rules. The Canadian players didn't understand the use of interference because rugby didn't allow it, and American players hadn't defended against serial laterals, let alone made them. As would be expected, Carlisle won the first half 44 to 0. What was surprising was that they also won the second half 5 to 1. Toronto's point was scored when Thorpe fielded a kick behind his goal line and touched the ball to the ground for a rouge[13].

Shortly after the game, the Indians caught the train home to prepare for Saturday's game with once-beaten Lehigh, the conqueror of Navy. The team, except for Welch, was in the pink. Although far from one-hundred percent, he was expected to play limited minutes against the Brown and White. Thorpe was a one-man wrecking crew, making four touchdowns, an extra

---

[13] A rouge is a rugby play similar to a safety in American football but worth one point.

be tacklers along the way. A series of short gains advanced the ball to the Army four-yard line. Bergie, who had been shifted from center to fullback to take Powell's place, bulled through the left side of West Point's line for Carlisle's first score. Thorpe's kick was true, putting Carlisle ahead 7-6. Army attempted to complete a forward pass three times before the first half ended but failed each time.

The second half had barely started when Thorpe was hit with a crushing tackle. With Jim lying on the field motionless, the referee started to enforce the two-minute rule. Army Captain Leland Devore interceded, "Nell's bells, Mr. Referee. We don't stand on technicalities at West Point. Give him all the time he needs." He soon regretted saying that.

Jim didn't like hearing what Devore said and got to his feet to resume play. Later, two Army defensive backs, Dwight David Eisenhower and Charles Benedict, decided to knock Thorpe out of the game by both hitting him at once. Jim stopped short causing them to slam into each other headfirst. When they staggered to their feet, Army's Coach Capt. Ernest Graves pulled them out of the game.

Army had to punt from deep in their territory early in the second half, giving Carlisle good field position. The Indians moved the ball all the way to the West Point one, but they lost it on downs. Army punted from its endzone to Welch at midfield. Thorpe carried the ball from scrimmage, leaving defenders sprawled across the field in his wake, as he flew around right end for twenty-five yards. Carlisle then punched the cadet line with short, powerful jabs to move the ball to Army's four-yard line. Arcasa carried it across for his first touchdown. Thorpe kicked the extra point to increase Carlisle's lead to 14-6. Arcasa fielded the ensuing kickoff on his thirty-yard line, where he was downed. The Indians then marched down the field, gaining five to fifteen yards at a clip. Army fought fiercely at their twenty to slow the assault, but the Indians summoned reserve energy and pounded away. Driving as if he was a human bullet, Arcasa piled through and over the goal line. Thorpe again made the kick to give Carlisle a commanding lead of 21-6.

ARMY ELEVEN IN A ROUT

Carlisle Indians Take the Measure of Cadets.

THORPE IN EVERY PLAY

On Attack and Defence He Is in Thick of Fray—Devore Banished from Field.

point, and a field goal. Carlisle's criss-cross, double pass, and tackle plays bewildered the Lehigh defenders, allowing Thorpe and Arcasa to circle the ends and Powell to plunge through the line. Big Jim got so cocky that he would tell the defense where the play was going. Even knowing that, they couldn't stop the Indian attack. Warner complained that Carlisle's secondary was unable to intercept passes, thus allowing Lehigh to score twice via the aerial route and close the final score to Carlisle 34–Lehigh 14.

The following Saturday brought a trip to once-beaten West Point. Warner had changed plays twice during the season and was about to unveil his third set. Included was the double-wingback formation he had kept secret and was about to unleash. Pop was always worried about a letdown and, at 9-0-1, the Indians were ripe for one. None of the current players had been on the team and most hadn't been at the school yet in 1905 when their predecessors beat Army, so Warner gave them a pep talk before the game.

Pete Calac remembered how excited the coach was. "He stood at the end of the locker room facing the team, who were standing up on the benches, and he began to pace back and forth and then up and down the aisle between the men to give them individual instruction. By golly! I didn't think we had a chance against Army that year. They were very big, much bigger than we were. They thought we'd be a pushover." Gus Welch said, "He reminded the boys that it was the fathers and grandfathers of these Army players who fought the Indians. That was enough!"

It didn't look that way early in the second quarter when Army, with the aid of the penalty accompanying Powell's ejection and one for holding, put the ball over on an end sweep by Hobbs for the game's first score. Pritchard's kick went under the crossbar to limit Army's lead to 6-0. After a punt exchange, Arcasa made a fair catch of Hobbs's short kick on the Army forty-five-yard line to put Carlisle in business. Thorpe ran for thirty yards, warding off would-

The Indians got stronger as the game wore on, and Army never figured out how to stop Warner's unbalanced line, which had two linemen on one side of the center and four blockers on the other. Carlisle's fourth drive was interrupted by a penalty and fumble but they regained the ball at midfield. The Indians chewed up the yardage, moving the ball down to the Army ten-yard line. The cadets made one of their noted goal-line stands at the one and got the ball back. But they had no luck. Coffin's punt from the end zone struck the goal post and veered out of bounds on the ten-yard line. Calac made a short gain on a tackle-carry criss-cross. Arcasa took the ball the next three times, going around West Point's right end the last time for his third touchdown. Thorpe's kick went wide due to his not having his kicking shoes with him. The game ended in darkness with the score Carlisle 27–Army 6.

Although scoring only extra points, Thorpe's performance received rave reviews. *The New York Times* gushed, "Standing out resplendent in a galaxy of Indian stars was Jim Thorpe. The big Indian captain added more lustre to his already brilliant record, and at times the game itself was almost forgotten while the spectators gazed on Thorpe, the individual. To wonder at his prowess. To recount his notable performances in the complete overflow of the Cadets would leave little space for other notable points of the conflict. He simply ran wild, while the Cadets tried in vain to stop his progress. It was like trying to catch a shadow."

The 1912 Penn Quakers had lost four games in a row but were fresh off a 27–21 victory over Michigan. The Indians were predictably flat for the Penn game, and Warner let that be known afterward. "If Carlisle had played as good as they have played in almost any other game this season, they would have won this important game, but the work of Carlisle's backs was the worst exhibition of football (handling the ball and poor generalship) which any Carlisle team has shown in many years. Some excellent work was done also, as Carlisle's four touchdowns proved, but all the good work was more than nullified by the costly mistakes." Warner pointed out one play in particular: "One of the touchdowns which Pennsylvania made was on a long pass. I thought Thorpe could have knocked down the pass if he had tried. After the game I asked him about this and he said, 'Oh yes, sure, I could have knocked that down. I didn't think the receiver could go to it.'" The final score on the Indians' first loss was Penn 34–Carlisle 26.

Thorpe redeemed himself in the next two games, playing arguably some of the best football of his life. When Pop was setting up the 1912 schedule, he desired a convenient game before the annual Thanksgiving game with Brown, which by definition, was played with two fewer days of preparation and healing

than other big games. The International YMCA College (today Springfield College) was located in Springfield, Massachusetts handy to Providence, Rhode Island. That Warner's friend James "Doc" McCurdy coached their team made setting up the game trivial. McCurdy relentlessly attacked the Indians with line shifts, speed, and forward passes, defending the last of which had plagued the Indians in earlier games. According to Warner's plan, Jim Thorpe was to play the first quarter then sit out the remainder of the game to rest up for Brown. He scored early, but the YMCA College jumped into a 14-7 lead. Thorpe stayed in the game and scored a second touchdown just before the end of the first half to tie the score.

The YMCA College fought hard in the second half but couldn't contain the big Indian. On defense, he was often the last man between a runner and the goal line. Springfield kept coming but Thorpe was relentless. They scored ten second-half points but he made sixteen. Tacklers trying to take him down got stiff-armed for their trouble. Jim ended up scoring all of Carlisle's points in their 30-24 victory.

Instead of returning to Carlisle after the game, they checked into the Leicester Inn and practiced on Leicester Common. When Thorpe was interviewed by the press, he announced that he was retiring from college athletics after the Brown game. His sole reason for quitting was, "the utter abhorrence of the public gaze and the large amount of notoriety he has received for his various stunts in the athletic world." This may have been his plan all along as he viewed baseball as the only sport in which it was possible to earn significant money.

Weather conditions for the Brown game varied depending on the source of the game coverage. *The Boston Globe* described the scene: "The countryside was picturesque with snow and the air was nipping and frost-laden." The *Brown Daily Herald's* coverage began: "In a blinding snowstorm and piercing norwester." It said, "The driving snow was hard on the spectators as well as the teams, but the best part of the throng remained until the finish of the game." The college's newspaper also estimated the size of the crowd as over 10,000, probably the largest attendance at a football game in Providence, and that several hundred more were turned away because the stadium's capacity had been exceeded.

In either weather condition, footing would have been poor, a factor that helps the offense because they know where they're going—or at least trying to go—and makes drop and placement kicking difficult. Frequent fumbles of the wet ball impeded both teams' drives. The first quarter ended scoreless with Brown in possession of the ball at midfield. Carlisle soon took over on downs on her forty-yard line. Thorpe circled left end for thirty-two yards. Then Goesback and Thorpe pounded Brown's line with Thorpe scoring the first touchdown. He missed what would have been an easy kick on a dry field. Brown moved the ball with steady advance to Carlisle's half-yard line but were offside when they put it over, causing Tenney's touchdown to be called back. Carlisle got the ball on downs after an incomplete forward pass. Later, Carlisle got the ball on downs on its own forty-one. Thorpe carried the ball around left end for his fifth long dash of the game (so far) to put the ball on Brown's ten-yard line. On fourth down, Goesback hit Guyon with a pass for the Indians' second touchdown. Bergie fumbled the punt out so no extra point could be tried. The half ended with Carlisle ahead 12-0.

Early in the second half, Brown drove down to Carlisle's thirteen-yard line, but the Indians held and took over on downs. Wheelock and Thorpe rushed the ball on end runs and tackle skin plays the length of the field with Thorpe plowing through guard for the touchdown. He kicked the extra point from an angle. On Brown's next possession, Crowther punted to Thorpe on his own forty-yard line. Thorpe ran the ball back, dodging the entire Brown team until Crowther caught him on the fifteen-yard line. A fumble on a later play ended the drive. The third quarter ended with Carlisle in possession on the Brown eighteen and ahead 19-0. In the fourth quarter, Brown blocked Thorpe's field goal attempt. When Brown's drive stalled, Crowther punted to Arcasa. Thorpe and Wheelock smashed through Brown's line, moving the ball to the Brunonians' forty. Then Arcasa passed the ball to Thorpe on the twenty-three. Wheelock and Bergie bulled through the tackles and guards with Wheelock carrying the ball over. Thorpe kicked the extra point. Later, Brown's Bartlett punted out of bounds, giving Carlisle possession at midfield. Thorpe's pass to Wheelock moved the ball to the twenty-five-yard line. Thorpe gained on a plunge through center, but Bergie was stopped at guard. Thorpe then skinned left tackle for an eighteen-yard touchdown. Powell's kick failed. The game ended with Carlisle ahead 32-0.

A BOSTON CARTOONIST'S IDEA OF CARLISLE'S THANKSGIVING DINNER.—*Boston Post*

Walter Camp again selected Jim Thorpe for his All-America Team First Eleven at Halfback, saying, "Thorpe showed once more the greatest individual prowess of any back on the gridiron. When I selected him last year I believed him capable of all this from his work in previous years. This he demonstrated in every department in 1912." He mentioned Guyon at tackle and Bergie at center but didn't place them on any of his All-America teams.

Camp praised Carlisle's offense for scoring 360 points but downgraded its defense for giving up so many points. George Orton ranked Carlisle third in the East behind Harvard and Penn State. "Offensively, the eleven was the best in the country. They had a great variety of plays and had them working like a well-oiled machine. Bergie at center, Guyon at tackle and Welch at quarterback were the best of the men, excepting Thorpe, and all of these were mentioned for All-America honors, Defensively, the team was comparatively weak as is shown by the fact that 114 points were scored against them." He raved about Thorpe: "In Thorpe, Coach Warner had the greatest footballer that has ever been in the game. As a back he has never been equaled."

Hamilton Fish considered Thorpe "...the most valuable all-round player in the game, and probably the greatest halfback that has ever played football."

Would Thorpe return to the reservation and go "back to the blanket" or would he do something different?

1912 Season Summary

Date	Opponent	Location	Indians	Opp.
Sep. 21	Albright College	Indian Field, Carlisle Barracks, PA	50	7
Sept. 25	Lebanon Valley College	Indian Field, Carlisle Barracks, PA	45	0
Sep. 28	Dickinson College	Biddle Field, Carlisle, PA	34	0
Oct. 2	Villanova College	Island Park, Harrisburg, PA	65	0
Oct. 5	Washington & Jefferson College	College Field, Washington, PA	0	0
Oct. 12	Syracuse University	Archbold Stadium, Syracuse, NY	33	0
Oct. 19	University of Pittsburgh	Forbes Field, Pittsburgh, PA	45	8
Oct. 26	Georgetown University	Georgetown Field, Washington, DC	34	20
Oct. 28	University of Toronto Old Boys	Toronto Stadium, Toronto, Canada	49	1
Nov. 2	Lehigh University	Lehigh Field, S. Bethlehem, PA	34	14
Nov. 9	Army	The Plain, West Point, NY	27	6
Nov. 16	University of Pennsylvania	Franklin Field, Philadelphia, PA	26	34
Nov. 23	International YMCA College	Pratt Field, Springfield, MA	30	24
Nov. 28	Brown University	Andrews Field, Providence, RI	32	0

Won 12; Lost 1; Tied 1

"BIG JIM" THORPE, OF CARLISLE, THE WORLD'S GREATEST ALL-AROUND ATHLETE, TO QUIT

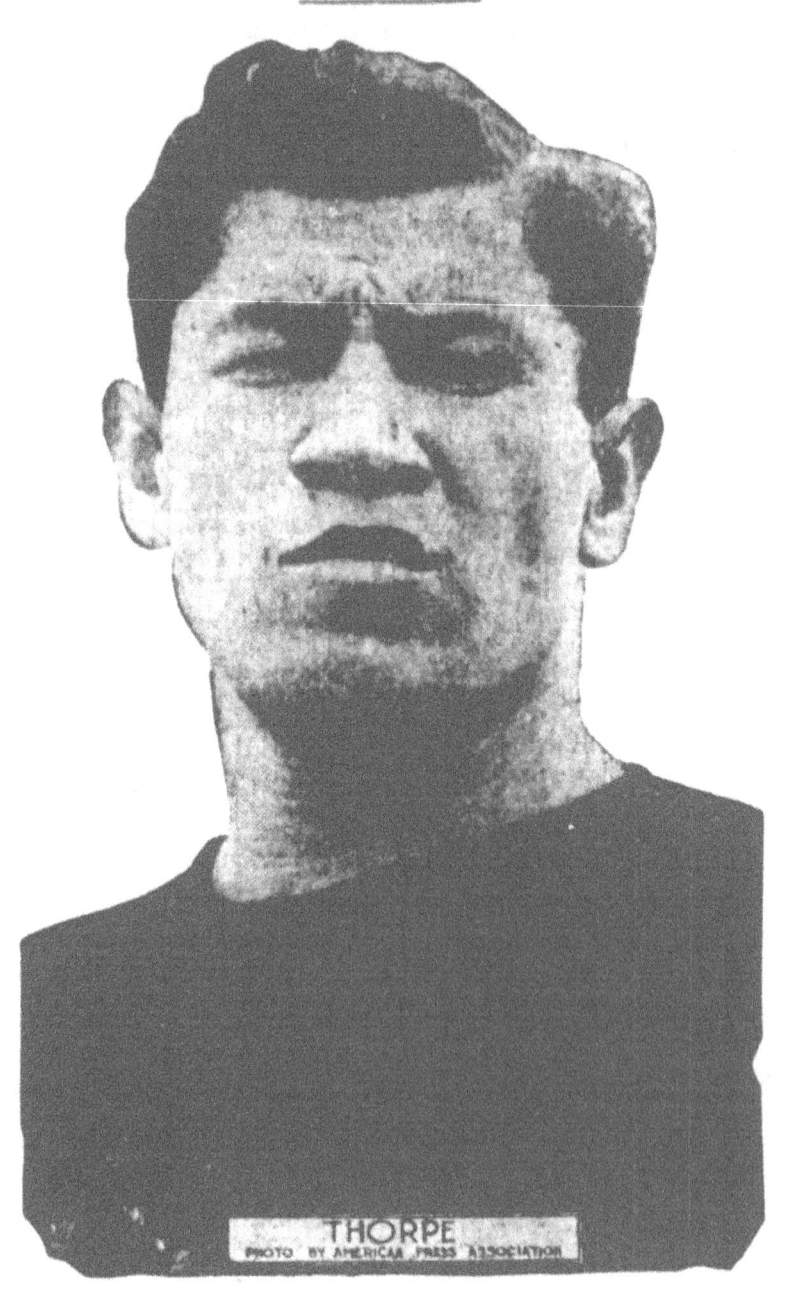

THORPE
PHOTO BY AMERICAN PRESS ASSOCIATION

18

Three in a Row

Rule changes for 1913:

A substituted player may be returned once at the beginning of any period, or at any time during the fourth or last period.

Language allowing the ball to be snapped by the center with his foot was removed.

Kicks/punts can be made from any distance behind the line of scrimmage, returning quarterback/onside kicks from scrimmage to the game.

Advancing a punt out beyond the goal line earns the penalty of repunting five yards further from the nearest goal post.

Entire 1913 Squad with Coaches Warner and Dietz.

Pop Warner expected to have a challenge replacing Jim Thorpe and the other starters whose eligibility had expired, but he was blindsided by what hit him. It all started in January 1913 when Charles Clancy, Manager of the Winston-Salem baseball team, sat down with Roy Ruggles

BASEBALL MAN SAYS THORPE IS PROFESSIONAL

Manager Charles Clancy of Winston-Salem Team Makes the Charges

SAYS HE LIKED GOOD TIME

Claims He Signed Athlete as Pitcher in Carolina Association

Johnson, County Editor and Reporter for the *Worcester Telegram*. Clancy, who was wintering in nearby Southbridge, thought it was for a friendly off-season chat. Possibly bragging and not thinking about the consequences of his actions, he told Johnson that Thorpe had played for his team. Johnson then found Jim on a team photo in the Reach baseball guide and wrote an article exposing Thorpe for having played a little minor league baseball. Clancy immediately denied having said what he said. Pop Warner and Moses Friedman denied knowing Thorpe had done this. Soon, writers claimed other Carlisle football players played professional baseball, William Newashe and William Garlow in particular.

Within a week, Thorpe wrote, or at least signed, a confession, quite possibly written by Warner. In it he mentioned that, being naïve, he played under his own name where the more sophisticated college boys playing alongside him used pseudonyms. He returned his medals and trophies and looked to his future. Many felt Warner and Friedman had betrayed him. Losing his amateur status was the one good thing about this mess. The AAU would not be able to exploit Jim by having him perform on a series of track and field events they had planned for the spring. He would now have to be paid to perform.

"I Was Only an Indian Schoolboy," Thorpe in His Confession to A.A.U.

Various professional sports were very much interested in Thorpe, for his promotion potential as well as his athletic attributes. A Canadian hockey team even made an offer. The only sport he took seriously was baseball because it was the only one in which he thought a player could possibly make enough to support himself. The Cincinnati Redlegs and New York Giants both offered contracts. Acting as Thorpe's agent and attorney, Warner negotiated a lucrative contract for Jim with the Giants and wrote the agreement himself, rather than using a standard contract used by baseball clubs. An important difference was that the standard contract included a clause that allowed a team to cut a player and stop paying him. Pop didn't include the cut clause in Thorpe's contract. Jim soon left Carlisle and joined the Giants at spring training.

On March 1, an article datelined Carlisle, Pa., and likely approved by Warner, circulated on newspapers around the country. "Carlisle Has Another Star: Young Athlete May Be a Second Thorpe." Pop was introducing Joe Guyon to the sporting world, possibly to strengthen Carlisle's position in negotiating appearance guarantees.

Pete Calac   Joe Guyon

Captain J. M. Beacham visited Carlisle to arrange a game between West Point and the Indians. Both sides signed a contract to play a post-season game on November 29, following the annual Thanksgiving game against Brown. The reason given was, "all possible efforts had been exhausted in arranging a game between the Army and the Navy." When the arrangement was announced and the Secretaries of War and the Navy became aware of it, they were not amused. In short order, a game between the military academies was set up for November 29 at the Polo Grounds in New York City and the Army-Carlisle game was canceled.

On September 1, Warner announced that practice had started and that he expected to again have a strong team, losing only two starters from the 1912 squad, Thorpe and fullback Powell. A contrary opinion circulated in the press around the country. Pundits thought Thorpe had left a hole too large to fill. Warner, however, was already cognizant of Guyon's and Calac's abilities. But he hadn't figured on Bergie, Arcasa, Large, and Joel Wheelock leaving. Pop enlisted Albert Exendine and Lone Star Dietz to assist him in training the green players who would have to fill the holes created by the departing players. Gus Welch led the team as captain.

As had become their habit, the Indians kicked off their season a week before other eastern powers. Albright brought their heaviest and strongest squad to date and posed a greater challenge than ever before. Even without Welch suited up and numerous new men getting significant playing time, Carlisle prevailed 25-0. Calac scored two touchdowns, Guyon and Goesback one each. Guyon succeeded on one of the extra-point kicks.

The following Wednesday, under almost unbearably sultry conditions, the Indians hosted Lebanon Valley for their annual contest. This time Joel Wheelock was lined up at right end against his old teammates, but the outcome was only marginally better for the Dutchmen than in previous years. Ahead 26-0 at halftime on Guyon's four touchdowns and two extra points, Joe looked like another Thorpe on the field. Warner was able to substitute liberally in the second half but LVC was strong enough to hold the backups scoreless.

West Virginia Wesleyan, unbeaten in 1912, was Carlisle's opponent on Saturday. Led by future Hall-of-Famer Earle "Greasy" Neale, the boys from Buckhannon came confident of victory. They held the Indians to six points in the first half on a freak play by John Wallette who fielded a Wesleyan kick in their end zone. The extra point was missed. Warner's impassioned halftime pep talk energized the Indians. Guyon, Calac, and Crane scored touchdowns, and Guyon kicked an extra point in the 25-0 rout. The only Carlisle player seriously injured was Goesback, whose face was badly cut when he was run over while sitting on the bench.

Carlisle jumped out to a seven point lead over Lehigh on the second play of the game when Gus Welch spied a hole on the right side of the line, dashed through it, and romped sixty yards for a touchdown. The little quarterback shook off tackler after tackler, unnerving the Engineers and practically decided the game. Garlow kicked the point after touchdown for a 7-0 Carlisle lead. In the second quarter, Guyon and Calac moved the ball downfield making clumps of yardage at a time. With the ball on the Lehigh five-yard line, the Indians shoved Guyon over for the score. Garlow again kicked the extra point.

> **REDSKINS SCALP LEHIGH SCOUTS**
>
> Indians Get Jump on Rivals and Score in First Half Minute--- Total, 21-7
>
> Bethlehem Boys Take Brace in Second Period, But Rally Comes Too Late

Lehigh came alive in the third quarter. Chenoweth floated a pass from thirty yards from midfield to Green, who eluded the Indian defenders surrounding him and dashed twenty-five yards for the Brown and White's score. Hoban kicked the extra point. Lehigh continued outplaying Carlisle until late in the fourth quarter, when Guyon broke loose for thirty yards, landing on Lehigh's ten. An Engineer penalty moved the ball to the five. Fullback Calac pounded the ball over for the last score of the game. Garlow again kicked the extra point to boost the final score to Carlisle 21-Lehigh 7.

With the schedule getting tougher, the Indians invaded Ithaca for a game with Cornell. Five minutes into the game, Goesback skirted right end for twenty yards. Then, Guyon plunged into the line three straight times, scoring on the third. Garlow kicked the extra point. The Indians never menaced the Cornell goal line again, but the same couldn't be said about the Big Red. They rushed to Carlisle's three-yard line in the second quarter, but Welch intercepted a pass to halt the drive. In the third quarter, Cornell drove down to Carlisle's one-foot line where quarterback Barrett was thrown back for a loss. In the fourth quarter, Barrett attempt a double pass from the ten-yard line, Barrett to Fritz to O'Hearn, but Fritz's pass fell lifeless to the ground in the end zone. Carlisle held on to win 7-0.

The Tuesday morning after the Cornell game, Jim Thorpe squeezed in time between the World Series and the Giants' around-the-world tour to return to Carlisle and marry former Indian School student Iva Miller. The elaborate affair was held at St. Patrick's Church, the oldest parish west of the Susquehanna River and the only one east of the Mississippi with a majority Indian congregation because of the 200 Catholic Carlisle students.

Possibly because they had covered the recent World Series and were going to film the tour, two movie companies bought the rights from Thorpe to film his wedding celebration. Many of his former teammates were in the wedding party, including Gus Welch who was his best man. Superintendent Friedman gave away the bride as he and the previous superintendents often did when students married. After the hour-and-a-half-long ceremony, the wedding party and invited guests, which included several of his Giants' teammates, adjourned to the adjacent hall built by Mother Katherine Drexel for the Catholic students at the Indian School. Mr. and Mrs. Friedman hosted a reception for the newlyweds in the afternoon before they caught a train for New York. No mention was made if Warner gave the players time off from practice to attend the festivities.

A week later in a fierce battle with Pitt, both teams spent the first quarter playing defense, much like prize fighters measuring their foes. The Indians mounted a long drive featuring runs by Welch and Guyon. At the Pitt fifteen, Welch faked a pass and ran the ball in for a touchdown. Garlow's kick went wide by a few inches. The half ended with no further scoring. The Panthers got stronger in the second half, and the Indians couldn't make first downs and retain possession of the ball. Pitt made good yardage via the aerial route. The third quarter ended with the Panthers knocking on the Indians' door at the six-yard line. Unable to gain on the ground, Williamson hit Smith with a forward pass for a touchdown. Williamson's kick missed, leaving the score tied at 6-all. Carlisle worked the ball to Pitt's thirty where Garlow attempted a field goal but failed. Welch misplayed a long, low, bouncing punt that Pitt's Wagner pounced on, giving the ball to the Panthers on Carlisle's six-yard line. The Indians rallied but Pitt pushed Heil over for their second, and winning,

touchdown. Dillon missed the kick after. The game ended Pitt 12-Carlisle 6 for Carlisle's first loss.

Carlisle wanted to erase the previous year's defeat by Penn but Mother Nature intervened by soaking the field with rain. Between the pools of water were dry spaces—until players' feet turned them to mud. For once, the lighter Indians outplayed their heavier opponents on a mucky field. This year's edition of the Quaker eleven was considered to be much better than last year's, the one that spoiled the Indians' 1912 record, but they put Penn on defense throughout the game. With poor footing and a slippery ball, the Indians resorted to line plunges and short end runs, with Guyon, Bracklin, and Calac making most of the gains. Charles Pratt and George Vedernack didn't allow a yard to be made around end, and Welch's generalship was the best of his career. The Indians made first downs almost at will and held the Quakers to only two of them, but frequent fumbles kept the scoring low. The Indians drew first blood in the second quarter when Bracklin went over for the Indians' touchdown. (Newspaper accounts attributed the score to Guyon but Warner later corrected that.) Garlow's low kick hit the crossbar but bounced over for a 7-0 Carlisle lead at halftime.

Penn quarterback Marshall fumbled Guyon's kickoff to open the second half into a pool of water at his twenty-five-yard line. While his interference formed, he recovered the ball. Following it, he dashed seventy-five yards down the field for Penn's touchdown. He made the easy extra point kick to tie the

score at 7-all. The Indians tried to score in the fourth quarter via Garlow's toe but a Penn defender knifed through the Carlisle blockers to deflect the ball less than a foot after it left holder Welch's fingers, leaving the final score a tie: Carlisle 7–Penn 7. After the game, Carlisle alum and Cooperstown-bound Athletics hurler Charles Albert "Chief" Bender congratulated each member of the underdog Indian team for his fine play.

The Blue and Gray of Georgetown had the unenviable task of facing Carlisle the following Saturday. The Indians took the lead three minutes in and never relinquished it. They gained four times as much yardage as the overmatched Hilltoppers with Warner's version of the criss-cross play doing much of the damage and Bracklin being the most reliable ground gainer. Guyon scored three touchdowns; Bracklin and Calac had one each. Garlow kicked four extra points in the 34-0 drubbing.

Whether Warner's intention in starting Garlow at quarterback against Johns Hopkins was to give Welch some rest or to let him come in later at halfback for some of the glory is unknown. Regardless, Calac undid Johns Hopkins with his line plunges, end runs, and open-field running. The Black & Blue defenders could not stop him. The Indians didn't have to punt a single time in this lopsided 61-0 victory. *The Baltimore Sun* gave Calac the lead in scoring with four touchdowns. Welch followed with three. Guyon and Bracklin had one each. Guyon kicked five extra points and Calac kicked two. *The Philadelphia Inquirer* allocated five touchdowns to Calac and two to Welch. Inconsistencies in newspaper coverage of games was still common.

The next Saturday, the Indians met 7-0-0 Dartmouth for what pundits expected to be one of the biggest games of the year. With wins over Princeton and Penn, Dartmouth was vying for Harvard for the mythical national championship. As an experiment, Dartmouth's players wore numbers on their jerseys. Even though the Indians didn't participate in the test, sportswriters considered it a success. Carlisle scored first ten minutes into the game after Wallette blocked a Dartmouth punt and smothered it on their thirty-five-yard line. Guyon, Calac, and Bracklin repeatedly shredded the right side of the Green line with Bracklin going over for the score. Garlow kicked an easy extra point to put Carlisle ahead 7-0. But that lead didn't last long. Dartmouth recovered a Carlisle fumble and drove to the Indian thirty-five-yard line, where the drive stalled. From there, Hogsett dropkicked a field goal to put the Hanoverians on the scoreboard. On the first play after the kickoff, Carlisle received a fifteen-yard penalty that put the ball dangerously close to their goal line. Guyon punted from his end zone to Ghee at the forty-three-yard line. Ghee's twenty-yard return put Dartmouth in a good position to score.

Vedernack's elbow was wrenched so badly he had to be carried off the field on a red blanket by four substitutes. Pratt came in for him for Carlisle's only substitution in the game. Line plunges had advanced the ball to the five-yard line when time expired.

Whitney started the second quarter by making a first down at the three. Two line plunges and an end run broken up by Welch put the Green in the position of having to make the decision whether to go for the touchdown or to kick another field goal. They took the aggressive choice. Ghee hit Loudon with a short forward pass to put Dartmouth ahead. Loudon's kick made the score Dartmouth 10-Carlisle 7. Hogsett attempted another field goal with time running out in the half but it missed.

In his autobiography (as edited by Mike Bynum), Warner recalled the scene during the intermission. A gambler, Warner had bet $300 on the Indians at five-to-three odds. Not wanting to lose the bet, he offered his players five dollars each from his winnings to spend at a stop in New York on their way home—if they won. (His memory was unclear about this because he said the game was played in Boston when it was actually at the Polo Grounds. The team wouldn't stop off in New York because they were already there.)

Whether the bonus provided the motivation or not, his team played inspired football when they came out for the second half. The Indians jumped in front within three minutes after the start of the second half and kept their feet on the gas. Dartmouth had no answer for Warner's double-wing formation and his revamped reverses. Guyon and Calac each made two touchdowns after which Garlow kicked the extra points for an overwhelming 35-10 Carlisle win.

Back in Carlisle, exuberant students celebrated what Warner considered one of his greatest victories. That night, several hundred boys dressed in nightshirts marched toward the town square headed by the school band and

All Carlisle Turns Out to Celebrate Indians' Victory

Dickinson College Students, Whose Team Also Wins, Join Hands with Redskins.

four "medics" carrying a stretcher holding a scalped dummy wearing a green sweater. Dickinson College's team also had a big away-game that day against Swarthmore. The Red and White defeated the Little Quakers 12-7, spawning a celebration similar to that of the Indian students. Their band led their procession of college students in nightshirts as they marched toward the square. The two processions met at the corner of Pitt and Main (High today) Streets, a block from the courthouse. Students danced the tango and did serpentines as the bands played.

Townspeople crowded the sidewalks to enjoy the spectacle. An anonymous citizen wrote a letter to the editor in which he said, "[The parade] was heartily enjoyed by the large crowd of spectators." He went on to complain that the Indian School band played only one tune, "Hail! Hail! The Gang's All Here," and far worse, boys on the sidewalk joined in, substituting vulgar words as they sang along.

Dartmouth's season was over but Carlisle's wasn't. The Indians had two more contests scheduled, and offers for post-season affairs in the West and South poured in. But the administration decided against a long post-season trip.

Syracuse, even at 5-3, was always a challenge for the Indians because they usually collided late in the season when players were worn down and field conditions were lousy. The Orange scored within minutes of the opening kickoff in the hotly contested battle when halfback Castle raced sixty yards for a touchdown. He also kicked the extra point. The Indians roared back but the Orangemen held the onslaught three times on their half-yard line. Then Guyon mustered all his strength in a final effort and carried the ball across the goal line. Garlow made the kick after. Calac soon tallied a score of his own to put the Indians up 14-7 at the end of the first quarter. Toward the end of the half, Syracuse drove from its own forty, with Kingsley carrying the ball over from twenty yards out. Castle kicked the extra point to tie the game.

The score seesawed back and forth with the teams alternating scoring touchdowns until Syracuse failed to make the extra point after their third. From then on, Carlisle was in the lead. Bracklin, Guyon, and Welch all scored in the second half with Garlow making the extra points. Their last touchdown was made with two minutes remaining. Syracuse threw pass after pass, trying to score again while the clock rapidly ticked. The whistle blew when they had moved the ball to the Carlisle eight-yard line. The final score was Carlisle 35-Syracuse 27.

With only five days until the annual Thanksgiving brawl with Brown, Warner kept the Indians east instead of returning to Carlisle between the Syracuse and Brown games. He sequestered his team at The Tavern in Mansfield, Massachusetts and practiced at Lowney Common. With two of 4-4 Brown's losses to Harvard and Yale, the Brunonians turned out to be tougher than the Indians expected and kept Carlisle out of the scoring column until the second quarter. Taking possession on their thirty-four-yard line, the Indians moved the ball down to the Brown ten, making five successive first downs along the way. Bracklin then made five yards and Calac carried it over. The extra point wasn't made. The next and last score was made in the fourth quarter after Bracklin intercepted a Brown pass from the twenty-yard line and returned it five yards. Guyon made five and Calac smashed through for a short gain and again for a touchdown. Garlow made the kick after. The game was closer than the 13-0 score indicated. The Indians gained 300 yards to Brown's 260 and made fifteen first downs to Brown's twelve.

This season had arguably been Warner's greatest effort as a coach. He had started with several green players and had molded them into a team that lost only one game for the third season in a row. This was quite a feat since they had just lost Jim Thorpe and the major groundgainers, Guyon and Calac, had been tackles the previous year.

BRACKLIN, KNOWN AS "DEERFOOT" BECAUSE OF HIS SWIFT RUNNING

Walter Camp selected Elmer Busch as a guard and Joe Guyon as a halfback for his All-America Team Second Eleven. He also said that Guyon could easily replace either of the first-team halves. "Busch of the Indians made a strong bid for first place among the guards and was only shut out by two such men as Pennock and Brown, with their great possibilities. Busch is a better man at leading interference than either of them." William Garlow and Gus Welch received mention at center and quarterback, but Camp didn't place them on his All-America teams. Parke Davis named Guyon to his All-America team at halfback.

George Orton gave Warner high marks: "Coach Warner deserves the greatest credit for the way in which Carlisle was developed as most of the players were rather raw material at the beginning of the season. In addition, the team was light. This explains the comparatively poor showing in their last two games, as by that time, the men were pretty well wearied out through their hard contests with Cornell, Pittsburgh, Pennsylvania and Dartmouth, all of which had heavier elevens. In the matter of defensive play Coach Warner showed a distinct advance over his team of 1912."

Then something happened during the season off-field that would change the course of Carlisle football forever.

1913 Season Summary

Date	Opponent	Location	Indians	Opp.
Sep. 20	Albright College	Indian Field, Carlisle Barracks, PA	25	0
Sep. 24	Lebanon Valley College	Indian Field, Carlisle Barracks, PA	26	0
Sep. 27	West Virginia Wesleyan College	Indian Field, Carlisle Barracks, PA	25	0
Oct. 4	Lehigh University	Taylor Stadium, S. Bethlehem, PA	21	7
Oct. 11	Cornell University	Percy Field, Ithaca, NY	7	0
Oct. 18	University of Pittsburgh	Forbes Field, Pittsburgh, PA	6	12
Oct. 25	University of Pennsylvania	Franklin Field, Philadelphia, PA	7	7
Nov. 1	Georgetown University	Georgetown Field, Washington, DC	34	0
Nov. 8	Johns Hopkins University	Homewood Field, Baltimore, MD	61	0
Nov. 15	Dartmouth College	Polo Grounds, New York, NY	35	10
Nov. 22	Syracuse University	Archbold Stadium, Syracuse, NY	35	27
Nov. 27	Brown University	Andrews Field, Providence, RI	13	0

Won 10; Lost 1; Tied 1

19

A Cure for All Diseases

Rule changes for 1914:

No one, including the head coach, can walk up and down the sidelines.

The Field Judge is brought back as an optional official as an assistant to the Referee and Linesman in big games.

A penalty is added for roughing the passer.

If a ball from a forward pass ends up out of bounds, possession goes to the defending team.

Both receiver's feet must be inside the end line and side lines for the catch to be legal.

The kick out after a touchback or safety is removed. The ball must be put in play from the twenty-yard line in all cases.

The intentional grounding penalty is added.

During a shift, a player may not move into the neutral zone.

Late in the 1913 football season, upset by what he perceived as mistreatment of his friend Jim Thorpe by the Indian School officials over the Olympics scandal and Warner's gambling, Gus Welch circulated a petition around the YMCA. It criticized the management of and conditions at the school. Two-hundred-seventy-six students signed the petition, which former student Montreville Yuda then delivered to the Secretary of the Interior.

Judge Cato Sells, new commissioner of Indian affairs, apparently at the urging of the Indian Rights Association and Welch's petition, began an investigation of Superintendent Moses Friedman's management of the Carlisle Indian Industrial School in January 1914. It seems that Cumberland County Judge Sadler (it is not clear whether it was Wilbur or Sylvester because the hereditary judgeship transferred from father to son that year) meted out a sixty-day jail sentence, possibly at Friedman's urging, to an Indian girl and boy for an infraction punishable only by a fine under Pennsylvania law. The infraction was not stated but debauchery is a definite possibility. This action did not sit well with the Philadelphia-based Indian Rights Association. Indian boys were found drinking alcohol in the town of Carlisle and had been arrested. According to Indian School staff and other students, the usual suspects "negro bootleggers" were to blame, not tavern owners. The timing could not have been worse for Carlisle as the walrus-mustachioed Judge Sells was on a rampage to stop the scourge of alcohol on his wards while trying to clean up the corrupt government agency.

On Friday, February 6, 1914, a joint commission of Congress under the direction of Inspector E. B. Linnen arrived unannounced in Carlisle to interview staff and students at Carlisle in an attempt to investigate the accusations. It was not a pretty sight. Superintendent Friedman made an unauthorized trip to Washington to plead his case, blaming Gen. Richard Pratt, founder of Carlisle Indian School, with meddling but was told to get back to his post. Local newspapers ran editorials supportive of Friedman, but several students and faculty members criticized his leadership. Meanwhile Inspector J. Linnen interviewed numerous witnesses. Sen. Joe T. Robinson of Arkansas chaired the questioning of witnesses.

Outing Manager Rosa B. LaFlesch testified that discipline: "...is better now than when I first came here, although it is lax yet." She went on to say, "They [students] have no respect for him [Supt. Friedman]." Wallace Denny, assistant disciplinarian (and Pop Warner's long-time trainer), gave four reasons or causes for student dissatisfaction:

1. Superintendent Friedman reduced the number of receptions and sociables per month to one each.
2. Students were given more difficult [academic] work.
3. Food was of a poor quality.
4. Employees did not work in harmony with Superintendent Friedman.

Principal Teacher John Whitwell reported that Outing Agent David H. Dickey found Pop Warner drunk with Gus Welch. Whitwell also claimed that students wrote "the Jew" and other such things on a blackboard in reference to Moses Friedman. He accused Friedman of carrying almost 200 students who were no longer at the school on the roll.

Miss [redacted in original] testified about the Friedmans' (perceived) misbehavior:

> ...And it just so happened some of the boys were playing on their trombones, and she started on her skirt-dance, and she went on—well, she carried it a little too far, and after Mr. Friedman got up on the porch they started to play peek-a-boo around those pillars there, and they acted what I would call silly for a man that was ruling over the

students that are here....At these dances when the orchestra is playing Mrs. Friedman goes around with her skirt up to her knees.

Native Art Teacher Angel DeCora presented the commission with a list of twenty-eight girls who had been "ruined" and sent home. Band Director Claude M. Stauffer was accused of beating a seventeen-year-old female student, Julia Hardin, at the insistence of Matron Hannah H. Ridenour.

Pop Warner was accused of mishandling athletic funds, so considerable time was spent interviewing William H. Miller, the school's financial clerk, who also served as secretary/treasurer of the Athletic Association. His and Warner's signatures were required on all checks. They were written only after Superintendent Friedman approved the expenditures. One of the charges was that the athletic association paid Hugh R. Miller, sports editor for *The Carlisle Sentinel*, and E. L. Martin to publicize the Carlisle team in the cities in which they played. Chairman Robinson and Rep. Charles D. Carter of Oklahoma paid particular attention to one expense item.

Chairman: "I see here under date of January, 1908, a check, No. 552, 'Camera, $140.68, for Mr. [Hugh] Miller.' Was that a moving picture camera?"

William H. Miller: "No, sir. It was a camera that was purchased for him to take pictures of games. It was a large box camera."

Rep. Carter: "Where is that camera now?"

William H. Miller: "In his possession. He always has had it."

Rep. Carter: "Is he a member of the [athletic] association?"

William H. Miller: "He is not. He is a newspaper man."

The fact that the hundreds paid out for PR resulted in thousands in increased gate receipts seemed to escape the commission. Or, it appeared unseemly to the senators and congressmen for the school to pay for publicity when they had franking privileges and reporters constantly asked them for stories. It appeared that Warner had pioneered another innovation: the sports information department.

Warner was found to have kept scrupulous records but was criticized for how some of the money was spent. He argued that he was getting the best value for the school when he purchased canned goods from his family's Springfield Canning Company. The coach also mentioned disbursing some of the money to the players. "At the close of the season the boys are given a twenty-five dollar suit of clothes and a twenty-five dollar overcoat; that is, the first team. And the first team also gets a souvenir of some kind." This explained some of the twenty-five- and fifty-dollar chits and log entries at Wardecker's Men's Wear (formerly Blumenthal's). Merchants sometimes gave gold watches and other awards of value to winners of important races and to star players. Many of these "trinkets," as Warner described them, came from out-of-town merchants.

When asked about numerous checks not relating to the Athletic Department but to the School proper, William H. Miller described the Athletic Fund as "a cure for all diseases" because it was used to cover expenses the government wouldn't, such as construction of some new buildings. He also stated that the fund had $25,000 in it at that time.

Warner was also criticized for recruiting star athletes from reservations, something he adamantly denied. He countered that many of his best players had never seen a football before arriving at Carlisle. Not stated was that Pratt's early attempts at recruiting from the reservations had proved fruitless. The flood of players from Haskell to Carlisle began after the 1904 game played at the St. Louis World's Fair during the period Warner was back at Cornell and a few months after Major Mercer took over as superintendent.

Commissioner Sells dismissed Friedman and Stauffer, bringing charges against Friedman for theft of funds. Oscar Lipps was brought in as acting superintendent. During his trial, Friedman claimed it was Chief Clerk Siceni J. Nori who embezzled the money and destroyed the records. State charges against Friedman were dropped and moved to federal court when it was learned that Nori, who was going through a divorce, needed the money to make support payments for his estranged wife and children. Friedman was acquitted, resigned, and took a job that paid $3,000 a year. A cook was suspended for taking an Indian boy into a saloon and buying him liquor. That infraction netted the cook a fine and imprisonment. The commission recommended that Warner, although he wasn't a government employee, be dismissed. But he had a year left on his contract with the Athletic Association and stayed on as athletic director.

A result of the Congressional Investigation was a major change in the curriculum, stricter requirements for admission, limited student ages to between 14 and 21, and a reduction of the enrollment period to three years. Athletic funds could not be used to pay travel expenses for students to come to the school, and prospective students had to complete reservation courses available to them before transferring to off-reservation schools. Transfers between off-reservation schools were also limited.

A number of the faculty changed and many students did not return in the fall. The investigation brought out the fact that, although Angel DeCora and her husband, Lone Star Dietz, had not been teaching native arts for about two years due to curriculum changes made after Leupp left the bureau, Superintendent Friedman had kept them on because he thought they were assets to the school. Dietz taught mechanical drawing at the time, illustrated school publications, and assisted with coaching football, but DeCora had no specific duties. They also operated a kennel of prize-winning Russian Wolfhounds behind their apartment on campus. The commission apparently agreed with Friedman and did not recommend their dismissal. Complaints of students loitering in the former Native Art Department led to the Leupp Art Building being reassigned to the new Alumni Association. Students would no longer make or decorate things to be sold by the school. Resale items were to be purchased from vendors in New York.

At the beginning of the 1914 football season, evidence appeared that Warner's PR department was still functioning. An article, probably written by Hugh Miller or E. L. Martin, titled, "Carlisle Indian Stars Are Teaching the Palefaces How to Play Football Game," circulated in newspapers around the country. Bemus Pierce, Albert Exendine, Frank Mt. Pleasant, Frank Cayou, William Gardner, Wilson Charles, William Garlow, Emil Hauser (better known as Wauseka), Pete Hauser, Charles Guyon (also known as Wahoo), Fritz Hendricks, Ed Smith, Antonio Lubo, Joseph Scholder, and St. Germaine were or had been coaching football at colleges and high schools around the country. Jimmie Johnson, Gus Welch, Lone Star Dietz, and several others had or were assisting in Carlisle by 1914. The schedule was similar to the previous year's except Georgetown, Johns Hopkins, and Dartmouth were replaced by Holy Cross, Notre Dame, and Dickinson College. Charles Guyon, aka Wahoo, soon arrived on campus to arrange a postseason game in Atlanta.

The 1914 team was again led by Head Coach Warner, who was assisted by Lone Star Dietz. John McGillis assisted former player Antonio Lubo with the reserves. Elmer Busch was elected captain at the end of the 1913 season, likely due to Walter Camp's endorsement for All-American recognition. Forty-five prospects turned out for the early practices. Gus Welch left a large hole to fill at quarterback. He was attending Dickinson School of Law and earned some income by coaching the Conway Hall team.

Leaving a larger hole was tailback Joe Guyon. He had joined former Carlisle students Peter Jordan and Leon Boutwell at Keewatin Academy in Prairie du Chien, Wisconsin despite Superintendent Oscar Lipps' pleas to return to Carlisle. In his letter to Gus Beaulieu, who wore many hats as an activist, editor of *The Tomahawk*, and mentor of the motherless Guyon at the White Earth Agency in Minnesota, Lipps explained that he had been lobbying the Commissioner of Indian Affairs to have two years added to Carlisle's curriculum, "...thus making Carlisle a preparatory school for agricultural and mechanical colleges."

Beaulieu wrote to Commissioner Sells and to Senator Moses Clapp protesting Carlisle's attempts to have Guyon return. Beaulieu also claimed that Warner was blackmailing Keewatin by threatening to advertise that they were giving Guyon free tuition when he was paying it. Assistant Commissioner Edgar Briant Meritt directed Lipps to not insist on Joe's return. "If it were not for the possible misconstruction that would be placed upon our action should we require his return, because his case is tied up with the desire of the Carlisle Athletic Association to procure football players, we would certainly ask that he observe his agreement to return to the Carlisle School."

1, Ranco; 2, Hawk Eagle; 3, Morrin; 4, Hill; 5, Pratt; 6, Martelle; 7, Wallette; 8, Welmas; 9, Calac, Capt.; 10, Busch; 11, Lookaround; 12, Ellman; 13, Broker; 14, Wofford; 15, Bird.   Hensel, Photo.

The 1914 edition of the Carlisle team started weaker than in previous years because they didn't score on Albright College in the first quarter. Perhaps the extreme heat had something to do with it. Warner had to shuffle his starting line-up and insert second-stringers before the game because Joe Guyon hadn't returned from his summer break, and some other players were nursing injuries. Albright was stronger than usual and the Indians' win hinged on three plays. James Crane started the scoring when he leaped high into the air to snare a fumble that had been launched skyward. Pete Calac and John Wallette each scored one of their own, and Philip "Woodchuck" Welmas kicked two extra points in Carlisle's 20-0 win.

On Wednesday, a day unfit for football, the game with Lebanon Valley was shorted to eight-minute quarters due to the sweltering heat. LVC attempted to score first—twice—but Keating missed both short field goal attempts. The Indians scored the winning, and only, touchdown in the fourth quarter when Calac ripped through the line for a score and Welmas kicked the point after to defeat the Dutchmen 7-0. Carlisle's light team was again outweighed by the visitors. Calac and Pratt stood out for the Indians but William Winnieshiek's work at center was criticized. Carlisle alum Joel Wheelock again stood out for LVC. Their home schedule completed for the year, the Indians took to the road, a very long one this year.

On Saturday, they opened West Virginia Wesleyan's season with a defensive battle kept scoreless until late in the game when Calac broke through the Orange and Black line at the fifty-yard line and raced down the field for the game's only score: Carlisle 6-Wesleyan 0. Their opponents' unexpectedly good showing was attributed to the coaching of former Carlisle stars Frank Mt. Pleasant and William Garlow.

The Lehigh game was decided by fumbles. Carlisle made twelve, recovering seven, where Lehigh only made one. Poor tackling by the defensive secondary yielded three touchdowns to the Engineers. Carlisle had a chance to score in the second quarter but Fred Broker's field goal attempt failed. Calac's third quarter touchdown was too little, too late. The final score was Lehigh 21-Carlisle 6.

By this time it was clear, more than clear, that Joe Guyon wasn't returning. He was tearing up the Midwest while playing for Keewatin Academy, a prep school in Prairie du Chien, Wisconsin. Perhaps he found the school's winter campus in St. Augustine and the opportunity to play sports year round enticing.

The next week's headlines scowled, "Ithacans Scalp Carlisle Indians." In the second quarter against Cornell, the Indians made a desperate effort to score—so desperate that quarterback Crane was injured so badly he had to be taken out of the game. Eventually, they turned over the ball on downs on the Cornell three-yard line. The Big Red scored three unanswered touchdowns for the final score of Cornell 21-Carlisle 0.

Pete Calac was elected captain in an unusual move to replace Elmer Busch in midseason. Perhaps this change became necessary because Gus

Welch was not on the field. The wily quarterback later related that Busch was an excellent player but didn't always play to his potential. To motivate the underperforming guard, Welch would provoke him by biting his leg in a pile up and blame the other team for doing it. Angry, Busch would then play like a demon.

The Indians' next foe was unbeaten Pitt, which already had wins over Cornell and Navy. An early fumble by Fred Broker on his eighteen-yard line set up Pitt's first score: a Hastings dropkicked twenty-five-yard field goal. Calac fumbled on the first play of Carlisle's next possession, this time on the Pitt twenty-four, but no score resulted from this miscue. Early in the second quarter, Calac hit Fred Broker on the goal line with a well-executed spiral. The Carlisle touchdown was called back for offsides. On Calac's second try, Pitt star Peck tipped the ball to Miller for an interception to end the threat. Later, Calac missed a field goal from the forty-yard line by inches. Still in the second quarter, with the ball at the Carlisle twenty-eight, DeHart, aided by Miller's interference, circled his right end, and after shaking off three Indian tacklers, raced across the goal line for a touchdown. Hastings kicked the extra point for a 10–0 Pitt lead. Pitt's attempt for another field goal failed. The first half ended with no further scoring.

Early in the third quarter, Hastings attempted a field goal from midfield but it fell ten-yards short. A little later, Calac barely missed one from the Pitt thirty-yard line. Carlisle got the ball at midfield early in the fourth quarter. When their drive bogged down, Calac dropped back to the thirty-yard line, from where he kicked a goal from placement, putting Carlisle on the scoreboard with three points before the game ended with Pitt ahead 10-3. Warner was pleased with their effort, calling it "...the best football the team has shown this year." Pitt would only lose one game that year, 13-10 to Washington & Jefferson, a team that beat Yale and whose only loss was by one point to Harvard.

Fumbles and poor kicking dashed Carlisle's hopes of beating Penn. Warner was encouraged because Crane and Calac did surprisingly well despite playing hurt and the "...determined effort on the part of every man which enabled Carlisle to outplay their heavier and more experienced opponents." In the fourth quarter, Penn's Avery hit teammate Merrill in stride with a forward pass, placed such that it allowed him to dodge the left side of the Indians' line and avoid their secondary for a touchdown, breaking a scoreless tie for the 7-0 Penn win.

The Indians next met Syracuse, a team with only one loss and a victory the week before over Michigan. The game was an unmitigated disaster. Carlisle's offense was impotent and the defense leaky. Syracuse thrashed the Indians 24–3.

Rumors circulated that Pitt had made Warner a tempting offer. When confronted, a member of their athletic committee owned up to it: "We believe we have the greatest bunch of football material in the country at Pitt now, and we want the greatest football general of the country to handle them for us." That could not have helped Carlisle's morale.

Holy Cross was a new opponent for the Indians but the outcome didn't improve. Had it not been for the field goal against Syracuse, the Indians would have been shut out three weeks in a row. They could do no better than a scoreless tie. Both left halfbacks, Fred Broker and Jesse Wofford, were knocked out of action during the game, forcing Warner to call up underweight reserve Grant White to fill in until they were healthy enough to play again.

Having a year of eligibility left and the Indians needing a good quarterback and field general, Gus Welch rejoined the team. After having circulated a petition with the objective of getting Warner fired, Welch's relationship with him would have been strained at best, but the old coach needed him. Whether Welch suited up out of loyalty to his school and old teammates or for the glory of playing in a big game wasn't mentioned. Guyon, then enrolled at Keewatin Academy in Wisconsin, watched from the Comiskey Park stands but didn't suit up.

Outweighed by twenty pounds per man, the Indians didn't have a chance against Notre Dame but they put up a good fight in the first half. Had it not been for Welch's fumble late in the second quarter that led to a touchdown for the Catholics, the Indians would only have been down 10–6 at halftime.

Early in the third quarter, Welch was knocked unconscious when tackling Eichenlaub and immediately sent to Chicago's Mercy Hospital. The tired Indians had no chance after that. Carlisle suffered its worst defeat in a decade, losing 48 to 6.

Gus Welch was injured so badly that he remained behind when the team returned to Carlisle. School administrators wrote Gus that his brother, James, would not be visiting him because James was in the hospital in Philadelphia over concern that he had a tubercular knee. Fortunately, their fears were not realized and James made a full recovery, just not in time to visit Gus in Chicago.

> **BULLETIN.**
> 1 o'clock a. m.—The nurse in charge of Gus Welsch at Mercy hospital announced that he was conscious and resting easily with no apparent change in his condition from that of the early evening.

Six days after the Notre Dame, Gus wrote Oscar Lipps, the acting superintendent, telling him that he was feeling fine and expected to return soon. Welch's attending physician Dr. W. E. Morgan wrote Lipps the next day stating, "He not only sustained a fracture of the cheek-bone (which he feels) but he had also a fracture of the base of the skull in front (which he don't feel) but which requires absolute rest to insure a future without invalidism, such as epilepsy, paralysis, deafness or loss of sight, any one of which might develop in after years from recklessness or negligence at this time." Two days later, Dr. Morgan wrote, "Mr. Gus Welch still continues with his gradual improvement and seems more contented than before. I believe he has decided to be good and mind the doctor. Has promised me to-day to do just as I say. He's a fine fellow and I can't take any chances with him." The next day the good doctor wrote, "I am sorry to say that our patient Gus Welch deliberately kicked over the traces to-day and in spite of all advice to the contrary, left his bed, and dressed himself, declaring that he would assume all responsibility." Gus pulled into Carlisle on November 30th while the team was away on a long road trip, injured too badly to ever suit up for the Indians again.

Carlisle renewed competitions with Dickinson College the Saturday after the Notre Dame game but it was another mismatch—this time in the Indians' favor. Twelve-minute quarters kept the scoring down a bit. The Indians jumped out to a thirteen-point lead in the first quarter on two Calac touchdowns and one successful kick after. In the second quarter, Charles Pratt fielded a kickoff on his own five-yard line and made a spectacular ninety-five-yard run for a touchdown. Calac kicked the extra points for that and the two

> **"Let Football Stars Alone, Girls,"**
> **Pleads College Dean With Co-Eds**
>
> Evanston, Ill., Nov. 14.—Disheartened over successive defeats of the Northwestern university football team, Dean Thomas Holgate today issued this appeal to co-eds of the university: "Let football players alone."
>
> "Don't keep football stars up late, girls," pleaded the dean. "Don't feed them rarebits and candy that put them out of condition. Make that 200-pound boy who comes to call feel cheap if he hasn't tried out for the eleven—and one last word, don't set the football men to dreaming about you when they ought to be rehearsing signals."

touchdowns he scored in the second and fourth quarters, respectively. Warner substituted players liberally in the second half. The final score was Carlisle 34–Dickinson 0.

Five days later, the Indians suited up for the annual end-of-season Thanksgiving Day game with Brown. The Indians outplayed the Brunonians but fumbling two of Gordon's punts deep in Indian territory led to two easy touchdowns for Brown, without which they would have lost the game. Calac scored two touchdowns late in the game and kicked both extra points. The final score was Brown 20–Carlisle 14. The Indians' regular season was over, and newspaper accounts assumed that Warner was going to be coaching Pitt in 1915.

> **Glenn Warner Signs To Coach Pitt Team**
>
> Wizard of Football Will Instruct the Local College Champions for the Next Three Years. Great Record Is Recounted.

The Indian School newspaper only made vague references to post-season games but no coverage. Fortunately, regular newspapers covered them in detail.

Former Harvard All-American Hamilton Fish assembled a team of predominately former Ivy League All Stars to challenge Pop Warner to a charity game benefitting the Children's Island Sanitarium the Saturday after the Brown game. Finding it convenient for the Indians to remain in New England for a couple more days, Warner accepted the challenge. Not known was his reason for taking on this challenge when he had such a weak team.

The Fenway Park field was in poor shape for a football game. The ground was frozen hard in the shade of the stands and wet and slippery farther out where the sun shone on it. An early Carlisle fumble by Wallette gave the All-Stars the ball at the forty-yard line. Ten powerful smashes later, Snow carried the ball across and kicked the extra point. In the second quarter, the Indians threatened at the All-Star seven-yard line but Dartmouth's Snow

intercepted their fourth-down forward pass to end the drive. The Indians threatened the entire third quarter but didn't score. In the fourth quarter, Huntington blocked Henry Broker's punt. Witherington gathered it in at the twenty and raced to the end zone for a touchdown. He missed the extra point. The All-Stars led 13–0.

When the Indians got the ball back, Fred Broker, who was filling in for Calac at fullback most of the game, made most of the rushes on the drive and carried the ball over for an Indian touchdown. His brother, Henry, missed the extra point. With little time remaining, the Indians tried to chew up yardage with forward passes but failed to complete them. The final score was All-Stars 13-Carlisle 6.

> **ALABAMA IS AFTER ASSISTANT COACH OF INDIANS**
>
> Dietz Announces That He Has Received Offer to Succeed Graves

On Wednesday, the Indians made a rare trip south to Birmingham, Alabama, where the Crimson Tide played their big games instead of at home in Tuscaloosa. Right halfback Pratt did the most damage, scoring touchdowns in each of the first two quarters. His replacement, Richard Johnson, scored one in the third quarter. Grant White kicked two extra points. Alabama got on the scoreboard with a fourth-quarter Vandergraff field goal. The final score was Carlisle 20-Alabama 3.

When approached about possibly coaching the Thin Red line, Dietz responded, "Alabama has just as good material as Carlisle, but they are not well coached on open play. I believe I could whip the team into shape to win games next year., and would consider the proposition from Alabama if the salary consideration could be arranged."

Bama's athletic authorities insisted on multiple occasions that they and the student body were pleased with D. V. "Tubby" Graves' work and they wanted to retain him. They blamed an anonymous writer for publishing articles aimed to undermine Graves and stated that they had never considered Lone Star for the job. Thomas Kelley took the reins in 1915 after Graves moved on to Texas A & M.

Saturday found the Indians in Atlanta playing what many thought was Auburn's best team ever. On a dreary day, unbeaten and unscored-upon The Plainsmen took on the Indians on a muddy field. Pratt and Calac gained considerable yardage but couldn't put the ball across the goal line as the poor footing hampered their attack. Although Auburn put on its best performance of the year, the game remained scoreless until the fourth quarter, when Orange and Blue unveiled their passing attack for the first time. Hairston threw to Robinson, but Kearley knifed across to snag the ball deep in Carlisle territory. A Carlisle offside moved the ball five yards closer to paydirt. Hairston then ran it across for an Auburn touchdown. Carlisle players were chagrined to end their season and their coach's tenure in a loss.

This game may have been the origin of Auburn's War Eagle cheer. According to this story, there was a lineman, possibly a tackle, named Bald Eagle on the Indians' team. Attempting to exhaust that player, Auburn's team began running multiple plays directly at his position. Without even huddling, the Auburn quarterback Lucy Hairston would yell "Bald Eagle," letting the rest of the team know that the play would be run at the tackle. Spectators, however, thought the quarterback was saying "War Eagle," and began to chant that. Carlisle had no player named Bald Eagle but they did have a guard named Thomas Hawkeagle. Hairston yelling "Hawkeagle" could be misunderstood to be War Eagle as easily as could Bald Eagle. This 1914 game could well have originated the "War Eagle" yell.

1914 Season Summary

Date	Opponent	Location	Indians	Opp.
Sep. 19	Albright College	Indian Field, Carlisle Barracks, PA	20	0
Sep. 23	Lebanon Valley College	Indian Field, Carlisle Barracks, PA	7	0
Sep. 26	West Virginia Wesleyan College	Union Park, Clarksburg, WV	6	0
Oct. 3	Lehigh University	Taylor Stadium, S. Bethlehem, PA	6	21
Oct. 10	Cornell University	Percy Field, Ithaca, NY	0	21
Oct. 17	University of Pittsburgh	Forbes Field, Pittsburgh, PA	3	10
Oct. 24	University of Pennsylvania	Franklin Field, Philadelphia, PA	0	7
Oct. 31	Syracuse University	Federal Field, Buffalo, NY	3	24
Nov. 7	College of the Holy Cross	Textile Field, Manchester, NH	0	0
Nov. 14	University of Notre Dame	Comiskey Park, Chicago, IL	6	48
Nov. 21	Dickinson College	Biddle Field, Carlisle, PA	34	0
Nov. 26	Brown University	Andrews Field, Providence, RI	14	20
Nov. 28	All Stars	Fenway Park, Boston, MA	6	13
Dec. 2	University of Alabama	Rickwood Field, Birmingham, AL	20	3
Dec. 5	Auburn University	Piedmont Park, Atlanta, GA	0	7

Won 5; Lost 9; Tied 1

Charge of the Grid Brigade By APPY

HALF A YARD, half a yard
　　Half a yard onward!
　See the brave quarterback
　　Prone and face downward,
Bearing upon his back
Struggling and fighting pack
Heaped in a human stack
　　Weighing six hundred.

　Half a yard, half a yard,
　　Half a yard forward,
Crawled the bold quarterback
　Sou-east by nor-ward,
Plowing his noble mush
Deep in the mud and slush
Wriggling beneath the crush
　　Steadily score-ward.

Thick flew the verbal shells,
　Shrapnel and dum-dum,
Thick on him foemen fell,
　Driving him rum-dum.
Stormed at by rooters' yell,
Bravely he crawled and well,
Flat on his little bel—
　(Pardon me, tum-tum).

Half a leg, half a leg,
　Half a leg sundered,
Hamstrung and stringhalted,
　Windbroke and foundered;
Spiked shoes astride of him,
Knots tied inside of him,
Scars on the hide of him,
　More'n a hundred.

Rahs for the quarterback
　Volleyed and thundered;
Why his back didn't crack
　All the world wondered.
Rah for the human skid,
Rah for the stunt he did,
Full half a yard he slid,
Burned up the bloody grid,
Sure is the candy kid,
　Rahs by the hundred!
　　　　—G. S. APPLEGARTH.

20

The Decline

Rule changes for 1915:

Field Judge is mandatory. Forward passes going out of bounds on a fly are now incomplete passes. Previously, was a turnover at the spot the ball went out of bounds. (Teams passed the ball out of bounds rather than punt.)
Running into and roughing the punter distinguished with separate penalties.
Center must snap and release the ball in one continuous motion.

On February 15, 1915, Pop and Tibb Warner were honored with an elaborate farewell reception, which was attended by the school's administrators as well as those involved in athletics. This event marked the end of Warner's tenure at Carlisle. He left for his home in Springville, New York a week later to get some rest before starting his new job as head football coach for the University of Pittsburgh with a salary reputed to be $4,500. Even before this, the papers were filled with conjectures as to who would be Carlisle's next head football coach.

The first name mentioned was Lone Star Dietz, Pop's primary assistant the last two seasons. Dietz was a logical choice but he didn't want the job. Speculation then had Al Exendine taking Warner's place if he could be released from his contract with Georgetown. Next was Frank Mt. Pleasant, who chose the University of Buffalo instead. Gus Welch was at least one writer's choice if Dietz wasn't available. Several former players, including Charles Guyon, Bemus Pierce, Frank Hudson, and Frank Cayou, applied for the job and others were mentioned by the media. But none of the Carlisle stars was chosen. In February, newspapers reported that Commissioner Cato Sells had hired well-known Indian lawyer and former Texas A & M quarterback, Victor M. "Choc" Kelley (often spelled Kelly) as athletic director at a salary of $4,000. Choc had also been at Carlisle for a short while. Gus Welch later charged that Kelley's hiring had been a political decision. The fact that Kelley's appointment was made by Commissioner of Indian Affairs Cato Sells supports this contention.

Warner received a request from Washington State College for a reference on E. R. Wingard of Maine, who had applied to fill their vacant head football coach position. Warner gave him a lukewarm recommendation and suggested they seriously consider Lone Star Dietz. WSC offered Dietz the job and he accepted it. Dietz had a lot to do before heading out to Pullman, Washington. Angel wasn't accompanying Dietz to Pullman, Washington. Her career was in the East and his job was only for the football season. She resigned and moved into an apartment in town with no place for a kennel. Liquidating Orloff Kennel meant selling the prize-winning Russian Wolfhounds. One pup's sale made the local newspaper, probably because it brought $700, more than a year's salary for many people. She wanted $1,000 for Khotni, that year's Best in Breed winner at Westminster but it's not known if she got it. Before leaving, Dietz predicted that Kelley would not be successful as the new Carlisle head coach.

New superintendent Oscar Lipps was dealing with more off-campus discipline problems than Pratt had experienced. He wrote, "I find that a large number of our students have more money than the average white boys and girls, and we have no way on knowing what their financial condition is, except through superintendents of the reservations from which they come." With more reservation land split among members of the tribes under the allotment system, many students owned or inherited plots. They would receive modest rent from a farmer or rancher or larger sums by selling it. Some tribes received cash annuities as part of treaties with the government. Young people not previously having access to significant amounts of money hadn't developed skills in managing it. Shady white and Black people eagerly took it, often illegally selling the young Indians alcohol. Athletes were affected as much as other students.

When the Indians' schedule was published, pundits poked the Crimson, saying, "The Carlisle Indians have been tamed sufficiently to play Harvard. It was said when the redskins were dropped that they were a trifle too strenuous."

L-to-R: Gus Welch & Victor Kelley

Cornell, Penn, Syracuse, and Notre Dame were replaced by Bucknell, Fordham, and Harvard in a move to soften Carlisle's schedule somewhat.

Coach Kelley arrived in late August to take the reins of the football team. Gus Welch, who had a successful year of coaching at Conway Hall, Dickinson College's preparatory school, agreed to assist Kelley with the varsity.

Ninety-three boys turned out for the first practice. Thirty of them were on the 1914 varsity or were substitutes, but the rest had little or no experience. Several of last year's players returned from Detroit where they had worked as apprentices at the Ford plant over the summer. Former stars including Welch, Garlow, Guyon, and Busch would never be in the line-up again.

Kelley began a winnowing process to find the best players. John McGillis coached the reserves with Leo Rocque, former Haskell halfback, assisting him. Pete Calac served as captain again. Hot weather prevented the coaches from working the players hard during the first week of practice.

Starting like the Carlisle teams of old against Albright College, Calac scored the Indians' first touchdown of the season on a series of end runs within two minutes of the opening kickoff. Before the first nine-minute quarter was over, he had scored again. Philip "Woodchuck" Welmas made both kicks after touchdown to put Carlisle ahead 14-0. Albright outplayed Carlisle in the second quarter and came close to scoring as the first half ended with Albright in possession on the Indians' two-yard line. Grant White was substituted into the game in the third quarter and scored Carlisle's third touchdown. Welmas's

1915 Squad

kick was good. Albright's Benfer threw a thirty-five-yard pass to Hoffman, who after catching the ball, ran thirty yards for only the second touchdown the Red and White had scored in fourteen years of playing the Indians. Benfer kicked the extra point. The Indians scored three more touchdowns but they were all called back for penalties, usually offsides. The final score was Carlisle 21–Albright 7.

On Sunday, the day after the Albright game, Charles "Uncle Charley" Moran arrived on campus to serve as trainer. "Choc" Kelley knew him as his head coach at Texas A&M. Moran immediately set about rubbing strained muscles.

The next Saturday, the Indians ran into a hornets' nest in the form of Lebanon Valley's defense. Guy Dickerson and Calac played the best games in the scoreless tie that featured numerous fumbles, incomplete passes, and penalties. Former Carlisle halfback Joel Wheelock assisted in coaching the Dutchmen that year. His familiarity with Carlisle's offense may have helped to defend against it. Their home schedule complete, the Indians took to the road for the bulk of their contests.

Backfield errors sealed the Indians' fate against Lehigh by giving up two touchdowns early in the first quarter. Poor defense against an end run and a fumble by a running back paved the way for the scores. The rest of the game, played on a muddy field, was a defensive struggle with no further scoring. Fred Broker played well for the Indians. Calac did the best he could on an injured knee. The final score was Lehigh 14–Carlisle 0. The band and student body greeted the team when its train arrived in Carlisle late that night.

Despite outgaining the Crimson 275 yards to 175, the outweighed Indians lost to Harvard because of fumbles, penalties, and intercepted passes. *The Boston Globe* was unimpressed by Harvard's effort: "The superiority of Haughton's men was by no means indicated by the difference that existed in the score, for Carlisle put up a more aggressive game than Harvard and only the queer breaks in luck for the Indians, coupled with the alertness of the Crimson team,

permitted the Cambridge eleven to emerge an ultimate winner." Jesse Wofford finally put the Indians on the scoreboard in the third quarter on a ten-yard run around end on a double pass Dickerson called when Harvard was expecting another line buck. Calac kicked the extra point. But it was too little too late. After all this, Carlisle's coaches thought they had played their best game of the season in the 29–Carlisle 7 loss.

The Indians could not have looked forward to the next game with undefeated Pitt. It was against their old coach's new team. Warner would have been familiar with many of the Carlisle players and was the man who invented their offensive scheme. To make matters worse, Pop inherited a highly skilled set of experienced players who had beaten a stronger set of Indian players the year before. Ed Morrin, Gus Lookaround, Wofford, and Calac played good games in spite of the overwhelming opposition in the 45–0 skinning.

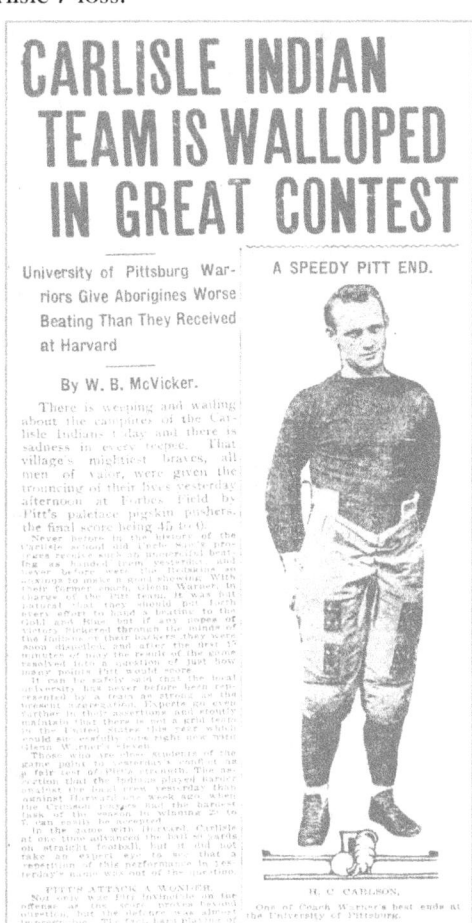

The Indians stayed at home to play Bucknell. Evenly matched, the teams played to a scoreless tie. Injuries and poor play led the coaches to constantly try new men. They elevated several players from the Second Team and tried new men throughout the season. The administration added participation on the school's athletic teams to the curriculum, a move that supplied an almost never-ending supply of players for the scrubs.

On the road again to play West Virginia Wesleyan, the Indians faced another team coached by one of their former teammates, William Garlow. After a scoreless first half, the Methodists took advantage of two opportunities to score. When the Indians failed to break up a forward pass in the third quarter, they gave up a touchdown. A punt return in the fourth quarter yielded a second score for the opponents. Three Carlisle drives stalled on the Wesleyan five-yard line when the Indians weren't able to put the ball into the end zone, allowing West Virginia Wesleyan to shut them out 14-0.

After a string of four losses and two scoreless ties, the Indians hoped to bounce back against Holy Cross, Dickinson, and Fordham. Gus Welch claimed that he was put in charge at that time due to Kelley's lack of coaching ability, saying, "There was a meeting three weeks before Thanksgiving at which Superintendent Lipps, Manager Meyer, Kelley, Capt. Calac and myself were present. It was decided then that Kelley was to be dismissed as head coach." Kelley claimed that he only turned over the conduct of practice to Welch, and that was done after concluding that some of the players weren't putting out their best efforts and, since Welch had been undermining him, they might perform better for his assistant.

A new player, 1914 All-Missouri Valley quarterback Henry Flood, had arrived from Haskell Institute on October 1st to enroll at Conway Hall in preparation to studying for a law degree. It wouldn't be inconceivable for him to have noticed that Carlisle presented an opportunity for a good athlete wanting to further his education and took advantage of it. Welch inserted him into the starting line-up at quarterback against Holy Cross. This was a game of opposite halves. The Indians could do nothing wrong in the first half, and the Sagamores could do nothing right. Fred Broker scored two touchdowns and Dickerson scored one. Broker kicked one extra point. Calac kicked another, plus a field goal, to put the Indians ahead 23-0 at halftime. Holy Cross made the game exciting by turning the tables in the second half. They also made three touchdowns but only one extra point. Tackling Flood in his end zone for a safety brought their point total to 21. Had their quarterback not fumbled within field goal range in the fourth quarter, Holy Cross might have pulled off a come-from-behind win. Carlisle held on for a 23-21 victory.

The Dickinsonians were poised to upset the Indians the next Saturday and their fans turned out in mass, hoping to see them beat Carlisle for the first time since 1893. The Red and White drew first blood early when Puderbaugh recovered an Indian fumble and raced twenty yards for a touchdown. McWhinney kicked the extra point. Later, Dickinson recovered another Carlisle fumble on the twenty-yard line and attempted a field goal that missed. In the second quarter, the Indians worked the ball down to the Dickinson two-yard line from where White ran the ball in for an Indian touchdown. Calac's extra-point attempt missed. Late in the half, Dickinson advanced the ball to the Indian four-yard line. They fumbled the ball away, losing the chance to score. The first half ended with Dickinson holding a slim 7–6 lead.

In the third quarter, Calac's thirty-five-yard dropkick attempt went wide by a foot. In the fourth quarter, McWhinney scooped up an Indian fumble and ran it fifty yards to the Indian one-yard line. Palm plunged over for the Dickinson touchdown. McWhinney's extra point gave the Red and White a commanding 14–6 lead. But the Indians weren't done. After a punt exchange, they drove the ball down to the Dickinson ten-yard line with a series of hard line plunges. Four short plunges later, Flood carried the ball in for a Carlisle touchdown. Calac's extra point brought the Indians to within striking distance. Down 14–13, time was running out. After receiving a Dickinson punt, the Indians fought with a fury, moving the ball down into field goal range. Denied a first down on three attempts, Dickerson fooled the defenders by circling his right end and twisting and sidestepping tacklers for a twenty-yard run to paydirt. Calac kicked the extra point with only thirty seconds remaining on the clock. The 20–14 Carlisle victory ended with Dickinson completing a twenty-five-yard pass to the Indian twenty-yard line. *The Philadelphia Inquirer* gave kudos to Calac, Flood, Dickerson, and the Morrin brothers, Edward and Joseph, on the Indians' side and to Palm, Dalton, Puderbaugh, Brown, and the Masland brothers, Robert and Frank, for their good play.

The game against Fordham started badly for Carlisle when the Bronxites' Captain Dave Dunn grabbed Flood's fumble and rambled eighty-five yards behind excellent interference to score a touchdown. Yule kicked the extra point. In the second quarter with the ball on Carlisle's twenty-yard line, Yule dropped back to attempt a field goal. Fortunately for Carlisle, his kick into the wind fell short by several yards. Using Calac as a battering ram, the Indians pounded the Fordham line for five consecutive first downs, putting the ball on the Rams' forty. The fullback then dropped back and split the uprights with a clean field goal for the Indians. After receiving the following kickoff, Fordham had moved the ball down to the Carlisle 8-yard line when the first half ended with them ahead 7–3.

In the third quarter, with fourth down and twelve yards to go for a first down, instead of kicking, Yule straight-armed, jumped over, and slipped through the entire defense while plowing forward for Fordham's second touchdown. He also kicked the extra point to put the Rams ahead 14–3. Calac countered with a touchdown and extra point for Carlisle. Going into the fourth quarter down 14–10, the Indians made things interesting. When the Indians had first and goal on Fordham's five-yard line, the home team's fans rose to their feet to cheer the defense on. Only able to gain but a yard on four tries, the Indians turned the ball over on downs, ending their last hope for a victory. Not unlike some previous contests, six Carlisle players were knocked out of the game with injuries. Fordham prevailed 14-10.

Five days later, the weakened Indians took on a strong Brown team that had already beaten Yale. Led by future College and Pro Football Hall-of-Famer and the first Walter Camp African-American All-American Fritz Pollard, the Brunonians overwhelmed the outmanned Indians. They moved the ball at will and scored at least one touchdown in every quarter. Carlisle's only score came late in the game via a field goal by Fred Broker from a difficult angle. The final score was Brown 39-Carlisle 3. The Indian School's athletic program was in disarray, and its future was in doubt.

Superintendent Oscar Lipps requested to have two years added to the school's new curriculum in order to attract more students. A larger and older student body could only help the school athletic program.

Their season over, several players left for Detroit the Monday after the Brown game to work at the Ford plant. Three others who had started in January were promoted in July to receive pay of $5.00 per day. Six who started in June were scheduled to be promoted in December. When Henry Ford had doubled his workers' pay to $5.00 a day in 1914, he shocked the industry. Former footballer Joseph Gilman, one of those already receiving that large salary, had recently broken the factory record for assembling a Model T by five minutes!

But Brown's season wasn't over. The Tournament of Roses administration had extended an invitation to them to play in an East vs West Championship Game largely on their defeat of perennial champion Yale. Pasadena, California locals had held a New Year's morning floral parade annually for decades and wanted a major event to round out the afternoon's activities. Other types of events, such as chariot races and donkey polo games, had been tried and found unacceptable, so they took a flyer on football. Brown's opponent, Washington State College, hadn't had a winning season in ages until Carlisle alum Lone Star Dietz arrived in August. Installing the Warner system, he led the formerly floundering team to an undefeated season, generating headlines across the country.

Snow fell in Pasadena two days before the game and rain poured down on New Year's day. With muddy field conditions, Dietz had to throw out the razzle-dazzle and run line bucks against the heavier Brown team. His protégés limited Pollard to forty yards rushing and almost drowned him in a mud puddle. Shutting out Brown 14-0 after an undefeated season caused some pundits to consider Washington State for the hypothetical national championship.

Lonestar Dietz's idea of Southern California college life.

California men will never be able to compete with anyone because they may never learn to walk. They ride in motorcars to cross the street. As a result, they are soft and never fit to play real football.   Lone Star Dietz

Numerous commentators recommended the University of Pittsburgh and Cornell for this honor. Dietz's mentor, Pop Warner, had taken over an improving Pitt team and led his charges to an impressive 8-0 season. Warner's alma mater, Cornell, also went undefeated but declined an offer to play Pitt to determine the Eastern Championship.

It might not have been a coincidence that Carlisle's former head coach and his first assistant both went undefeated in 1915, and that their teams were considered for the national championship. The change in coaching surely had a significant effect on Carlisle's performance in 1915.

Gus Welch claimed that Victor Kelley's lack of personality and inability to coach football kept Kelley from being successful. He asserted that in a letter of protest against Kelley, signed by sixteen varsity players, and presented it to the superintendent. Kelley accused Welch of torpedoing his efforts, relating that a friend of Welch's had wagered Welch would begin undermining him within ten days of his arrival. The Indian School administration supported Kelley. Welch countered that the team went 2-2 in the four games in which he was in charge, a far better record than when Kelley was calling the shots. Kelley also claimed that Welch's undermining of Warner led to the poor 1914 showing. A battle between a head coach and his first assistant wasn't likely to create anything good. Better coaching could possibly have turned three of the losses and two ties into wins. The turnaround at Washington State that Dietz engineered and Warner's success at Pitt were testaments to what good coaching can accomplish.

Professional football was a ragtag business in 1915, but a couple of Carlisle alums were involved in something that impacted football history forever. Jack Cusack, as owner and manager of the Canton, Ohio semi-pro football team, had agreed with the Massillon Tigers' manager to renew the Canton-Massillon rivalry games at the end of the season. The two teams were located ten miles apart and would play a game on each team's home field. When he got wind of Massillon loading up on former All-Americans, Cusack put in motion something that would change the course of professional football. He dispatched former Carlisle Indian School end William Gardner, who was playing for Canton at the time, to Bloomington, Indiana to offer Jim Thorpe, who was coaching the Indiana University backfield, $500 a game to play for Canton. Thorpe agreed. When word got out what Cusack had done, other team managers said he'd go broke. Sure, ringers had been paid large amounts to play in a big game here and there, but no one had been paid this kind of money to play every game of the season.

The rest, as they say, is history. Attendance more than doubled at every game in which Thorpe was to appear and professional football became a marginally profitable business. Thorpe's interactions with Massillon's ringer, Knute Rockne, are legends in themselves.

Rockne often told of his first encounter with Thorpe. When Big Jim carried the ball around Rockne's end, Knute tackled him for a loss.

Thorpe said, "You mustn't do that, Rock. These fans paid to see Old Jim run. Be a good boy and let Old Jim run."

Rockne didn't heed the advice and tried to tackle Thorpe the next time he came his way. Flat on his back, Knute watched Thorpe run fifty yards for a touchdown. After the play, Jim came back to check on Rockne's condition. He handed the still-groggy downed end a wet towel, smiled, and said, "That's a good boy, Rock. You let Old Jim run."

1915 Season Summary

Date	Opponent	Location	Indians	Opp.
Sep. 18	Albright College	Indian Field, Carlisle Barracks, PA	21	6
Sep. 25	Lebanon Valley College	Indian Field, Carlisle Barracks, PA	0	0
Oct. 2	Lehigh University	Taylor Stadium, S. Bethlehem, PA	0	14
Oct. 9	Harvard University	Harvard Stadium, Cambridge, MA	7	29
Oct. 16	University of Pittsburgh	Forbes Field, Pittsburgh, PA	0	45
Oct. 23	Bucknell University	Indian Field, Carlisle Barracks, PA	0	0
Oct. 30	West Virginia Wesleyan	League Park, Martins Ferry, WV	0	14
Nov. 6	College of the Holy Cross	Fitton Field, Worcester, MA	23	21
Nov. 13	Dickinson College	Biddle Field, Carlisle, PA	20	14
Nov. 20	Fordham University	Fordham Field, Bronx, NY	10	14
Nov. 25	Brown University	Andrews Field, Providence, RI	3	39

Won 3; Lost 6; Tied 2

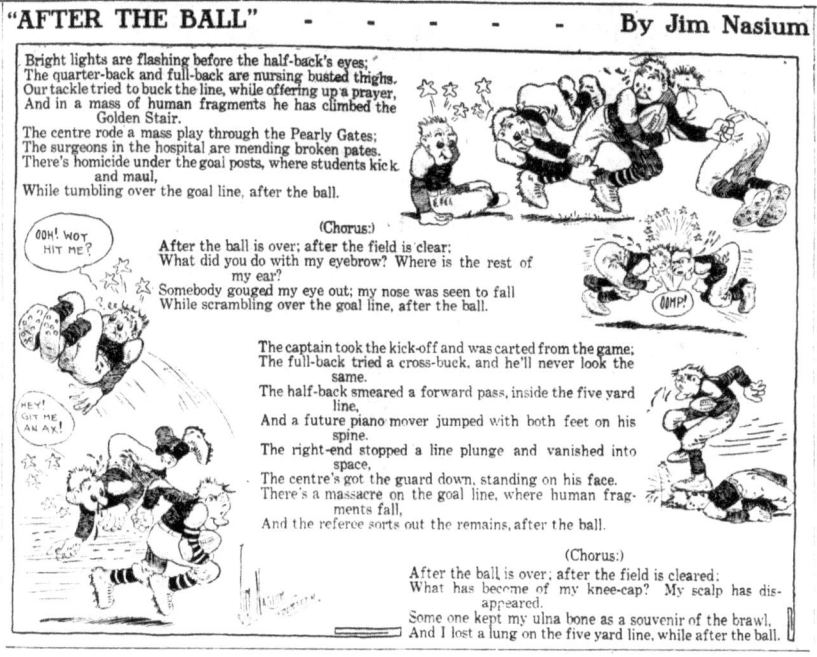

Lone Star Dietz, coach of the undefeated Pacific Coast champions

21

The Season That Almost Wasn't

Rule changes for 1916:

The safety rule was clarified to eliminate a player being pushed back into the end zone being a safety as the forward progress rule overruled that.

Defensive penalties in the end zone would give the team on offense a touchdown.

A quarterback is ineligible to receive a forward pass unless he is at least a yard back from the line of scrimmage when the ball is snapped.

Players on defense cannot interfere with the person trying to catch the punt-out.

The rule against striking an opponent with locked hands has been expanded to all players in all situations.

Striking a player in the face with the heel of the hand is now considered unnecessary roughness.

Another issue raised by the 1914 joint congressional investigation was that players sometimes received chits for merchandise at local stores. These awards continued to flow after the investigation, but were now issued by the superintendent instead of the coach. Football players also received "trinkets," which were often gold watches, clothing, or tailoring for their efforts on the gridiron. But they no longer came from the coach or athletic director; they came directly from the school's administration. Although no fan of football, Superintendent Oscar Lipps must have agreed with Warner and others that students often needed things the government didn't supply them. The underfunded school didn't have the means to pay students even small stipends. Earnings from outing periods served that function for students old enough to work off-campus at farms or businesses. Football players couldn't go on outings during the fall and were often asked to speak at meetings while away from school. The chits were often used to buy suits of what they called "citizens' clothing" they could wear on such occasions.

Shortly after the 1915 season ended, newspapers across the country blared headlines stating that Carlisle was dropping football. Secretary of the

Interior Lane cited one reason: of seventeen students participating in the training program at Ford that led to earning $5.00 a day, thirteen interrupted their automobile work to return to school to play football, sacrificing educational opportunities and wages at Ford. Colleges then jockeyed to replace Carlisle's position on other teams' schedules. As one example, Georgetown University, then coached by Carlisle alum Albert Exendine, lobbied to play against Brown in their annual Thanksgiving game previously played against Carlisle. No one played Brown that year. Thanksgiving came late on November 30 in 1916, and Brown had finished its season before that. Georgetown didn't play anyone that day but they had two games in December, the last of which was against Tulane in New Orleans.

> **POOR LO NOW IS BUSY LO**[14]
>
> Indians at Carlisle School Earned $35,169.42 Working Part Time During the Year.
>
> Carlisle, Pa.—How the Indian is taking his place as a citizen of this country and fitting himself to be a self-sustaining wage-earner is shown in the report of the work of the students of the Carlisle Indian school under the "outing system" for 1916, recently made public.

Victor Kelley's name soon appeared in newspaper articles across the country as being considered by various schools in the Southwest and Far West. Carlisle had not drawn up a schedule for the upcoming season, and he would not be returning. Coaches of teams Carlisle had played against bemoaned their disappearance from the gridiron. Some credited them with saving the game.

At the start of the new school year in September, students were quarantined to campus due to an infantile paralysis (polio) epidemic in the Northeast, as were the town children. Two cases had been reported in the county along with a dozen cases of typhoid fever, the latter attributed to bad ice cream from a Harrisburg dairy. Especially irritating for the students was not being allowed to attend the Carlisle Fair.

Gus Welch took an assistant disciplinarian position at the Large Boys Quarters on campus because, as an orphan, he needed the income to support himself and to pay his law school tuition. Gus also coached the Conway Hall prep school team, for a small amount of pay, one assumes. He spent his Saturdays starring at halfback on the Dickinson College team.

---

[14] In old U. S. slang, Lo was a generic name for an Indian or Indians collectively.

On September 30, after Dickinson held Navy to a scoreless tie at Annapolis, students gathered wood for a bonfire, organized a drum corps, and paraded through the town with the freshmen leading in their nightshirts. A freshman led the parade on horseback, holding up a banner displaying the game's score. They soon heard music coming in from North Hanover Street. The Indian School band led the battalion of cadets and merged into the parade already formed. When asked why the Indians were celebrating, one responded, "We want to show the authorities that we still like football and, if we can't have a team of our own, we will help Dickinson celebrate her victories." George May had been elected captain of the football team at the end of the last season but had no team to lead. After school started, Nick Lassa was elected cheerleader for the year but cross country, the only sport Carlisle was competing in this fall, didn't lend itself to his type of support.

Spurious articles began appearing in newspapers. One had Carlisle as Yale's first opponent for the year. It was false but something was happening. The Carlisle administration stated that the Secretary of the Interior had been misunderstood: "Secretary Lane did not issue an order forbidding football at Carlisle, but he did let it be known that in the future football must be subordinated to the educational features of the school. It has never been the intention to drop the game at Carlisle, but under present rules governing the enrollment of students in Indian schools Carlisle can no longer compete with the large universities on anything like equal terms. For this reason it will be content to develop the very best teams possible under the restrictions now prevailing and to play only such school teams as may fairly be considered in its class. While we can afford no high salaried coach and no expensive training tables, still we shall continue to play good football."

> **Carlisle Indians Hand Out Football Surprise; Return to Gridiron Sport**

Merton L. Clevett, hired as physical director after Warner left, was assigned the duties of head football coach. Since the season had already started, it was too late to put together a cohesive schedule; games would be arranged on an ad hoc basis. The first game the Indians played was "quietly planned and few except the enthusiastic student body here, headed by its band, saw the game." The light Carlisle team, consisting of almost all new men, defeated the Lebanon Valley College Reserves 20 to 6 on a Tuesday afternoon. Press coverage was less detailed than for varsity games in the past.

Many former players had dispersed to other schools and semi-pro teams after the announcement that Carlisle was dropping football. Last year's star Pete Calac had transferred to West Virginia Wesleyan and Joe Guyon was on Georgia Tech's freshman team. Nine of the previous year's eleven working at Ford formed a "Carlisle Indian" team in Detroit and played independent teams. Older former players turned pro. For example, William Garlow teamed with Jim Thorpe at Canton and Joe Bergie was with Pitcairn.

On Saturday, the Indians took on the Conway Hall squad that was coached by Gus Welch. They played at the Indian School instead of Biddle Field because Dickinson College was playing Ursinus there that day. Although the teams were equal in size, the prep school boys were no match for Carlisle's new varsity squad. The Indians were much quicker "with as brilliant an exhibition of open playing as has ever been seen on Indian Field." The features of the 20 to 0 blowout were Thomas Miles' two touchdowns and Captain May's seventy-six-yard run through the entire Conway Hall defense for another one.

On Wednesday, Clevett reinstituted a staple of Warner's training regime: mid-week scrimmages with Dickinson College.

The next Saturday at Selinsgrove, the Carlisle varsity suffered its first defeat at Susquehanna University by being shut out 12 to 0. While that game was going on, the Carlisle third string pounded Cumberland Valley State Normal

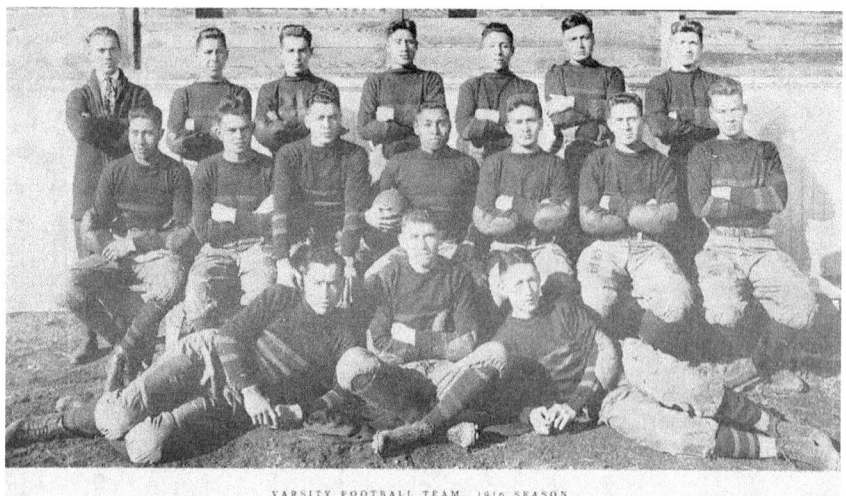

VARSITY FOOTBALL TEAM 1916 SEASON
M. L. Clevett, G. Francis, J. White, C. Walker, B. Spears, G. Tibbetts, D. Noti, J. Flinchum, L. Godfrey, G. May—Capt., W. Eshelman, Tacalesse, Ojibway, J. LeRoy, J. Herman, T. Miles.

School 33-0 on Indian Field. Indian end runs and forward passes from Earl Wilber to Leon Miller overwhelmed the boys from Shippensburg 32-0.

The varsity's next game proved to be a disaster. Their opponents were a semi-pro team from Conshohocken, Pennsylvania, and the game was played on their field. Coach Clevett served as umpire for the game and warned both teams that he would not stand for fighting. Rough play, mostly from the Conshohocken team, happened during the first half but there was no punching. The half ended with the score tied 6-6. Early in the second half, one of the Carlisle halfbacks tackled Conshohocken's left end after he caught a long pass. A fight broke out between them. After the pugilists were pulled apart, Clevett pulled his team off the field. He was instantly surrounded by several hundred spectators who threatened him for stopping the game. The fans may have been enraged because Carlisle fullback Jacob Herman had scored the first touchdown against the home team in three years.

Conshohocken Manager Crawford demanded that Clevett return the guarantee of $166 Carlisle received before the game. When Clevett refused, he was escorted to the police station. After a long negotiation, he returned eighty-three dollars in order to be released. Upon return to Carlisle, he enlisted Attorney William Kramer to sue for $10,000 in damages for false arrest and imprisonment. Conshohocken denied there was an arrest even though two policemen took him into custody. Conshohocken eventually settled by sending Carlisle the eighty-three dollars they had extorted from Clevett for his release.

> **CARLISLE INDIAN COACH, JAILED, WILL SUE FOR $10,000 AS DAMAGES**
>
> M. L. CLEVETT IS INDIGNANT OVER TEAM'S TREATMENT
>
> Calls Game With Conshohocken Saturday Because of Roughness and Is Taken To Jail—Indians Outplay Their Opponents

The Saturday after the Conshohocken debacle, Carlisle crossed the North Mountain to play Carson Long in the neighboring county. The November 10 edition of the school newspaper announced that enrollment was almost to capacity and that the "Hot Shots," Carlisle's second team, were to play Bloomfield Academy the next day. By that time, the military school's name had been changed to Carson Long Institute. The Hot Shots, referred to by newspapers as Reserves, thrashed the cadets 47-13.

A week later, the varsity traveled to Annville to take on the Lebanon Valley varsity after having trounced its reserves a month earlier. The Indians held the Dutchmen scoreless in the first quarter, keeping the ball in LVC territory. When Mackert was substituted into the Annville backfield in the second quarter, LVC came to life and scored twenty points. The Indians held them scoreless in the third quarter but couldn't stop them in the fourth when the Dutchmen scored thirteen more. For the first time in fifteen tries, Lebanon Valley beat Carlisle and by the decisive score of 33-0. Lined up at center for LVC was former Carlisle player and band member William Winneshiek. On the sidelines assisting LVC Head Coach Roy Guyer was former Carlisle halfback and band member Joel Wheelock. At the same time in Carlisle, the LVC Reserves beat the Carlisle Reserves 12-7.

Mother Nature didn't smile on the Indians when they took on the Purple and Gold of Alfred University the following Saturday when she dumped two inches of snow on the players. To make matters worse, the wind reached gale force at times. In spite of the weather, the Indians started strong. John LeRoy intercepted an Alfred forward pass and returned it eighty yards for a Carlisle touchdown. Jacob Herman made the kick after. Later in the first half, he kicked a field goal to put the Indians ahead 10-7 at halftime.

Early in the second half, Alfred pushed Witter over to put them ahead 14 to 10. The Indians came back using a combination of forward passes and rushes to move the ball down the field to send Tom Miles over for a touchdown. His extra point put Carlisle in front 17-14. The tide turned against the Indians when Alfred's quarterback and captain, King, intercepted a forward pass and followed great interference to score a pick six. Behind 21-17, the Indians were still in the game, but Alfred retained possession and pushed Williams over for a decisive touchdown. Alfred won 27-17. The *Elmira Star-Gazette* had one complaint: "There was just one thing to mar the afternoon and that was the discourtesy shown at times by Henderson of Syracuse, who umpired, to newspaper men."

ALFRED UNIVERSITY LIFTS SCALPS OF CARLISLE INDIANS

King Accounts for All but Six of Winning Eleven's Twenty-seven Points.

A Thanksgiving Day game to close the season was arranged with Winchester Athletic Club. A heavy rain caused the game against the semi-pros to be postponed until the Saturday after Thanksgiving. The Reserves, however, met Conway Hall in a rematch on Turkey Day and Conway Hall avenged their earlier loss to Carlisle's varsity 6 to 0. The Winchester A. C. game received scant coverage in the press. About all is known is that the Indians lost 20-6.

The players elected George Tibbetts for Captain of the 1917 team and the local press predicted that Leo "Deed" Harris would be next year's head coach. A piece circulating around the country related that, in a meeting with Superintendent Lipps, thirty experienced players announced their intention to return next year when the football schedule was planned to go back to "the scale of games played many years ago when the Indians first made their reputations on the gridiron."

1916 Season Summary

Date	Opponent	Location	Indian	Opp.
Oct. 17	Lebanon Valley College Reserves	Indian Field, Carlisle Barracks, PA	20	6
Oct. 21	Conway Hall	Indian Field, Carlisle Barracks, PA	26	0
Oct. 28	Susquehanna University	Warner Field, Selinsgrove, PA	0	12
Oct. 28*	Cumberland Valley State Normal School	Indian Field, Carlisle Barracks, PA	32	0
Nov. 4	Conshohocken Athletic Association	Conshohocken Community Field, Conshohocken, PA	6	6
Nov. 11*	Carson Long Institute	Academy Field, New Bloomfield, PA	47	13
Nov. 18	Lebanon Valley College	Annville Field, Annville, PA	0	33
Nov. 18*	Lebanon Valley College Reserves	Indian Field, Carlisle Barracks, PA	7	12
Nov. 25	Alfred University	Gridiron, Alfred, NY	17	27
Nov. 30*	Conway Hall	Biddle Field, Carlisle, PA	0	6
Dec. 2	Winchester Athletic Club	Yale Bowl, New Haven, CT	6	20

*Denotes games played by Carlisle's Reserves.

Varsity Results

Won 2; Lost 4; Tied 1

Reserves Results

Won 2; Lost 2; Tied 0

Shows "Dead Indian" Play

W. H. (Lone Star) Dietz, crafty coach at the Haskell Indian institute, is shown above. Sketches show famous "Dead Indian" play, which Dietz has abandoned, but which may be revived at any time for a vital touchdown. The ball carrier shown downed in position 1, passes ball (position 2) while prone before opposing backs have returned to their stations. The trick has earned many touchdowns. Dietz formerly coached at Washington State.

22

The Last Dance

Rule changes for 1917:

To prevent coaching from the sidelines, incoming substitutes are not allowed to communicate with their teammates until the first play is over. If the substitute is the quarterback, he may call the signals.

Place kicks must be kicked from the ground. Earth may be scraped up to create a tee but artificial tees are banned.

On kick offs and free kicks, players may be in motion in any direction provided they are not off side when the ball is kicked.

The penalty for pass interference is the loss of the ball to the offended side at the spot of the foul.

Penalties for running into or roughing the kicker are now measured from the spot where the ball was put into play.

On January 19, Physical Director Merton Clevett announced the year's ambitious football schedule: Albright College, Mount St. Mary's College, Alfred University, Princeton University, Johns Hopkins University, Bucknell University, Catholic University, Harvard University, University of Pennsylvania, and Rochester University. Playing three of the Big Four was a huge jump for a young team that just completed a losing season against a lower level of opposition. Did Clevett have delusions of grandeur or was he setting an impossibly high standard for the new coach to meet? Leo "Deed" Harris was selected for head football coach later that month and drove his automobile to campus, where he took John LeRoy and Jacob Herman for a ride. They had met earlier at a basketball game in Harrisburg where he lived, having coached one of the best prep elevens in the country at Central High School. Harris was a long-term friend of Pop Warner and follower of his methods.

Months before football season was to start, the United States Congress declared war on Germany, entering the country into World War I, an event that would have a huge impact on everyone in America including Carlisle. Since college and professional sports were played largely by young men of draft age, college football and Major League Baseball were seriously impacted

Gus Welch in officer's uniform.

by the war. In May after graduating from law school, Gus Welch left for officers training school at Ft. Niagara, New York. He would be far from the last Carlislian to enlist. Numerous others quickly followed. Although school publications applauded students who were serving in the military, privately administrators counseled them to continue their education. If the boys were minors, school officials insisted they have written parental consent before joining up.

The Commencement Edition of *The Carlisle Arrow* listed the names of ten boys who joined the Navy, twelve who joined the Army, and five who had been working for Ford who joined the Sixth Regiment, Engineer Reserve Corps. Patriotic boys leaving to do their part in the war would be a fact of life for schools and teams across the country. It would have more of an impact on Carlisle because American Indians served in our wars at a higher rate than any other ethnic group. Even though non-citizen Indians—some had accepted citizenship at this time but most hadn't—were not subject to the draft, a number went to Canada to join the British forces before the U. S. entered the war.

Not having experience leading football teams and little budget to hire assistants, Physical Director Clevett would serve as Harris's assistant. To improve his football skills—gymnastics was his specialty—he attended a summer course at the University of Illinois conducted by their Head Coach Robert Zuppke.

In August, Princeton dropped football for the 1917 season, creating a hole in Carlisle's schedule. Others soon followed. Many other schools reduced or eliminated their athletic programs during the war years and several military units fielded teams of their own. Carlisle's schedule would have to be adjusted accordingly.

Pop Warner spent five days at Carlisle in early September working with coaches Harris and Clevett and their team. He predicted a positive future: "While the school and its friends should not expect great things of the team this year, I feel sure that a very creditable showing will be made and that the coming season will start the Carlisle Indian football team on the right road to regain its former prestige. A great football team cannot be developed in one season with the material at hand. It may take two or even three seasons of steady development to reach a place near the top, but I feel sure that the right kind of start has been made and that the Indians are going to 'come back' in football."

The season opener with Albright College started with Carlisle making some "inexpensive" fumbles as the Red and White didn't capitalize on them. Captain George Tibbets at left halfback and John LeRoy at fullback exhibited some fancy footwork resembling that of famous Carlisle stars of the past. Right halfback Jacob Herman duplicated Thorpe's feat of zigzagging though the entire Albright team for a touchdown. Metoxen made some fine gains around end and up the middle. Carlisle's defense was not as well developed as its offense. The second string performed as well in the second half as the starters did in the first. Tibbets scored four touchdowns. LeRoy, Louis Godfrey, Herman, Charles Walker, and Emerson Metoxen scored one each. LeRoy kicked five extra points; Herman kicked one. Carlisle won 60-0.

A press special, probably released by E. L. Martin but possibly by Clevett, applauded the work of the team against Albright: "Notwithstanding the Redskins' losses to the Army and Navy, the youngsters who average only a little over 17 years of age, are showing such form that Carlisle will have one of the most spectacular teams in its history."

After the Franklin and Marshall College game, Coach Harris would write that ninety percent of Carlisle's players were in their nineteenth year and were the youngest and lightest team to ever represent the school. Whether the press release was wrong or that the team had been decimated by players leaving for the war was unclear. Coach Harris focused on blocking out two men at once and on the kicking game in the Wednesday scrimmage with Dickinson College.

Their home schedule finished, the Indians traveled to Lancaster, Pennsylvania to take on a heavier, but slower, F&M team. Carlisle's play improved, especially that of left tackle Nick Lassaw, aka Long Time Sleep because of his proclivity to sleep late. Carlisle's thirty first downs opposed to F&M's two sums up the game. Tibbets scored three touchdowns; LeRoy and Herman two apiece; Miles and Walker had one each. LeRoy kicked the extra points but missed a field goal attempt. The final 63-0 score suggested that Carlisle was back.

At Morgantown, on the field with no official name the students referred to as "Splinter Stadium," perhaps referring to the condition of the boards in the bleachers, the Indians took on a new opponent, West Virginia. Prior to the Indians coming, they had lost to Pitt and had beaten Navy. Neither team moved the ball well, remaining scoreless through the end of the third quarter. However, West Virginia had the ball to Carlisle's six-yard line at that time. The home team was threatening to score after a twenty-seven-yard penalty on Long Time Sleep and dashes of five, seven, and four yards by Harris, Rodgers and King, respectively. Rodgers bucked the ball over to start the fourth quarter and to put West Virginia on the scoreboard. He also kicked the extra point.

Shortly after the Indians received the kickoff, Rodgers intercepted a Carlisle forward pass and ran it back to the Indians' twenty-five-yard line. Lentz made three yards and Harris fifteen before King ran it in for the second score. Rodgers again made the kick after. On the first play of West Virginia's next possession, Rodgers heaved a pass thirty yards down the field to Mills who carried it twenty yards for the third and final touchdown. Rodgers again made the kick. The final score was West Virginia 21-Carlisle 0. *The Carlisle Arrow and Red Man* described the field as "very slippery and unfit to play on as the fence was 1 yard from the side lines and bleachers practically up against the goal post." It also blamed the loss on penalties and suggested that West Virginia didn't play cleanly.

The next Saturday the Indians ran into a buzzsaw in Annapolis. Navy's new coach, future Hall-of-Famer "Gloomy" Gil Dobie, had gotten his sea legs a week earlier against Maryland State after losing to West Virginia in the Midshipmen's previous outing. Led by former Colgate halfback and future All-American Wolcott "Wooky" Roberts, the Middies blasted holes through and ran around the Carlisle line at will. With a 61-0 lead, Dobie inserted his second string in the fourth quarter and the Indians allowed no further scoring. Carlisle's only bright spot was Lassaw's tackling. Navy went on to win their next four games, scoring eighty or more points against all opponents but Georgetown! Carlisle's defeat didn't look as bad when put into perspective.

The Indians bounced back against Johns Hopkins. Hometown sportswriter C. Star Matthews summed up the game: "Playing a slashing, fighting article of football, Johns Hopkins held the Carlisle Indians to a 15-to-7 score yesterday afternoon at Homewood Field...the Black and Blue gridders fought for every inch of ground. Carlisle deserved to win. She had the better team and only had it not been for two fumbles, both very near the goal line of the varsity, the score would have been much larger."

LeRoy opened the scoring with a thirty-yard field goal from placement, putting the Carlisle ahead 3-0. In the second quarter, the Indians staged a sixty-eight-yard drive consisting at first of end runs, later on line bucks. Jacob Herman gained four off-tackle before squeezing between Hopkins' right tackle and end for a Carlisle touchdown. LeRoy missed an easy extra point. The Indians led 9-0 at halftime.

Sheffy thrilled Hopkins' supporters when he returned LeRoy's kickoff to start the second half eighty yards to set up his touchdown a few plays later. Schmidt kicked the extra point. His field goal attempt later in the third quarter fell below the crossbar. LeRoy's forty-five-yard attempt also failed. The third quarter ended with Carlisle ahead 9-7. Getting the ball at midfield in the fourth quarter, line plunges by LeRoy and Tibbetts advanced the ball down to the Hopkins' eight-yard line. LeRoy muscled the ball over for the last score of the game. He again missed an easy extra point.

Next up was Bucknell, a team the Indians hoped to beat. But a heavy field and penalties did in Carlisle. Bucknell's Waddell kicked a field goal from the thirty-yard line to put the home team ahead 3-0 at halftime. And Waddell hit Kostos with a forward pass in the end zone for a fourth-quarter touchdown. Hall kicked the extra point. LeRoy's unsuccessful field-goal try ended the game with Bucknell winning 10-0.

Stinging from their loss to Notre Dame a week earlier, the Cadets at West Point played their best game of the year against the Indians. Oliphant scored two touchdowns and kicked the extra points in the first half. Wicks scored two more in the second half and Barlett kicked the extra points. Herman made some long runs but fumbled away any advantage gained. LeRoy's third-quarter forty-two-yard-field-goal attempt failed. The final score was Army 28-Carlisle 0.

Scheduling Georgia Tech's Golden Tornado was probably the result of Charles "Wahoo" Guyon's lobbying. He had apparently arranged for a job as

an assistant to Coach John Heisman to get his brother, All-America halfback Joe Guyon, to enroll at Tech and convinced their old alma mater Carlisle to come to Atlanta to play. The game against the consensus National Champions was a total mismatch, resulting in Carlisle suffering its worst loss in school history. Before being taken out midway in the second quarter, quite possibly by his own request, Joe Guyon had reeled off runs of twenty-five, twenty-two, twenty, fifteen and fifteen yards, scored a touchdown, and completed the only pass he threw that day. A Georgia Tech assistant once said that tackling Joe was akin to "grabbing ahold of an airplane propeller." The score when the final, merciful whistle blew was Georgia Tech 98–Carlisle 0.

A Thanksgiving Day game with Boston College was canceled by Carlisle management after the Georgia Tech game. The Indians were already banged up from the Army and Georgia Tech games, and would be worse after the upcoming Penn game. Coach Harris was trying to replace injured players with new men and was trying others at different positions in an attempt to put together a viable lineup. Making that more difficult was the fact that forty-seven Carlisle boys had joined the Army and Navy so far and ten more were expected to go within ten days.

Carlisle's annual rival Penn was up next. The Quakers had only lost to Heisman's men by 41–0, indicating that they were a far better team than that

year's Indians, even if they had been healthy and their ranks not depleted by the war. The Indians surprised the Quakers, or at least one Philadelphia sportswriter, by holding Penn to sixteen points in the first half. Carlisle even threatened to score at the end of the second quarter when they advanced the ball to Penn's fifteen-yard line. Denizens of The City of Brotherly Love must have expected the Indians to be even weaker than they were after hearing the Georgia Tech score. Carlisle couldn't move the ball after receiving the kickoff to open the second half, and Miles punted the ball away. Quigley returned the ball twenty yards to the Indian forty-yard line. On play after play, Penn's backs pounded the Indian line until Light tore through for another Penn touchdown. Quigley kicked the extra point. In the fourth quarter, Penn's attack became jumbled deep in Carlisle's territory but they salvaged something when Quigley kicked an eighteen-yard field goal from placement. The Indians gave the Quakers a scare late in the game when, using long end runs and forward passes drove the Penn defenders backward to their own five-yard line. But LeRoy fumbled and Rosenau recovered the ball to end the threat. The final score was Penn 26–Carlisle 0.

There was a sad denouement to the game. Louis Godfrey, Chippewa from the Fond du Lac Reservation in Cloquet, Minnesota, had to leave the game in the second quarter after being tackled by an opponent. His nose was broken and a previously injured knee was sprained. He later returned to the game and played to the finish. The next day in Carlisle, he walked to the hospital on campus where the physician suggested he take to bed and rest his leg. Apparently thinking his injuries were small, Louis insisted on leaving the hospital. The physician allowed him to leave, thinking Godfrey was returning to his quarters. Instead, he walked a distance of two miles to get a newspaper in town.

His leg hurt mightily that Sunday afternoon, so he was taken to the hospital where he was admitted. The injured knee swelled rapidly and his pain increased. The treatments he was given weren't working, so, on Friday, the physician on campus consulted with a doctor in

LOUIS GODFREY. Right guard of the Carlisle Indians, who died Wednesday from blood poisoning, due to an injury received during the season. Godfrey played here against Tech.

Carlisle. Louis was then diagnosed with Synovitis—inflammation of the synovial membrane in his knee—complicated with Phlebitis. The doctors considered it inadvisable to give the knee active treatment at that time. On Monday morning, with the swelling increased further and the pain not subsiding, a specialist from Harrisburg was brought in. He determined that an operation was needed and that it should be performed at the hospital in Carlisle rather than the one on campus because it was a difficult one to perform. The surgery took place at 7:00 a.m. on Tuesday and appeared to be successful because Louis rallied when he came out from under the ether with the pain and swelling relieved. He continued to improve until 12:30 p.m. Wednesday when he cyanosed and died suddenly. The cause of his death was determined to have been an embolism of the brain caused by a blood clot from a vein in his inflamed knee, which broke loose and moved to his brain, killing him.

A priest was with Louis when he died and a funeral was held the next day at St. Patrick's Church in Carlisle. His body was shipped home as his mother directed and his brother Frank, also a student at Carlisle, accompanied it.

Washington Times sportswriter Louis A. Dougher opined or passed on gossip as to the reason for the difficulty of Carlisle's 1917 schedule: "It is whispered that the 1916 outgoing management, not caring to be of considerable assistance to the incoming management, made up a schedule that would have taxed the strength of Jim Thorpe's or Frank Mount Pleasant's elevens...One thing is certain, if Coach Harris is to be believed, the Carlisle eleven of 1918 will cut down its traveling expenses, and will not attempt to be a chopping block for all the strong teams willing to give it a date."

The players elected John Flinchum for Captain of the 1918 team. Physical Director Clevett left Carlisle in December to take the position of Physical Director with the Y. M. C. A. at the Ambulance Camp at Allentown, Pennsylvania. Several former football players then in the military played on football teams for their units. Eschewing his annual college elevens because of the war, Walter Camp named one of them, former Carlisle end

Arlene French & William Gardner

William Gardner, to his All-America Service Elevens First Team at end. Gardner played for the Camp Custer, Michigan team and served as an officer in charge of recent immigrants from Poland who had enlisted in the Army.

1917 Season Summary

Date	Opponent	Location	Indian	Opp.
Sep. 29	Albright College	Indian Field, Carlisle Barracks, PA	60	0
Oct. 6	Franklin & Marshall College	Williamson Field, Lancaster, PA	63	0
Oct. 13	West Virginia University	Splinter Stadium, Morgantown, WV	0	21
Oct. 20	Navy	Worden Field, Annapolis, MD	0	61
Oct. 27	Johns Hopkins University	Homewood Field, Baltimore, MD	15	7
Nov. 3	Bucknell University	Athletic Field, Lewisburg, PA	0	10
Nov. 10	Army	The Plain, West Point, NY	0	28
Nov. 17	Georgia Institute of Technology	Grant Field, Atlanta, GA	0	98
Nov. 24	University of Pennsylvania	Franklin Field, Philadelphia, PA	0	26
Nov. 29	Boston College	Canceled by mutual agreement		

Won 3; Lost 6; Tied 0

Lieutenant Mt. Pleasant is one of the best known athletes in this country. He graduated from Carlisle and holds records for the quarter-mile, 100-yard, 220-yard dashes, and for the broad jump. He was a former football player and represented the United States in the Olympic games in Europe in 1909. He graduated from the academic department of Dickinson College in 1910 and was the first Indian to get a diploma and degree from this college. He was football coach for the Franklin and Marshall teams. He also coached the football teams at the Indiana Normal School and at West Virginia Wesleyan.

LIEUT. FRANK
MT. PLEASANT
AND TRENCH DOG

Mt. Pleasant is not only an athlete but also a student and a man who makes good at whatever he does. His winning of a commission as first lieutenant in a camp of 1,000 men at Fort Niagara is proof of this. He is serving with the 153rd Depot Brigade. He is the same bundle of muscle and sinew that he was in his school and college days, and Carlisle feels that the first Boche who tries to climb the delicate frame of this American soldier will have the surprise of his life and it will be necessary for the Kaiser to order up heavy re-enforcements to stop the rough stuff started in the American lines.

23

The End of It All

Rule changes for 1918:

The Rules Committee made no changes to the rules for the 1918 season.

Although schools such as Harvard, Yale, and Princeton did not field teams in 1917, more games were played that year than any before. This was due to the addition of numerous military units and Student Army Training Corps at colleges and universities across the country forming teams to represent them. Military teams replaced colleges in the annual New Year's game played in Pasadena, disappointing Carlisle alum Lone Star Dietz whose Washington State team had gone unbeaten again. Normally, they would have defended the honor of the West in that game. Military teams composed of former college stars were so popular that the Mare Island Marines and Camp Lewis Army teams, both from the West Coast, were invited instead.

1918 Lacrosse Team

In early January of 1918, six more Carlisle Indian School students enlisted in the Navy, bringing the total who had volunteered since war was declared to nearly sixty, about fifteen percent of the male student population. Most went into the Navy, Army infantry, or Cavalry. Some were in unit bands and a few were buglers. The majority of the boys remaining at the school were between sixteen and nineteen years of age. Only a half dozen of these were old enough or citizens liable to the draft. The rest were underage or weren't citizens. (The first of three draft registrations for WWI was held on June 5, 1917 and was limited to men between the ages of twenty-one and thirty-one.) The school's newspaper was filled with lists of names of students and former students in the military, notes from them, and a few photos of them in uniform.

Carlisle's basketball season continued well into the new year and baseball coach Duran was being hired as last year's coach, Eugene Hanks, had returned to Mercersburg Academy. (Carlisle had reinstituted baseball the previous year after a hiatus of several years from the sport.) Wallace Denny had the track boys training indoors until weather permitted them to go outdoors. The fiery Canadian Lacrosse coach Bill O'Neil led the team to have a good season. The Indians only lost one game, an early match against Navy. On May 24, the 1918 football schedule was released. The nine-game schedule was front-loaded with hard games against Pitt, Army, and Lafayette appearing early on their schedule. A better season was expected in 1918 because few of the lettermen were graduating and most were years too young to be drafted.

FOOTBALL SCHEDULE—1918.

Next year's football schedule is complete and is as follows:
Sept. 28. Albright, at Carlisle, Pa.
Oct. 5th. Pittsburgh University, at Pittsburgh, Pa.
Oct. 12th. Army, at West Point, N. Y.
Oct. 19th. Lafayette, at Harrisburg, Pa.
Oct. 26th. University of Detroit, at Detroit, Mich.
Nov. 2d. Bucknell University, at Lewisburg, Pa.
Nov. 9th. Villanova, at Carlisle, Pa.
Nov. 16. Holy Cross, at Worcester, Mass.
Nov. 28. Georgetown University, at Washington, D. C.

On Memorial Day, the Carlisle Indian School band took the Cumberland Valley Railroad to Shippensburg where they played a major role in the more-elaborate-than-usual Memorial Day parade. This time, the parade ended at a monument in Spring Hill Cemetery. The monument was unveiled to reveal that it was a memorial to William Cloyd Ashwell, the first local boy to die in World War I. He served in the U. S. Coast Artillery Corps and died in France at age twenty-two.

Carlisle celebrated its fortieth commencement exercises on June 2nd to 6th. Although the number of students on campus was smaller than usual due to the war effort and more boys being out on farms than in other summers, the administration expected to have a successful event. They included the annual inter-class track meet, the awarding of letters for spring sports, concerts, the granting of diplomas, and much speechifying. Nearly a thousand visitors and townspeople attended the graduation ceremony at which eight of the new graduates were also made American citizens. Congress and President Coolidge made noncitizen Indians citizens in 1924. This may be why Coolidge was photographed wearing a war bonnet so frequently. Many non-citizen Indians lived, and their descendants still do, on land belonging to Indian nations that negotiated treaties with the U. S. government.

John Francis, Jr., who had taken over as superintendent a year earlier when Oscar Lipps was promoted, left campus right after commencement to test for a commission as an officer in the Army. The second WWI draft registration was held on June 5, 1918 for those who had turned twenty-one after the first draft. This draft did not likely affect any Carlisle students or staff. Most students were younger or not citizens and staff would have been older.

Even with the superintendent focused on other matters, the school didn't shut down completely over the summer. In mid-June, school administrators submitted a request to the Bureau of Indian Affairs to lengthen the course of study from three to five years. After completing the expanded curriculum, Carlisle graduates would be eligible to enter American colleges and universities without attending prep schools. Students from other Indian schools desiring to advance their education would likely transfer to Carlisle to take advantage of the new offerings. Both keeping students two more years and attracting additional students would increase the school's prestige along with the size and average age of Carlisle's student body. A bonus would be allowing Carlisle athletes to get more experience than they were currently and would attract more-seasoned ones wanting to continue their education to transfer to the school. Carlisle students awaited a decision from the government that could significantly impact their lives.

Those still on the campus over the summer remained active. The baseball team played games against other teams in Central Pennsylvania. Students and faculty donated time and money to the Red Cross in the form of 300 pillows and unsterilized pads in July. Indian School Band Director James Riley Wheelock, referred to as "the Red Rival of Sousa," put together "a big municipal orchestra of truly great proportions" composed of amateur and professional musicians from all local musical organizations, including bands and churches as well as some not affiliated with a formal organization. The orchestra performed on the evening of July 4th on the Dickinson College campus in front of a large audience.

On the fifth of July, John Francis left for Fort Niagara, New York where the new first lieutenant joined the infantry unit he was to command. Claude V. Peel was assigned as temporary superintendent to replace Francis.

Business as usual at Carlisle came to a crashing halt on July 17, when Secretary of the Interior Franklin Knight Lane dropped a bomb on the Indian School. He announced that Carlisle Barracks was needed again by the Army and was being returned to them. Commissioner of Indian Affairs Cato Sells stated that Carlisle Indian School would cease to exist and its students would be transferred to other schools. It had always been an endangered species so to speak, underfunded by the government and with western politicians wanting to take its budget for their states. Richard Henry Pratt, then a brigadier general in retirement, had fought constantly to keep his creation alive and was a master press agent for it. It took a world war to defeat him and kill his school.

The next day, the War Department announced that Carlisle Barracks would be adapted to serve as "a hospital for sick and wounded soldiers and also a place for the education and rehabilitation of maimed and incapacitated men." The fifty buildings and property were valued at about $250,000. A month earlier, an Army officer had inspected the site and submitted a report to the authorities in Washington. The Indian School was given until September 1st to shut down and disperse students.

With only six weeks to close the school and to transfer students and employees to other locations, a flurry of activity occurred. The condition of files found in the National Archives suggests that the saving of records was done in a hurried and haphazard way. Numerous student files were lost, and many that were saved are incomplete. There may have even been some pilfering of documents from the National Archives as it later became necessary to only make photocopies of some files available to the public because original documents were disappearing from certain folders.

In the midst of this, the Indian School Band participated in the parade honoring 133 men of Cumberland County who were leaving for Camp Lee, Virginia to prepare to fight in the war. The first notice of an employee transfer was announced on July 30 with Dr. Menger, the government physician at the school, moving to Haskell Institute in Lawrence, Kansas. Others followed soon after that. On August 2nd, plans began for a permanent canteen to serve servicemen on the truck trains that passed through Carlisle. It was also announced that Carlisle students then on outings in the country would return on August 28 and would depart for their homes from Carlisle the next day.

James Riley Wheelock, brother of the famous band leader and composer Dennison Wheelock, passed the examination for bandmaster in the U. S. Army and reported to Camp Meade, Maryland. On the 12th, twenty-five Carlisle students, all under the draft age of twenty-one at that time, enrolled in the shipbuilding school at Hog Island near Philadelphia. There they would be instructed in riveting, chipping, caulking, and ship carpentry by Carlisle alum Montreville Yuda. He had been working at the New York Shipbuilding Corporation plant but had recently changed jobs to work at Hog Island as an instructor.

On August 19, Army Major A. C. Backmayer, who was in charge of transitioning Carlisle Barracks to function as a hospital, released construction plans to begin before winter set in. Existing shop buildings would be adapted for vocational training. The new buildings would be erected east of the then existing campus on Farm Number 1, the one closest to the campus. The first of the new buildings would be of tile, two and a half stories high, to accommodate 2,000 patients. Equipment was expected to arrive around September 1.

Survivors of the famous Civil War unit Company A of the 209th Regiment, Pennsylvania Volunteers, held their annual reunion on the Carlisle Indian School bandstand on Monday, August 26. That evening, a fitting farewell to the students and faculty was held. Citizens gathered at the town square at 7:30 to proceed by car and on foot to Carlisle Barracks. The procession was marshalled by H. A. Ewing, a funeral director, and headed by the Carlisle Town Band and Home Defense Police. Following them were members of Company G, about fifty veterans of the Spanish-American War, and thirty automobiles filled with townspeople. One assumes the elderly Civil War veterans joined the procession when it reached the campus. The band played lively airs as it marched up to the superintendent's residence. Various local people took their turns at speechifying. H. B. Miller sang the verse to the Carlisle School song, which was written by Pop Warner in 1907, while Indian School students sang the chorus. Pop Warner spoke next, getting an enthusiastic reception. Not physically able to attend the event, Gen. Pratt sent a telegram that was read aloud. At the end, S. M. Goodyear presented James Riley Wheelock with a silver wristwatch. So moved by the gesture, all Wheelock could say was "Thank you." The formal proceedings over, the band gave a concert from the bandstand and an orchestra played for dancing in the gymnasium until late at night.

Famous Carlisle Indian School band at Carlisle Barracks bandstand.

Reports that Wheelock had been assigned to Siberia were either incorrect or were changed because he was sent to France as bandmaster of the 808th (colored) Regimental Band. Gus Welch was a captain assigned to the same regiment. Former Superintendent Major Mercer was promoted to colonel for, starting in April 1917, recruiting over 7,000 volunteers from the state of Connecticut, one of the first states to meet its quota under President Wilson's call for volunteers.

Students left in bunches. Large groups were segregated by sex, boys on one train, girls on another in special coaches reserved for them with overflowing luggage cars. The few who remained on August 31 sang "Old Carlisle" with tears in many of their eyes as they left the school for the last time.

The girls of the Susan Longstreth Society donated their library of several hundred books to be sent to soldiers in camps in America and abroad. Much of the work of closing down the school must have fallen onto Wallace and Nellie Robertson Denny, long-time employees of the school who started as students in 1896 and 1880, respectively. Mrs. Denny had the longest tenure of any person at Carlisle, arriving a year after the school was founded and staying after it closed. She and her husband were the only Indian School staff members to remain at Carlisle Barracks when it became the Army's General Hospital Number 31.

The Carlisle Sentinel proclaimed, "There should be either at the school grounds or in in the town of Carlisle a building erected or set apart as a memorial of the school...This should be provided by the government...."

Neither the government nor the town ever built such a memorial.

A Carlisle Revival?

Many Carlisle alums were not pleased that the school was closed. Warner thought athletics, if managed properly, could have funded the school's operation, making government largesse unnecessary. That concept wasn't explored.

After WWI ended, several attempts were made to have it reopened. In January 1919, Herbert K. Welch, president of the Indian Rights Association, made an urgent appeal to reopen Carlisle Indian School. A year after the Army took back Carlisle Barracks, prominent Indian leaders met with Indian Commissioner Major General Hugh C. Scott, retired, in Syracuse, New York to get his support to reestablish the school. In December, a report was circulated announcing a meeting of Dr. Erl Bates, physician and originator of the Indian Extension Program at Cornell, with the Indian Commission in Washington about reopening Carlisle. "[B]ut will be devoted to teaching trades—not professions, to make carpenters, farmers and mechanics rather than doctors, lawyers and ministers. Dr. Bates may be chosen as its head." In 1920, the Society of American Indians passed a resolution demanding that the government reopen Carlisle or that another, comparable facility be established. In late-December 1926, Everette Burgess Howard, a newly elected representative from Oklahoma, announced his intention to submit a bill in the upcoming congress to re-establish Carlisle Indian School. The Carlisle Alumni

Association headed by Albert Exendine had started the movement to reopen the school but in Oklahoma instead of Pennsylvania.

The last known attempt to reopen Carlisle Indian School happened on March 14, 1935 when Charles Dillon, the football player made famous for his role in the 1903 hidden-ball trick, returned to Carlisle. He announced his intent to bring about 200 Indians from across the country to town to urge reopening the school and left for Washington to parley a little New Deal money to seed the project. He said he would return the following week with a committee that included Jim Thorpe, Gus Welch, Charles Albert "Chief" Bender, and Asa Sweetcorn claiming, "Our aim is to build a college with Indian money, to be conducted by and for Indians."

He didn't return with or without the committee or with any funding. A Montana newspaper editor reported that Charles Dillon had died on a Montana reservation the previous April. Apparently, the imposter was a purported Iroquois chief who called himself Charles Dillon or Clear Sky and traveled around the country giving lectures to school children about American Indians and their customs.

With Pratt unavailable to champion the cause, none of the attempts to reopen the school were successful. Even if he had been able to lead the fight, there were too many obstacles against it. Carlisle Barracks was owned by the Army and, after it reclaimed the base, it has never let it go idle again. When it

Wallace, Roberstson & Nellie Robertson Denny
The Dennys assisted with the transition to an army hospital and continued to work at Carlisle Barracks for a number of years after that.

was no longer needed as a hospital to treat those injured in World War I, it was converted to host the Medical Field Service School. More than 30,000 officers and NCOs passed through the school in its twenty-six years of operation. From 1946 to 1951, Carlisle Barracks housed six different Army schools. Then, the U. S. Army War College was moved to Carlisle Barracks, where it remains to this date.

A number of temporary Army camps were closed after the end of WWI. One of them would have been a possible place to locate a revived Carlisle Indian School. However, significant funding would have been required to repurpose a camp and politicians from western states would likely have opposed spending the money in the East. The Bureau of Indian Affairs would probably have considered Haskell Institute adequate for the purpose at that time and they wouldn't have received the increased budget appropriation necessary to expand Haskell or convert an idle Army camp.

Carlisle alumni were scattered across the country and were not organized in any way to spearhead the task. Many were already leaders of their tribes and nations at this time and focused their energies on local matters. Those wanting their children to attend government Indian schools had a number of them closer to home to choose from. A considerable number of former Carlisle students had gone "back to the blanket" and were opposed to the school. The bulk of the more successful alumni had integrated into white society and were focused on their businesses or careers.

By Congress making all Indians citizens in 1924, the majority population likely felt the need for Carlisle no longer existed and no politician championed the cause. Carlisle closed with the bang of World War I and its whimpers were not heard.

> *Football will never be a great national game, for a variety of reasons. The season is shorter, not so many games are possible as in baseball, for instance; and the game is not so open or spectacular. But, in my opinion, one of the main reasons why it will never be a popular sport, is the fact that it depends too much on careful coaching.*
> Glenn Warner

Halls of Fame

Carlisle Indians Inducted into the College Football Hall of Fame

Player*	Position	Year Inducted
Albert Exendine	End	1970
Joe Guyon	Halfback/Tackle	1971
James Johnson	Quarterback	1969
Ed Rogers	End	1968
Jim Thorpe	Halfback	1951†
Gus Welch	Quarterback	1975
Glenn S. "Pop" Warner	Coach	1951†
Lone Star Dietz	Coach	2012

Carlisle Indians Inducted into the Professional Football Hall of Fame

Player	Position	Year Inducted
Jim Thorpe	Halfback	1963†
Joe Guyon	Halfback	1966

Carlisle Indians inducted into Citizens Savings (originally Helms) Athletic Foundation Hall of Fame

Player	Position	Year Inducted
Jim Thorpe	Halfback	1950†
Glenn S. Pop" Warner	Coach	1951
Lone Star Dietz	Coach	1976

†Charter member.

Epilogue

The story of American Indians excelling in sports didn't end with the closing of Carlisle Indian School. Although Harvard, Yale, Princeton, Cornell, and several other schools canceled interscholastic football for 1918, a college football season was played by many schools and military teams. However, it was disrupted by the Great Influenza Epidemic. Warner's Pitt Panthers, for example, delayed their first game until November 9, cutting their eight-game schedule in half. His consensus National Co-Champion's greatest win was the 32-0 skunking of the 1917 champion Georgia Tech. Albert Exendine's Georgetown team went 3-2 against four military teams and Fordham. With no Washington State team to coach, Lone Star Dietz led a Mare Island Marines team loaded with his former players to a 10-0 season not unlike *The Perils of Pauline*. First, they were quarantined on base in Vallejo, California from September 28 until November 2 during the 1918 Influenza Pandemic. When released, the team took a 3,500-mile bus trip around the Northwest to recruit more Marines and rack up enough victories to land a berth in the New Year's game in Pasadena. The battle against George Halas's Great Lakes Navy team could be a chapter in itself. Jim Thorpe's Canton pro team didn't play in 1918, but his New York Giants baseball team did. Gus Welch was serving in France during the season, as were William Gardner, Frank Mt. Pleasant, and numerous lesser-known Carlisle Indians.

Although many Carlisle athletes joined in the war effort, a number of them continued playing football at other schools or professional teams, largely on those in states bordering the Great Lakes. With Carlisle closed, the American Indian athletics mantle was passed to Haskell Institute in Lawrence, Kansas where several former Carlisle students transferred. Haskell lost both of its games in an abbreviated 1918 season but went 8-1-1 with victories over Oklahoma A&M, Kansas State, and St. Xavier in 1919. In 1920, they went 3-1-1 against lesser opponents under new coach Matty Bell. Haskell went 5-5 in 1921, beating small colleges but losing to powers like Notre Dame and Nebraska. In 1922, the Indians rose to prominence going 8-2 under first-year coach Dick Hanley. Hanley had played at Washington State and the Mare Island Marines under Lone Star Dietz and used the Warner system, as did Dietz. Hanley led the "Lords of the Prairie" against strong teams from coast to coast and even in Hawaii. After he departed to lead Northwestern in 1927, Haskell fielded mediocre teams until 1929, when Lone Star Dietz took over as head coach and was dubbed "Miracle Man" for turning the team around. Haskell's prominence ended in 1932 when, at the height of the depression, the government slashed its funding. Dietz left to coach the Boston NFL team. Gus Welch followed him at Haskell as he had at Washington State but didn't have the success Lone Star had at either school.

In 1920, owners of several professional teams in the Great Lakes states formed the American Professional Football Association (APFA) in the showroom of Ralph Hay's Hupmobile dealership in Canton, Ohio. Jim Thorpe was elected President of the league as the original Pete Rozelle, so to speak, but he was allowed to continue playing for one of the teams because of the additional ticket revenue his presence created. Two years later, the APFA was renamed the National Football League.

In 1922, Jim Thorpe teamed with Walter Lingo, owner of Oorang Dog Kennels in LaRue, Ohio, to start an NFL team. A franchise at that time cost less than the price of a King Airedale, the best type of dog Lingo bred and sold for $150. The team was staffed with former Carlisle and Haskell players, some of whom were long in the tooth at this time. The Oorang Indians, in their orange and maroon jerseys, performed stunts and skits before games and at halftime to promote mail order sales of Lingo's dogs. The team lasted only two years. But Thorpe, Guyon, and Calac continued playing.

The NFL is still in business as of this writing, but of the fourteen original teams, only two have survived: the Chicago Cardinals (today's Arizona Cardinals) and Decatur Staleys (today's Chicago Bears). The other thirty current NFL teams were created later and are spread from coast to coast and north to south.

Wallace Denny rejoined Pop Warner at Stanford in 1922 to again serve as his trainer. The two would work together until Warner retired decades later.

Numerous Carlisle players coached teams around the country but none had success approaching Lone Star Dietz's. He was inducted into the College Football Hall of Fame as a coach. Jim Thorpe, Gus Welch, Albert Exendine, Edward Rogers, Joseph Guyon, and James Johnson were all enshrined as players. Pop Warner's work at Carlisle laid the foundation for his induction. George Woodruff's 7-2 1905 season leading the Indians served as a capstone for his Hall-of-Fame career. Jim Thorpe and Joe Guyon were also enshrined in the Pro Football Hall of Fame in Canton, Ohio. Starting in 1986, The Jim Thorpe Award has been given to the best defensive back in college football each year.

In 1933, Gus Welch brought his Haskell Institute team to Carlisle Barracks to tour the site of the former Carlisle Indian School and to practice on the same field on which the famous Carlisle Indians played. Two days later, in a confrontation that couldn't have been welcomed by either of them, Welch matched wits with his old mentor, Pop Warner, by taking on the Temple Owls in Philadelphia. After leading the Carlisle Indians for so many years, the Old Fox had never been up against an Indian team before. However, Haskell was coming to visit for the third year in a row in a meeting arranged by the teams' former coaches: Heinie Miller and Lone Star Dietz. Warner and Welch were each in his first year at their respective institutions and, given their personal history, would not likely have set up this game. Welch's August hiring made changing the schedule difficult. Pop's squad beat his former player's team 31–0.

In 1941, twenty-five years after the school closed, Carlisle alums Adam Spring (Tonawanda Seneca), Isaac Lyon (Onondaga), and Daisie Doctor Snyder (Tonawanda) organized the first, and last, reunion of Carlisle alumni at the New York State Fair in Syracuse. They selected the annual Indian Day for the event. Three hundred and eighty Carlislians attended along with Pop Warner. Spring (sixty-five), a distance runner, and Pop (seventy) reminisced about a two-mile race held at Bucknell University. When Spring finished the eighth lap around the track well ahead of his competitors, he headed for the clubhouse, thinking he had won. Warner chased after him, telling him to get back in the race. He had two more laps to go because Bucknell had a fifth-mile track instead of the usual quarter-mile around a football field. Spring ran back to the track and won the race. Warner and Thorpe both died in the 1950s and the others who had survived this long soon followed. No other reunion was held.

Although fired from his position as superintendent in 1904, Gen. Pratt periodically returned to visit the school. On those occasions, he received a hero's welcome. The academic/workdays were cut short for the presentation of special programs to honor him. When he died twenty years after his dismissal, a group of his former students approached his widow, begging for the honor of raising a monument to him at his grave in Arlington Cemetery. She consented with the stipulation that all donations had to be nominal. The granite slab at the base of his marker bears the inscription, "ERECTED IN LOVING MEMORY BY HIS STUDENTS AND OTHER INDIANS."

Over a number of years, superintendents Pratt, Mercer, and Friedman had each mailed questionnaires to former football players no longer at Carlisle, apparently to refute the widely held belief that athletes "never amount to much after leaving school." Who received the questionnaires is unknown as is who returned them. What is known is some players did return them, and some of these responses still exist in student files. The results found comprise no scientific study but do represent the thinking of some individuals.

Charles Guyon responded, "I owe my success to the training I have received in the two schools I have attended [Haskell and Carlisle], and to make it short—I am working for something higher—to the highest goal." Caleb Sickles frankly stated, "From my own experience, I think that the pupil who has attended Carlisle should never go back to the reservation to live. If he has holdings I would advise him to sell them, put the money in the bank, and seek employment or attend a school and obtain a professional or technical education." From Minnesota, Cass County Attorney Ed Rogers answered, "What little degree of success I have attained I attribute entirely to my early training at Carlisle" and offered, "I might add although the subject is not mentioned nor no opinion is requested that to abolish non-reservation schools is a mistake and would be a serious detriment to the progress and welfare of the future young Indians."

APPENDICES

A
Origin of the School

Richard Henry Pratt (seated), Susan Longstreth, Spotted Tail. In rear: Mary Anna Longstreth, Rebecca Haines

The Carlisle Indian football team was unlike any that came before or since. It was the product of the school, its superintendent, the coach, and the players themselves. Carlisle Indian School would not have existed had it not been for a special man having radical beliefs and the conviction to act on them. At eighteen, he apprenticed himself to a tinsmith and worked at that trade for three years until the Confederates shelled Fort Sumter.

Eight days later, he enlisted in the 9th Indiana Regiment. When his three-month enlistment expired, he re-enlisted, this time as a sergeant in the 2nd Regiment Indiana Cavalry. Among other places, he fought at Chickamauga. On April 12, 1864, he was commissioned as a 1st lieutenant in the 11th Indiana Cavalry. The hostilities over, Richard Henry Pratt mustered out on May 29,

1865. He and Anna Laura Mason, whom he had married in 1864 while home on a recruiting trip, returned to Logansport, Indiana to operate a hardware store. But that didn't work out. So, Pratt returned to military life as a 2nd lieutenant with brevet ranks of 1st lieutenant and captain for meritorious service during the Civil War. Assigned to the 10th United States Cavalry, he led a newly formed unit of African-American enlisted men with white officers. The Indians they were fighting dubbed the troops "Buffalo Soldiers" because of the perceived similarity of the soldiers' hair with bison fur. Although quickly promoted to 1st lieutenant, further promotions were a long time in coming. However, he was often addressed or referred to as Captain Pratt to honor his brevet rank.

In 1875, Lt. Pratt was assigned the task of transporting seventy-two Cheyenne, Kiowa, Comanche, Arapaho, and Caddo Indian prisoners taken in the Red River War to Fort Marion (renamed Castillo de San Marcos) in St. Augustine, Florida and served as their jailer. Most of the prisoners were men, but the group included one Cheyenne woman prisoner—Buffalo Calf Woman, the wife of Medicine Water—who had killed a farmer. Also transported were a number of wives and children who had refused to be separated from their husbands and fathers. Eleven of the Comanche and Kiowa prisoners were actually Mexican captives who had been raised as tribal members.

After eight years of working directly with Indian scouts and former slaves as soldiers, Pratt developed a philosophy that guided him the rest of his days. He believed that all Indians and African-Americans needed to compete on equal terms with whites were: "The rights of citizenship include[ing] fraternity and equal privilege for development." Equal opportunity for Indians became the great crusade of his life.

Pratt used the Fort Marion incarceration as a laboratory to demonstrate that wild Indians could be converted into peaceful, enlightened citizens. He immediately replaced the army guards with a group of prisoners he selected to perform that duty. He dressed the inmates in military uniforms and offered them classes in English language, art, guard duty, and craftsmanship. Experienced educators Misses Sarah Mather and Rebecca Perrit, who lived in St. Augustine, volunteered to conduct the classes as did Mather's friend Harriet Beecher Stowe. He allowed inmates to teach archery and sell artwork, bows and arrows, polished sea beans, and other trinkets to visitors. He also encouraged townspeople to hire his wards for jobs they could do. When fire struck buildings close to the fort in the middle of the night, Pratt marched a troop of

Indians with buckets and blankets to help put it out. The residents were grateful as the town had no fire department.

Pratt's program soon became well-known across the country. Distinguished visitors, including Harriet Beecher Stowe and others, came from a variety of places. The U.S. commissioner of education and the president of Amherst College wanted to see firsthand what Pratt was doing for the Indians. The lieutenant's experience convinced him that putting them in "civilized environments" was the only way to totally assimilate Indians. He wrote, "[the Indian] is born a blank, like all the rest of us. Transfer the savage born infant to the surroundings of a civilization and he will grow to possess a civilized language and habit." By the end of the three-year sentences, he had erased any doubts he might have previously held about the conversion. He was completely convinced assimilation was the only way for Indians to survive in a modern society. Others considered Indians "a vanishing race" and thought it pointless to waste money and energy on them.

In his memoir, he wrote of an early example of assimilation that was working too well. "One of the prominent young ladies of St. Augustine was a special friend to the youngest Cheyenne." The girl kept the boy out after curfew and Pratt punished him. "A light stick of wood was given to him to carry on his shoulder [in lieu of a rifle] in front of the guard tent until midnight. I awakened at daylight and, looking out of the tent, saw the boy still carrying the stick of wood. Calling for the sergeant of the guard, who belonged to the same tribe, I asked why he had not relieved the young Indian. The sergeant of the guard replied that it was a very bad thing the boy had done and that my punishment was not severe enough, so he had kept him up all night."

When their confinement ended, Lt. Pratt convinced seventeen of his former prisoners to pursue further education at Hampton Institute (now Hampton University). The Hampton, Virginia school had been founded a decade earlier by Gen. Samuel Chapman Armstrong as a boarding school to educate recently freed slaves by training "the head, the hand, and the heart." Educating African-Americans and American Indians, although segregated from each other as well as the townspeople, was controversial to some as many thought Blacks and Indians were not educable. He differed from Armstrong, thinking full emersion into the majority culture was the key to Indians' long-term survival and left Hampton after a year. However, the experiment was successful enough that Hampton Institute continued its Indian division until 1923.

Richard Henry Pratt, son of a singing Methodist mother, summarized his philosophy as, "Kill the Indian, save the man." He viewed the reservations as ghettos in which Indians were denied the rights and opportunities enjoyed by citizens. Residents were afflicted by several pathologies prevalent on the reservations. Alcoholism, idleness, disease, violence, and polygamy were all too common. Many children were missing a parent, some two, and the tribes had few resources for orphans. One of the things that made Carlisle attractive to girls was that being hundreds or thousands of miles from home would make being married off to an old man as his second, third, or fourth wife difficult. To Pratt, killing the Indian meant stripping him of or keeping him from assimilating these pathologies. He viewed Indians being the same as other human beings and capable of accomplishing what any other race can. An important step was teaching the boys, and some girls, trades with which they could support themselves and not have to rely on meager government handouts for survival.

Pratt formulated a model similar to that being used at Hampton and successfully lobbied the government to set up a school just for Indians at an unused Army post adjacent to Carlisle, Pennsylvania. The former cavalry school had been abandoned in 1872 after local residents petitioned the War Department to stop Sunday dress parades. Fearful the townspeople would reject a school for Indians in their midst, Secretary of War George Washington McCrary directed Pratt to go to Carlisle and get a petition for the school. In Harrisburg while waiting for the Cumberland Valley RR train to Carlisle, Pratt told Gen. Chapman Biddle, then treasurer of the railroad, of his mission. Biddle told him to return to Washington saying, "I will send the Secretary a petition signed by every man and woman in Carlisle." Pratt did as Biddle suggested and received the petition a few days later. The railroad executive probably told merchants about the commerce the school would bring and townspeople the jobs it would create.

Congress approved the use of Carlisle Barracks by the Department of the Interior and detailed Pratt for Indian education duty. The War Department issued the order and Lt. and Mrs. Pratt were on their way to Carlisle. No sooner were Mrs. Pratt and the children settled in and a builder arranged to make necessary repairs and improvements, Pratt traveled to the Dakotas to recruit students for the school. His orders called for him to get thirty-six pupils each from the Rosebud and Pine Ridge Reservations and to get enough more from the Indian Territory tribes (Oklahoma) to bring the total to 120 students.

Miss Sarah Mather, then considered aged at sixty-three, urged him to let her accompany him on the trip to help with the girls.

Pratt and Mather took a train to Yankton where they caught a boat that took them up the Missouri River to a landing one-hundred miles from Rosebud Reservation. The new agent there sent a two-seated spring wagon to meet them. The Indian driver brought four blankets for his use and none for his passengers. Pratt recalled:

> I determined to make the trip in two days, so sat with the driver, used the 'black snake' whip, and kept the mules at the necessary speed. When halfway, we stopped for the night. We made Miss Mather an army bed in the bottom of the wagon, taking out the seats, using a cushion for a pillow, and giving her two of the blankets which, by folding, we made into a camp bag bed with two thicknesses above and two below. The Indian and I slept under the wagon using the other two blankets, one to sleep on and one over us. We all slept in our clothing. It was a frosty night and we suffered from the cold. There being no other way, we had to hitch the mules to the wagon. Wolves came near and howled, and once I got up with my revolver to drive them away, but they were too far off to shoot. Sleep was practically impossible for me. The cold led us to start long before daylight. During the afternoon Miss Mather became wretchedly seasick and we had to stop several times. We reached the agency before dark and the very capable agency physician soon restored her equilibrium.

Initially, the agency employees and chiefs objected to sending the children so far away but, after passing a ceremonial pipe around a circle of forty chiefs and elders, Pratt made his pitch. Spotted Tail, the principal chief, spoke against their children learning the white man's wicked ways. Pratt countered with the argument that, had the Indians been able to read and write, they wouldn't have been cheated when signing treaties. After talking among themselves, the chiefs agreed to send their children to Carlisle.

The next morning, Pratt set out for the Pine Ridge Agency. This time he asked for a light wagon and two ponies. The driver, who spoke no English, navigated the hundred-mile trip more quickly than had the previous driver. When darkness fell, they followed the stars and arrived well before midnight. Red Cloud was old and had no young children. However, he agreed to send a grandson. Pratt was able to enroll only sixteen, mostly boys, from Pine Ridge.

When he returned to Rosebud, ninety children waited to enroll. The agency physician and his wife gave the children careful physical examinations before Pratt would accept them. He only took fifty-six of them because he was only authorized a total of seventy-two from the Dakotas. He later decided to add ten more in accordance with the Indian Bureau's idea that having the children in white men's hands would be a deterrent to war. When he called roll on the boat at the landing, two additional boys from Pine Ridge were found to be stowaways. When Pratt attempted to put them ashore, the Pine Ridge agent convince him to let them stay. He now had eighty-four students enrolled, twelve more than were authorized.

Pratt noticed that nearly all of the boys were smoking cigarettes as they steamed down the river. He then bought all that were for sale and handed them out to the boys with this admonition: "Between here and Carlisle, as we will be traveling on the boat and as on the [train]cars the boys will be in a separate car from the girls, we can all have a goodbye smoke all the way to Carlisle, but when we reach Carlisle we will all quit." He knew he would have to break his twelve-year habit when he reached the school and broke it cold turkey.

Around midnight on October 6, 1879, hundreds of people from the town greeted Pratt and the first contingent of students to arrive at the school. The townspeople escorted the tired travelers on the walk from Carlisle Junction to the barracks. The first group of students were largely sons of Lakota chiefs (boys had little economic value when confined to reservations because they could no longer hunt buffalo or make war, but families could still receive a bride price for girls, often in ponies). America's second-oldest military facility—the one that housed Hessian troops captured at Trenton by Gen. George Washington after crossing the Delaware—now housed the children of warriors who only three years earlier had defeated Custer at the Battle of the Little Bighorn.

Shortly after the students from Indian Territory arrived, three Quaker ladies came for a visit: Miss Susan Longstreth and her sister Mary Anna, then retired after operating a famous school for young ladies in Philadelphia for 50 years, and a Miss Brown, one of their former students. After a tour of the school, Miss Longstreth asked, "Captain, thee is undertaking a great work here. Thee will need many things. Thee must remember if thee would receive thee must ask. Will thee take thy pencil and put down some of the things thee needs very much just now and the cost?"

Pratt listed tools needed for the various shops for the trades the students would study. The women took his list and huddled. Pratt heard them say, "I will take this" and "I will take that." Miss Longstreth handed him back the list, saying, "Buy all and send us the amount of each bill, and we will send checks to pay." He felt the same rush of blood to his brain and heart forty-two years afterward as he did when it happened. The Quaker ladies from Philadelphia continued to support Pratt and Carlisle until their deaths.

Carlisle Indian Industrial School students divided their days between academic studies and vocational training. They dressed in military uniforms and lived regimented lives. Free-time activities included music, athletics, and literary or debating societies. Although Carlisle Indian Industrial School was essentially a trade school coupled to elementary and high school academics, Pratt envisioned some of his students advancing to college and professional schools.

Rather than returning to their reservations during school breaks, Pratt wanted his students kept away from tribal influences as long as possible, ideally their entire enrollment periods. During their "outing" periods working off-campus at farms and businesses to further immerse them in the dominant culture, students received practical experience and made some money of which they were forced to save a significant portion. Pratt kept his charges away from their families and tribes three, four, or five years at a time, depending on when they enrolled. In 1883, explaining his philosophy, he wrote, "In Indian civilization I am a Baptist, because I believe in immersing the Indians in our civilization and when we get them under holding them there until they are thoroughly soaked." The government saved money by not having to house and feed the children when they were away.

As the school's superintendent, Pratt constantly battled Congress for funding and did not fare well. He was not shy about publicly criticizing the government's stinginess and other shortcomings, particularly those in the Bureau of Indian Affairs. The outing period wasn't enough to keep costs within budget; other funding sources were needed. Donations from individuals helped immensely.

Extracurricular activities, particularly the literary and debating societies, helped prepare higher-level students for further academic work as well as to think more critically and to communicate more clearly, skills that would serve future leaders well. Although Pratt desired that his former students assimilate into the dominant culture, many returned to their tribes and used the skills learned at Carlisle to become effective tribal leaders. Others returned to their former ways.

Soon, the girls and boys each had two societies from which to select: the Susan Longstreth Literary Society, the Mercer Literary Society, the Standard Literary Society, and the Invincible Debating Society, respectively. These societies were much more than what their names implied as some of them formed bands, played sports, held dances, and put on plays. They also had their own colors and elected officers as did the freshman, sophomore, junior and senior classes. Carlisle's classes (freshman et al) did not correspond to public high school classes of the same names. Besides the usual officers, these groups elected a Critic, whose function may not be obvious to modern readers. The author found a definition in the *1918 Quittapahilla,* Lebanon Valley College's yearbook: "Over each meeting presides the Critic and he, by mode of criticism, points out the strength and weakness of the respective numbers with special reference to errors in style, English grammar, elocution, logic, literary structure and the speakers' manner on the floor." While some of the details may vary between schools and organizations, the description will hold in the main.

The boys loved playing games and sports. In the early years of the school, they played the games they had played on the reservations. Over time, they adopted the sports schoolboys across the country enjoyed. At Carlisle, each shop had its own athletic teams that competed in intramurals with the others on campus. The annual shop football championship was a major event. In 1890, some of the boys played off-campus against the Dickinson College team. Having had little direct experience with football and seeing occasional victims of the game's violence, Captain Pratt was not disposed to encourage its playing. When Stacy Matlock suffered a compound fracture of his lower leg in the Dickinson game, Pratt carried him from the carriage to the operating table. He helped hold the boy while the doctor set the break. Revulsed by what he saw, Pratt decreed, "This ends outside football for us."

B
Players with Years Played

Identifying all the players who at one time were on the varsity squad, including second and third teams, reserves, and scrubs, was a difficult task. The Carlisle student files were incomplete, newspaper accounts were inaccurate, and no one who was alive at that time was available to consult. The likelihood that some of the information that follows is inaccurate is high in spite of the author doing everything he could do to ensure completeness and accuracy.

The same approach was taken for each chapter in which games were covered:

1. School newspaper accounts of games, awards banquets, photographs, and snippets about the team and players were searched first.

2. Newspapers were searched for coverage of the games played in the year(s) covered, drawings, and photographs.

3. Carlisle student records were searched for the names—often last name only—of players identified in the above steps to determine exactly who these people were and to find out their tribes or nations, Indian names, and nicknames, if any.

4. Knowledgeable people were consulted to help in correcting errors and identifying people from photographs.

A list of players that couldn't be identified and the years in which they played follows. Hopefully, readers will be able to shine some light on them. Some may be nicknames, others may be misspellings, still others may have been heard incorrectly by the reporter.

Hyrock, 1900
Childs, 1901, 1902
Freeman, 1902
Easterling, 1903
Colt, 1905
Chestnut-in-the-fire, 1905
Strongarm, 1905
Wholes, 1905

O'Bline, 1908
Canfield, 1911
Early Bird, 1911
Moy, 1913
Oneida/O'Neida, 1913
Robbin, 1913
Mann, 1913
G. Morin, 1913

Hemlock, 1913
Skundooli/
Skundooh, 1913
Barie, 1913
Firestine, 1914
Cogan, 1915
Leonard, 1915

Full Name (Tribe/Nation)	Years Played			
Addison, Burdick (Arapaho)	1914			
Aiken, John (Osage)	1907	1908		
Albanez, Stephen (Mission)	1905			
Alexander, Peter (Ottawa)	1898			
Allen, Grover (Kickapoo)	1913			
Allen, John (Clallam)	1899			
American Horse, Benjamin (Sioux)	1894			
Andrews, Frank (Puyallup)	1904			
Aragon, William (Shoshone)	1908	1909	1910	
Arcasa, Alexander (Colville)	1909	1910	1911	1912
Archambault, Harry (Sioux)	1907			
Archambault, Leo (Sioux)	1913			
Archiquette, Chauncey (Oneida)	1896	1897	1898	1905
Arquette, Mitchell W. (Mohawk)	1913			
Austin, Anthony (Piegan)	1893	1894		
Azure, Ovilla (Chippewa)	1911			
Baine, John (Sioux)	1899	1900		
Baine, William (Sioux)	1899	1900		
Baird, Charles (Oneida)	1915			
Baker, Joseph (Winnebago)	1903	1904		
Balenti, John (Cheyenne)	1907	1908		
Balenti, Michael (Cheyenne)	1905	1906	1907	1908
Barrel, Napoleon (Chippewa)	1908			
Bear Horse, John (Sioux)	1913			
Bearlouse, Solomon (Cheyenne)	1904			
Beartail, John (Creek)	1917			
Beaver, Frank (Winnebago)	1898	1899	1900	1901
	1902			
Bellefeuille, Theodore (Chippewa)	1915			
Bender, Charles Albert (Chippewa)	1900	1901		
Bergie, Joseph (Chippewa/Sioux)	1910	1911	1912	
Bettleyoun, Isaac (Sioux)	1915			
Big Top, Fred (Piegan)	1913			
Bigbear, Samuel (Winnebago)	1911	1912		
Billy, Nicodemus (Seneca)	1904	1905	1906	
Bird, David (Cherokee)	1913	1914	1915	
Bird, Sampson (Piegan)	1908	1909	1910	1911
Blackbird, Charles (Omaha)	1914	1915		
Blackchief, Lyman (Seneca)	1900			
Blaine, James G. (Pawnee)	1908			
Bouchard, John (Kootenai)	1912	1913		
Bowen, Nicholas (Seneca)	1900	1901	1902	1903
	1904	1905	1906	1907
Boyd, Oscar (Piegan)	1909			
Bracklin, Edward (Chippewa)	1910	1912	1913	1914

Full Name (Tribe/Nation)	Years Played			
Bradby, Walter (Pamunkey)	1912			
Bradley, Johnson (Cherokee)	1900	1901	1902	1903
	1904			
Brave Eagle, Silas (Sioux)	1914			
Bravethunder, William (Sioux)	1905	1906		
Broker, Fred (Chippewa)	1911	1912	1913	1914
	1915			
Broker, Henry (Chippewa)	1911	1912	1914	1915
Brophy, John (Chippewa)	1917			
Brought Plenty, John (Sioux)	1912			
Brown, Alonzo (Mashpee)	1910			
Bruce, Robert (Chippewa)	1912			
Bruner, William (Creek)	1916	1917		
Bryant, Cecil (Osage)	1917			
Buck, Charles W. (Piegan)	1893	1894		
Burr, Sidney (Alaskan)	1899			
Burton, Roy (Osage)	1914	1915		
Busch, Elmer (Pomo)	1911	1912	1913	1914
Calac, Peter (Mission)	1912	1913	1914	1915
Campeau, Edward (Chippewa)	1895			
Caswell, Benjamin F. (Chippewa)	1893	1894		
Cayou, Francis Mitchell (Omaha)	1893	1894	1895	1896
	1897	1898		
Charging Whirlwind, Daniel (Sioux)	1909			
Charles, Foster (Paiute)	1902	1904		
Charles, Reuben (Seneca)	1910			
Charles, Wilson (Oneida)	1900	1901	1902	1903
	1904	1905	1906	
Chase, Daniel (Gros Ventre)	1915			
Chatfield, Peter (Chippewa)	1900	1901		
Chesowah, Lum (Osage)	1900	1901		
Clairmont/Claymore, Philip (Sioux)	1915			
Clifford, Henry (Sioux)	1916			
Coleman, Charles (Mission)	1901			
Coleman, Francis (Chippewa)	1909	1910		
Connor, Andrew (Chippewa)	1916			
Coons, Louis (Chippewa)	1914			
Cornelius, Casper (Oneida)	1906			
Cornelius, Joel (Oneida)	1898	1900	1902	
Cornelius, Phillip (Oneida)	1908	1909	1911	1912
Cornelius, Samson (Oneida)	1900			
Crane, James (Umatilla)	1910	1911	1912	1913
	1914	1915		
Cries-for-Ribs, Harry (Ponca)	1908			
Crowe, Boyd (Cherokee)	1913	1914	1915	1916
Crows Ghost, Morgan (Artikaree)	1910			

Full Name (Tribe/Nation)	Years Played			
Cueller, Andrew (Shawnee)	1917			
Curly Bear, Charles (Piegan)	1901			
Daniels, Albert (Ute)	1904	1905		
Davis, Jesse (Nez Perce)	1904			
Decora, Nathaniel (Winnebago)	1900	1901		
DeGrass, Alfred (Mashpee)	1910			
Degray, George (Sioux)	1904			
DeMarr, Edward (Chippewa)	1901			
Dennis, Edward (Chippewa)	1912			
Denny, Wallace (Oneida)	1903	1904	1905	
Dewey, Scott (Shoshone)	1913	1914		
Dickerson, Guy (Choctaw)	1915			
Dietz, William Henry (Sioux)	1907	1908	1909	1910
	1911			
Dillon, Charles (Sioux)	1900	1901	1902	1903
	1904	1905	1906	
Donnell, Antoine (Chippewa)	1894			
Downwind, Xavier (Chippewa)	1913	1915		
Doxtator, Benjamin (Oneida)	1893			
Doxtator, Frank (Seneca)	1903	1904		
Dubois, Alfred (Chippewa)	1905	1906		
Dunbar, James (Piegan)	1911			
Dupuis, Louis (Iowa)	1909	1910		
Dutton, Frank (Chippewa)	1902			
Eagle Man, Thomas (Sioux)	1904	1905	1906	
Ear, Seth (Sioux)	1904			
Earth, George (Chippewa)	1911	1912		
Eastman, Christian E. (Sioux)	1897			
Eastman, Peter (Sioux)	1912	1913	1915	
Edmonds, Taylor (Caddo)	1916	1917		
Edwards, Eustace (Delaware)	1915			
Emmett, Robert (Assiniboine)	1898			
Eshelman, Wilfred (Pawnee)	1915	1916		
Evans, James (Piegan)	1917			
Exendine, Albert (Delaware)	1902	1903	1904	1905
	1906	1907		
Felix, Louis (Sioux)	1907			
Fielder, Isaac (Sioux)	1901			
Fischer, Adam (Winnebago)	1903	1904		
Fisher, Eugene (Cheyenne)	1902	1903		
Flinchum, John B. (Choctaw)	1916	1917		
Flood, Henry (Sioux)	1915			
Flores, Louis (Mission)	1901	1902	1903	1904
Fly, Felix (Sioux)	1914			
Foote, Stephen (Sioux)	1915			

Full Name (Tribe/Nation)	Years Played			
Forte, Bruce (Sioux)	1910			
Fox, Edward (Shawnee)	1910			
Francis, George (Penobscot)	1915	1916		
Freemont/Fremont, Francis (Omaha)	1902	1904	1905	
French, Meroney (Cherokee)	1916	1917		
Friday, Moses (Arapaho)	1908			
Gaddy, Peter (Delaware)	1910			
Gardner, George (Chippewa)	1905	1906	1907	1908
Gardner, William (Chippewa)	1904	1905	1906	1907
Garlow, James (Onondaga)	1911			
Garlow, William (Onondaga)	1908	1909	1910	1911
	1912	1913		
George, David (Oneida)	1912			
George, Lewis (Klamath)	1909			
Gibson, John (Pima)	1913			
Gilman, Joe (Chippewa)	1912	1913	1914	
Giroux, William (Sioux)	1910	1911	1912	
Godfrey, Francis (Miami)	1905	1906		
Godfrey, Frank John (Chippewa)	1917			
Godfrey, Louis (Chippewa)	1916	1917		
Goesback, Bruce (Arapapaho)	1908	1911	1912	1913
Gokee, Jr., John (Chippewa)	1913			
Green, Edward (Seneca)	1902	1903		
Grinnell, George (Gros Ventre)	1908			
Guyon, Benedict (Chippewa)	1915	1916		
Guyon, Charles Mayo (Chippewa)	1905			
Guyon, Joseph (Chippewa)	1912	1913		
Half Town, Ora (Seneca)	1911			
Hare, Nelson (Seneca)	1899	1900	1901	
Harris, Buddy (Choctaw)	1917			
Harrison, Benjamin (Pueblo)	1915	1916		
Has Knife, Alfred (Sioux)	1903			
Hauser, Emil (Cheyenne)	1906	1907	1908	1909
	1910			
Hauser, Herman Peter (Cheyenne)	1907	1908	1909	1910
Hawk Eagle, Thomas (Sioux)	1913	1914	1915	
Hawk, Thomas (Hidatsa)	1916			
Hayes, Noah (Nez Perce)	1917			
Hazlett, George or Stuart (Piegan)	1897	1898		
Helms, Joseph (Pottawatomie)	1914			
Hendricks, Fritz (Caddo)	1903	1904	1905	1906
	1907	1908	1909	
Hendricks, Richard (Papazo)	1898			
Henry, Noah (Tuscarora)	1912			
Herman, Jacob (Sioux)	1915	1916	1917	
Hill, Levi E. (Oneida)	1909			

Full Name (Tribe/Nation)	Years Played			
Hill, Robert (Tuscarora)	1911	1912	1913	1914
Hinman, Richard (Ponca)	1908			
Hodge, William (Klamath)	1909	1910	1911	1912
	1913			
Hoff, Joseph (Sioux)	1903			
Holstein, James (Chippewa)	1914	1916	1917	
Hood, Oscar (Shawnee)	1917			
Houk, G. Presley (Piegan)	1894			
Howling Wolf, William (Cheyenne)	1900			
Huber, Charles (Hidatsa)	1904			
Hudson, Frank (Laguna Pueblo)	1894	1895	1896	1897
	1898	1899	1905	
Huff, Morris (Seneca)	1912			
Hunt, Oscar (Wyandotte)	1905	1906	1907	
Iron Whiteman, Alex (Sioux)	1917			
Irons, Thomas (Sioux)	1911			
Irwin, Joseph (Gros Ventre)	1893	1894	1895	1898
Isham, William G. (Chippewa)	1904			
Island, Louis (Oneida)	1906	1907	1910	
Jackson, Jack (Cherokee)	1911			
Jackson, Jonas (Cherokee)	1905			
Jackson, Peter (Shoshone)	1916			
Jackson, William B. (Cheyenne)	1903	1904		
Jacobs, Luther (Cherokee)	1912	1913		
James, Laban (Apache)	1893			
James, Leslie (Chippewa)	1911	1914		
James, Moses (Covelo)	1902	1903		
Jamison/Jimerson, Jacob (Seneca)	1895	1896	1897	
Jimerson, Albert (Seneca)	1911			
Jimerson/Jamison, Roger Tandy	1904			
John, Herbert E. (Seneca)	1905			
Johnnyjohn, Mitchell/Michael (Seneca)	1910			
Johnson, Clifford (Cherokee)	1915	1916		
Johnson, James (Stockbridge)	1898	1899	1900	1901
	1902	1903		
Johnson, Richard (Cherokee)	1914			
Jones, Amos (Mohawk)	1917			
Jones, William C. (Sioux)	1904	1905		
Jordan, Dewey (Mohawk)	1916			
Jordan/Jourdan, Peter (Chippewa)	1907	1908	1909	1910
Jude, Frank (Chippewa)	1902	1903	1904	1905
Kelley, Victor M. (Choctaw)	1908			
Kelly, Calvin Lee (Sioux)	1908			
Kelsey, Charles (Winnebago)	1912	1913		
Kenjockety, Jesse (Cayuga)	1905	1906	1908	

Full Name (Tribe/Nation)	Years Played			
Kennedy, Alvin (Seneca)	1910			
Kennedy, Charles M. (Seneca)	1897	1899	1903	1904
	1905			
Kennedy, Patrick (Sioux)	1904			
Kennerly, Jerome (Piegan)	1907	1908	1909	1910
Kettle, Francis (Seneca)	1913			
King, Kenneth (Sioux)	1914			
Kipp, George (Piegan)	1917			
Knocks-Off-Two aka Knox, Augustine	1913	1916	1917	
Komah, Walter (Comanche)	1904			
La Mere, Oliver (Winnebago)	1902			
La Rocque, Paul (Chippewa)	1904	1905	1906	1907
	1908			
LaFleur, Mitchell (Colville)	1910			
Lambert, Frank (Sioux)	1908			
Large, Roy (Shoshone)	1910	1911	1912	
Larrabee aka Larvie, David (Sioux)	1913			
Lassaw, Nicholas (Flathead)	1914	1915	1916	1917
Lay, Kelley (Seneca)	1900			
LeClaire, Peter Michael (Ponca)	1908	1909		
Leighton, William Morris (Crow)	1895			
Lemieux, John (Chippewa)	1898			
Leo, Edward (Ottawa)	1913			
Leroy, John (Stockbridge)	1915	1916	1917	
Leroy, Louis (Stockbridge)	1901			
Libby, Archie (Chippewa)	1903	1904	1905	1906
Libby, Joseph (Chippewa)	1905	1906	1907	1908
	1909	1910		
Little Hawk, James (Sioux)	1913			
Little Old Man, David (Cheyenne)	1904	1905	1906	1907
	1908			
Little Wolf, William (Cheyenne)	1907	1908		
Littlechief, Charles (Sioux)	1916			
Locklear, George (Cherokee)	1910			
Lone Elk, Charles (Sioux)	1909			
Lone Wolf, Delos (Kiowa)	1894	1895	1896	
Long Roach, William (Cheyenne)	1911	1912		
Long, Grover (Wyandotte)	1904	1905	1906	1907
Lookaround, August (Menominee)	1912	1913	1914	1915
Lorentz, Albert (Wichita)	1911			
Loud Bear, Joseph (Sioux)	1910			
Lubo, Antonio (Mission)	1900	1901	1902	1903
	1904	1905	1906	1907
	1914			
Luna, Joe B. (Mission)	1902			
Lyon, Isaac (Onondaga)	1907	1908		

Full Name (Tribe/Nation)	Years Played			
Machukay, Martin (Apache)	1904			
Martell, Grover (Shawnee)	1911	1912	1913	1914
	1915			
Martell, William (Chippewa)	1908			
Martin, Michael (Caddo)	1910	1911		
Mathews, Walter (Osage)	1902	1903		
Matlock, Elmo (Pawnee)	1913	1914		
Matlock, Louis (Pawnee)	1905			
Matlock, Stacy (Pawnee)	1905			
May, George (Wichita)	1914	1915	1916	
McClean, Robert (Sioux)	1908			
McDonald, Lewis (Ponca)	1898	1899		
McDowell, John (Lummi)	1915			
McFarland, David (Nez Perce)	1894	1895	1896	1897
McLean, Robert (Sioux)	1907	1908	1909	
McLean, Samuel (Sioux)	1907	1908		
Metoxen, Emerson (Oneida)	1917			
Metoxen, James (Oneida)	1904			
Metoxen, Jonas (Oneida)	1893	1894	1895	1896
	1897	1898	1899	
Miguel, Ambrose (Yuma)	1905	1906	1908	
Miguel, Jefferson (Yuma)	1907	1908		
Miles, Thomas C. (Sac & Fox)	1915	1916	1917	
Miller, Artie (Stockbridge)	1895	1896	1897	1898
	1899			
Miller, Edwin (Miami)	1916	1917		
Miller, James (Chippewa)	1900			
Miller, Leon (Cherokee)	1910	1911	1916	
Mitchell, Frank (Penobscot)	1916			
Mitchell, Jonas (Ottawa)	1896	1897	1898	
Monchamp, Charles (Chippewa)	1910			
Monhart, John (Klamath)	1907			
Moore, Edwin (Sac & Fox)	1898			
Moore, Job J. (Oneida)	1903			
Moore, Philip (Creek)	1917			
Morin, Solomon (Chippewa)	1913			
Morrin, Edward (Chippewa)	1913	1914	1915	
Morrin, Joseph (Chippewa)	1913	1915		
Morrison, Daniel W. (Chippewa)	1896			
Mt. Pleasant, Franklin Pierce (Tusc.)	1902	1904	1905	1906
	1907			
Nahtailish, Vincent (Apache)	1898			
Needham, Simon (Chippewa)	1912	1913		
Nelson, Ezra (Navajo)	1911			
Nephew, Arthur (Seneca)	1913			

Full Name (Tribe/Nation)	Years Played			
Nephew, Lloyd (Seneca)	1901	1902	1903	1904
	1905			
Nephew, Percy (Seneca)	1908			
Newashe, William (Sac & Fox)	1908	1909	1910	
Nicolar, J. Frederick (Penobscot)	1903	1904		
No Shin Bone, Henry (Crow)	1901			
Noble, Jonah (Pima)	1904			
Nori, Davis (Pueblo)	1913	1915	1916	1917
Northrup, Joseph (Chippewa)	1908			
Ojibway, Francis (Chippewa)	1916	1917		
Owl, Theodore (Cherokee)	1906	1907		
Owl, William J. (Cherokee)	1908	1909	1910	
Paisano, James (Pueblo)	1908			
Palmer, Jesse (Sioux)	1900	1901		
Pambrum, Francis (Piegan)	1912	1913		
Parker, Ely (Seneca)	1900	1902		
Paul, Edward (Nez Perce)	1911			
Paulin, Louis (Flathead)	1912	1913	1915	
Payne, Albert (Umatilla)	1907	1908		
Peake, George C. (Chippewa)	1907	1908		
Peconga, Willis (Miami)	1905			
Penny, Benjamin (Nez Perce)	1905	1906	1907	1908
Peters, Edward (Chippewa)	1898			
Phillips, Daniel (Sioux)	1909	1910		
Phillips, James (Cherokee)	1901	1902		
Pico, Carlos (Mission)	1901	1903		
Pierce, Bemus (Seneca)	1893	1894	1895	1896
	1897	1898	1904	1905
Pierce, Hawley (Seneca)	1895	1896	1897	1898
	1899	1900	1904	
Poodry, Aaron (Seneca)	1914			
Porter, Scott (Chippewa)	1905	1906	1907	1908
Powell, Stansill (Cherokee)	1908	1909	1910	1911
	1912			
Pratt, Charles (Pottawatomie)	1911	1912	1913	1914
	1915			
Printup, Harrison (Onondaga)	1894	1895	1896	
Purse (Pierce), Howard (Seneca)	1908	1909		
Quick Bear, Ernest (Sioux)	1908			
Quick Bear, Levi (Sioux)	1913			
Ramsey, John (Nez Perce)	1911			
Ranco, Everett (Penobscot)	1913	1914	1915	
Red Tomahawk, Francis (Sioux)	1902	1903	1904	1906
Redwater, Thaddeus (Cheyenne)	1896	1897	1898	1899
	1900			
Reed, Amos (Oneida)	1896			

Full Name (Tribe/Nation)	Years Played			
Reed, Lloyd (Cherokee)	1910			
Rickard, Edward (Tuscarora)	1898			
Ricketts, Paul (Delaware)	1906			
Roberts, Charles (Chippewa)	1899	1900		
Roberts, George (Pawnee)	1914			
Roberts, Henry E. (Pawnee)	1911			
Robinson, David (Klamath)	1909			
Robinson, William Jr. (Chippewa)	1911			
Roe, Charles (Ottawa)	1916			
Rogers, Edward L. (Chippewa)	1896	1897	1898	1899
	1900	1904		
Rolling Bull, Rutherford (Cheyenne)	1911			
Roundstone, Fred (Cheyenne)	1907			
Roussian, John (Chippewa)	1908	1909		
Roy, Joseph (Chippewa)	1912			
Roy, Robert Charles (Chippewa)	1904	1905		
Ruiz, Joseph (Pueblo)	1900	1901		
Runnels, Lewis (San Poil)	1909			
Sage, Alexander (Arikaree)	1905			
Sampson, John (Creek)	1915			
Sat-on, Russell (Seneca)	1905	1906		
Saul, Alfred (Sioux)	1904			
Saul, Thomas (Sioux)	1901	1903	1904	1905
	1906	1907	1908	
Saunook, Jackson (Cherokee)	1901	1902	1903	
Saunook, Stillwell (Cherokee)	1910			
Saunooke, Samuel (Cherokee)	1905			
Schenandore, Fred S. (Onondaga)	1910			
Schildt, Joseph (Piegan)	1899			
Scholder, Joseph (Mission)	1899			
Schweigman, Louis (Sioux)	1911			
Scott, Frank (Seneca)	1896	1897	1898	1899
	1905			
Scrogg, Solomon (Seneca)	1899	1901		
Seneca, Isaac (Seneca)	1895	1896	1897	1898
	1899	1900		
She Bear, David (Cheyenne)	1908	1910	1911	
Shelafo, George (Chippewa)	1894	1895	1896	
Sheldon, Arthur (Nez Perce)	1900	1901	1902	1903
	1904	1905		
Shell, Huckleberry (Cherokee)	1915	1916		
Shemamey, James (Caddo)	1912			
Shomin, Sebastian (Ottawa)	1900			
Short Bear, Bert (Arickaree)	1906			

Full Name (Tribe/Nation)	Years Played			
Shouchuk, Nekifer (Aleut)	1901	1902	1903	1904
	1905	1906	1907	
Sickles, Caleb (Oneida)	1898	1899		
Silverheels, Stephen (Seneca)	1904			
Simpson, Albert (Arickaree)	1904	1905	1906	
Simpson, John (Pawnee)	1908			
Skenandore, Benjamin (Oneida)	1913	1914		
Skenandore, Fred (Oneida)	1912	1913	1914	
Skenandore, Thomas A. (Oneida)	1894	1895		
Smith, Chester (Osage)	1896			
Smith, Claude (Sioux)	1914	1916	1917	
Smith, Edwin (Clallam)	1894	1896	1897	1898
	1899	1900		
Smith, Jefferson (Gros Ventre)	1909	1910	1911	1912
Snow, James (Sioux)	1904	1905		
Solomon, David (Mohawk)	1909			
Sousa, Eloy (Mission)	1909	1910	1911	
Spears, Benjamin (Chippewa)	1916			
Spearson, Albert (Piegan)	1917			
Spybuck, Thomas (Shawnee)	1916	1917		
Squirrel, John (Chippewa)	1911	1912	1913	
St. Germaine, Thomas (Chippewa)	1909			
Stabler, George (Omaha)	1905	1906		
Stevenson, Nuss (Wichita)	1910			
Stranger Horse, Moses (Sioux)	1910			
Sumner, Joseph (Chippewa)	1913	1914	1915	
Sundown, Fayley (Seneca)	1910			
Sutton, Ernest (Seneca)	1905	1906	1907	
Sweetcorn, Asa (Sioux)	1909	1910		
Tahquechi, Norton (Comanche)	1915	1916	1917	
Tall Crane, Fred (Sioux)	1907	1908		
Tarbell, Peter (Mohawk)	1915			
Tatiyopa, Henry (Sioux)	1901			
Teesatesky, Welch (Cherokee)	1915	1916		
Thomas, Dennis (Kiowa)	1917			
Thomas, Frank (Cowlitz)	1898			
Thomas, George (Onondaga)	1905	1906	1907	1908
	1909			
Thompson, George (Mashpee)	1907	1908		
Thompson, John (Chippewa)	1905			
Thompson, Noble (Pueblo)	1905	1908		
Thompson, Norman (Pomo)	1911	1912	1913	
Thorpe, James Francis (Sac and Fox)	1907	1908	1911	1912
Tibbetts, George (Chippewa)	1914	1915	1916	1917
Tramper, Ammons (Cherokee)	1911			
Traversie, Alexander (Sioux)	1916			

Full Name (Tribe/Nation)	Years Played			
Tupper, Hobson K. (Choctaw)	1916	1917		
Twin, Joseph (Winnebago)	1905			
Two Hearts, Joseph (Sioux)	1905	1906	1907	1908
	1909			
Valandra, Louis (Sioux)	1917			
Vedernack, George (Chippewa)	1909	1910	1911	1912
	1913			
Vielle, John (Piegan)	1917			
Vigil, Clement (Pueblo)	1917			
Vincent, Henry (Ottawa?)	1909			
Walker, Benjamin (Omaha)	1900			
Walker, Charles Amos (Omaha)	1915	1916	1917	
Walker, Fred (Omaha)	1915	1916	1917	
Walker, Thomas (Omaha)	1900			
Walletsie, John (Umatilla)	1901			
Wallette, John (Chippewa)	1910	1911	1912	1913
	1914			
Warner, Harvey D. (Omaha)	1893	1894		
Warren, John B. (Chippewa)	1898	1899		
Wasase, David (Seminole)	1915			
Washington, Alex (Shawnee)	1914	1915	1916	1917
Washington, Wesley (Creek)	1917			
Waupoose, William (Menominee)	1912			
Webster, Lewis (Oneida)	1898			
Weeks, William (Gros Ventre)	1908			
Welch, Gustave (Chippewa)	1910	1911	1912	1913
	1914			
Welch, James (Chippewa)	1913	1914		
Welmas, Philip (Mission)	1910	1911	1912	1913
	1914	1915		
Wheeler, Harry (Nez Perce)	1905	1906	1907	1909
	1910	1911		
Wheelock, Hugh (Oneida)	1907	1908	1909	1910
	1911	1912		
Wheelock, Joel (Oneida)	1908	1909	1910	1911
	1912			
Wheelock, Martin (Oneida)	1893	1894	1895	1896
	1897	1898	1899	1900
	1901	1902		
Whipple, Samuel (Sioux)	1900			
White Crow, Titus (Sioux)	1902	1903	1904	1905
	1906			
White Dog, Henry (Piegan)	1917			
White Fox, George (Crow)	1910	1911	1912	
White Thunder, Clarence (Sioux)	1894			

Full Name (Tribe/Nation)	Years Played			
White, Chauncey (Winnebago)	1913			
White, Grant (Pawnee)	1913	1914	1915	
White, John (Mohawk)	1914			
White, Joseph (Mohawk)	1916			
White, William H. Jr. (Crow)	1899	1900	1901	1902
	1903	1904		
White, William S. (Digger)	1905	1906	1907	1908
Whiteface, Henry (Sioux)	1901			
Wilber, Earl (Menominee)	1915	1916		
Wilde, Byron (Arikaree)	1897	1898		
Wilkie, Michael (Chippewa)	1914			
Williams, Charles (Caddo)	1909	1910	1911	1912
	1913			
Williams, Charles (Stockbridge)	1899	1900	1901	1902
	1903	1904		
Williams, Chauncey (Sioux)	1914	1915		
Williams, Joseph (Nez Perce)	1911			
Wilson, Samuel B. (Caddo)	1910			
Winneshiek, William (Winnebago)	1912	1913	1914	1915
Winnie, William (Seneca)	1905	1906	1907	1908
Wizi, John (Sioux)	1901			
Wofford, Jesse (Cherokee)	1914	1915		
Wolfe, Tarquette (Cherokee)	1908			
Woodbury, Clarence (Chippewa)	1908			
Wounded Eye, Davis (Cheyenne)	1908	1909	1910	1911
Wright, Ellis (Cherokee)	1917			
Wynaco, George (Yakima)	1911	1913		
Yankee Joe, William (Chippewa)	1906	1907	1908	1909
Yarlott, Frank (Crow)	1900	1901	1902	
Yellow Elk, William (Sioux)	1909			
Yellow Head, Joseph (Sioux)	1916			
Youngbird, Wesley (Cherokee)	1917			
Yukkanini, Karl (Apache)	1903			

Notes

In the earliest years of Carlisle's football history, school publications included little about the games, eliminating the school's view of what transpired. Newspapers were about the only source covering these games. In a few years, school publications started covering the games but commercial newspapers remained the primary source for information about what happened on and off the field. Since the coverage of games varied greatly from source to source, it was necessary to sort through the accounts, analyze them, and synthesize the most likely parts of each into a cohesive narrative. For a few games only the scores were known, eliminating any discussion of what happened. The approach taken made attributing statements to specific sources impossible, so all the sources reviewed are listed for each chapter.

Introduction

Pop Warner: Football's Greatest Teacher, edited by Mike Bynum, 1993.

Chapter 1

1893

Battlefield and Classroom: An Autobiography by Richard Henry Pratt, edited by Robert M. Utley, 1964.
Pratt: The Red Man's Moses, Elaine Goodale Eastman, 1935.
The Sentinel, November 10, 1893, Caswell captain.
The Sentinel, November 10, 1893, Harrisburg High.
Patriot, November 13, 1893, p2.
Patriot, November 15, 1893, p3, 16-4 score.
Philadelphia Inquirer, November 13, 1893, p3.
Philadelphia Inquirer, December 1, 1893, p5, Educational Home.
The Sentinel, December 1, 1893, Educational Home.
Carlisle Weekly Herald, December 7, 1893, Patrolman injured.
The Dickinsonian, December 1893, Carlisle practice game.

1894

The Sentinel, September 21, 1894, to play Hbg High.
The Times, September 29, 1894, season schedule.
Harrisburg Daily Independent, October 5, 1894, Sixth Street Grounds.
Epitome Yearbook 1896, October 6, 1894, Athletic Grounds, Still Looking for You.
The Philadelphia Inquirer, October 7, 1894, Central High.
The Times, October 7, 1894, Line-ups for Central High game.
The Patriot, October 8, 1894, p2, Hbg game coverage.
The Sentinel, October 8, 1894, game write up.
The Philadelphia Inquirer, October 10, 1894, can absorb civilization.
The Sentinel, October 11, 1894, p1, to play Dickinson.
The Sentinel, October 11, 1894, to play F&M on Nov 3.
The Philadelphia Inquirer, October 10, 1894.
The Sentinel, October 15, 1894, Dickinson game.
The Times, October 21, 1894, Surprised Lehigh.
The Philadelphia Inquirer, October 21, 1894, Indians play well against Lehigh.
Philadelphia Inquirer, October 21, 1894, p3, Lehigh game.
The Sentinel, October 22, 1894, snappy game.
The Patriot, November 1, p2, Indians will play Yale.

The Times, November 1, 1894, Navy.
The Patriot, November 3, 1894, p1, team attended Yale talk.
The Philadelphia Inquirer, November 4, 1894, F&M.
The Times, November 4, 1894, collapsed in 2nd half.
The Sentinel, November 5, 1894, Metoxen's Marvelous Strength.
The Daily New Era, November 5, 1894, F&M's Greatest Victory.
Washington Times, November 6, 1894, p4, CAC game being arranged.
The Gazette, November 10, 1894, YMCA ministers object to Thanksgiving Day.
The Gazette, November 11, 1894, fewer object to Thanksgiving game.
The Philadelphia Inquirer, November 11, 1894, lose 10-0 at Bucknell.
The Pittsburgh Press, November 14, 1894, game with Carlisle added.
The Pittsburgh Press, November 15, 1894, played great against Bucknell.
The Philadelphia Inquirer, November 15, 1894, possible game.
Public Press, November 16, 1894, Bucknell wins.
The Pittsburgh Press, November 16, 1894, Indians to play PAC.
The Pittsburgh Press, November 17, 1894, (1) PAC Park.
The Pittsburgh Press, November 17, 1894, (2) PAC should have hair short.
The Pittsburgh Press, November 17, 1894, Indians in Pittsburgh.
The Pittsburgh Press, November 18, 1894, PAC play by play.
Pittsburgh Daily Post, November 18, 1894, Lack teamwork.
The Philadelphia Inquirer, November 18, 1894, Indian boys engrossd in game.
The Sentinel, November 19, 1894, finest tackling.
The Indian Helper, November 23, 1894, Vol. 10, No. 9, New Captain.
Pittsburgh Post Gazette, November 24, 1894, injured hand.
The Sentinel, November 24, 1894, play CAC.
Washington Times, November 24, 1894, p3,Ticket ad.
Washington Times, November 24, 1894, p4, National Baseball Park.
Washington Times, November 25, p4, Fail to score.
The Times, November 25, 1894, CAC 18-0.
Washington Times, November 25, 1894, p3, CAC wins 15-0.
The Sentinel, November 26, 1894, CAC 18-0.
The Sentinel, November 27, 1894, p1, Rockafellow.
The Sentinel, November 27, 1894, will play Thanksgiving Day.
Lewisburg Journal, November 28, 1894, Indians civilized.
The Sentinel, November 29, 1894, Leave for York.
The Times, November 30, 1894, better line-ups.
The Philadelphia Inquirer, November 30, 1894, YMCA game line-ups.
The Sentinel, November 30, 1894, YMCA tie.
The Indian Helper, December 7, 1894, Vol. 10, No. 11, Cayou.
The Patriot, December 10, p2, Hbg season recap.
Washington Times, November 24, 1894, p4, National Baseball Park.
Washington Times, November 25, p4, Fail to score.
Washington Nationals Ballparks History | Washington Nationals (mlb.com)

1895

Spalding's Official Football Guide for 1895, September 1895.
The Red Man, September & October 1895, v13, n4.
The Indian Helper, October 4, 1895, v11, n1.
The Philadelphia Inquirer, October 06, 1895, p7, Gettysburg.
The Sentinel, October 7, 1895, Dickinson decline Carlisle rise.
The Pittsburgh Press, October 11, 1895, CCA game.
The Pittsburgh Press, October 13, 1895, avenged.

The Pittsburgh Press, October 13, 1895, 16-4 McCormick plays for Chicago.
The Pittsburgh Press, October 13, 1895, CAC play by play.
Harrisburg Daily Independent, October 15, 1895, -1 McCormick.
The Philadelphia Inquirer, October 16, 1895, p4 Windsor Hotel.
The Philadelphia Inquirer, October 17, 1895, p1, Lose to Penn 36-0.
Evening Journal, October 17, 1895, p5, Wilmington DE Penn game.
The Sentinel, October 17, 1895, lost 36-0.
The Philadelphia Inquirer, October 17, 1895, more cartoons.
The Philadelphia Inquirer, October 17, 1895, p1.
The Sentinel, October 19, 1895, Dickinson playing.
The Times, October 20, 1895, Penn team drawing.
The Philadelphia Inquirer, October 20, 1895, Indians as football players.
The Sentinel, October 21, 1895, to play Yale.
The Philadelphia Inquirer, October 22, 1895, negotiating w Yale.
The Philadelphia Inquirer, October 22, 1895, taunts Yale.
The Sentinel, October 23, 1895, careful training.
The Philadelphia Inquirer, October 27, 1895, Navy 4 - Inds 2.
Sun & New York Press, October 27, 1895, p9. Navy.
The Baltimore Sun, October 28, 1895, Navy.
The Sentinel, November 7, 1895, Yale.
Morning Journal & Courier, November 07, 1895, p7, Yale.
New York Tribune, November 07, 1895, p4, Yale.
The Philadelphia Inquirer, November 17, 1895, Bucknell.
Carlisle Evening Herald, November 18, 1895, Bucknell.
The York Daily, November 18, 1895, York YMCA.
Pittsburgh Daily Post, November 18, 1895, Bucknell new interference.
The Gazette, November 21, 1895, York YMCA.
New York Tribune, November 21, 1895, p3, Crescent A. C.
The York Daily, November 21, 1895, No signals.
The York Daily, November 22, 1895, York YMCA.
The Times, November 22, 1895, York YMCA.
The Sentinel, November 22, 1895, cold day.
New York Tribune, November 29, 1895, p3, Manhattan YMCA.

Chapter 2

1896

The Philadelphia Inquirer, September 27, 1896, Short halves.
The Times, September 27, 1896, p1, 15 & 20 minute halves.
The Times, September 27, 1896, Bemus Pierce Redwater.
Pittsburgh Daily Post, October 4, 1896, Duquesne CAC.
The Philadelphia Inquirer, October 4, 1896, Duquesne CAC.
The Sentinel, October 5, 1896, DCAC college men.
New Haven Register, October 7, 1896, p7, McKees Rocks Indians.
The Philadelphia Inquirer, October 9, 1896, p4, Princeton adds bleachers.
The Boston Globe, October 31, 1896, Hickok - busts.
The Red Man, September & October 1896, v13, n12, p2, Bemus Pierce quote.
The Times, November 1, 1896, Harvard game.
The Philadelphia Inquirer, November 1, 1896, Harvard.
The Sentinel, November 2, 1896, Harvard.
The Pittsburgh Press, November 8, 1896, Army game canceled.
The Times, November 8, 1896, Penn Smith.
Sunday News, November 8, 1896, Yale Slugging.

The Boston Globe, November 8, 1896, Penn.
The Philadelphia Inquirer, November 8, 1896, Penn.
Pittsburgh Daily Post, November 13, 1896, to play Penn State.
The Cincinnati Enquirer, November 15, 1896, Cincinnati.
The Pittsburgh Press, November 15, 1896, Cincinnati.
The Times, November 18, 1896, West Point.
The Philadelphia Inquirer, November 18, 1896, Cayou to Princeton.
The Sentinel, November 19, 1896, West Point.
The Sentinel, November 20, 1896, Brown.
The Patriot, November 20, 1896, p2, Brooke.
The Sentinel, November 21, 1896, Penn State.
The Pittsburgh Press, November 22, 1896, Penn State.
Philadelphia Times, November 22, 1896, p9, Bass Yale TD.
Pittsburgh Daily Post, November 22, 1896, Penn State.
The Patriot, November 23, 1896, p2, Penn State.
New York Evening Journal, November 24, 1896, p3, Brown.
New York Evening Journal, November 26, 1896, pp1&2, Brown.
The Boston Globe, November 27, 1896, Brown Mitchell.
The New York Times, November 27, 1896, Mitchell.
Evening Bulletin, November 27, 1896, p8, Brown.
The Red Man, November 1896, v14, n1.
Sun & New York Press, December 6, 1896, p9, Wisconsin challenged.
The Patriot, December 9, 1896, p5, Wisconsin.
The Philadelphia Inquirer, December 17, 1896, p7, Depart for Chicago.
The Inter Ocean, December 18, 1896, Wrong Wheelock.
Chicago Tribune, December 19, 1896, Chicago tour.
Chicago Record, December 19, 1896, p6, Gave up against Princeton.
Daily Illinois State Journal, December 20, 1896, p1, Wisconsin.
Denver Rocky Mountain News, December 20, 1896, p6, Wisconsin.
Pittsburgh Daily Post, December 20, 1896, Wisconsin.
The Chicago Chronicle, December 20, 1896, Sketches Wisconsin.
The Chicago Chronicle, December 21, 1896, Tour U of Chicago.
Milwaukee Journal, December 21, 1896, p8, Wisconsin.
The Philadelphia Inquirer, December 22, 1896, Stagg.
The Inter Ocean, December 26, 1896, Stagg.
The Free Lance, December 1896, pp134-5, Penn State.

1897

Denver Post, August 11, 1897, McFarland locked up.
Minneapolis Journal, September 2, 1897, p10, Billy Bull.
Aberdeen Daily News, September 22, 1897, p4, Layton.
The Philadelphia Inquirer, September 23, 1897, Bull & McCormick.
Minneapolis Journal, September 29, 1897, p10, Layton derelict.
Denver Post, September 29, 1897, p11, Denver AC.
The Philadelphia Inquirer, October 4, 1897, Schedule.
The Sentinel, October 4, 1897, Dickinson.
The Sentinel, October 7, 1897, Prepare for Princeton.
The Bloomsburg Daily, October 8 Bloomsburg ad.
The Philadelphia Inquirer, October 10, 1897, Bloomsburg.
The Bloomsburg Daily, October 11 Bloomsburg game.
The Scranton Tribune, October 11, 1897, Bloomsburg.
The Plain Dealer, October 17, 1897, p10, Princeton.

The Philadelphia Inquirer, October 22, 1897, Princeton slugged.
New York Evening Journal, October 23, 1897, Yale.
New York Daily Tribune, October 24, 1897, p9, Yale.
The Philadelphia Inquirer, October 31, 1897, Gettysburg.
Chicago Tribune, November 14, 1897, Brown.
The Cincinnati Enquirer, November 26, 1897, Cincinnati.
San Francisco Chronicle, November 27, 1897, p8, Carlisle to California.
Daily Illinois State Journal, November 28, 1897, p2, Ohio Med.
Kansas City Daily Journal, November 28, 1897, p16, Medics.
The Philadelphia Inquirer, November 28, 1897, Ohio Medical School.
Chicago Record, November 29, 1897, p6, McCormick.
The Red Man, September-December, 1897, v14, n7.

1898

The Sentinel, January 27, 1898, Attempt to defund Carlisle.
Philadelphia Times, September 25, 1898, Bloomsburg.
The Gazette, September 25, 1898, 10 games scheduled.
Chicago Tribune, October 2, 1898, Susquehanna.
The Sentinel, October 3, 1898, Susquehanna.
Detroit Free Press, October 4, 1898, Season schedule.
The Champaign County News, October 5, 1898, p8, extra points.
Democrat & Chronicle, October 9, 1898, Cornell.
The Sun, October 16, 1898, Williams College.
The Boston Globe, October 30, 1898, Harvard.
The Boston Globe, October 30, 1898, p2, Harvard.
Dayton Daily News, November 1, 1898, Cincinnati.
Cincinnati Commercial Tribune, November 2, 1898, p3, Demand $800.
Philadelphia Times, November 6, 1898, Dickinson.
The Sentinel, November 7, 1898, Dickinson.
Dayton Daily News, November 10, 1898, Carlisle greedy.
Philadelphia Times, November 12, 1898, p8, Expect to score.
Philadelphia Times, November 13, 1898, Penn.
The Philadelphia Inquirer, November 13, 1898, p14, Dickinson line-up.
The Philadelphia Inquirer, November 17, 1898, p6, Dickinson line-up.
The Saint Paul Globe, November 20, 1898, Illinois.
Cincinnati Commercial Tribune, November 20, 1898, p3, Illinois.
The Patriot, November 21, 1898, p2, last game on Saturday.
Chicago Record, November 21, 1898, p6, Carlisle not in good shape.
Los Angeles Daily Herald, November 21, 1898, p8, $10,000.
Milwaukee Journal, November 23, 1898, p8, Wisconsin game off to play Cincinnati.
Plain Dealer, November 24, 1898, p8, Cincinnati.
The Columbus Telegram, November 24, 1898, 3rd touchdown.
The Philadelphia Inquirer, November 24, 1898, Cayou with Dickinson.
The Sun, November 24, 1898, Carlisle at Cincinnati.
Cleveland Leader, November 24, 1898, p8, Cincinnati.
Omaha Daily Bee, November 24, 1898, p4, Wisconsin.
The Patriot, November 25, 1898, p2, Carlisle played Cincinnati.
The Philadelphia Inquirer, November 25, 1898, p5, Cayou plays for Dickinson.
Scranton Tribune, November 25, 1898, p2, Dartmouth loses.
The Baltimore Sun, November 25, 1898, Carlisle scrubs.
The Philadelphia Inquirer, November 25, 1898, 2nd team.
The Sentinel, November 25, 1898, Did not play.

The Cincinnati Enquirer, November 28, 1898, Kentucky All-Stars.
The Sun, November 28, 1898, Harrisburg.
Cincinnati Commercial Tribune, December 2, 1898, p3, Money due.
The Baltimore Sun, December 2, 1898, Players not returning.
The Bourbon News, December 6, 1898, All-Kentucky team.
New York Evening Journal, December 10, 1898, p7, Carlisle in demand.
Plain Dealer, December 15, 1898, p10, Hudson Rogers Cayou not leaving.
The Red Man, December 1898, v15, n3, pp4-5.
Spalding's Official Football Guide 1899, August 1899.

Chapter 3 1899

Battlefield and Classroom: An Autobiography by Richard Henry Pratt, edited by Robert M. Utley, 1964.
Pop Warner: Football's Greatest Teacher, Glenn S. Warner, edited by Mike Bynum, 1993.
Pop Warner: A Life on the Gridiron, Jeffrey J. Miller, 2015.
The Sentinel, August 23, 1899, Baine etc.
The Sentinel, September 25, 1899, Gettysburg.
The Philadelphia Inquirer, October 15, 1899, Penn.
The Sentinel, October 23, 1899, Dickinson.
The Dickinsonian, October 28, 1899.
The Philadelphia Inquirer, October 29, 1899, Harvard.
Star Gazette, November 1, 1899, Hamilton congressman.
The Baltimore Sun, November 1, 1899, No BMC game.
Democrat and Chronicle, November 5, 1899, Hamilton College.
The Buffalo Times, November 5, 1899, Hamilton College.
The New York Times, November 5, 1899, Hamilton College.
The Philadelphia Inquirer, November 26, 1899, Oberlin.
Philadelphia Inquirer, November 26, 1899, p12 Columbia.
The Sentinel, November 27, 1899, Oberlin.
The Red Man, September-November, 1899, v15, n8.
The Indian Helper, December 8, 1899, v15, n7.
The Evening Transcript, December 28, 1899, Visit Perris.
Albuquerque Citizen, December 30, 1899, Las Cruces.
The Red Man, December, 1899, v15, n9.
The San Francisco Examiner, January 2, 1900, 83-6.
The York Dispatch, January 2, 1900, 86-6.
Arizona Republican, January 1, 1900, Phoenix ad.
Arizona Republican, January 2, 1900, 83-6.
Spalding's Official Football Guide 1900, August 1900.
San Francisco Chronicle, October 26, 1902, Schildt.
Statesman Journal, October 14, 1903, Big Joe Schildt.
Spokane Chronicle, January 15, 1904, Schildt boxer.

Chapter 4 1900

The Buffalo Commercial, June 28, 1893, Scientific Course.
Democrat and Chronicle, June 28, 1893, Genesco Normal School.
The Meriden Morning Record and Republican, September 18, 1900, First Names.
The Times, September 23, 1900, Bender & Thomas Walker.
The Boston Globe, September 23, 1900, LVC.
The Red Man & Helper, September 28, 1900, LVC & Dickinson.
The Philadelphia Inquirer, September 23, 1900, LVC.
The Times, September 23, 1900, LVC.

The Sentinel, September 24, 1900, LVC.
The Sentinel, September 25, 1900, game played at Indian School.
The Philadelphia Inquirer, September 30, 1900, Susquehanna.
The Philadelphia Inquirer, October 7, 1900, Gettysburg.
Washington Times, October 14, 1900, UVA.
The Baltimore Sun, October 16, 1900, Maryland.
Harrisburg Daily Independent, October 22, 1900, Reserves vs Steelton YMCA.
Harrisburg Telegraph, October 22, 1900, Reserves vs Steelton YMCA.
The Boston Globe, October 27, 1900, More first names.
The Boston Globe, October 28, 1900, p2, Cartoon.
The Boston Globe, October 28, 1900, Harvard.
The Red Man & Helper, November 9, 1900, Pine Grove.
The Gazette, November 11, 1900, Yale.
New York Tribune, November 11, 1900, Yale.
Yale Daily News, November 12, 1900, no. 40, Yale.
The Philadelphia Inquirer, November 18, 1900, p14 Penn.
The Pittsburgh Press, November 25, 1900, W&J.
Pittsburgh Daily Post, November 25, 1900, W&J.
New York Tribune, November 30, 1900, Columbia.
Spalding's Official Football Guide 1901, August 1901.

Chapter 5 1901

Evening Star, February 5, 1901, p5, Pratt Lt Colonel.
Topeka Weekly Capital, March 5, Ft Leavenworth.
New York Daily Tribune, March 10, 1901, p6, To 15th Cavalry.
The Red Man & Helper, September 13, 1901, Steelton YMCA game rescheduled.
The Red Man & Helper, September 20, 1901, Steelton YMCA game for Sep 14 called off.
Arizona Republican, September 22, 1901, First game of season.
The Philadelphia Inquirer, September 22, 1901, LVC.
The Indianapolis News, September 23, 1901, Pan Am Grounds.
Evening Report, September 24, 1901, LVC.
Boston Journal, September 25, 1901, p8, only 4 return.
The Patriot, September 25, 1901, p4, Gettysburg at Island Park.
The Patriot, September 25, 1901, p8, Steelton athletic field.
Democrat and Chronicle, September 25, 1901, LVC 27 men.
The Patriot, September 26, 1901, p4, Steelton offside.
The New York Times, September 26, 1901, Runs back opening kickoff.
Carlisle Evening Herald, September 26, 1901, Steelton YMCA.
The Philadelphia Inquirer, September 26, 1901, Steelton Athletic Field.
The Sentinel, September 30, 1901, Gallaudet.
The Patriot, October 3, 1901, p4, Gettysburg.
The Philadelphia Inquirer, October 3, 1901, Gettysburg.
The Sentinel, October 3, 1901, Gettysburg.
New York Daily Tribune, October 06, 1901, p12, Dickinson.
The Red Man & Helper, October 10, 1901, p4, Gallaudet Warner assesses team.
The Philadelphia Inquirer, October 13, 1901, Athletic Park.
Buffalo Courier, October 13, 1901, Bucknell.
The Philadelphia Inquirer, October 16, 1901, p9, Fortnightly Club.
The New York Times, October 17, 1901, Haverford.
Jersey Journal, October 17, 1901, p10, scrubs play Dick prep.
Buffalo Courier, October 20, 1901, Cornell.
The Buffalo Times, October 20, 1901, Cornell.

The New York Times, October 20, 1901, Cornell.
The Buffalo Times, October 20, 1901, Shouchuk.
The Washington Times, October 20, 1901, Women & Children trampled.
The Philadelphia Inquirer, October 24, 1901, Reserves vs Dickinson.
Boston Post, October 27, 1901, Harvard Phillips.
Chicago Daily News, November 2, 1901, p2, Michigan lineups.
Denver Post, November 2, 1901, p7, Indians crippled.
Michigan Daily, November 3, 1901, Michigan game.
Detroit Free Press, November 4, 1901, Michigan.
Livingston County Daily Press and Argus, November 6, 1901, Detroit Bennett Park.
The Baltimore Sun, November 10, 1901, Navy.
The Washington Times, November 10, 1901, p9, Navy.
Boston Herald, November 10, 1901, p41, Connors returns.
The Times, November 12, 1901, Navy rough.
The Times, November 17, 1901, Penn.
The Pittsburgh Press, November 24, 1901, W&J.
The Baltimore Sun, November 27, 1901, Reserves vs Gettysburg.
Spalding's Official Football Guide 1902, August 1902.

Chapter 6 1902

The Patriot, September 18, 1902, Bender w As.
The Sentinel, September 22, 1902, LVC Shouchuk.
The Daily News, September 22, 1902, LVC.
Carlisle Evening Herald, September 22, 1902, LVC.
The Philadelphia Inquirer, October 12, 1902, Bucknell.
The Pittsburgh Press, October 12, 1902, Bucknell.
The Philadelphia Inquirer, October 16, 1902, Bloomsburg.
The Philadelphia Inquirer, October 19, 1902, Cornell.
New York Tribune, October 19, 1902, Cornell.
The Buffalo Sunday Morning News, October 19, 1902, Cornell.
The New York Times, October 19, 1902, Cornell write up.
The New York Times, October 19, 1902, Cornell.
The Philadelphia Inquirer, October 20, 1902, Cornell.
The Philadelphia Inquirer, October 20, 1902, p1, Harvard.
New York Tribune, October 26, 1902, 107 yard run.
The Philadelphia Inquirer, October 26, 1902, Medico-Chi.
The Arrow, October 27, 1905, Frank Doxtator JV.
Harrisburg Telegraph, October 29, 1902, Reserves vs Hbg Students.
The Boston Globe, November 2, 1902, p1,6, Harvard.
The Philadelphia Inquirer, November 9, 1902, Susquehanna.
The Philadelphia Inquirer, November 16, 1902, p1, Penn.
Carlisle Evening Herald, November 17, 1902, Penn crossbar.
The Red Man & Helper, November 21, 1902, Penn Game - Phillips hit by crossbar.
The Norfolk Landmark, November 23, 1902, p1, Virginia.
The Norfolk Landmark, November 23, 1902, p8, Virginia.
The Baltimore Sun, November 28, 1902, Georgetown.
The Philadelphia Inquirer, December 6, 1902, Stauffer.
The Red Man & Helper, June 18, 1903.
Spalding's Official Football Guide 1903, August 1903.

Chapter 7 1903

Evening Star, January 30, 1903, p17, Pratt promoted to Colonel.

Evening Star, February 7, 1903, p1, Pratt requests promotion.
Evening Star, February 14, 1903, p2, Pratt retired.
Evening Star, February 17, 1903, p2, Pratt stays at Carlisle.
The Washington Times, February 18, 1903, p10, Pratt xferred to 13th Cavalry.
The Washington Times, February 19, 1903, p10, Not fit for Cavalry duty.
Evening Star, February 25, 1903, p13, Scheme to retire old officers.
Evening Star, March 2, 1903, p7, Pratt complains.
The Red Man & Helper, September 18, 1903.
Harrisburg Telegraph, September 21, 1903, LVC.
The Philadelphia Inquirer, October 4, 1903, Bucknell.
Harrisburg Daily Independent, October 9, 1903, Reserve players.
The Philadelphia Inquirer, October 11, 1903, F&M.
Harrisburg Daily Independent, October 12, 1903, Reserves vs Hbg Students.
The New York Times, October 14, 1903, Bemus light team.
The Sun, October 18, 1903, Princeton.
The Philadelphia Inquirer, October 25, 1903, Swarthmore.
The Washington Times, November 8, 1903, Georgetown.
Boston Post, November 1, 1903, pp1&12, Harvard.
The Baltimore Sun, November 8, 1903, Georgetown.
The Philadelphia Inquirer, November 15, 1903, Penn.
The Fresno Morning Republican, November 15, 1903, Will Play New Year's Day.
The Philadelphia Inquirer, November 20, 1902, Little Quakers.
The Norfolk Landmark, November 22, 1903, pp2&6, Virginia.
Chicago Tribune, November 27, 1903, Northwestern.
The Inter Ocean, November 27, 1903, Northwestern.
The Red Man & Helper, November 27, 1903, Reserves vs Dickinson Seminary.
The Sentinel, November 30, 1903, Northwestern celebration.
The Los Angeles Times, December 1, 1903, Sherman Institute.
The San Francisco Call, December 1, 1903, Stanford.
The Washington Times, December 1, 1903, Cornell wants Warner back.
Berkeley Daily Gazette, December 4, 1903, Reliance A C.
The Salt Lake Herald, December 11, 1903, Utah.
San Francisco Chronicle, December 12, 1903, Western trip.
The Salt Lake Tribune, December 13, 1903, Utah.
Salt Lake Telegram, December 20, 1903, Utah.
The San Francisco Examiner, December 26, 1903, Reliance.
The Evening Bee, December 26, 1903, Reliance.
Los Angeles Express, January 1, 1904, Sherman Institute.
The Los Angeles Times, January 2, 1904, Sherman Institute.
Pop Warner: A Life on the Gridiron, Jeffrey J. Miller, 2015.
Spalding's Official Football Guide 1904, August 1904.

Chapter 8 Captain Leadership

The Kansas City Star, November 19 & 20, 1924, J. P. Glass and George Byrnes interviewed Pop Warner for a syndicated column that was distributed nationally by the North American Newspaper Alliance (NANA).

Chapter 9 1904

The Boston Globe, February 12, 1904, Warner to return.
Springville Journal, February 18, 1904, $3500 at Carlisle.
Washington Times, May 16, 1904, p2, Pratt stands pat.
The York Daily, May 24, 1904, Move to Montana.

The Morning Post, May 25, 1904, Brig General.
Evening Star, June 11, 1904, p3, Pratt detatched.
Harrisburg Telegraph, June 13, 1904, McDowell Heirs.
Washington Times, June 20, 1904, p4, Curt Order.
Lancaster Intelligencer, July 23, 1904, $140,000 in gifts.
The Arrow, August 25, 1904, v1, n1, Superintendent Mercer.
The Times Tribune, September 1, 1904, Carlisle coaches.
The Philadelphia Inquirer, September 18, 1904, LVC.
The Washington Post, October 3, 1904, Bearlo La Roque.
The Sentinel, October 3, 1904, Gettysburg.
The Sentinel, October 6, 1904, Susquehanna.
The Baltimore Sun, October 10, 1904, team photo.
The Indiana Gazette, October 10, 1904, Bucknell.
Harrisburg Daily Independent, October 10, 1904, Bucknell.
The Sentinel, October 17, 1904, Albright.
The Wellsboro Gazette combined with Mansfield Advertiser, October 19, 1904, Buster Morris Bucknell.
The Arrow, October 20, 1904, v1, n9, team photo.
The Boston Globe, October 22, 1904, Bucknell slugging.
The Boston Globe, October 22, 1904, Harvard preview.
The Boston Globe, October 23, 1904, p8, Harvard.
The Norfolk Virginian, October 30, 1904, Virginia.
The Philadelphia Inquirer, November 6, 1904, Ursinus.
The Philadelphia Inquirer, November 13, 1904, p1&13, Penn.
St. Louis Post Dispatch, November 27, 1904, Haskell.
The Ohio State Lantern, November 30, 1904.
Spalding's Official Football Guide 1905, August 1905.

Chapter 10 1905

Letter from Capt. W. A. Mercer to Commissioner of Indian Affairs, January 12, 1905, William White expelled.
The Minneapolis Journal, February 6, 1905, Rogers not returning.
The Salt Lake Herald, May 21, 1905, Sheldon to Northwestern.
Rutland Daily Herald, June 2, 1905, WG Thompson.
Chicago Tribune, July 30, 1905, Sheldon freshman.
The Sentinel, August 24, 1905, Gen Pratt in Denver.
The Philadelphia Inquirer, September 3, 1905, Woodruff 1st practice.
The Gazette, September 23, 1905, Kinney.
Wilkes Barre Times Leader & The Evening News, September 27, 1905, to play Villanova.
Lebanon Daily News, September 29, 1905, Albright cancels.
The Philadelphia Inquirer, October 1, 1905, Villanova.
The Pittsburgh Press, October 8, 1905, special dining car.
The Philadelphia Inquirer, October 8, 1905, Full roster.
The Pittsburgh Press, October 8, 1905, p22 Players' names.
Harrisburg Daily Independent, October 9, 1905, Penn State.
The Sentinel, October 9, 1905, Coach Kinney.
The Washington Post, October 10, 1905, Roosevelt threatens.
The Times Dispatch, October 15, 1905, pp1&29, Virginia.
The Washington Post, October 22, 1905, Indians Hide Injuries.
The Gazette, October 22, 1905, Dickinson Fight.
The Philadelphia Inquirer, October 22, 1905, Dickinson.
The Pittsburgh Press, October 22, 1905, Big Long Horn.

The Sentinel, October 23, 1905, Dickinson.
Harrisburg Daily Independent, October 23, 1905, Carlisle's faults.
The Pittsburgh Press, October 24, 1905, Dickinson.
The Philadelphia Inquirer, October 29, 1905, Penn.
The Philadelphia Inquirer, November 1, 1905, Working hard for Harvard.
The Boston Daily Globe, November 5, 1905, Harvard.
The Philadelphia Inquirer, November 5, 1905, Mt. Pleasant slow.
The New York Times, November 8, 1905, West Point.
The New York Times, November 12, 1905, Army.
The Sun, November 12, 1905, Army.
The Philadelphia Inquirer, November 12, 1905, Reserves vs Dickinson Seminary.
The Philadelphia Inquirer, November 12, 1905, Winnie at QB.
The Standard Union, November 16, 1905, Players on western trip.
News Journal, November 16, 1905, Massillon.
The Arrow, November 17, 1905, v2, n13, Oysters.
The Stark County Democrat, November 17, 1905, Massillon.
The Topeka State Journal, November 18, 1905, Indian Names.
The Cincinnati Enquirer, November 19, 1905, Cincinnati.
Fall River Daily Evening News, November 21, 1905, Boxing injury.
News Journal, November 23, 1905, Canton.
Pittsburgh Daily Post, November 23, 1905, Canton.
Harrisburg Telegraph, November 23, 1905, Canton.
The Stark County Democrat, November 24, 1905, pp1-2, Canton.
The Pittsburgh Press, November 26, 1905, W&J.
Arkansas Democrat, November 29, 1905, Broken nose.
Buffalo Morning Express & Illustrated Buffalo Express, November 29, 1905, Nose better than new.
Central City Record, November 30, 1905, Trampled.
Clyde Voice Republican, November 30, 1905, Suggested rule changes.
The Honolulu Advertiser, November 30, 1905, Teddy Jr knocked out of game.
The Nashua Reporter, November 30, 1905, Surgery.
The Washington Post, November 30, 1905, Broken nose.
Wayne County Herald, November 30, 1905, Hero of Cambridge.
The Ashton Gazette, November 30, 1905, Roosevelt's reform platform.
The South Bend Tribune, December 2, 1905, Football injuries.
The Atlanta Constitution, December 3, 1905, Too Rough for Teddy.
The Washington Post, December 31, 1905, Indians' year.
The Pittsburgh Press, December 31, 1905, Soccer.
Evening Star, January 1, 1906, Ranked 8th.
The Arrow, January 19, 1906, v2, n21, football roster.
Buffalo Courier, September 28, 1906, Carlisle squad.
Letter from Chauncy Archiquette to Major W. A. Mercer, January 21, 1907.
The Arrow, December 13, 1907, p2, Employee athletes explained.

Chapter 11 1906

The New York Times, January 13, 1906, Rules committees merge.
The New York Times, January 29, 1906, New Rules drafted.
The New York Times, April 15, 1906, New rules passed.
Washington Times, June 2, 1904, p3, Gen. Pratt.
The Brooklyn Daily Eagle, September 2, 1906, Carlisle strong.
The Minneapolis Journal, September 2, 1906, Early start.
The Arrow, September 7, 1906, v3, n3, Warner assists Indian coaches.

Boston Evening Transcript, September 15, 1906, Smaller squad.
Buffalo Courier, September 16, 1906, Smaller squad than last year.
The Arrow, September 21, 1906, v3, n4, Indian coaches.
Pop Warner: A Life on the Gridiron, Jeffrey J. Miller, 2015.
The Sentinel, September 27, 1906, Villanova.
Nashville Banner, September 29, 1906, New Rules Favor Indians.
The Philadelphia Inquirer, October 6, 1906, Team Photo.
The Philadelphia Inquirer, October 7, 1906, Reflections on New Rules.
Williamsport Sun Gazette, October 7, 1906, Penn State.
State Collegian, October 11, 1906, Penn State.
Pittsburgh Post Gazette, October 21, 1906, WUP.
The Philadelphia Inquirer, October 28, 1906, Penn.
The Philadelphia Inquirer, November 4, 1906, Reserves vs Susq Wholes.
The New York Times, November 4, 1906, Syracuse.
The Boston Globe, November 11, 1906, Harvard.
Williamsport Sun Gazette, November 12, 1906, Reserves vs Dick Sem.
The Minneapolis Journal, November 18, 1906, pp30-31, Minnesota.
The Times, November 21, 1906, White headgear.
Nashville Banner, November 22, 1906, Vanderbilt.
The Nashville American, November 23, 1906, pp1&7, Vanderbilt.
Pittsburgh Daily Post, November 25, 1906, Cincinnati.
Pittsburgh Daily Post, November 30, 1906, Virginia.
The Baltimore Sun, November 30, 1906, Virginia.
The Cornell Daily, December 14, 1906, Warner accepts Carlisle position.
Pop Warner: A Life on the Gridiron, Jeffrey J. Miller, 2015.
The Arrow, December 21, 1906, v3, n17, Warner returns.
Spalding's Official Football Guide 1907, August 1907.

Chapter 12 1907

The Pittsburgh Press, September 1, 1907, Toughest schedule.
The Pittsburgh Press, September 22, 1907, McLeans & Roundstone.
The Philadelphia Inquirer, September 22, 1907, LVC.
The Sentinel, September 23, 1907, LVC sea of mud.
Pittsburgh Post Gazette, September 29, 1907, Reserves vs Mercersburg.
The Philadelphia Inquirer, September 29, 1907, Monhart etc.
The Courier, September 29, 1907, Villanova.
Pittsburgh Daily Post, September 29, 1907, Villanova.
Pittsburgh Daily Post, October 3, 1907, Susquehanna.
The Pittsburgh Press, October 6, 1907, Penn State.
Williamsport Sun Gazette, October 7, 1907, Penn State.
The Philadelphia Inquirer, October 13, 1907, Reserves vs Wyo Seminary.
Buffalo Courier, October 13, 1907, pp25&32, Syracuse.
Chicago Tribune, October 14, 1930, Warner Minnesota.
The Philadelphia Inquirer, October 20, 1907, Syracuse Bucknell.
The Philadelphia Inquirer, October 27, 1907, pp15&26, Penn.
The Brooklyn Daily Eagle, November 3, 1907, Princeton.
The Philadelphia Inquirer, November 3, 1907, Reserves vs Frankford AC.
The Philadelphia Inquirer, November 3, 1907, Team Photo.
Harrisburg Telegraph, November 8, 1907, Reserves vs Steelton YMCA.
The Boston Globe, November 10, 1907, p1, Harvard.
Harrisburg Telegraph, November 11, 1907, Reserves vs Steelton YMCA.
The Arrow, November 15, 1907, v4, n11, Nightshirt parade.

The Philadelphia Inquirer, November 17, 1907, Reserves vs Susquehanna.
Star Tribune, November 17, 1907, p42, Minnesota.
Cornell Alumni News, November 22, 1905, Player dismissed from the team.
The Baltimore Sun, November 24, 1907, Chicago.
The Arrow, November 29, 1907, v4, n13, Mercer's test ride.
The Des Moines Register, November 30, 1907, No transcontinental trip.
Lewisburg Journal, December 6, 1907, $$$$.
Spalding's Official Football Guide 1908, August 1908.

Chapter 13 1908

The Oklahoma State Capital, January 2, 1904, Leupp investigates.
The Kansas City Star & The Kansas City Times, May 14, 1904, Pratt rails against Indian bureau.
The New York Times, June 12, 1904, Hitchcock fires Pratt.
Star Tribune, July 12, 1904, Jones forced out.
St Louis Globe Democrat, July 16, 1904, Jones resigns.
The Kansas City Star & The Kansas City Times, September 6, 1904, Leupp gives verbal report.
Chicago Tribune, November 20, 1904, Leupp starts on 1-1-1905.
Salt Lake Telegram, November 21, 1904, Leupp appointed.
The Standard Union, November 21, 1904, Leupp intimate friend of Roosevelt.
The Oklahoma State Capital, November 22, 1904, Leupp offered position.
Lehigh Leader, December 1, 1904, Leupp investigated Randlett.
Spokane Chronicle, December 8, 1904, Leupp background.
Sioux City Journal, January 1, 1905, Leupp more independent.
The Oklahoma State Capital, January 3, 1905, Inaugural parade.
The Champaign Daily News, February 6, 1905, Train to be soldiers.
The Valley Times Star, February 23, 1905, Lobby President to attend graduation.
The Scranton Republican, March 2, 1905, Indians in inaugural parade.
The Sentinel, May 20, 1905, Quakers oppose military training.
Carlisle Evening Herald, June 22, 1905, Seek funds for new hospital.
The Washington Post, February 7, 1906, DeCora hired.
The Philadelphia Inquirer, March 21, 1906, Leupp presents diplomas.
Harrisburg Telegraph, March 23, 1906, No plans to move school.
The Kansas City Star & The Kansas City Times, January 11, 1907, Senate bill to close Carlisle.
The Daily News, January 22, 1907, Carlisle saved.
The Washington Bee, May 11, 1907, Art Building.
The Wichita Daily Eagle, December 8, 1907, Leupp wants to close Carlisle.
The Arrow, December 27, 1907, v4, n17, Mercer resigns.
The Washington Herald, January 1, 1908, Carlisle Endangered.
The Washington Post, September 2, 1908, Nebraska land.
The Pittsburgh Press, January 2, 1908, Football May Save Carlisle.
Carlisle Evening Herald, January 3, 1908, Off-reservation schools endangered.
The Press Herald, January 3, 1908, Mercer resigns.
Harrisburg Telegraph, January 11, 1908, Pratt petition.
Carlisle Evening Herald, January 13, 1908, no appropriation for Carlisle.
New York Tribune, January 21, 1908, Temporary superintendent.
The Decatur Herald, January 23, 1908, Pratt defends Carlisle.
Harrisburg Daily Independent, January 29, 1908, Fighting Leupp.
Intelligencer Journal, January 29, 1908, States to take over Indian schools.
Reading Times, January 30, 1908, Bill to turn over Carlisle to PA.

The Independent Record, January 31, 1908, Albert Nash.
The Iola Daily Index, January 31, 1908, PA delegation fights Leupp.
Lancaster Intelligencer, February 1, 1908, Clause inserted into bill.
Carlisle Evening Herald, February 12, 1908, Olmstead opposes Leupp.
Harrisburg Telegraph, February 15, 1908, Wm Hazlett ltr to TR.
The Kansas City Star, February 16, 1908, Wm Hazlett defends Carlisle.
The Arrow, March 6, 1908, v4, n27, Friedman appointed.
The Sentinel, March 6, 1908, Moses Friedman selected.
The Semi Weekly New Era, March 14, 1908, Skeptical over Friedman.
The Arrow, March 27, 1908, v4, n30, Friedman arrives.
Evening Star, April 3, 1908, Leupp threat.
Harrisburg Telegraph, April 3, 1908, Leupp pleased.
Pittston Gazette, April 3, 1908, Leupp misunderstood.
The Philadelphia Inquirer, April 4, 1908, Leupp challenged.
The Sentinel, August 4, 1908, Paris track meet.
The Buffalo Enquirer, September 19, 1908, Players names.
The Washington Post, September 20, 1908, Conway Hall.
The Washington Post, September 24, 1908, LVC.
The Philadelphia Inquirer, September 27, 1908, Reserves vs Mercersburg.
The Philadelphia Inquirer, September 27, 1908, Villanova.
The Pittsburgh Press, September 27, 1908, Winthrup Grogan Wolf.
The Philadelphia Inquirer, October 4, 1908, Penn State.
The Philadelphia Inquirer, October 11, 1908, Reserves vs Swatara.
Harrisburg Daily Independent, October 12, 1908, 2nd Team vs Swatara.
The Philadelphia Inquirer, October 24, 1908, Reserves vs Wyo Seminary.
The Philadelphia Inquirer, November 8, 1908, 3rd Team vs Gettysburg.
The Pittsburgh Press, November 12, 1908, Wore Numbers.
The Philadelphia Inquirer, November 14, 1908, Reserves vs Walbrook AA.
The Baltimore Sun, November 15, 1908, Reserves vs Walbrook AA.
Pittsburgh Daily Post, November 17, 1908, Cage.
Star Tribune, November 17, 1908, Football cage.
Star Tribune, November 18, 1908, Cage.
The Philadelphia Inquirer, November 22, 1908, Reserves vs Muhlenberg.
Lawrence Daily World, November 23, 1908, Possible Haskell game.
The Allentown Leader, November 23, 1908, Reserves vs Muhlenberg.
The Daily Sentinel, November 24, 1908, Denver.
The Daily Gazette, November 28, 1908, Haskell.
The Philadelphia Inquirer, November 29, 1908, Reserves vs Union Club.
Carlisle Evening Herald, December 1, 1908, Carlisle Plays Haskell.
The Sentinel, December 1, 1908, Carlisle defeats Haskell.
Daily Utah State Journal, December 2, 1908, Mt Pleasant punt block.
The Arrow, December 4, 1908, v5, n13, Haskell game omitted.
The Sun, December 6, 1908, Safe stolen & recovered.
Harrisburg Telegraph, December 8, 1908, Leupp drops plan to close Carlisle.
The Sentinel, December 8, 1908, Measle epidemic.
Omaha Daily Bee, December 8, 1908, Indian Schools not needed.
The Augusta Daily Gazette, December 8, 1908, Carlisle saved.
The News Journal, December 9, 1908, Carlisle Saved.
The Sentinel, December 10, 1908, measles.
The Hutchinson Gazette, December 24, 1908, Warner rankings.
Evening Star, December 26, 1908, Leupp to resign.
The Chandler Tribune, January 1, 1909, Leupp to resign.
The Daily Oklahoman, January 1, 1909, Leupp impractical.

Evening Star, January 2, 1909, Leupp recommends that his office be abolished.
The Washington Times, March 14, 1909, Leupp's backing.
Lincoln Journal Star, March 16, 1909, Roosevelt's backing.
The Shawnee Daily Herald, March 17, 1909, Requested to remain.
The Norfolk Weekly News Journal, March 19, 1909, Leupp to remain.
The Weekly Chieftain, March 19, 1909, Withdraws resignation.
Evening Star, March 30, 1909, Leupp to remain.
Daily News Democrat, March 31, 1909, Will remain if health permits.
Portage Daily Democrat, April 2, 1909, Now endorses Carlisle.
The Post Star, April 15, 1909, 10 Newspaper reporters in administration.
The Tulsa Democrat, April 15, 1909, Leupp reconsidered.
The Daily Ardmoreite, May 10, 1909, Jones wants to succeed Leupp.
The Morning News, June 14, 1909, Recommends Valentine.
Corsicana Daily Sun, June 15, 1909, Valentine is successor.
Spalding's Official Football Guide 1909, August 1909.

Chapter 14 1909

The Vinita Daily Chieftain, March 13, 1909, Leupp withdraws resignation.
The Carlisle Arrow, March 26, 1909, v5, n29, 1909 football schedule.
Detroit Free Press, September 5, 1909, Warner disagrees.
Harrisburg Telegraph, September 10, 1909, Thorpe to return.
The Carlisle Arrow, September 10, 1909, v6, n1, New athletic quarters.
The Philadelphia Inquirer, September 19, 1909, Steelton players.
Harrisburg Daily Independent, September 20, 1909, Steelton Players.
Harrisburg Telegraph, September 20, 1909, Steelton AC.
The Philadelphia Inquirer, September 23, 1909, LVC.
The Philadelphia Inquirer, September 26, 1909, Scrubs.
The Philadelphia Inquirer, September 26, 1909, Villanova.
The Philadelphia Inquirer, October 3, 1909, Bucknell.
The Philadelphia Inquirer, October 10, 1909, Penn State Lonestar.
The Philadelphia Inquirer, October 10, 1909, Scrubs vs Middletown.
Pittsburgh Post Gazette, October 10, 1909, PSU.
The Philadelphia Inquirer, October 10, 1909, PSU.
The Evening News, October 11, 1909, PSU.
Wilkes Barre Times Leader & The Evening News, October 11, 1909, PSU rough play.
Buffalo Evening News, October 16, 1909, Syracuse.
The Sun, October 16, 1909, Maoris.
The Philadelphia Inquirer, October 17, 1909, Scrubs vs Gettysburg.
New York Tribune, October 17, 1909, Syracuse.
The Brooklyn Daily Eagle, October 17, 1909, Syracuse.
The New York Times, October 17, 1909, Syracuse.
The Philadelphia Inquirer, October 17, 1909, Syracuse.
The Sun, October 21, 1909, Maori challenge.
Pittsburgh Daily Post, October 24, 1909, pp1-2, Pitt & Warner's comments.
The Philadelphia Inquirer, October 31, 1909, pp1&32, Penn.
The Philadelphia Inquirer, November 7, 1909, Bloomsburg.
The Washington Herald, November 7, 1909, pp1&32, GWU.
The Baltimore Sun, November 14, 1909, Scrubs vs Walbrook.
The Philadelphia Inquirer, November 14, 1909, Gettysburg.
Harrisburg Telegraph, November 15, 1909, team photo.
The Boston Globe, November 21, 1909, Brown.
The Brooklyn Daily Eagle, November 21, 1909, Brown.

The Allentown Leader, November 26, 1909, Scrubs Muhlenberg.
The Philadelphia Inquirer, November 26, 1909, Scrubs Muhlenberg.
The Morning Call, November 27, 1909, Scrubs Muhlenberg.
Carlisle Evening Herald, December 3, 1909, 14 Gold Watches.
Spalding's Official Football Guide 1910, August 1910.

Chapter 15 1910

Austin American Statesman, January 2, 1910, Indian Bureau ban.
The Berkshire Evening Eagle, January 18, 1910, Leak from Warber.
The Carlisle Arrow, June 24, 1910, v6, n42, Intercollegiate baseball ended.
Harrisburg Telegraph, September 1, 1910, Villanova.
Harrisburg Daily Independent, September 19, 1910, Lone Star dwgs.
Harrisburg Telegraph, September 19, 1910, p6, Lone Star dwgs.
Harrisburg Telegraph, September 19, 1910, p1, Trophy.
The Sentinel, September 19, 1910, Beauty Spot.
Harrisburg Daily Independent, September 20, 1910, p10, Lone Star dwgs.
Harrisburg Telegraph, September 22, 1910, LVC & Villanova.
The Philadelphia Inquirer, September 22, 1910, LVC.
The Sentinel, September 22, 1910, LVC & Lone Star.
Harrisburg Daily Independent, September 23, 1910, pp1&5, Villanova.
Harrisburg Telegraph, September 24, 1910, Villanova.
The Courier, September 25, 1910, pp1&6, Villanova.
Carlisle Evening Herald, September 26, 1910, Villanova.
The Morning Call, September 29, 1910, Muhlenberg.
The Philadelphia Inquirer, September 29, 1910, Muhlenberg.
The Philadelphia Inquirer, October 6, 1910, Dickinson.
The Philadelphia Inquirer, October 9, 1910, Bucknell.
Harrisburg Telegraph, October 10, 1910, 3rd Team vs Tech.
The Philadelphia Inquirer, October 12, 1910, Gettysburg.
The Sentinel, October 12, 1910, Gettysburg.
Democrat and Chronicle, October 16, 1910, Syracuse.
The Philadelphia Inquirer, October 22, 1910, Bloomsburg.
New York Tribune, October 23, 1910, Princeton.
The Philadelphia Inquirer, October 30, 1910, pp46&48, Penn.
The Daily News, October 31, 1910, LVC.
The Sentinel, November 1, 1910, Direct Snap Only.
Harrisburg Daily Independent, November 4, 1910, Hbg Academy.
The Philadelphia Inquirer, November 6, 1910, Phoenixville.
The Washington Post, November 6, 1910, pp1&18, Virginia.
Pittsburgh Daily Post, November 7, 1910, Princeton fools Indians.
The Carlisle Arrow, November 11, 1910, v7, n10, Penn rough & lucky.
The Philadelphia Inquirer, November 12, 1910, 3rd Team vs Mercersburg.
The Baltimore Sun, November 13, 1910, Walbrook.
New York Tribune, November 13, 1910, Navy.
The Baltimore Sun, November 13, 1910, Navy.
The Boston Globe, November 17, 1910, pp1&6 Harvard Law.
The Baltimore Sun, November 20, 1910, Johns Hopkins.
Intelligencer Journal, November 21, 1910, Millersville.
The Daily New Era, November 21, 1910, Millersburg.
The Boston Globe, November 25, 1910, Brown.
The Philadelphia Inquirer, November 25, 1910, Brown.
The Morning Call, November 26, 1910, Muhlenberg.

College News, Lebanon Valley College Publication (Fall 1910) .html.
Spalding's Official Football Guide 1911, August 1911.

Chapter 16 1911

The Evening News, March 25, 1911, Schedule.
The Sentinel, August 31, 1911, Thorpe back.
The Evening News, September 4, 1911, Pat O'Brian.
The Pittsburgh Press, September 13, 1911, Hauser GA Tech.
Hartford Courant, September 15, 1911, Warner & coaches.
The Charlotte News, September 15, 1911, Hauser GA Tech.
The Hutchinson Gazette, September 15, 1911, Hauser GA Tech.
The Tennessean, September 15, 1911, Vanderbilt.
The Carlisle Arrow, September 15, 1911, v8, n1, Thorpe returns.
Pittston Gazette, September 16, 1911, Thorpe back.
The Sandusky Star Journal, September 16, 1911, Sam Bird.
The Pittsburgh Press, September 17, 1911, Lots of material.
The Sun, September 17, 1911, Veterans return.
The Philadelphia Inquirer, September 24, 1911, LVC.
The Philadelphia Inquirer, September 24, 1911, LVC.
Carlisle Evening Herald, September 25, 1911, LVC.
Harrisburg Telegraph, September 28, 1911, Muhlenberg.
The Philadelphia Inquirer, September 28, 1911, Muhlenberg.
The Courier, September 29, 1911, Lafayette.
Harrisburg Telegraph, October 2, 1911, Dickinson.
The Sentinel, October 2, 1911, Dickinson.
Harrisburg Telegraph, October 7, 1911, Mt St Marys.
The Evening Sun, October 7, 1911, Mt St Mary's.
The Washington Post, October 7, 1911, Mt St Mary's.
The Washington Times, October 7, 1911, Mt St Mary's.
The Philadelphia Inquirer, October 8, 1911, Reserves vs Bloomsburg.
The Philadelphia Inquirer, October 8, 1911, Mt St Marys.
The Pittsburgh Press, October 8, 1911, Mt St Marys.
The Washington Post, October 8, 1911, Mt St Mary's.
The Washington Herald, October 15, 1911, pp35-36, Georgetown.
Pittsburgh Post Gazette, October 22, 1911, p18, Pitt.
The Pittsburgh Press, October 22, 1911, pp1& 15, Pitt.
Pittsburgh Post Gazette, October 29, 1911, Lafayette.
The Lafayette Weekly, October 31, 1911, Lafayette.
Harrisburg Telegraph, November 4, 1911, Large team photo.
The Courier, November 5, 1911, Penn.
The Philadelphia Inquirer, November 5, 1911, Penn.
The Boston Globe, November 12, 1911, pp1&16, Harvard.
The Philadelphia Inquirer, November 19, 1911, Syracuse.
Pittsburgh Daily Post, November 26, 1911, Johns Hopkins.
The Baltimore Sun, November 26, 1911, Johns Hopkins.
The Boston Globe, December 1, 1911, Brown.
Spalding's Official Football Guide 1912, August 1912.

Chapter 17 1912

The Lafayette Weekly, May 28, 1912, Track.
The Carlisle Arrow, July 4, 1912, v8, n41, Olympians depart.
The Carlisle Arrow, September 13, 1912, v9, n2, Olympians' triumphant return.

The Philadelphia Inquirer, September 15, 1912, Novel workout.
The Washington Post, September 15, 1912, Little Yahoo.
The Courier, September 22, 1912, Villanova.
The Philadelphia Inquirer, September 22, 1912, Albright.
Carlisle Evening Herald, September 23, 1912, p1, Albright.
Carlisle Evening Herald, September 23, 1912, p5, Albright.
Harrisburg Daily Independent, September 26, 1912, LVC.
Harrisburg Telegraph, September 26, 1912, LVC.
Lebanon Daily News, September 26, 1912, Scalped.
The Philadelphia Inquirer, September 26, 1912, LVC.
Pittsburgh Post Gazette, September 29, 1912, Reserves vs Mercersburg.
The Philadelphia Inquirer, September 29, 1912, Dickinson.
Pittsburgh Daily Post, October 3, 1912, Villanova.
Carlisle Evening Herald, October 3, 1912, Dickinson.
Carlisle Evening Herald, October 3, 1912, Villanova.
Harrisburg Daily Independent, October 3, 1912, Villanova.
Harrisburg Telegraph, October 3, 1912, Belle Story.
Harrisburg Telegraph, October 3, 1912, Villanova.
Pittsburgh Daily Post, October 6, 1912, pp37&39, W&J.
Carlisle Evening Herald, October 7, 1912, Reserves vs Conway Hall.
The Sentinel, October 7, 1912, Reserves vs Conway Hall.
Harrisburg Telegraph, October 7, 1912, W&J.
Carlisle Evening Herald, October 12, 1912, Roster.
Buffalo Morning Express & Illustrated Buffalo Express, October 13, 1912, Syracuse.
Democrat and Chronicle, October 13, 1912, Syracuse.
The New York Times, October 13, 1912, Syracuse.
Harrisburg Daily Independent, October 14, 1912, 3rd Team vs Tech.
The Standard Union, October 14, 1912, Warner's book.
Press and Sun Bulletin, October 16, 1912, Michigan.
Pittsburgh Daily Post, October 20, 1912, p37, Pitt.
Pittsburgh Daily Post, October 20, 1912, p38, Pitt.
The Philadelphia Inquirer, October 27, 1912, Albright.
The Baltimore Sun, October 27, 1912, Georgetown.
The Washington Herald, October 27, 1912, pp1&39&41, Georgetown.
Star Gazette, October 29, 1912, Toronto w line-ups.
The Philadelphia Inquirer, October 29, 1912, Toronto.
The Ottawa Citizen, October 29, 1912, Toronto.
The Philadelphia Inquirer, October 29, 1912, Toronto.
The Sentinel, October 29, 1912, Toronto.
The Philadelphia Inquirer, November 2, 1912, Lehigh.
Pittsburgh Post Gazette, November 3, 1912, Lehigh.
The Philadelphia Inquirer, November 3, 1912, Lehigh.
The Allentown Leader, November 4, 1912, Reserves vs LVC.
Carlisle Evening Herald, November 4, 1912, Lehigh.
The Philadelphia Inquirer, November 4, 1912, New Plays.
The Sentinel, November 4, 1912, Lehigh.
Latrobe Bulletin, November 6, 1912, Latrobe Wappoose.
The Sun, November 10, 1912, pp17&18, Army.
The Philadelphia Inquirer, November 17, 1912, pp1&16 Penn.
The Wilkes Barre Record, November 18, 1912, Reserves vs Hillman Academy.
The Boston Globe, November 24, 1912, Springfield YMCA.
The Philadelphia Inquirer, November 24, 1912, YMCA.
The Boston Globe, November 26, 1912, Leicester.

The Philadelphia Inquirer, November 26, 1912, Thorpe to quit.
Brown Daily Herald, November 29, 1912, Brown.
Carlisle Evening Herald, November 29, 1912, Brown.
Fall River Daily Evening News, November 29, 1912, Brown.
The Boston Globe, November 29, 1912, Brown.
Williamsport Sun Gazette, November 30, 1912, Carlisle Reserves over the years.
The Carlisle Arrow, December 20, 1912, v9, n16, All-Americans.
Fall River Daily Globe, January 25, 1913, Clancy denies.
Spalding's Official Football Guide 1913, August 1913.

Chapter 18 1913

Harrisburg Telegraph, February 6, 1905.
Worcester Telegram, January 22, 1913, Roy Ruggles Johnson Thorpe.
Springfield Daily News, January 23, 1913, p6, Clancy denies.
Springfield Union, January 23, 1913, p15, Clancy charges.
The Carlisle Arrow, January 24, 1913, v9, n21, Thorpe returns w brother.
The Boston Globe, January 25, 1913, AAU Thorpe.
The Evening Herald, January 25, 1913, Charges false.
Greensboro Daily News, January 27, 1913, Thorpe baseball.
Boston Herald, January 28, 1913, p7, Thorpe confesses.
Detroit Free Press, February 2, 1913, Jackson baseball.
The Daily Herald, February 13, 1913, Roy Ruggles Johnson.
The Courier, March 1, 1913, Guyon.
The Carlisle Arrow, March 21, 1913, v9, n29, Marlin, TX.
The Berkshire County Eagle, August 20, 1913, Army-Navy cancel.
Harrisburg Telegraph, September 1, 1913, Only 2 players lost.
Pittsburgh Post Gazette, September 21, 1913, Albright.
The Courier, September 21, 1913, Albright.
The Philadelphia Inquirer, September 21, 1913, Albright.
The Spokesman Review, September 21, 1913, Weak.
Carlisle Evening Herald, September 22, 1913, Albright.
Harrisburg Daily Independent, September 25, 1913, LVC.
The Carlisle Arrow, September 26, 1913, v10, n4, New players.
The Philadelphia Inquirer, September 28, 1913, Mercersburg.
The Philadelphia Inquirer, September 28, 1913, WV Wesleyan.
Carlisle Evening Herald, September 29, 1913, WV Wesleyan.
Harrisburg Telegraph, October 2, 1913, Dickinson Scrimmage.
The Philadelphia Inquirer, October 5, 1913, Conway Hall.
The Philadelphia Inquirer, October 5, 1913, Lehigh.
The Philadelphia Inquirer, October 12, 1913, Cornell.
The Daily News, October 13, 1913, Albright vs Reserves.
The Sentinel, October 14, 1913, Thorpe wedding.
The Philadelphia Inquirer, October 19, 1913, Pitt.
The Philadelphia Inquirer, October 26, 1913, Bloomsburg Robbin.
The Philadelphia Inquirer, October 26, 1913, Penn.
The Philadelphia Inquirer, October 27, 1913, Penn.
The Philadelphia Inquirer, November 2, 1913, Georgetown.
The Washington Herald, November 2, 1913, Georgetown.
The Baltimore Sun, November 9, 1913, Johns Hopkins.
The Philadelphia Inquirer, November 9, 1913, Johns Hopkins.
Wilkes Barre Times Leader & The Evening News, November 10, 1913, Hillman Academy.
The Philadelphia Inquirer, November 16, 1913, Muhlenberg Oneida.

The Philadelphia Inquirer, November 16, 1913, Dartmouth.
The Allentown Democrat, November 17, 1913, Muhlenberg O'Neida.
The Sentinel, November 17, 1913, Biggest football night.
The Sentinel, November 17, 1913, Vulgar words.
Democrat and Chronicle, November 23, 1913, Syracuse.
Pittsburgh Post Gazette, November 23, 1913, Syracuse.
The Buffalo Sunday Morning News, November 23, 1913, Syracuse.
The New York Times, November 23, 1913, Syracuse.
Star Gazette, November 24, 1913, Syracuse.
The Evening Herald, November 25, 1913, Brown.
The Philadelphia Inquirer, November 28, 1913, Holmesburg Moy Deerfoot.
The Philadelphia Inquirer, November 28, 1913, Brown.
The Sun, November 23, 1913, Syracuse.
The Carlisle Arrow, December 19, 1913, v10, n16, All-Americans.
Spalding's Official Football Guide 1914, August 1914.

Chapter 19 1914

Hearings before the Joint Commission of the Congress of the United States Sixty-Third Congress Second Session to Investigate Indian Affairs, February 6-9 & March 25, 1914, Carlisle Indian School.
The Carlisle Arrow, February 27, 1914, v10, n26, Lipps in place.
The Philadelphia Inquirer, September 20, 1914, Albright.
Evening Public Ledger, September 21, 1914, No Weaker.
The Daily News, September 21, 1914, Albright.
The Sentinel, September 21, 1914, Albright.
Harrisburg Daily Independent, September 24, 1914, LVC.
The Pittsburgh Press, September 27, 1914, WV Wesleyan.
The Daily Telegram, October 1, 1914, WV Wesleyan.
The Philadelphia Inquirer, October 4, 1914, Lehigh.
Lebanon Daily News, October 5, 1914, Reserves vs LVC no Wowru.
Carlisle Evening Herald, October 5, 1914, Reserves vs LVC Wowru.
The Brooklyn Daily Eagle, October 11, 1914, Cornell.
The Carlisle Arrow, October 16, 1914, v11, n7, Pratt visits.
The Philadelphia Inquirer, October 18, 1914, Reserves vs Albright Deerfoot Firestine.
Pittsburgh Daily Post, October 18, 1914, p35&36, Pitt.
The Carlisle Arrow, October 23, 1914, v11, n8, Calac captain.
The Philadelphia Inquirer, October 25, 1914, Penn.
Buffalo Courier, November 1, 1914, p88, Syracuse.
Pittsburgh Daily Post, November 8, 1914, Pitt wants Warner.
The Boston Globe, November 8, 1914, Holy Cross.
The Philadelphia Inquirer, November 8, 1914, Holy Cross.
Chicago Tribune, November 15, 1914, p19&21, Notre Dame.
Harrisburg Daily Independent, November 16, 1914, Reserves vs Middletown AC.
The Philadelphia Inquirer, November 22, 1914, Reserves vs Susquehanna.
The Philadelphia Inquirer, November 22, 1914, Dickinson.
The Sentinel, November 23, 1914, Dickinson.
The News Journal, November 27, 1914, Reserves vs Delaware May.
The Boston Globe, November 27, 1914, Brown.
The Boston Globe, November 29, 1914, All Stars.
The Atlanta Constitution, December 6, 1914, Auburn.
Pop Warner: A Life on the Gridiron, Jeffrey J. Miller, 2015.
The Montgomery Advertiser, December 6, 1914. Lone Star Dietz

The Tuscaloosa News, December 6, 1914. Lone Star Dietz
Spalding's Official Football Guide 1915, August 1915.

Chapter 20 1915

Oakland Tribune, January 3, 1915, Lone Star.
The Journal and Tribune, January 3, 1915, Harvard.
Muskogee Daily Phoenix, February 27, 1915, Kelley.
The Carlisle Arrow, March 8, 1915, v11, n26, Warner's farewell.
Pop Warner: A Life on the Gridiron, Jeffrey J. Miller, 2015.
The Spokesman Review, May 23, 1915, Dietz.
The Washington Herald, September 5, 1915, Practice starts.
The Carlisle Arrow, September 10, 1915, v12, n2, Kelley arrives.
Evening Public Ledger, September 18, 1915, p1, Albright.
The Baltimore Sun, September 19, 1915, Preseason.
The Philadelphia Inquirer, September 19, 1915, Albright.
Carlisle Evening Herald, September 20, 1915, pp1&7, Albright.
The Philadelphia Inquirer, September 26, 1915, LVC.
Carlisle Evening Herald, September 27, 1915, Reserves vs Mercersburg.
Carlisle Evening Herald, October 4, 1915, Reserves vs Conway Hall.
Carlisle Evening Herald, October 4, 1915, Lehigh game.
Pittsburgh Daily Post, October 10, 1915, Harvard.
The Boston Globe, October 10, 1915, pp1&11, Harvard.
Lebanon Daily News, October 11, 1915, Reserves vs LVC.
The Pittsburgh Press, October 17, 1915, Reserves vs Bellefonte.
Pittsburgh Daily Post, October 17, 1915, pp39&40, Pitt.
The Washington Times, October 23, 1915, Reserves photo.
The Washington Times, October 23, 1915, Reserves vs Gallaudet.
The Washington Post, October 24, 1915, Reserves vs Gallaudet.
Daily Intelligencer, October 30, 1915, p8, WVWC.
Pittsburgh Daily Post, October 31, 1915, WVWC.
Carlisle Evening Herald, November 6, 1915, Holy Cross Groker.
Carlisle Evening Herald, November 6, 1915, Reserves for Bloomfield.
The Boston Globe, November 7, 1915, Holy Cross.
Carlisle Evening Herald, November 8, 1915, pp1&8, Holy Cross.
The Berkshire Evening Eagle, November 9, 1915, Refused goal.
The Boston Globe, November 11, 1915, Thorpe.
The Philadelphia Inquirer, November 14, 1915, Dickinson.
Public Opinion, November 16, 1915, Reserves vs Ship Normal.
The Gazette, November 17, 1915, Reserves vs Ship Normal.
The New York Times, November 21, 1915, Fordham.
Fall River Daily Globe, November 26, 1915, Brown Crane not Leonard.
Carlisle Evening Herald, November 26, 1915, Brown Leonard.
The Boston Globe, November 26, 1915, Brown.
Delaware County Daily Times, December 1, 1915, Kelley.
The Daily New Era, December 1, 1915, Kelley.
Pittsburgh Daily Post, December 2, 1915, Kelley.
The Los Angeles Times, December 2, 1915, Kelley.
The Washington Times, December 2, 1915, Kelley.
The Carlisle Arrow, December 3, 1915, v12, n14, Season summary.
The Los Angeles Times, December 21, 1915, Kelley.
The Carlisle Arrow, January 7, 1916, v12, n17, Dietz & Warner undefeated.
Spalding's Official Football Guide 1916, August 1916.

Chapter 21 1916

The New York Times, December 1, 1915, Lipps.
The Washington Post, December 4, 1915, Lane.
The Wilkes Barre Record, December 4, 1915, Canceled.
The Washington Times, January 6, 1916, Dietz.
Chicago Tribune, January 7, 1916, Guyon.
Carlisle Evening Herald, March 28, 1916, Guyon.
The Atlanta Constitution, April 7, 1916, Guyon.
Pittsburgh Post Gazette, July 18, 1916, Govt foul up.
The Carlisle Arrow, July 21, 1916, v13, n1, enrollment calculations.
Star Tribune, September 6, 1916, Guyon.
Carlisle Evening Herald, September 9, 1916, Polio typhoid fever.
Harrisburg Telegraph, September 20, 1916, LVC.
The Atlanta Constitution, September 20, 1916, Guyon brothers.
Knoxville Sentinel, September 22, 1916, Guyon.
The Carlisle Arrow, September 22, 1916, v13, n3, first practice.
The Sentinel, September 23, 1916, Conway Hall.
The Atlanta Constitution, September 24, 1916, Guyon eligible.
Chattanooga Daily Times, September 29, 1916, Guyon brothers.
The Pittsburgh Press, October 1, 1916, Calac.
Carlisle Evening Herald, October 2, 1916, pp1&6, Band parades.
Pittsburgh Daily Post, October 3, 1916, WVWC Guyon.
New Castle Herald, October 6, 1916, WVWC Guyon.
Akron Evening Times, October 9, 1916, Pro team.
The Sentinel, October 14, 1916, LVC reserves.
Harrisburg Telegraph, October 18, 1916, LVC.
The Chattanooga News, October 18, 1916, Guyon.
The Carlisle Arrow, October 20, 1916, v13, n7, not interfere w Dickinson game.
The New York Times, October 22, 1916, Conway Hall.
The Philadelphia Inquirer, October 22, 1916, Conway Hall.
Carlisle Evening Herald, October 23, 1916, Home game.
Carlisle Evening Herald, October 26, 1916, Midweek scrimmage.
The Sentinel, October 27, 1916, Shippensburg Normal.
St Louis Post Dispatch, October 28, 1916, Guyon.
The News Journal, October 28, 1916, Welch protested & F&M.
The Philadelphia Inquirer, October 29, 1916, Shippensburg.
The Philadelphia Inquirer, October 29, 1916, Susquehanna.
Carlisle Evening Herald, October 30, 1916, Shippensburg Reserves.
Carlisle Evening Herald, October 30, 1916, Susquehanna.
The Atlanta Constitution, November 1, 1916, Guyon ineligible.
The Carlisle Arrow, November 3, 1916, v13, n9, football not banned.
Carlisle Evening Herald, November 6, 1916, p6, Conshohocken.
Nashville Banner, November 6, 1916, Guyon GA Tech.
The Sentinel, November 6, 1916, Conshohocken.
Norwich Bulletin, November 9, 1916, p3, Govt approves football.
The Philadelphia Inquirer, November 12, 1916, Carson Long.
Carlisle Evening Herald, November 13, 1916, Dickinson.
The Philadelphia Inquirer, November 19, 1916, LVC reserves.
The Daily News, November 20, 1916, LVC.
Star Gazette, November 25, 1916, Alfred.
The Sentinel, November 27, 1916, Alfred.
The Sentinel, November 27, 1916, Conshohocken.

Fiat Lux, November 28, 1916, Alfred.
The Sentinel, December 1, 1916, Conway Hall.
The Carlisle Arrow, December 3, 1916, v13, n13, subordinated.
Star Gazette, December 7, 1916, No post-season trip.
The Brattleboro Daily Reformer, December 11, 1916, Full schedule in 1917.
Harrisburg Telegraph, December 16, 1916, Harris will coach.
The New York Sun, December 17, 1916, New Coach.
Dickinson College Bulletin: The Catalogue 1916-17, May 1917, p78, Law School fees.
https://carlisleindian.dickinson.edu/sites/all/files/docs-ephemera/NARA 1326 b119 f4821.
Spalding's Official Football Guide 1917, August 1917.

Chapter 22 1917

The Carlisle Arrow, January 5, 1917, v13, n17, students enrolled.
The Sentinel, January 13, 1917, Harris coach.
The Carlisle Arrow, January 19, 1917, v13, n19, new coach to be hired.
Carlisle Evening Herald, January 19, 1917, Harris hired.
The Carlisle Arrow, March 9, 1917, v13, n26, Full schedule.
The Carlisle Arrow, June 15, 1917, v13, n36, Boys in army & navy.
The News Journal, August 17, 1917, Princeton drops football.
The Carlisle Arrow, September 14, 1917, v14, n1, Warner visits.
Harrisburg Telegraph, September 17, 1917, New players' names.
The Philadelphia Inquirer, September 30, 1917, Albright.
The Sentinel, October 1, 1917, Albright.
The Carlisle Arrow, September 14, 1917, v14, n1, Warner visits.
The Carlisle Arrow and Red Man, October 5, 1917, v14, n4, Lt. Welch.
The Philadelphia Inquirer, October 7, 1917, F&M.
The Philadelphia Inquirer, October 7, 1917, Practice game.
Pittsburgh Daily Post, October 14, 1917, Reserves vs Indiana.
The Philadelphia Inquirer, October 14, 1917, West VA.
The Pittsburgh Press, October 21, 1917, Players' names.
Pittsburgh Post Gazette, October 21, 1917, Navy.
The Philadelphia Inquirer, October 23, 1917, George Kipp.
Carlisle Evening Herald, October 25, 1917, James Evans.
The Baltimore Sun, October 28, 1917, Johns Hopkins.
The Pittsburgh Press, November 4, 1917, Bucknell.
Carlisle Evening Herald, November 5, 1917, Reserves vs Ship.
The Carlisle Arrow and Red Man, November 9, 1917, v14, n9, Pratt visits.
Pittsburgh Daily Post, November 11, 1917, Army.
The Philadelphia Inquirer, November 18, 1917, Reserves vs LVC.
The Philadelphia Inquirer, November 18, 1917, GA Tech.
Carlisle Evening Herald, November 19, 1917, Reserves vs LVC.
Carlisle Evening Herald, November 22, 1917, Losses to war effort.
The Boston Globe, November 22, 1917, Boston College canceled.
The Kansas City Star, November 22, 1917, Boston College game canceled.
The Campus, November 22, 1917, U of Rochester cancels Carlisle game.
Evening Public Ledger, November 24, 1917, pp1&6, Penn.
The Courier, November 25, 1917, Improving.
The Philadelphia Inquirer, November 25, 1917, Penn.
Carlisle Evening Herald, November 26, 1917, Reserves vs Hbg Acad.
Harrisburg Telegraph, November 26, 1917, Reserves vs Hbg Acad.
The Evening News, November 26, 1917, Reserves vs Hbg Acad.
The Boston Globe, November 27, 1917, Boston College.

The Washington Times, November 29, 1917, Rough schedule.
The Pittsburgh Press, December 2, 1917, Nicknames.
The Sentinel, December 5, 1917, Godfrey dies after Penn game.
The Carlisle Arrow and Red Man, December 7, 1917, v14, n13, Louis Godfrey.
The Marshfield News & Wisconsin Hub, December 20, 1917, Join military.
Pittsburgh Post Gazette, December 23, 1917, Baseball again.
Carlisle Evening Herald, July 31, 1918, p8, Employees transferred.
College Football Historical Society, February 1, 1988, Guyon GA Tech 1917.
https://carlisleindian.dickinson.edu/sites/all/files/docs-ephemera/NARA 1326 b150 f5838 0, Louis Godfrey student file
Spalding's Official Football Guide 1918, August 1918.

Chapter 23 1918

The Washington Herald, January 2, 1918, More games played.
The Washington Herald, January 2, 1918, No Rules Changes for 1918.
The Miltonian, January 3, 1918, 60 boys enlisted.
The Evening News, February 25, 1918, Baseball coach.
The Carlisle Arrow, May 24, 1918, Football schedule.
Carlisle Evening Herald, June 1, 1918, Commencement.
Harrisburg Telegraph, June 1, 1918, Football schedule.
The Sentinel, June 1, 1918, Baseball.
The Sentinel, June 1, 1918, Large number out on farms.
The Philadelphia Inquirer, June 2, 1918, Football schedule.
The Evening News, June 3, 1918, Lafayette at Island Park.
The Philadelphia Inquirer, June 5, 1918, Letters awarded.
The Pittsburgh Press, June 5, 1918, Pitt to open against Carlisle.
The Chronicle, June 6, 1918, pp1&4, Band in big Shippensburg parade.
Carlisle Evening Herald, June 7, 1918, 1000 at commencement.
The Sentinel, June 8, 1918, Francis to join army.
Pittsburgh Daily Post, June 9, 1918, to play Pitt at Forbes Field.
The Sentinel, June 13, 1918, Choctaw drafted.
Harrisburg Telegraph, June 14, 1918, Lacrosse record.
The Gettysburg Times, June 14, 1918, request to expand Carlisle.
Carlisle Evening Herald, June 18, 1918, Management changes.
The Sentinel, June 28, 1918, Longshore buried.
Carlisle Evening Herald, July 3, 1918, 4th of July concert.
The Sentinel, July 3, 1918, Wheelock big band.
The Gettysburg Times, July 5, 1918, Francis joins Army.
The Sentinel, July 6, 1918, Medical supplies.
The Pittsburgh Press, July 9, 1918, Francis encourage Indians to join.
The Pottsville Republican, July 17, 1918, School abandoned.
Carlisle Evening Herald, July 18, 1918, To be hospital.
Harrisburg Telegraph, July 18, 1918, details of closing.
The Washington Post, July 18, 1918, 700 students.
Harrisburg Telegraph, July 22, 1918, Arranging transfer.
Carlisle Evening Herald, July 23, 1918, Parade.
Harrisburg Telegraph, July 25, 1918, Changes start.
The Morning Call, July 29, 1918, Chilocco.
The Sentinel, July 30, 1918, Doctor to Haskell.
Carlisle Evening Herald, July 31, 1918, p1, Employees transferred.
Harrisburg Telegraph, August 2, 1918, Canteen for Soldiers.
The Sentinel, August 2, 1918, Students depart end of August.

The Sentinel, August 9, 1918, J R Wheelock Army bandmaster.
The Sentinel, August 9, 1918, Put Carlisle on the map.
Evening Public Ledger, August 12, 1918, Hog Island.
Lebanon Daily News, August 13, 1918, Wheelock commissioned.
Evening Star, August 15, 1918, Bandmaster confused.
The Sentinel, August 15, 1918, Reception at C of C.
Harrisburg Telegraph, August 19, 1918, Hospital plans.
The Gettysburg Times, August 19, 1918, Patients to arrive.
The Sentinel, August 24, 1918, Sequence for reception.
Harrisburg Telegraph, August 26, 1918, Civil War reunion.
Altoona Times, August 27, 1918, Returning students pass through Altoona.
Carlisle Evening Herald, August 27, 1918, Longstreth Library.
Carlisle Evening Herald, August 27, 1918, pp1&8 Reception.
Harrisburg Telegraph, August 27, 1918, Reception.
The Sentinel, August 27, 1918, p6, Reception.
The Sentinel, August 28, 1918, Mercer Wheelock.
The Sentinel, August 29, 1918, Should build memorial.
The Sentinel, August 30, 1918, A dozen students remain.
The Sentinel, August 30, 1918, Few remained.
Harrisburg Telegraph, August 31, 1918, Singing.
The Philadelphia Inquirer, January 23, 1919, Reopen Carlisle.
Lancaster New Era, March 14, 1935, Dillon in Carlisle.
Shamokin News Dispatch, March 14, 1935, Dillon leaves for DC.
The York Dispatch, March 22, 1935, Reopen school Dillon.
The Sentinel, April 5, 1935, Dillon Imposter.
The News Chronicle, April 9, 1935, Dillon dead.
Spalding's Official Football Guide 1919, August 1919.

Epilog

Carlisle Evening Herald, July 26, 1919, Reopen Carlisle.
The Evening World, April 18, 1922, Wallace Denny.
The Los Angeles Times, April 18, 1922, Wallace Denny.
Pop Warner: A Life on the Gridiron, Jeffrey J. Miller, 2015.
Sapulpa Herald, December 16, 1926, Sapulpa to get Carlisle.
The Cushing Daily Citizen, December 28, 1926, Exendine.
Poughkeepsie Eagle News, August 30, 1941, Reunion.
The Ithaca Journal, August 30, 1941, Reunion.
The Sentinel, 1987, F E Masland ltr to editor.

Appendix A Origin of the school

Battlefield and Classroom: An Autobiography by Richard Henry Pratt, edited by Robert M. Utley, 1964.
Pratt: The Red Man's Moses, Elaine Goodale Eastman, 1935.

Illustrations

Cover

Artwork created by Lone Star Dietz for cover of *Football for Players and Coaches* by Glenn S. Warner, 1912.

Frontispiece

Drawing done by Lone Star Dietz for 1909 Athletic Banquet frontispiece.

Introduction

Pratt with student photo courtesy of U. S. Army Military History Institute, Carlisle, PA.
Carlisle Indian School admin building photo from postcard.

Chapter 1 1893-1895

Football field layout from Foot-Ball Rules and Referee's Book, revised by Walter Camp, Secretary of Advisory Committee, authorized and adopted by the American Intercollegiate Association, 1893.
1894 Team photo by John N. Choate, Carlisle, PA.
Cartoon by Charles M. Payne, member of Duquesne Country and Athletic Club, 1895
After Quaker Scalps, On the Warpath, and The Modern Hiawatha cartoons from *The Philadelphia Inquirer*, October 17, 1895.

Chapter 2 1896-1898

Team photo from *Spalding's Official Football Guide for 1896*.
"Big Four" from *The Philadelphia Inquirer*, November 15, 1896.
Awaiting the Signal from *New York Evening Journal*, November 26, 1896.
Large untitled cartoon from *Pittsburgh Daily Post*, October 4, 1896.
Team sketch from *Chicago Tribune*, December 19, 1896.
New York's Only Big Game from *New York Evening Journal*, October 23, 1897.
Penn game cartoon from *The Philadelphia Inquirer*, November 7, 1897.
When the Ball cartoon from *The Cincinnati Enquirer*, November 26, 1897.
Indian Skulking cartoon from *New York Journal*, October 24, 1897.
Harvard's First Touchdown cartoon from *The Boston Globe*, October 30, 1898.

Chapter 3 1899

Warner coaching photo courtesy of U. S. Army Military History Institute
The Philadelphia Times, October 15, 1899
The Philadelphia Inquirer, October 15, 1899
The San Francisco Call, December 26, 1899

Chapter 4 1900

Cartoon from *The Philadelphia Inquirer*, November 18, 1900.
Cartoon from *The Boston Globe*, October 28, 1900.
Team photo by Choate & Co. for *Spalding's Official Football Guide for 1901*.

Chapter 5 1901

Team photo from *Columbia Daily Spectator,* December 3, 1901.
Progress chart from *The Boston Post*, October 27, 1901.
Cartoon from *The Philadelphia Inquirer*, November 14, 1901.

Chapter 6 1902

When the Crown Prince of Siam from *Boston Post*, October 29, 1902.
Team photo from *New York Daily Tribune*, October 13, 1902
Indians Defeat Penn from *The Philadelphia Inquirer*, November 16, 1902.

Foster Charles photo from *The Evening World*, September 26, 1902.
James Phillips photo courtesy of Brown family collection.

Chapter 7 1903

Field diagram from *Spalding's Official Football Guide for 1903*.
Penn and Harvard Go Down from *The Philadelphia Inquirer*, November 15, 1903.
Northwestern Succumbs from *Chicago Tribune*, November 27, 1903.
Carlisle Indian Gridiron Hero Weds from *The Tacoma Times*, December 31, 1903.
Tin shop and Shoe shop photos courtesy of Library of Congress.

Chapter 8 Captain Leadership

Martin Wheelock photo courtesy of U. S. Army Military History Institute, Carlisle, PA.
Antonio Lubo photo courtesy of U. S. Army Military History Institute, Carlisle, PA.
The Atlanta Constitution, November 30, 1924.
Carlisle Barracks map courtesy of National Park Service.

Chapter 9 1904

Field diagram from *Spalding's Official Football Guide for 1904*.
Photo of Pratt on horseback taken by Frances Benjamin Johnston courtesy of the Library of Congress.
Photo of Mercer courtesy of Denver Public Library.
Bemus Pierce sketch from *The Philadelphia Times*, September 27, 1896.
Cartoon from *The Philadelphia Inquirer*, November 13, 1904.
Cartoon from *The Lantern*, November 30, 1904.

Chapter 10 1905

Ed Rogers photo courtesy of U. S. Army Military History Institute, Carlisle, PA.
Kicked-in-the-Jaw from *The Philadelphia Inquirer*, October 22, 1905.
George Woodruff photo courtesy of U. S. Forestry Service.
Query cartoon from *The Boston Daily Globe*, November 4, 1905.
Redskins Scalp West Point from *The Philadelphia Inquirer*, November 12, 1905.
Violence cartoon from *Judge* magazine, 1905.

Chapter 11 1906

Football is Tackled cartoon from *The Boston Daily Globe*, November 30, 1905.
Next! Cartoon courtesy of the Library of Congress, c1905.
Rival football committees cartoon, c1905.
Frank Hudson photo courtesy of U. S. Army Military History Institute, Carlisle, PA.
Early incarnation of single-wing formation diagram from Offense pamphlet from Warner's correspondence course, *Football for Players and Coaches*, 1908.
Mt. Pleasant throwing photos from *Football for Players and Coaches* by Glenn S. Warner, 1912.
How the Indians Line Up from *The Philadelphia Inquirer*, October 27, 1906.
Vandy Hands a Lemon cartoon from *The Atlanta Constitution,* November 23, 1906.
Angel De Cora photo courtesy of Swedish National Museums of World Culture

Chapter 12 1907

Villanova game ad from Carlisle Printing Company, 1907.
Indian Maidens from *The Philadelphia Inquirer*, October 27, 1907.
Poor John! Cartoon from *The Boston Globe*, November 10, 1907.
Hanging the Indian Sign cartoon from *Chicago Tribune*, November 24, 1907.
Carlisle stars collage from *The Joliet Evening Herald News*, November 25, 1907.

Chapter 13 1908

Football player cartoon from *The Washington Times*, October 18, 1908.
James Johnson photo courtesy of U. S. Army Military History Institute, Carlisle, PA.
Forward pass cartoon from *Star Tribune*, November 9, 1908.
Five Carlisle Stars from *Star Tribune*, November 17, 1908.
High treason cartoon from *The Philadelphia Inquirer*, November 2, 1908.
Numbers photo from Carnegie Library of Pittsburgh.

Chapter 14 1909

Lewis Tewanima photo courtesy of Library of Congress, c1911.
Halley Comet cartoon from *The Boston Globe*, November 15, 1909.
Cartoonist Winner's cartoons from *Pittsburgh Daily Post*, October 24, 1909.
Fun with the Indian cartoon from *The Philadelphia Inquirer*, November 1, 1909.
Captain Libby from *The Nebraska State Journal*, November 7, 1909.
Red Men Scalped collage from *St. Louis Globe Democrat*, November 26, 1909.
Poem cartoon from *The Philadelphia Inquirer*, November 2, 1909.
Ready for the Operation cartoon from *The Philadelphia Inquirer*, September 1, 1910.

Chapter 15 1910

Field diagram from *Spalding's Official Football Guide for 1910*.
Edward Bracklin photo courtesy of U. S. Army Military History Institute, Carlisle, PA.
Team in formation from Wardecker Collection.
Stars from *The Evening Sun*, November 17, 1910.
In Battle Array from *The Philadelphia Inquirer*, October 29, 1910.
Stars of Comet Type cartoon from *The Boston Globe*, November 17, 1910.
Hopkins Interference photo from *The Baltimore Sun*, November 20, 1910.

Chapter 16 1911

Team photo courtesy of Wardecker Collection.
Headlines from *Pittsburgh Daily Post*, October 22, 1911.
Battle with Penn from *The Philadelphia Inquirer*, November 5, 1911.
H vs C cartoon from *The Boston Globe*, November 11, 1911.
Thorpe kicking from *The Boston Globe*, November 12, 1911.
Comes the Injun! Cartoon from *The Boston Globe*, November 11, 1911.
The Saltine Warrior drawing from *The Syracuse Herald*, November 18, 1911.
In the Spotlight collage from *The Philadelphia Inquirer*, December 3, 1911.

Chapter 17 1912

Field diagram from *Spalding's Official Football Guide for 1912*.
Tewanima and Thorpe photos taken by Hensel Studio, 1912.
Line photo courtesy of Wardecker Collection.
When Jeff Eleven Holds from *Pittsburgh Daily Post*, October 20, 1912.
Four Indians from *The Washington Post*, October 24, 1912.
Carlisle Plunks cartoon from *The Washington Post*, November 3, 1912.
Army in Rout headlines from *New York Tribune*, November 10, 1912.
Rough Paleface cartoon from *The Philadelphia Inquirer*, November 18, 1912.
A Regular Clean-Up cartoon from *Boston Post*, November 28, 1912.
Big Jim photo from *The Fort Wayne Journal Gazette*, December 1, 1912.

Chapter 18 1913

Team photo courtesy of U. S. Army Military History Institute, Carlisle, PA.
Baseball man says from *Carlisle Evening Herald*, January 22, 1913.
I was only from *Chicago Examiner*, January 28, 1913.
Calac and Guyon photos courtesy of the Library of Congress.
Redskins Scalp headlines from *The Philadelphia Inquirer*, November 17, 1913.
"Next" cartoon from *The Philadelphia Inquirer*, October 22, 1913.
Tit for Tat cartoon from *The Philadelphia Inquirer*, October 26, 1913.

Georgetown Not Alone from *The Washington Times*, November 2, 1913.
Watch Me Pop cartoon from *The Philadelphia Inquirer*, November 15, 1913.
Have a Heart cartoon from *The Philadelphia Inquirer*, November 17, 1913.
All Carlisle Turns Out headlines from *Democrat and Chronicle*, November 17, 1913.
Thorpe's Successor sketch by Ripley from *Syracuse Herald*, November 21, 1913.
Bracklin photo from *Cincinnati American*, November 25, 1913.

Chapter 19 1914
Team photo courtesy of U. S. Army Military History Institute, Carlisle, PA.
NEXT cartoon from *The Pittsburgh Press*, October 18, 1914.
Ready for the Fray cartoon from *The Philadelphia Inquirer*, October 23, 1914.
Gus Welch photo courtesy of U. S. Army Military History Institute, Carlisle, PA.
Bulletin clipping from *Chicago Tribune, November 15, 1914.*
Let Football Stars Alone clipping from *The Pittsburgh Press*, November 14, 1914.
Glenn Warner Signs headline from *Pittsburgh Post Gazette*, December 6, 1914.
Can Old Timers Play cartoon from *The Boston Globe*, November 29, 1914.
Alabama After Dietz headlines from *The Montgomery Advertiser*, December 6, 1914.
Charge of the Grid Brigade poem from *The Pittsburgh Press*, October 10, 1915.
Lone Star Dietz photo from The Oregonian, October 1915.

Chapter 20 1915
Welch and Kelley photo courtesy of Wardecker Collection.
Team photo courtesy of Wardecker Collection.
Harvard Wins clipping from *The Boston Globe*, November 29, 1914.
Walloped clipping from *The Pittsburgh Press*, October 17, 1915.
The happy days cartoon from *The Providence Journal*, November 28, 1915.
Lonestar Dietz Tells cartoon from *Los Angeles Times*, January 4, 1916.
After the Ball poem from *The Philadelphia Inquirer*, November 12, 1914.

Chapter 21 1916
Poor Lo clipping from *The Champaign Daily Gazette*, September 29, 1916.
Return to Gridiron headline from *Harrisburg Telegraph*, October 18, 1916.
Team photo from *Fabulous Redmen* by John S. Steckbeck, 1951.
Coach Jailed headline from *Harrisburg Telegraph*, October 1, 1916.
Alfred University headline from *Democrat and Chronicle*, November 25, 1916
Dead Indian Play from *Spokane Chronicle*, November 23, 1931..

Chapter 22 1917
Gus Welch photo courtesy of Cumberland County Historical Society, Carlisle, PA.
Stung 98 Times cartoon from *The Technique*, November 20, 1917.
Today's Attractions cartoon from *The Philadelphia Inquirer*, November 24, 1917.
Dead Indian Star clipping from *The Atlanta Constitution*, December 7, 1917.
William Gardner wedding photo courtesy of Diane Garrard.
Mt. Pleasant clipping from *The Carlisle Arrow and Red Man*, March 22, 1918.

Chapter 23 1918
Lacrosse team photo courtesy of Winneshiek Collection.
Football schedule from *The Carlisle Arrow and Red Man*, May 24, 1918.
Band photo courtesy of Library of Congress.
Wallace Denny family photo courtesy of Cumberland County Historical Society, Carlisle, PA.

Appendix A
Photo courtesy of National Anthropological Archives, Smithsonian Institution

INDEX

Addison, Burdick, 325
Aiken, John, 177, 325
Albanez, Stephen, 129, 130, 134, 135, 325
Alexander, Peter, 325
Allen, Grover, 325
Allen, John, 325
American Horse, Benjamin, 17, 325
Andrews, Frank, 325
Aragon, William, 325
Arcasa, Alexander, 202, 204, 211, 213, 214, 215, 217, 218, 229-231, 233-235, 238, 244, 325
Archambault, Harry, 325
Archambault, Leo, 325
Archiquette, Chauncey, 123, 129, 130, 134, 325
Arquette, Mitchell W., 202, 218, 325
Austin, Anthony, 12, 15, 17, 69, 325
Azure, Ovilla, 325
Bache, R. Meade, 1, 2, 22
Backmayer, A. C., Major, 305
Bailey, Mary, 27
Baine, John, 65, 325
Baine, William, 65, 66, 69, 325
Baird, Charles, 38, 325
Baker, Joseph, 15, 96, 103, 325
Balenti, John, 325
Balenti, Michael, 135, 158, 169, 175, 177, 179, 182, 185, 186, 325
Barrel/Barril, Napoleon, 3, 177, 325
baseball, discontinued, 200
baseball, reinstituted, 302
Bear Horse, John, 325
Bearlouse, Solomon, 325
Beartail, John, 325
Beaver, Frank, 65, 72, 89, 111, 325
Bellefeuille, Theodore, 325
Bender, Charles Albert, 64, 71, 84, 142, 248, 308, 325
Benedict, Charles C., 234
Bergie, Joseph, 4, 222, 229, 231, 234, 237, 238, 239, 244, 286, 325
Bettleyoun, Isaac, 325
Biddle Field, 227, 286
Biddle, Chapman, Gen., 320
Big Top, Fred, 325
Bigbear, Samuel, 325
Billy, Nicodemus, 325
Bird, David, 325

Bird, Sampson, 182, 195, 200, 203, 211-216, 226, 227, 325
Blackbird, Charles, 325
Blackchief, Lyman, 325
Blaine, James G., 325
Blumenthal, Moses, 97, 258
Bouchard, John, 325
Bowen, Nicholas, 90, 96, 99, 118, 122, 126, 127, 129, 134, 207, 325
Boyd, Oscar, 325
Bracklin, Edward, 203, 206, 207, 212, 247, 248, 249, 252, 325
Bradby, Walter, 325
Bradley, Johnson, 78, 112, 114, 326
Brave Eagle, Silas, 326
Bravethunder, William, 326
Broker, Fred, 4, 214, 222, 261, 262, 264, 267, 274, 276, 278, 326
Broker, Henry, 213, 267, 268, 326
Brophy, John, 326
Brought Plenty, John, 326
Brown, Alonzo, 16, 326
Bruce, Robert, 326
Bruner, William, 326
Bryant, Cecil, 326
Buck, Charles W., 12, 326
Bull, William T., 36, 37
Burr, Sidney, 326
Burton, Roy, 72, 326
Busch, Elmer, 211, 253, 259, 261, 262, 273, 326
Butterworth, Frank S., 15
Bynum, Mike, 183, 250
Byrnes, George, 107
Calac, Pedro "Pete", 228, 233, 235, 244, 245, 247-253, 261-263, 265-268, 273, 274, 275, 276, 277, 286, 313, 326
Camp, Walter, 9, 13, 19, 51, 56, 61, 69, 75, 80, 84, 91, 98, 103, 104, 113, 127, 146, 150, 169, 174, 185, 223, 239, 253, 259, 278, 298
Campeau, Edward, 326
Carter, Charles D., Rep., 257
Caswell, Benjamin F., 8, 11, 12, 14-17, 326
Cayou, Francis Mitchell, 12, 22, 24, 28, 29, 31, 32, 33, 36, 38, 39, 42, 45-49, 52, 101, 259, 271, 326
Charging Whirlwind, Daniel, 326

Charles, Foster, 326
Charles, Reuben, 326
Charles, Wilson, 80, 85, 88, 90, 96, 120, 150, 259, 326
Chase, Daniel, 326
Chatfield, Peter, 72, 326
Chesowah, Lum, 326
Clairmont/Claymore, Philip, 326
Clancy, Charles A., 241, 242
Clevett, Merton L., 285-287, 291-293, 298
Clifford, Henry, 326, 329
Cochran, Garrett, 56, 57
Cochran, Thomas, 15
Coleman, Charles, 326
Coleman, Francis, 326
Connor, Andrew, 57, 326
Connors, George S., 64, 78
Conway Hall, 17, 95, 175, 179, 202, 212, 259, 273, 276, 284, 286, 289
Coons, Louis, 326
Cornelius, Casper, 326
Cornelius, Joel, 326
Cornelius, Phillip, 326
Cornelius, Samson, 326
Crane, James, 213, 244, 260-263, 326
Cries-for-Ribs, Harry, 326
Crowe, Boyd, 326
Crows Ghost, Morgan, 326
Cueller, Andrew, 326
Curly Bear, Charles, 327
Cusack, Jack, 280
Daniels, Albert, 327
Davis, Jesse, 130, 185, 253, 327
Decora, Angel, 101, 104, 142, 169, 174, 257, 259, 271
Decora, Nathaniel, 64, 65, 72, 327
DeGrass, Alfred, 327
Degray, George, 327
DeMarr, Edward, 76, 327
Dennis, Edward, 327
Denny, Wallace, 102, 118, 127, 256, 302, 307, 313, 327
Devore, Leland S., 234
Dewey, Scott, 327
Dickerson, Guy, 274, 275, 276, 277, 327
Dickey, David H., Outing Agent, 256
Dickinson College, 8, 10-12, 15, 19, 28, 31, 35, 37, 43, 45, 46, 49, 53, 54, 64, 65, 72-75, 84, 85, 91, 95, 104, 129, 130, 174-176, 178, 179, 200, 201, 203, 204, 212, 213, 227, 229, 250, 259, 265, 266, 273, 276, 277, 285, 286, 293, 304, 324
Dickson, Charles H., 171, 173
Dietz, William Henry, 61, 174, 188, 191, 194, 202, 203, 207, 211-213, 216, 217, 219, 227, 228, 244, 259, 268, 271, 272, 279, 280, 301, 310-314, 327
Dillon, Charles, 97, 118, 122, 129, 130, 136, 146, 150, 155, 170, 246, 308, 327
Donnell, Antoine, 327
Downwind, Xavier, 327
Doxtator, Benjamin, 12, 327
Doxtator, Frank, 122, 327
Drexel, Mother Katherine, 245
Dubois, Alfred, 130, 131, 327
Dunbar, James, 327
Dupuis, Louis, 194, 202-204, 209, 212, 327
Dutton, Frank, 327
Eagle Man, Thomas, 327
Ear, Seth, 327
Earth, George, 226, 327
Eastman, Charles, 94
Eastman, Christian E., 327
Eastman, Peter, 327
Eckersall, Walter H., 184
Edmonds, Taylor, 327
Edwards, Eustace, 327
Eisenhower, Dwight David, President, 234
Emmett, Robert, 327
Eshelman, Wilfred, 327
Evans, James, 327
Ewing, Hastings A., 305
Exendine, Albert, 88-90, 107-109, 111-113, 122, 123, 129, 130, 133, 145-148, 150, 151, 158, 161, 163, 167-170, 174, 212, 244, 259, 271, 284, 308, 310, 312, 313, 327
Fastbear, Esa aka Asa Sweetcorn, 204, 334
Felix, Louis, 327
Ferree, Minnie L., 95
Fielder, Isaac, 74, 327
Fischer, Adam, 48, 220, 327
Fish, Hamilton S., III, 185, 207, 208, 239, 266
Fisher, Eugene, 327
Flanders, C. L., 146
Flinchum, John B., 298, 327
Flood, Henry, 276, 277, 327
Flores, Louis, 327
Fly, Felix, 327
football-shaped patches, 180

Foote, Stephen, 327
Forte, Bruce, 327
Fox, Edward, 327
Francis, George, 328
Francis, John, Jr., 303, 304
Freemont/Fremont, Francis, 328
French, Meroney, 8, 328
Friday, Moses, 328
Friedman, Moses, 172, 173, 182, 242, 245, 255-259, 314
Gaddy, Peter, 202, 203, 328
Gardner, George, 328
Gardner, William, 122, 146, 147, 150, 158, 161, 163, 166, 168, 174, 200, 259, 280, 299, 312, 328
Garlow, James, 328
Garlow, William, 193, 194, 203, 206, 211, 212, 229, 242, 244-259, 261, 273, 275, 286, 328
George, David, 328
George, Lewis, 328
Gibson, John, 231, 328
Gilman, Joe, 278, 328
Giroux, William, 328
Glass, J. P., 107
Godcharles, Frederic A., Sen., 129
Goddard, R. H. Ives III, 24
Godfrey, Louis, 293, 297, 328
Goesback, Bruce, 226, 237, 244, 245, 328
Gokee, Jr., John, 328
Goodyear, Samuel M., 306
Graves, Ernest, 234, 268
Green, Edward, 328
Grinnell, George, 328
Guyon, Benedict, 328
Guyon, Charles Mayo, 123, 126, 136, 259, 295, 328
Guyon, Joseph, 123, 126, 136, 228, 237, 239, 242, 244-253, 259-261, 264, 271, 273, 286, 295, 296, 310, 311, 313, 315, 328
Half Town, Ora, 328
Hare, Nelson, 68, 72, 328
Harris, Buddy, 11, 294, 328
Harris, Leo F., 289, 291, 293, 296, 298
Harrison, Benjamin, 36, 328
Has Knife, Alfred, 328
Haskell Institute, 60, 61, 99, 121-123, 126, 183, 185, 200, 258, 273, 276, 305, 309, 312-315
Hauser, Emil, 3, 123, 146, 159, 174, 177, 183, 184, 189, 192, 201, 212, 259, 328

Hauser, Herman Peter "Pete", 122, 123, 157-159, 161, 163, 164, 166, 168-170, 177, 181-185, 188-191, 193-196, 201-206, 208-210, 212, 216, 259, 328
Hawk Eagle, Thomas, 328
Hawk, Thomas, 328
Hayes, Noah, 31, 68, 328
Hazlett, George or Stuart, 47, 328
Hazlett, William, 154
Heisman, John W., 14, 212, 296
Helms, Joseph, 328
Hendricks, Fritz, 97-99, 122, 134, 146, 158, 161, 174, 177, 185, 186, 188, 259, 328
Hendricks, Richard, 328
Henry, Noah, 328
Herman, Jacob, 287, 288, 291, 293, 328
Heston, William M., 77, 78
Hickok, William O. "Wild Bill", 15, 27-30
Hill, Levi E., 328
Hill, Robert, 328
Hinman, Richard, 328
Hitchcock, Ethan A., 117, 154
Hodge, William, 67, 329
Hoff, Joseph, 329
Holstein, James, 329
Hood, Oscar, 329
Houk, G. Presley, 16, 329
Howling Wolf, William, 329
Huber, Charles, 329
Hudson, Frank, 24, 32, 36-42, 44-49, 52, 54, 55, 59, 60, 61, 64, 72, 117, 118, 126, 133, 143, 271, 329
Huff, Morris, 329
Hunt, Oscar, 147, 150, 155, 329
Iron Whiteman, Alex, 329
Irons, Thomas, 329
Irwin, Joseph, 12, 56, 329
Isham, William G., 329
Island, Louis, 157, 160, 161, 166, 329
Jackson, Jack, 329
Jackson, Jonas, 329
Jackson, Peter, 329
Jackson, William B., 329
Jacobs, Luther, 329
James, Laban, 329
James, Leslie, 329
James, Moses, 329
Jamison/Jimerson, Jacob "Jakey", 22, 24, 29, 34, 37, 38, 42, 45, 329
Jimerson, Albert, 329
Jimerson/Jamison, Roger Tandy, 329

John, Herbert E. aka Kicked-on-the-Jaw, 329
Johnnyjohn, Mitchell/Michael, 329
Johnson, Clifford, 329
Johnson, James, 59, 60, 65, 66, 68, 69, 73, 78-80, 84-91, 95-99, 102-104, 107, 112-114, 118, 126, 150, 155, 159, 160, 174, 182, 241, 259, 268, 310, 313, 326, 329
Johnson, Richard, 329
Johnson, Roy Ruggles, 241
Jones, Amos, 329
Jones, William A., 117
Jones, William C. aka Two-Dogs-in-the-Snow, 329
Jordan, Dewey, 329
Jordan/Jourdan, Peter, 194, 207, 212, 218, 259, 329
Jude, Frank, 98, 118, 119, 121, 129, 132, 134, 135, 143, 329
Keewatin Academy, 259, 260, 261, 264
Kelley, Victor M., 180, 271-273, 279, 280, 284, 329
Kelly, Calvin Lee, 329
Kelsey, Charles, 329
Kenjockety, Jesse, 329
Kennedy, Alvin, 329
Kennedy, Charles M., 119, 121, 127, 128, 170, 329
Kennedy, Patrick, 329
Kennerly, Jerome, 191, 212, 330
Kettle, Francis, 330
Kicked-on-the-Jaw aka Herbert E. John, 127, 329
King, Kenneth, 56, 227, 288, 294, 313, 330
Kinney, Ralph P., 127, 133
Kipp, George, 330
Knocks-Off-Two aka Knox, Augustine, 330
Komah, Walter, 330
Kramer, William, 287
La Mere, Oliver, 330
La Rocque, Paul, 330
LaFlesch, Rosa B., Outing Manager, 256
LaFleur, Mitchell, 330
Lambert, Frank, 330
Lane, Franklin K., Interior Secretary, 284, 285, 304
Large, Roy, 244, 284, 306, 330
Larrabee aka Larvie, David, 330
Lassaw, Nicholas "Long Time Sleep", 293, 294, 330

Lay, Kelley, 65, 330
LeClaire, Peter Michael, 330
Leighton, William Morris, 330
Lemieux, John, 330
Leo, Edward, 273, 289, 291, 325, 330
Leroy, John, 330
Leroy, Louis, 76, 330
Leupp, Francis E., 115, 117, 125, 142, 153, 154, 155, 170-172, 181-183, 187, 259
Libby, Archie, 120-123, 128, 129, 134, 135, 143, 145-148, 150, 155, 158, 330
Libby, Joseph, 188-196, 201, 202, 206, 208, 209, 212, 330
Linnen, Chief Inspector, 256
Lipps, Oscar H., 258, 260, 265, 272, 276, 278, 283, 289, 303
Little Boy aka Scott Porter, 123, 134, 135, 145-147, 150, 159, 161-168, 183, 186, 188, 333
Little Hawk, James, 330
Little Old Man, David, 127, 177, 181, 182, 330
Little Wolf, William, 158, 330
Littlechief, Charles, 330
Locklear, George, 330
Lone Elk, Charles, 330
Lone Wolf, Delos, 33, 36, 330
Long Horn, 127, 333
Long Roach, William, 330
Long, Grover, 15, 127, 287, 288, 293, 294, 330, 333, 336
Longstreth, Mary Anna, 322
Longstreth, Susan, 307, 322, 323
Lookaround, August, 275, 330
Lorentz, Albert, 213, 330
Loud Bear, Joseph, 330
Louis of, Prince, 132
Lubo, Antonio, 85, 86, 88, 90, 107, 109-114, 118, 122, 129, 130, 146, 155, 159, 163, 166, 168, 174, 259, 330
Luckenbaugh, Nancy, 13
Luna, Joe B., 330
Lyon, Isaac, 159, 314, 330
Machukay, Martin, 330
Man-Who-Forgets, 127
Martell, Grover, 330
Martell, William, 330
Martin, E. L., 257, 259, 293
Martin, Michael, 331
Mather, Sarah Ann, 318, 320, 321
Mathews, Walter "Tex", 99, 133, 331
Matlock, Elmo, 331

Matlock, Louis, 331
Matlock, Stacy, 8, 173, 324, 331, 331
May, George, 228, 242, 285, 286, 292, 302, 318, 331
McClean, Robert, 331
McCormick, Vance C., 13, 15, 19, 21, 23, 27, 86, 129, 162
McDonald, Lewis, 331
McDowell, John, 331
McFarland, David, 15, 17, 19, 20, 28, 31, 32, 34, 36, 37, 40-42, 45, 331
McLean, Samuel aka Afraid-of-a-Bear, 168, 331
Mercer, William A., 117, 126, 132, 135, 142, 143, 146, 151, 153, 154, 155, 170-172, 205, 206, 216, 258, 306, 314, 323
Metoxen, Emerson, 293, 331
Metoxen, James, 331
Metoxen, Jonas, 12, 15, 17, 20, 22, 23, 29, 31-33, 35-37, 39-42, 45-49, 54, 55, 64, 331
Meyer, Harvey K., 276
Miguel, Ambrose, 331
Miguel, Jefferson, 331
Miles, Thomas C., 286, 288, 293, 297, 331
Miller Margaret Iva, 245
Miller, Artie, 32, 39, 41, 42, 45, 47, 64, 331
Miller, Edwin, 331
Miller, Hugh R., 2
Miller, James, 331
Miller, Leon, 287, 331
Miller, William H., 180, 257
Mitchell, Frank, 331
Mitchell, Jonas, 331
Moakley, John F., 64
Monchamp, Charles, 331
Monhart, John, 331
Montezuma, Carlos, M.D., 32, 57, 94, 155, 170
Moore, Edwin, 331
Moore, Job J., 99, 331
Moore, Philip, 331
Morgan, W. E., M.D., 265, 327
Morin, Solomon, 325, 331
Morrin, Edward, 275, 277, 331
Morrin, Joseph, 277, 331
Morrison, Daniel W., 331
Mt. Pleasant, Franklin Pierce, 121, 128, 129-136, 145-148, 150, 157-159, 161-164, 166-170, 173, 177-179, 200, 201, 259, 261, 271, 312, 331
Muma, Irwin J., 56, 57
Murphy, Michael C., 64
Nahtailish, Vincent, 331
NANA, North American Newspaper Alliance, 107
Nash, Albert H., 154
Neale, Alfred Earle, 244
Needham, Simon, 331
Nelson, Ezra, 68, 328, 331
Nephew, Arthur, 331
Nephew, Lloyd, 143, 331
Nephew, Percy, 331
Newashe, William, 192, 196, 204, 206-209, 211, 213, 214, 217, 218, 227, 242, 331
Nicolar, J. Frederick, 331
Niles, Rev. Dr. H. E., 17
No Shin Bone, Henry, 332
Noble, Jonah, 332, 335
Nori, Davis, 258, 332
Northrup, Joseph, 332
Ojibway, Francis, 332
Olmsted, Marlin E., Rep., Rep., 154, 155
Orton, George W., 104, 123, 185, 239, 253
Owl, Theodore, 158, 160, 332
Owl, William J., 332
Paisano, James, 332
Palmer, Jesse, 32, 33, 57, 64,-66, 72, 332
Pambrum, Francis, 332
Parker, Ely, 65, 89, 90, 163, 164, 332
Patterson, Thomas M., 181
Paul, Edward, 128, 131, 155, 330, 332
Paulin, Louis, 332
Payne, Albert, 156, 157, 159, 161, 163, 166, 176, 183, 184, 332
Payne, Charles, 29
Payne, Charles M., 20
Peairs, Hervey B., 99, 183
Peake, George C., 12, 332
Peconga, Willis, 332
Penny, Benjamin, 332
Penrose, Boies, Sen., 175
Peters, Edward, 332
Phillips, Daniel, 332
Phillips, James, 75, 76, 78, 85, 88, 89, 100, 104, 332
Pico, Carlos, 332
Pierce, Bemus, 12, 15, 17, 19, 20, 22, 24, 28, 29, 32-35, 37, 38, 40, 42, 45, 47-49, 52, 64-66, 69, 94, 95, 104, 117-

119, 122, 123, 126, 133, 134, 143, 259, 271, 332
Pierce, Hawley, 24, 28, 38, 45, 48, 64, 94, 119, 122, 332
Pine Grove Furnace, 66, 84, 320, 321
Pollard, Frederick D., 278, 279
Poodry, Aaron, 332
Powell, Stansill "Possum", 4, 191, 206, 207, 209, 211-216, 218, 219, 222, 229, 230, 233, 234, 238, 243, 332
Pratt, Charles, 247, 265, 332
Pratt, Richard Henry, 1, 3-6, 8-11, 13, 18, 25, 29, 32, 35, 46, 49, 51, 52, 54, 56, 57, 63, 64, 94, 116, 117, 125, 154, 170, 173, 187, 249, 256, 258, 261, 268, 272, 304, 306, 308, 314, 318-324
Printup, Harrison, 36, 332
Purse (Pierce), Howard, 332
Quick Bear, Ernest, 332
Quick Bear, Levi, 332
Ramsey, John, 332
Ranco, Everett, 332
Ransome, Thomas H., 45, 49
Red Cloud, 321
Red Tomahawk, Francis, 332
Redwater, Thaddeus, 38, 39, 55, 57, 64, 65, 332
Reed, Amos, 332
Reed, Lloyd, 332
Rice, Lawrence J., 151
Rickard, Edward, 332
Ricketts, Paul, 332
Ridenour, Hannah H., Matron, 257
Roberts, Charles, 59, 60, 64
Roberts, George, 332
Roberts, Henry E., 65, 211, 213, 217, 222, 333
Robinson, David, 333
Robinson, Joseph T., 256
Robinson, William Jr., 333
Rockne, Knute K., 280
Roe, Charles, 191, 333
Rogers, Edward L., 49, 60, 64, 65, 71, 117, 118, 122, 123, 125, 229, 310, 313, 315, 333
Rolling Bull, Rutherford, 333
Roosevelt, Theodore, President, 90, 94, 115-117, 121, 125, 132, 135, 139-142, 154, 155, 181, 183
Roosevelt, Theodore, Jr., 140
Roundstone, Fred, 333
Roussian, John, 333
Roy, Joseph, 333

Roy, Robert Charles, 143, 333
Ruiz, Joseph, 64, 74, 333
Runnels, Lewis, 333
Sage, Alexander, 333
Sage, Russell & Olivia, 29
Sampson, John, 195, 200, 212, 333
Sat-on, Russell, 333
Saul, Alfred, 333
Saul, Thomas, 333
Saunook, Jackson, 333
Saunook, Stillwell, 333
Saunooke, Samuel, 333
Schenandore, Fred S., 333
Schildt, Joseph, 333
Schoemaker, Ferdinand, M.D., 126, 180
Scholder, Joseph, 60, 333
Schweigman, Louis, 333
Scott, Frank, 37, 41, 123, 134, 146, 183, 192, 206, 307, 333
Scrogg, Solomon, 333
Sells, Cato, 255, 256, 258, 260, 271, 304
Seneca, Isaac, 39, 45, 52, 56, 60, 61, 64, 333
She Bear, David, 333
Shelafo, George, 333
Sheldon, Arthur, 34, 88, 89, 96, 97, 98, 103, 118-120, 126, 128-131, 134, 135, 143, 333
Shell, Huckleberry, 333
Shemamey, James, 333
Sherman, James S., Rep., 45, 95, 101, 102, 104, 118, 154
Shomin, Sebastian, 333
Short Bear, Bert, 333
Shouchuk, Nekifer, 75, 76, 78, 85, 90, 119, 122, 159, 334
Sickles, Caleb, 315, 334
Silverheels, Stephen, 334
Simpson, Albert, 334
Simpson, John, 334
Skenandore, Benjamin, 334
Skenandore, Fred, 334
Skenandore, Thomas A., 334
Smith, Chester, 334
Smith, Claude, 334
Smith, Edwin, 259, 334
Smith, Jefferson, 334
Smith, Marcus A., Rep., 154
Snow, James, 334
Soldiers, Buffalo, 1, 8, 318
Solomon, David, 195, 196, 334
Sousa, Eloy, 211, 213, 214, 216, 222, 304, 334

Spears, Benjamin, 334
Spearson, Albert, 334
Spotted Tail, 321, 334
Spybuck, Thomas, 334
Squirrel, John, 226, 334
St. Germaine, Thomas, 334
Stabler, George, 334
Stagg, Amos Alonzo, 33-35, 36, 168, 169, 184
Stanwix, Col. John, 8
Stauffer, Nathan P., 86, 91, 129, 136
Stevenson, Nuss, 334
Stowe, Harriet Beecher, 319
Stranger Horse, Moses, 334
Strong Arm, 127
Stuart, Gen. J. E. B., 8
Sumner, Joseph, 334
Sundown, Fayley, 334
Sutton, Ernest, 334
Sweetcorn, Asa aka Esa Fastbear, 204, 207, 212, 308, 334
Taft, William Howard, 117, 187
Tahquechi, Norton, 334
Tall Crane, Fred, 334
Tarbell, Peter, 334
Tatiyopa, Henry, 334
Teesatesky, Welch, 334
Tewanima, Lewis, 173, 188, 202, 203, 218, 225-227
Thomas, Dennis, 334
Thomas, Frank, 334
Thomas, George, 143, 158, 334
Thompson, George, 334
Thompson, John, 334
Thompson, Joseph H., 216
Thompson, Noble, 334
Thompson, Norman, 334
Thompson, William G., 10, 32, 33, 38, 57, 61, 90, 123, 135, 136, 155
Thorpe, Hiram, 156
Thorpe, James Francis, 4, 131, 156, 157, 159-162, 164, 166, 169, 175-188, 197, 200, 201, 211-216, 218-223, 225-239, 241-245, 253, 255, 280, 286, 293, 298, 308, 310-314, 334
Tibbetts, George, 289, 295, 334
Trachoma eye disease, 4
Tramper, Ammons, 334
Traversie, Alexander, 334
Tupper, Hobson K., 335
Turkish Trophy cigarettes, 156
Twin, Joseph, 335
Two Hearts, Joseph, 158, 334

Two-Dogs-in-the-Snow aka William C. Jones-in-the-Snow, 127
Valandra, Louis, 334
Vedernack, George, 4, 222, 247, 249, 334
Venne, Alfred M., 142, 143
Vielle, John, 334
Vigil, Clement, 335
Vincent, Henry, 169, 335
Walker, Benjamin, 335
Walker, Charles Amos, 293, 335
Walker, Fred, 335
Walker, Thomas, 65, 335
Walletsie, John, 335
Wallette, John, 244, 249, 261, 266, 335
Warner, Glenn S. "Pop", 2, 5, 9, 10, 28, 46, 51-68, 71-80, 83-86, 88, 90, 91, 94-98, 101-107, 112-114, 116, 118, 143, 144, 148, 150, 151, 153, 155-157, 159, 164-170, 173, 174, 176, 177, 179-185, 187-192, 194, 195, 200-204, 208-214, 218, 219, 221, 222, 225-229, 231, 233-236, 239, 241-244, 246-248, 250, 252, 253, 255-260, 263, 264, 266, 271, 275, 279, 280, 283, 285, 286, 291, 292, 306, 307, 309-314
Warner, Harvey D., 12, 183, 184, 335
Warner, Tibb Smith, 63, 102, 151, 180, 271
Warner, William J., 75, 84, 86, 91, 94, 95, 107, 108, 110, 113, 116, 195
Warren, John B., 60, 335
Wasase, David, 335
Washington, Alex, 335
Washington, Wesley, 335
Waupoose, William, 335
Webster, Lewis, 335
Weeks, William, 40, 77, 132, 335
Welch, Gustave "Gus", 211-217, 219, 221, 222, 226, 229-234, 239, 244-250, 252, 253, 255, 256, 259, 262, 264, 265, 271-273, 276, 279, 280, 284, 286, 292, 306, 308, 310, 312-314, 335
Welch, Herbert K., 307
Welch, James, 265, 335
Welmas, Philip, 261, 273, 335
West Point U. S. Military Academy, 8, 31, 56, 125, 131, 132, 172, 233, 234, 235, 243, 295
Wheeler, Harry, 38, 55, 57, 204, 207, 335
Wheelock, Dennison M., 27, 33, 305
Wheelock, Hugh, 211, 227, 335
Wheelock, James R., 304-306

Wheelock, Joel, 58, 202-204, 206, 209, 211-213, 215-217, 219, 238, 244, 261, 274, 288, 335
Wheelock, Martin, 12, 28, 33, 41, 47, 52, 55, 58-61, 64, 65, 73, 76, 78-80, 84-88, 91, 107, 110-114, 335
Whipple, Samuel, 57, 58, 335
White Crow, Titus, 335
White Dog, Henry, 335
White Fox, George, 335
White Thunder, Clarence, 335
White, Chauncey, 336
White, Grant, 336
White, John, 336
White, Joseph, 336
White, William H. Jr, 90, 126, 158, 336
White, William S., 336
Whiteface, Henry, 336
Whitney, Caspar W., 61, 91, 104, 136, 150, 170, 185, 250
Whitwell, John, Principal Teacher, 256
Wilber, Earl, 287, 336
Wilde, Byron, 336
Wilkie, Michael, 336
Williams, Charles (Caddo), 222, 336
Williams, Charles (Stockbridge), 4, 46, 49, 78, 84-86, 89-91, 95, 98, 99, 104, 107, 112, 113, 126, 288, 336
Williams, Chauncey, 336
Williams, Joseph, 336
Wilson, Samuel B., 336
Winneshiek, William, 288, 336
Winnie, William, 164, 180, 336
Witmer, Lightner, 1
Wizi, John, 336
Wofford, Jesse, 264, 274, 275, 336
Wolfe, Tarquette, 336
Wolfenberger, Joseph W., 155
Woodbury, Clarence, 336
Woodruff, George W., 2, 22, 125, 127, 129, 131, 132, 136, 137, 313
World Series of Football, 94
Wounded Eye, Davis, 336
Wright, Ellis, 99, 135, 336
Wynaco, George, 336
Yankee Joe, William, 191, 196, 336
Yarlott, Frank, 64, 65, 336
Yellow Elk, William, 336
Yellow Head, Joseph, 336
Yost, Fielding H., 76, 144, 158
Young, Bill, 16
Youngbird, Wesley, 336
Yuda, Montreville S., 255, 305
Yukkanini, Karl, 336

www.ingramcontent.com/pod-product-compliance
Lightning Source LLC
Chambersburg PA
CBHW071952110526
44592CB00012B/1066